American Stories

Case Studies in Politics and Government

James R. Bowers, who holds a Ph.D. from Northern Illinois University, is an assistant professor of political science at St. John Fisher College in Rochester, New York, where he regularly teaches undergraduate courses on American political institutions and processes, public policy, public administration, and constitutional law. His research interests include abortion politics and policy, family policy, legislative-executive relations, the exercise and control of administrative discretion, and constitutional theory. Among his published books and articles are *Regulating the Regulators: An Introduction to the Legislative Oversight of Administrative Rulemaking* (Praeger, 1990), "Establishing the Constitutional Legitimacy of OMB's Regulatory Review," and "Classical Liberalism, the Constitution, and Abortion Policy: Can Government Be Both Pro-Choice and Anti-Abortion?" In addition to an active teaching and research agenda, Professor Bowers also contributes twice-monthly political commentaries on national, state, and local politics to WXXI-1370, the Rochester area National Public Radio Affiliate.

American Stories

Case Studies in
Politics and Government

James R. Bowers
St. John Fisher College

Wadsworth Publishing Company
Belmont, California
A Division of Wadsworth, Inc.

Acquisitions Editor: Cynthia C. Stormer
Editorial Associate: Cathleen S. Collins
Production Coordinator: Fiorella Ljunggren
Production: Lifland et al., Bookmakers
Manuscript Editor: Quica Ostrander
Permissions: Marie DuBois
Interior Design: Quica Ostrander
Cover Design: Roy R. Neuhaus
Author's Photograph: Bill McDowell
Cover Illustration: Erin Mauterer/Bluewater A & D
Typesetting: Bookends Typesetting
Printing and Binding: Malloy Lithographing, Inc.

1 2 3 4 5 6 7 8 9 10—97 96 95 94 93

Printed in the United States of America

Library of Congress Cataloging-in-Publication Data

Bowers, James R.
    American stories : case studies in politics and government / James
R. Bowers.
      p. cm.
    Includes bibliographical references.
    ISBN 0-534-14502-7 :
    1. United States—Politics and government. I. Title.
JK21.B65 1992   92-17211
320.973—dc20   CIP

FOR JAN,
BECAUSE OF HER INSPIRATION, PATIENCE, ENDURANCE,
AND—MOST IMPORTANTLY—HER LOVE

Preface

THOSE OF US WHO REGULARLY TEACH INTRODUCTORY COURSES ON AMERICAN NATIONAL GOVERNMENT AND POLITICS UNDERSTAND THE NEED FOR good, readable, interesting, and informative case studies about our political system. We know good case studies can help us describe and explain American government and politics to our students. We also know that through good case studies we can help students develop a fuller understanding and appreciation of our political order by encouraging them to see the interrelationships among concepts, by fostering independent thinking, and by generating class discussion. In short, we know that case studies permit students to see how the materials presented in class fit into the real world of practical politics and government.

American Stories: Case Studies in Politics and Government is an attempt to incorporate into a textbook what we, as teachers of introductory courses in American government, know about the value of case studies. I hope that by providing a source of readable, informative, and interesting case studies, *American Stories* will give students a greater sense of the reality of American government and politics.

Organization and Content

American Stories is written and organized in a manner that makes it easy to use with almost any approach to the teaching of national government. It consists of twenty case studies organized in pairs in ten chapters. The case studies are somewhat longer than the selections in most supplementary readers used for courses in American national government. The somewhat longer readings are of sufficient depth to promote student understanding, and this emphasis on depth is important. Case studies convey meaning best when students can immerse themselves in the topic under discussion and participate in what Richard Fenno (1978, 249) refers to as "soaking and poking."

The content of *American Stories* is also tailored to follow closely the content of most American government textbooks. The case studies cover standard topics such as the Constitution, campaigns and elections, the media, Congress, and the president. Many of the case studies can also be read in connection with topics other than those designated in the table of contents. For instance, "The Making of a Delegate" could be incorporated into a discussion on the presidential nomination process as easily as one on political parties. Similarly, "Scripting the Video Presidency" could be included in a discussion on the media as well as one on the contemporary presidency. These are only a few of the possibilities.

To make *American Stories* even more compatible with the variety of ways in which American national government is taught, I have included mostly case studies that are nonideological. The main criterion for including a case study was whether it tells a "good story." A good story is one that illustrates fundamental themes and concepts in an interesting, informative, and readable manner. For the most part, then, the selections reflect my belief in the usefulness of the case study approach and the importance of emphasizing institutions and processes. This does not mean, though, that none of the case studies has an ideological slant. Some clearly do. But each case study's outlook is clearly secondary to the overall story it has to tell. Furthermore, the fact that this reader as a whole is nonideological does not mean that the individual case studies lack a point of view. Quite the contrary: All good case studies express a point of view. Some of the case studies in *American Stories* border on being exposés. Others are clearly critical of the institutions and processes they are examining. Such characteristics enhance these stories' usefulness because of the additional class discussion and independent thinking they are likely to generate.

In addition to presenting the kinds of case studies described above, each chapter of *American Stories* begins with an original introductory essay. These essays are designed primarily to assist students in understanding the case studies by defining and discussing the themes and concepts presented within the case studies and by introducing related concepts necessary for a clear comprehension of the topic. For example, the introductory essay in the chapter on the Supreme Court presents a brief overview of the politics of both Supreme Court appointments and Supreme Court decision making. This information helps prepare students to read the two case studies concerning early political opposition to the failed nomination of Robert H. Bork and competition in the 1940s between Justices Felix Frankfurter and Hugo Black for the intellectual and task leadership of the Supreme Court.

Each introductory essay concludes with a short annotated list of suggested readings. The introductory material also includes, at the beginning of each case study, a number of study questions for students to consider as they read each story. These questions frame the students' reading by directing them toward the important factual issues and material in each of the selections, thus helping them understand the concepts and themes presented in the case studies. The questions can also be used as the basis for class discussion on the case studies and as models for test questions.

On Using Case Studies

Although the case studies in *American Stories* can be easily incorporated into courses in American government, the use of case studies as a central component of a course admittedly takes practice. If case studies are to be successfully incorporated into introductory courses on American national government, students must approach the stories as more than another set of readings. The case studies should be used to focus students' attention on the topics being presented and discussed in class. To this end, I recommend using one of two approaches. First, the case studies can be read following formal lectures and discussions and after other assigned readings have been completed. Used in this manner, the case studies serve to summarize and reaffirm what students have already read. The students' principal responsibility is to read the case studies with an appreciation for how they illustrate previous readings, class lectures, and discussions.

A second approach with which I have been experimenting is to have the students read the case studies before completing any other assigned readings or attending formal lectures and discussions. In reading and discussing the case studies, students must deduce what the stories reveal about a general course topic. I find this approach interesting for several reasons. First, it helps students sharpen their ability to think analytically and critically. Second, students' comments and questions shape the formal lectures and discussions. Information in lectures and discussions is thus presented in light of the glimpses of political reality offered by the case studies rather than in the abstract or in isolation. Finally, when they are read before any formal introduction to the general topics, the case studies serve as focal points or extended examples that can be referred to throughout the ensuing lectures and class discussion.

Acknowledgments

A number of people provided indispensable assistance in developing *American Stories.* Dawn Burnam, district sales manager for Wadsworth, saw the merit in my original idea and helped me develop the prospectus on which *American Stories* is based. She also provided unwavering support in encouraging the Brooks/Cole division of Wadsworth, Inc. to agree to publish this book. Cindy Stormer, political science editor for Brooks/Cole, was also invaluable in the completion of the book. She taught me a great deal about the business of textbook publishing and provided level-headed advice throughout the project. Though there were times when I did not initially agree with her, I always came around to her point of view. *American Stories* is a much better book because of her persistence, insistence, and guidance.

My fellow teachers of American national government who reviewed the manuscript provided insightful comments on its structure and substance. These reviewers are W. Merrill Downer of Thiel College, Forest Grieves of the University of Montana, Robert Griffiths of the University of North Carolina at Greensboro, John Johannes of Marquette University, Thomas H. Little of The American University, Albert Nelson of the University of Wisconsin–La Crosse, Michael Nelson of Rhodes College, Jeffrey Orenstein of Kent State University–Stark Campus, Leonard Ritt of Northern Arizona University, John Roos of the University of Notre Dame, Robert Ross of the University of Northern Iowa, Jeffrey Sedgwick of the University of Massachusetts, William R. Shaffer of Purdue University, Stewart Shapiro of Bentley College, Bruce

Unger of Randolph-Macon College, Kenny Whitby of the University of South Carolina, and Stephanie Witt of Boise State University. My students in my introductory American government course at St. John Fisher College also provided vital assistance. They were the guinea pigs on whom I experimented.

Finally, my wife, Jan, was a rock throughout the development of *American Stories.* In addition to giving me general support, she also read, edited, and commented on all of the introductory essays. I dedicate this book to her.

James R. Bowers

Contents

American Stories

Case Studies in
Politics and Government

The Constitution

For more than two hundred years, the Constitution has provided the nation with a blueprint for government. It has also served as fundamental law for our nation longer than any of its counterparts in the world's democracies. As a statement of fundamental law, the Constitution has also remained relatively stable and unchanged throughout its existence. Since the formal ratification of the Bill of Rights (Amendments I through X) in 1791, the Constitution has been amended only sixteen times.

The Constitution's longevity is due, in part, to the pride and almost religious faith that many Americans have in it. For many Americans, belief in the Constitution is like a secular religion. Admittedly, though, our pride and faith in the Constitution have not always been evident in public attitude and government policies. In his book *A Machine That Would Go by Itself,* constitutional historian Michael Kaman (1986, 3) contends that "the Constitution occupies an anomalous role in American cultural history. For . . . two centuries it has been swathed in pride yet obscured by indifference: a fulsome rhetoric of reverence more than offset by the reality of ignorance."

Despite this popular, yet uninformed, public fervor for the Constitution, it is important for us to remember that the document was written by mortal men confronted with the earthly problem of how to structure a new national government. How then are we to approach and understand the events surrounding the drafting and ratification of the Constitution and the adoption of the Bill of Rights?

The activities at the Constitutional Convention are often interpreted from one of two perspectives. The Constitutional Convention is often described in terms of conflicts between the interests of the big states and those of the small states over such issues as proportional versus equal representation in Congress. Alternatively, the activities of the Philadelphia convention are discussed in terms of the members of an economic or propertied elite attempting to provide a framework for government that would protect their economic well-being, then being threatened by the domestic instabilities caused by the Articles of Confederation. American historian Charles A. Beard's still widely read book *An Economic Interpretation of the Constitution of the United States* (1913), is an excellent illustration of this second view.

Some thirty years ago, in response to perceived inadequacies of both the "big state versus small state" perspective and Beard's economic interpretation, political scientist John Roche proposed a third, more encompassing view of the Constitutional Convention, which can be applied equally to the ratification process for the Constitution and to the adoption of the Bill of Rights. In his article "The Founding Fathers: A Reform Caucus in Action" (1961), Roche suggested that the Constitutional Convention is best understood as a nationalistic reform caucus of like-minded men. Thirty-nine of the delegates to the Constitutional Convention had served in Congress under the Articles of Confederation. They were intimately aware of the general impotence imposed on the existing national government by the Articles. Possessing this continental outlook, these delegates hoped to establish a strong, yet accountable, central government that would not be plagued by the severe restrictions imposed by the Articles of Confederation.

If we accept Roche's perspective, we can understand and appreciate that the delegates at the Constitutional Convention were motivated as much by pragmatic political concerns as by political theory. Pragmatism shaped the debate at two levels. First, it motivated the delegates' discussions on how to structure and distribute authority within the new national government. Second, because the states were then the dominant partners in the national union, pragmatism drove the delegates' awareness that any new constitution proposing a stronger central government would have to be carefully presented if it were to gain acceptance.

Pragmatic concern about state power is also clearly illustrated by the delegates' strategy for ratification. The delegates knew that they had already exceeded their instructions by drafting an entirely new framework for government and national union. Congress had intended only a limited convention and had specifically instructed the delegates to offer revisions to the Articles of Confederation. Having already started a second American revolution and facing likely hostility from the states for their actions, the delegates also ignored congressional instructions on how any proposed changes to the Articles of Confederation would be ratified.

Originally, the work of the Convention was to be approved first by Congress and then by all of the states. Knowing that the new Constitution would be defeated under these conditions, the delegates made another calculated political decision to further ignore their congressional instructions. The delegates instead instructed Congress to submit the proposed constitution directly to the states, stipulating that it would go into effect after it was approved by nine state ratifying conventions.

The two stories presented in this chapter embrace Roche's perspective. They emphasize the political and pragmatic dimensions of drafting the Constitution and securing its ratification by the states. First, ''Decision in Philadelphia'' by Christopher and James Collier provides a vivid description of the raw politics that shaped so many of the debates and outcomes of the Constitutional Convention. It focuses on the important role that the slavery issue played at the Convention and how slavery politics created seemingly unnatural alliances among delegates who would not normally be aligned.

''The Cement of the Union'' by Alan Briceland continues the story of how the drafting and ratification of the Constitution was influenced by politics and pragmatic considerations. In describing the debate and activities at the state ratifying convention in Virginia, it provides a vivid and interesting account of the political strategies employed by both the Federalists in their efforts to secure ratification of the proposed constitution and the Anti-Federalists in their equally intense efforts to defeat ratification.

Suggested Reading

Becker, Carl. 1942. *The Declaration of Independence: A Study in the History of Political Ideas.* New York: Knopf. A classic and highly regarded work on the meaning of the Declaration of Independence.

Farber, Daniel A., and Suzanna Sherry. 1990. *A History of the American Constitution*. St. Paul, MN: West. A collection of original writings and historical documents tracing the historical development of the Constitution.

Feldman, Daniel L. 1990. *The Logic of American Government*. New York: William Morrow. An attempt to apply the Constitution to contemporary American politics in a way that encourages citizens to become involved in public policy making through the exercise of their constitutionally guaranteed rights.

Rossiter, Clinton. 1966. *1787: The Grand Convention*. New York: Macmillan. An interesting account of the 1787 Constitutional Convention told in terms of the men who made it happen, the conditions that gave rise to it, and the results that followed from the drafting and ratification of the Constitution.

Storing, Herbert. 1981. *What the Anti-Federalists Were For*. Chicago: University of Chicago Press. These counter-arguments to the *Federalist Papers* embody the political and philosophical ideas of those who opposed the ratification of the Constitution.

Woods, Gordon S. 1982. *The Creation of the American Republic*. New York: W. W. Norton. A thorough examination of American political thought prior to the Constitutional Convention.

Decision in Philadelphia

Christopher Collier
James Lincoln Collier

As you read this case study, consider the following questions:

1. Why was slavery an unavoidable issue at the Constitutional Convention?

2. What practical political considerations and compromises did delegates need to make as a result of the unavoidable nature of the slavery issue?

3. What was the relationship between slavery and other important issues such as taxation and the manner in which seats in the new Congress would be apportioned?

4. Why was Connecticut concerned about the big state–Deep South alliance?

5. What motivated Connecticut to align itself with South Carolina?

6. Why was the alliance between Connecticut and South Carolina so unnatural, and what factors overrode this mispairing of state delegations?

7. What was the basis of the compromise between Connecticut and South Carolina that eventually allowed a New England–Deep South alliance to emerge at the Constitutional Convention?

8. How does the constitutional requirement of a decennial census reflect a political compromise?

O VER THE TWO-HUNDRED-YEAR HISTORY OF THE UNITED STATES, PROB-
ABLY NO QUESTION HAS TROUBLED THE COUNTRY AS MUCH AS RACIAL
antagonism. It brought on a Civil War, which nearly wrecked the nation and left hundreds of thousands of young men dead; and it continues into the present day as a cesspool of bitterness and hatred. Good
men and bad have searched desperately for a way to end the enmity
between blacks and whites, and nobody has succeeded. Racial antagonism remains the most painful canker in American democracy, a
wound that nothing seems to completely heal.

The problem was already evident in 1787. As the wrangling over
the big-states–small-states issue moved into its final stages, it became
clearer and clearer to the delegates that Madison was right about at
least one thing: the major division in the country was between the
North and the South. Indeed, in 1787 these two great sections of the
country were already very different from each other in attitudes, lifestyles, and economics. . . .

But beyond all of these differences was one overriding one—
black slavery. It defined the South. You could not think about the South
without thinking first of the "peculiar institution." Economically,
politically, emotionally, slavery divided the American nation into two
distinct halves, and it continued to do so long after the Founding Fathers
were bones in the earth. . . .

Slavery was hardly an American invention, but at least some
authorities insist that American slavery was the worst the world has
ever known. Slaves carried to the Americas suffered horribly during
the long transatlantic voyage; many of them attempted suicide by fling-
ing themselves overboard, refusing to eat, or clawing their throats open
with their fingernails. . . . In New England, blacks represented only
2.5 percent of the population; in the South they were 40 percent. In
1790 in fifteen out of thirty-two South Carolina counties the black
population exceeded 70 percent. Sixty percent of southern families
owned slaves, and it was the possession of slaves that made the South
the wealthiest section of the nation.

To be black in the South was to be a plantation hand, enduring
long hours of hard, tedious work, eating at subsistence levels, and coarse
foods only, dressing in rags, and living a life controlled in detail from

above. Some masters were relatively kindhearted, but most of the slaves were driven by overseers who at times rode among them spurring them on with the lash. For most there was no escape and little joy. In addition, all slaves could be sold away from their friends and families at the whim of cash-short masters.

The slave trade in particular was deplored by many people who condoned slavery itself. Yet the trade was locked into the institution of slavery. In the miasmic coastal lowlands the life of a slave was likely to be short, and a constant supply of new ones was needed. In Virginia, on the other hand, where blacks reproduced themselves at nearly the same rate as whites, slavery was unprofitable: . . . the only way Virginians could make the peculiar institution profitable was to sell their surplus slaves to the planters of the deep South.

The foreign slave trade was of interest only to the three Deep South states; by 1779 all other states had outlawed the importation of slaves. South Carolinians imported 7,000 of them between 1783 and 1785. But in 1787 South Carolina temporarily closed down the trade, and a year earlier North Carolina had placed a prohibitive duty on slave importations. There was good enough reason to believe—if that is what you wanted to believe—that the trade was quickly drying up. . . .

It was clear that slavery would eventually be ended in the North. By 1787 the Massachusetts courts had abolished it, and the gradual abolition of slavery in other northern states, especially Pennsylvania, Rhode Island, and Connecticut, was under way. Surely slavery was a dying institution; why cause an uproar over it when it was bound to wither away soon enough?

But slavery was not a dying institution in 1787; indeed the demand for slaves was picking up, even before the great thrust given it by the invention of the cotton gin five years after the Convention. But many Americans believed—or chose to believe—that the death of slavery would automatically follow the end of importations. And importation had already been made illegal in ten states. At any event, the human capacity for self-deception is infinite, and northerners at the Convention were so strongly committed to union that it was easy for them to believe that slavery would shortly disappear. They did not like it, but it was not something they saw as a do-or-die issue. They very quickly discovered, however, that it was so enmeshed with a host of other problems that addressing it was unavoidable.

If, for example, the new legislature was to be based on proportional representation, as Madison so fervently wished, would slaves be counted? Would they be taxed as wealth? Furthermore, it was obvious that import duties must be a key source of revenue for the new government. Would newly arrived slaves be taxed as imports? Were slaves people or property?

Then there was the question of the new states that would inevitably be cut from the western lands. Neither side wanted to admit states allied with the other, and it was generally recognized that the determining factor in the alliance would be the presence or absence of slavery. Thus, should slavery be permitted in new states? Ought northern states allow southerners to cross their borders in search of runaway slaves? Should northern states be required to hunt down and arrest fugitives? Would a black traveling with his master into a free state become free? Were slaves items of interstate commerce?

The slavery question, then, ran into everything. Moreover, the issues it touched upon were themselves intermeshed. The first of these interrelated issues to arise substantially at the Convention was the question of whether slaves were to be counted as people or property. The issue was forced up during the tense battle over proportional representation: would the South be allowed to include their black slaves?

The question of whether slaves were people or property was not new. It had arisen first in the early days of the old Confederation, when a decision had to be made about how each state's financial contribution to the central government would be assessed. It was eventually decided to base the levies on population. And how would black slaves be counted? The South, of course, wanted the count as low as possible, the North as high, and eventually the issue was compromised: one slave would equal three-fifths of a person; five slaves would count as three whites. There was no particular reason for settling on this figure—it was simply the result of compromise. . . .

At Philadelphia the situation was different. Madison and his allies were attempting to establish the principle of proportional representation. As the debate on how black slaves should be counted progressed, it became clear to the delegates that the shoes had switched feet. If representation in the new Congress was to be based on population, it was now all to the South's advantage to count as many slaves as possible. And the North, of course, now took the opposite view: slaves could be bought and sold and had no free will of their own. . . . It was, therefore, the battle over proportional representation that first forced the slavery issue on the delegates to the Convention.

The issue arose on June 11, early in the debate over proportional representation, and it was Roger Sherman who raised it. Sherman, in the course of offering what would become the Connecticut Compromise, proposed that suffrage in the House of Representatives should be figured according to the ''numbers of *free* inhabitants'' in each state.

This, of course, was something the southerners would not like. However, it was not a southerner but James Wilson of Pennsylvania who proposed that the proposition should also include "three-fifths of all other persons not comprehended in the foregoing description"— that is, black slaves. This was precisely the language that had been used in the old Congress in determining how state levies should be calculated. Wilson had chosen it, obviously, because it was a formula familiar to both southerners and northerners. His proposal carried nine to two. Only New Jersey and Delaware voted against it, and that was because they objected to the whole idea of proportional representation.

It is not necessary to believe that Wilson and other delegates from the Big Three had made an explicit deal with the delegates from the Deep South.* At this point in the Convention, the Big Three were primarily concerned with getting proportional representation through. The delegates from the Deep South states, expecting to be big themselves soon enough, were their natural allies, and the men from the Big Three had to give them what they wanted in respect to slavery in order not to disrupt the alliance.

On June 11 few of the delegates had a clear idea of how the Convention was taking shape; they were only slowly becoming aware of the natural alliances and divisions among them. But by early in July it had become obvious to most of the delegates that the Big Three–Deep South alliance could dominate the Convention. And it occurred to Roger Sherman, if not to anyone else, that the only way his state rights–small-state bloc could avoid being crushed would be to break up the Big Three–Deep South alliance and put together a different one.

Connecticut . . . prided itself on its democratic ways. Because it was less controlled by a hereditary establishment than many other states, it had always had to govern itself by consensus. Horse-trading came naturally to Connecticut's leaders; only men who had a knack for creating consensus rose to the top in Connecticut politics. It is therefore not surprising to discover that all three of the Connecticut delegates to the Constitutional Convention were men who by temperament hated making waves.† . . .

Men of this stripe were almost by nature bound to seek alliances to gain their ends. And in the days after the Virginia Plan was pushed through the Committee of the Whole it was clear to the Connecticut men that they would need allies on a variety of issues. Unfortunately,

*Editor's note: The three states were Virginia, New York, and Pennsylvania.
†*Editor's note:* Roger Sherman, Oliver Ellsworth, and William Samuel Johnson were the Connecticut delegates.

their natural partners, the New England states and the small-states bloc, would not do. The small states' alliance was neither large enough nor firm enough to carry the day on most issues. Massachusetts was in the big-state camp, and the other two New England states, New Hampshire and Rhode Island, were not even present. So the Connecticut men took the bold step of reaching directly into the enemy camp for an ally: South Carolina.

These two states were very odd bedfellows. South Carolina, the leader of the Deep South group, was one of the most aristocratic of states; Connecticut was the most republican. Connecticut had already provided for the gradual abolition of slavery. Half the people in South Carolina were slaves and the other half were determined to keep them that way. South Carolina, the wealthiest of all the states, was dominated by great plantations and a one-crop economy, Connecticut was a land of small family farms and diversified agriculture. But despite these differences, the two states held in common one very important, if less obvious, interest. For both, the export trade was a critical part of their economies. . . . This common interest in the export trade bridged the deep division between the two states. Moreover, William Samuel Johnson's urbanity and membership in the Anglican Church made him attractive to southerners, and as a member of Congress since 1784 he had made many friends among them. And besides, Johnson owned slaves. . . .

Precisely how and when the Connecticut–South Carolina axis was formed we do not know. . . . Nor do we know when the two partners to the deal brought in their sectional allies—Connecticut, the New Englanders; South Carolina, the states of the Deep South. There can be no doubt, however, that an arrangement was made. . . .

. . . The coalition was not a monolith. The three New England and three Deep South states did not always vote together, nor was everybody in these six delegations part of the deal. But these six states acted together to carry many crucial issues.

If we do not know how the deal was made, we have a fairly clear idea of what the terms were. At bottom, the New England states agreed to support the Deep South on slavery questions, if the Deep South would support the New Englanders on matters bearing on shipping and trade.

In making the deal, the Connecticut men were thoroughly aware that the Convention could not interfere with slavery very much, if at all, if they hoped to keep the Deep South states in the union. In agreeing to support the Deep South on slavery issues, the Connecticut men must have believed that they were bargaining off something they could not have got anyway. From their viewpoint, they were getting something for nothing.

We must remember, too, that for most of the delegates the primary goal was to see that the Convention succeeded in producing a workable government. This was the great work they were charged with, and they were prepared to bend far to complete it. So the deal was made, and the Virginia nationalists, who had dominated the Convention in June, were by August isolated with their principal allies, the Pennsylvanians.

The new dominating alliance was quite different in tone from the one James Madison had put together in May. It was characterized less by high intellectualism than by a pragmatism bent on producing a nation in which the export trade could proceed unfettered. . . .

This approach was not entirely to the taste of all the delegates at the Convention. The Virginians especially had come into the Convention feeling strongly that a national government must be able to control the states to a substantial degree, and throughout the Convention they would consistently vote for curbs on state powers. They were supported in this by the smaller states. Once Maryland, New Jersey, and Delaware got equal suffrage in the Senate, which would give them a fighting chance to forestall legislation they did not like, these little states were eager to see a national govenment that would be able to control commerce in the United States, in order to prevent the larger states around them from preying on them. But on this point their former ally, Connecticut, had abandoned them. Connecticut wanted national controls over imports only; exports were to remain unfettered.

Connecticut had abandoned its former allies on the slavery issue, too. The middle states emphatically did not want to put anything in the Constitution that would tend to prolong slavery. Many of the delegates from these states were antislavery on principle, but whatever their principles, all of them knew that a document that seemed to support slavery would be hard to push past their constituents back home. And Virginians, for their own reasons, were eager to stop the importation of slaves. This group of states in the middle of the country, then, opposed both parts of the bargain struck between the Deep South and the New Englanders, and they would fight it.

We can pick up the story on July 2, when the proportional representation crisis peaked, and the despairing delegates sent off that select committee to produce a compromise acceptable to big states and small. On July 5, the committee delivered its report, which said, among other things, that the first branch of the national legislature should be made up of one representative for every 40,000 people in each state, and included the three-fifths formula, which had earlier been generally accepted.

But the formula left some men uneasy. Among them was Gouverneur Morris, who . . . believed that men of wealth, who had a "stake in society" and would inevitably be carrying a good deal of the expense of the govenment, ought to have a larger say in how their money was spent. And the next day, July 6, Morris proposed the establishment of a new committee, which would assign specific numbers of representatives to each of the thirteen states, taking into account wealth as well as population. The Convention accepted the proposal. . . . The composition of the committee showed how rapidly the old fight between big and small states was receding from everybody's minds: four of the five men were from the Big Three and the fifth was one of their allies from the Deep South. The balance now was between North and South.

On July 9 the committee brought in a formula that gave the North thirty-one representatives and the South twenty-five, basing the South's extra representation on the fact that it had more wealth. The debate that followed turned mainly on the question of whether wealth should be counted.

In fact, at this point in the debate the term "wealth" was being used as a euphemism for black slaves. What the argument was really all about was the extent to which the South would be allowed to count slaves when representation was calculated. If slaves were counted, it was perfectly obvious that the South could increase its number of congressmen simply by bringing in more slaves, which the Deep South states were doing in any case.

When we read the debates through July 9 we find William Paterson saying that he could "regard Negro slaves in no light but as property. They are no free agents, have no personal liberty, no faculty of acquiring property. . . ." And we find Gouverneur Morris saying that he "could never agree to give such encouragement to the slave trade as would be given by allowing [the South] representation for their Negroes. . . ."

The northerners, here, were concerned far less about the rights of blacks than to see that the South would not dominate any new Congress that came out of the Convention.

So the arguing went on. On July 9 the Convention sent out another committee, made up of one man from each state, to refigure congressional representation. The next day it brought in another set of numbers, which increased the total to sixty-five representatives but left the North-South ratio unchanged. The Convention was no better off than before, and once again the northerners set about fighting off the southerners. King of Massachusetts complained that the four "eastern" states were underrepresented in comparison with the four southernmost states. . . . Charles Cotesworth Pinckney responded that he didn't demand that the South get a majority in the new legislature, but insisted that it ought to have "something like an equality." Williamson of North Carolina made the central point. "The southern interest must be extremely endangered by the present arrangement. The northern states are to have a majority in the first instance and the means of perpetuating it."

This was the crux of the problem. Everyone was aware that at the start the North would have an edge in the new Congress—in the Senate because it had more states, in the House because it was more populous. The South could accept that, and bide its time until its population grew, but it had to make certain that the North would not be able to maintain its edge forever.

To insure that this would not happen, Randolph on July 10 moved "that in order to ascertain the alterations in population and wealth"— for which read slaves—a census ought to be taken regularly and the legislature adjusted accordingly. In other words, Congress would not be allowed to reapportion itself when it saw fit, which in a Congress controlled by the North might be never, but would be constitutionally required to reapportion at regular intervals.

Morris quickly objected, again worried about populous new western states, which might come to control the Congress if reapportionment was mandatory. Better to let the Congress do as it wanted. On July 11, Sherman urged that making reapportionment mandatory was "shackling the legislature too much, we ought to choose wise and good men, and then confide in them."

They bickered on, getting nowhere, delegates from North and South one after another making one case or another in favor of their own side. . . .

Of particular interest were two short speeches made by Roger Sherman, both on July 11. The first came after Rutledge spoke in favor of mandatory reapportionment. As soon as he sat down Sherman rose to say that although he had originally been against the rule requiring reapportionment, he had been convinced by "the observations" of the southerners to change his mind. The second occurred later in the day, after King of Massachusetts objected to the formula for reapportionment the last committee had brought in, with its overrepresentation for the South. Once again Sherman quickly rose to support the formula, breaking ranks with his fellow New Englanders. "In general the allotment might not be just, but considering all circumstances, he was satisfied with it.'' By ''all circumstances,'' Sherman simply meant that the South was going to have to be given extra weight if the business was to go forward. The Connecticut–South Carolina axis was by this moment surely in place.

But it was not yet in control. On the eleventh, the northern bloc pulled itself together and voted not to allow the South to count their slaves in the calculation at all—not as three-fifths, not as one-half, not as anything. The one northern state to break with its fellows and vote to keep the three-fifths formula was Connecticut. . . .

The Cement of the Union

Alan V. Briceland

As you read this case study, consider the following questions:

1. Why did many political observers of the time view the Virginia ratifying convention as the key to the entire ratification issue?

2. What was the main Federalist strategy in trying to get the convention to ratify the proposed constitution?

3. When the Anti-Federalists were confronted by a small Federalist majority, what tactics did they employ in trying to reverse that majority?

4. How did the issue of a bill of rights reflect the political posturing of the Federalists and Anti-Federalists?

5. What compromise did Madison and other leading Federalists ultimately accept in order to maintain unity among their ranks?

By Alan V. Briceland in *The Constitution and the States: The Role of the Original Thirteen in the Framing and Adoption of the Federal Constitution,* Patrick T. Conley and John P. Kaminski (Eds.). Copyright 1988 by Madison House Publishers, Inc. Reprinted by permission.

• • • IT WAS CLEAR FROM THE BEGINNING THAT THE RATIFICATION CONTEST IN VIRGINIA WAS GOING TO BE CLOSE AND HARD fought. Powerful men stood arrayed on both sides. George Washington and James Madison—who had no qualms about the Constitution— knew that success for the Federalist, or Constitution, cause depended on the votes of men such as Edmund Pendleton, who entertained doubts. A strategy was needed to unify all who were basically sympathetic to the Constitution. Washington and Madison determined whenever possible to shift the emphasis of the contest from the merits of the Constitution to the issue of union or disunion. Washington firmly believed that the only real choice lay between ''The Constitution or disunion.''

Patrick Henry, who declined to attend the Philadelphia Convention because he ''smelled a rat,'' led the largest group of Virginia Antifederalists, the ''Virginia First'' faction. The Henryites could countenance no subordination of Virginia's interests to national interest. George Mason, who attended the convention but refused to sign its handiwork, was the best known of the unregenerate radical faction of Antifederalists. Henry's primary loyalty was to Virginia, while Mason's was to the philosophical principles of revolutionary, egalitarian radicalism. Mason considered the proposed government not so much a threat to Virginia as to individual liberty. The national government would be not only too distant for the people to control but also too powerful to be restrained. Even before the Philadelphia Convention had adjourned, he had penned and begun to circulate his ''Objections.'' ''There is no declaration of rights,'' trumpeted the opening words. The author of the Virginia Declaration of Rights expected readers to comprehend immediately the profound and terrible significance of this omission. . . .

Between the Antifederalists and Federalists, Governor Edmund Randolph occupied the middle ground. He insisted that he was a friend to the Constitution (which he also refused to sign), but he argued that the way to prevent the document's outright rejection was to advocate prior amendments, particularly a bill of rights.

The Debate in Virginia

The period from the fall of 1787 to March 1788, when the elections for convention delegates were held, was essentially a drawn-out election campaign. Leading partisans wooed the support of locally prominent men, for it was from their ranks that the delegates would be chosen. Because of Virginia's great distances and poor roads, the ratification contest can best be understood by considering it not as a statewide contest but as many local contests. . . .

By mid-April the voting patterns were broadly evident. Tidewater, Northern Neck, the Shenandoah Valley, and the Alleghenies were overwhelmingly Federalist. Southside, the Southwest, and Kentucky were just as strongly Antifederalist. The Piedmont north of the James was something of a checkerboard.

In the wake of the election results, many observers became convinced that Virginia held the key to the whole ratification question. After six consecutive Federalist victories—Delaware, Pennsylvania, New Jersey, Georgia, Connecticut, and Massachusetts—the string had been broken when the New Hampshire convention had met in February and adjourned without decision until mid-June. Even if Maryland and South Carolina ratified in the interim, as it appeared they would do, there could be only eight of the needed nine ratifications by the time the Virginia convention met in June. Moreover, all of the remaining states—Virginia, New Hampshire, Rhode Island, New York, and North Carolina—were Antifederalism's strongest bastions.

A small bombshell of sorts exploded in mid-May at the Maryland convention. Although Thomas Jefferson was abroad, his support for tactics to force the inclusion of a bill of rights in the Constitution was made known through the unauthorized publication of a private letter. The event proved to be an embarrassment to Virginia Federalists, since Jefferson had implied that Virginia should withhold ratification in support of a bill of rights.

Thus by late May the talk in Virginia centered on the subject of amendments to the Constitution, although various groups in the ratification struggle viewed the prospect of amendments in different ways. The Henry faction planned to use prior amendments to gut the Constitution. The Mason-Lee faction sought them to protect individual rights, along the lines suggested by Jefferson. The Randolph faction sought them to garner enough votes to establish the Union. Believing a bill of rights unnecessary, the Madison-Washington faction thought that prior amendments would lead to disunion rather than union.

The Virginia Convention: The Opening

On an early June day in 1788, 170 specially elected delegates crowded into the Academy building on Shockoe Hill in the city of Richmond. They had journeyed from as far as the Ohio and Mississippi River valleys. In 1788 Virginia, the largest of the states, encompassed what is now West Virginia and Kentucky. . . .

One overriding fact colored the development of convention strategies on both sides—the knowledge that Federalists, with eighty-six votes, had a slim majority in delegate count. If the majority held, it meant victory. Antifederalists counted eighty firm adherents. Half a dozen votes won and the day would be theirs, but they had to win those crucial votes.

Henry's tactic was to excite and alarm, to expose the chains of tyranny lurking in every clause of the Constitution, and to fasten these imagined chains around every possible interest group. In speech after speech he played upon the fears and private interests of the delegates. "The trial by jury is gone," he thundered at the small debtor farmers. "British debtors will be ruined by being dragged to the federal courts," he told the larger planters. "The majority of congress is to the north, and the slaves are to the south," he warned the slaveholders. He threatened the men of the Shenandoah Valley with the loss of their lands and the men of the west with the loss of their navigation. He threatened everyone with the loss of individual liberty. Time and again he returned to the theme of northern dominance of the new government, with the consequent loss of southern rights.

Antifederal strategists believed the weakest link in the Federalist chain to be "the four Counties which lie on the Ohio between the Pennsylvania line and Big Sandy Creek." These were the counties of Greenbrier, Ohio, Harrison, and Montgomery, the first three of which were located in present-day West Virginia. How could they be turned against the Constitution? Over and over in the course of the convention, Henry reminded the delegates of the willingness of the northern commercial states to relinquish to Spain navigation rights on the Mississippi in return for commercial advantage for themselves.

Federalist leaders had their own problems. They had to avoid any action that could be construed as unfair. The slightest hint of manipulation could drive men with a strong sense of fair play into opposition and would strengthen the resolve of the Antifederalists to fight to the last ditch. "I have thought it prudent," Madison would explain, "to withhold, by a studied fairness in every step on the side of the Constitution, every pretext for rash experiments."

Knowing that they did not have the votes, Mason and Henry needed time—time for Mason's logic and Henry's passion to work upon those delegates who were only weakly committed to the Constitution. The Antifederalist convention strategy was one of delay and attrition. On June 3, immediately after convention preliminaries had been concluded, Mason sought recognition. He declared that "the fullest and clearest investigation" into the Constitution was "indispensibly necessary." He therefore moved that the convention should systematically examine and separately debate each and every section of the Constitution. To his great surprise, Madison rose immediately to support the proposal. The procedure was ideal for Madison's purpose of focusing the convention on the Constitution rather than on amendments. The Federalists' margin was too thin for them to risk an immediate vote. Discussion clause by clause would take time; but it was, from the Federalists' standpoint, less dangerous than an open-ended discussion dominated by Henry. . . .

To make absolutely certain that the debate would last several weeks, Mason moved that no vote for ratification should be taken "until the said Constitution shall have been discussed clause by clause, through all its parts." Again Federalists acquiesced, and the rule passed unanimously. The stage was set. Antifederalists would have the time they needed, but the fight was to be on grounds advantageous to Federalists.

Nonetheless, a clause-by-clause discussion of the Constitution did present a risk to the document's supporters. Madison feared that Antifederalists planned deliberately to "procrastinate the debates" until a weariness of debating, the heat of Richmond, and the convening of the state legislature at the end of June would provide an excuse for the members to "yield to a postponement of the final decision to a future day." . . .

The Virginia Convention: The Debate

Wednesday, June 3, was the first day for debating the Constitution and for discussing the proposed plan of government clause by clause in the committee of the whole. Before the clerk could read the first section, however, Henry sought and gained recognition. In disregard of the vote of the previous day, Henry intended single-handedly to shift the debate onto grounds favorable to his own position. He called for the reading of the "act of [the Virginia] Assembly appointing deputies to meet at Philadelphia to revise the Articles of Confederation—and other public papers relative thereto." Everyone now realized that Henry was laying the groundwork from which to challenge the legality of the proposal before the convention. He obviously was going to argue that the Philadelphia Convention had exceeded its authority by proposing a new government when it should have proposed only amendments to the Articles of Confederation. If he were successful, serious doubts might be raised, and a vote to reject might bring the proceedings to a quick end.

There was a stirring, and [Edmund] Pendleton was helped to stand with the aid of crutches to speak on whether the documents should be read. Whether the federal convention exceeded its powers "ought not to influence our deliberations," he declared. "Although those gentlemen were only directed to consider the defects of the old system, and not devise a new one," he continued, "if they found it so thoroughly defective as not to admit a revising, and submitted a new system to our consideration which the people have deputed us to investigate, [then] I cannot find any degree of propriety in reading those papers." The people were the key. The people were sovereign. Whether the Philadelphia Convention exceeded its instructions was of no consequence. One fact overrode all questions of legality: "The people have sent us hither to determine whether this government be a proper one or not." That, Pendleton declared, was the authority on which the convention and the Constitution, if ratified, would rest.

. . . Henry must have sensed that the power of Pendleton's logic had crushed any doubts he had raised, for he thereupon withdrew the request and took his seat. The clerk read the preamble of the Constitution and a part of Article I. George Nicholas of Albemarle County had agreed to speak in support of this section. His prepared speech lasted two hours. Such lengthy speeches would be the norm during the next twenty-one days.

After Nicholas concluded, Henry again sought recognition, but his objections were not addressed to the single section before the body. He had prepared himself to challenge the authority of the federal convention, and he was going to do so. "Who authorized them to speak the language of, *We, the people,* instead of *We, the states?*" Henry demanded. This was no confederation with which the people were comfortable. "If the states be not the agents of this compact, it must be one great, consolidated, national government, of the people of all the states," he reasoned. *Consolidated*—that was the scare word. It conveyed the impression that Virginia's affairs were being decided by outsiders. Time and again over the next three weeks, Federalists would have to parry this form of attack by explaining that they supported a federal system of divided or dual sovereignty, and not a consolidated or unitary system of national sovereignty.

Edmund Randolph now rose to speak. Randolph was the one man of real influence still able to join either side. His first speech was eagerly awaited. Randolph acknowledged that ever since Philadelphia he had believed in the necessity of amendments. The only question was whether they would best be adopted previous or subsequent to ratification. "The postponement of this Convention to so late a day has extinguished the probability of the former without inevitable ruin to the proposed Union," he declared. Since he believed the union to be "the anchor of our political salvation," his position now was that the Constitution must be ratified unamended. Those who, like himself, wished amendments must trust to subsequent alterations to improve the system.

After Randolph had spoken, Mason rose to refute the assertion that it was too late to amend the Constitution. It was not too late, nor would it ever be too late. "Its amendment is with me a *sine qua non* of its adoption." His words could not however, lessen the devastating blow of Randolph's defection.

On the following day Henry was back on his feet. . . .

Henry ranged far and wide, introducing the themes upon which he would play in the weeks to come. He attacked the executive: "If your American chief be a man of ambition and abilities, how easy is it for him to render himself absolute! The army is in his hands." He attacked the House of Representatives: "Virginia is as large as England. Our proportion of representatives [in the national House] is but ten men. In England they have five hundred and fifty-eight." He attacked the Senate: "The Senate, by making treaties, may destroy your liberty and laws." He attacked the national government's authority over the military: "A standing army we shall have, also, to execute the execrable commands of tyranny." He attacked the ability of the federal government to control the state militias: "My great objection to this government is, that it does not leave us the means of defending our rights, or of waging war against tyrants." What resistance could be made? "You will find all the strength of this country in the hands of your enemies; their garrisons will naturally be the strongest places in the country." . . .

Henry went on for three hours. . . .

Not since the first speech by George Nicholas had anyone spoken directly to Article I. For four days Henry had successfully sidetracked the convention, and he would have his way, choose his topics, and take his time for still another week. Not until Saturday, June 14, would the convention be able to begin the section-by-section analysis it had unanimously chosen almost two weeks before as the order of business.

The Antifederalist leadership was active in another way. If the convention was going to be diverted from ratification by the adoption of prior amendments, a list of suitable amendments had to be prepared and held in readiness for the proper moment of introduction. Near the end of the first week, an informal Antifederalist caucus led by Henry, Mason, and William Grayson began meeting for that purpose. It was not easy to get such a disparate group to agree on a single list of amendments. . . .

By June 11 a list of twenty provisions had been agreed upon and was ready for circulation. Since the adoption of any one amendment would serve Henry's immediate purpose of blocking ratification, he and Grayson had evidently allowed Mason to play the primary role in compiling the list. The entire document was in the nature of a bill of rights for the protection of the individual, but its adoption in this form would not have served Henry's larger purpose of restoring sovereignty to the states.

Latent frustrations ultimately surfaced on Monday, June 23, in a round of rhetoric that was both more intemperate and more personally abusive than any previously aired. The delegates had reached the boiling point. Hot, tired, living and working in close, uncomfortable quarters, equally divided over a momentous matter (if not to themselves, to their posterity), they were now trading barbs, insults, and threats. Fortunately, the last few sections of the Constitution had been read that afternoon. They had fulfilled their resolve to debate every section. Tomorrow would bring a showdown.

The Federalist leadership assessed the situation. The events of the day convinced them that it was time to force a vote on ratification. They had finished their explanations. Further delay would only aid Henry. An escalation of the day's name-calling might offend someone and lose his vote. Madison was of the opinion that "both sides [had by their actions] declared themselves ready for the question." It was time to move for a vote. That would not, however, be a simple matter. Henry and Mason were sure to "bring forward a bill of rights with sundry other amendments as conditions of ratification." "Should these fail or be despaired of," Madison predicted, "an adjournment will I think be attempted." The Federalists' count affirmed that they still held the narrow margin of "3 or 4; or possibly 5 or 6 votes." Madison translated the desperation evidenced by Henry and Mason into a validation of that count. Federalists were very concerned that illness, accident, or personal business might draw delegates away from the convention. With only a vote or two to spare, any kind of unpredictable circumstance could "endanger the result."

Before the June 24 session, Madison predicted the strategy both sides would use. Federalists would introduce a motion to ratify. The opposition would respond with a motion that the document be amended first. Federalists would then be prepared to introduce "a conciliatory declaration of certain fundamental principles in favor of liberty, in a form not affecting the validity & plenitude of the ratification." As a concession, they would recommend "a few amendments" for adoption *after* the Constitution was in operation. This procedure was a compromise within the Federalist ranks, necessitated, said Madison, "to conciliate some individuals who are in general well affected, but have certain scruples drawn from their own reflections, or from the temper of their Constituents."

George Wythe had been chosen to move adoption. As the session on June 24 opened, the chair immediately recognized the delegate from York County. Wythe briefly reviewed "the defects and inadequacy of the Confederation and the consequent misfortunes suffered by the people." He admitted that the proposed Constitution was not perfect, but he argued that experience would be the best guide to its improvement. As to the choice between previous and subsequent amendments, he contended that "the extreme danger of dissolving the Union rendered it necessary to adopt the later alternative"; necessary amendments "would be easily obtained *after ratification* in the manner proposed by the Constitution." He thereupon moved the unconditional approval of the Constitution.

Henry was on his feet to reply. One last time he raised the specter of northern domination. . . .

Henry asked the clerk to read two sets of amendments. One was the declaration of rights drawn up with Mason during the early days of the convention; the other was a set to amend "the most exceptional parts of the Constitution." The fourteen amendments in the second list were designed to ensure state supremacy in any conflict with national authority. Henry had earlier spoken of the purse, the sword, and the judiciary as the bulwarks of state supremacy. His amendments were directed primarily to those areas. In place of direct taxation, the Congress would have to requisition the states for funds in proportion to their populations. Only if a state refused to pay could Congress "assess and levy such State's Proportion." Federal revenue was expected to come primarily from tariff duties, but tariffs could adversely affect states like Virginia, which imported in quantity. One Antifederalist amendment required two-thirds majorities for passage of commercial legislation or commercial treaties. In time of peace no regular troops were to be raised except by a two-thirds vote, and terms of enlistment were limited to four years. State militias were to remain answerable to state authorities except in "time of War, invasion, or Rebellion." The federal judiciary would be limited to one supreme court and such courts of admiralty as Congress might establish. All cases except those involving a state or a foreign diplomatic representative would thus originate in state courts and be appealable only on the basis of law, not of fact.

After the clerk's reading, Henry launched into a general defense of his resolutions. When he concluded, Randolph attacked each of them in turn. John Dawson, a Spotsylvania lawyer, joined Grayson of Prince William County in Henry's defense. Then Madison received the nod of the chair. It was the crucial moment. Madison swallowed his pride in order to cut his losses. He announced his support for recommending most of Henry's proposals for subsequent adoption, "not because they are necessary, but because they can produce no possible danger." "No possible danger"—though they were as dangerous as a match in a powder magazine. But Madison had to provide assurance to a part of his faction that the convention would propose amendments.

The Virginia Convention: The Final Vote

On Wednesday, June 25, as the nine o'clock hour for convening approached, the galleries filled and all delegates, save two who had been called out of town, took their seats. George Nicholas received the chair's recognition. He bluntly confessed that the Constitution's friends "are convinced that further time will answer no end but to serve the cause of those who wish to destroy the Constitution." He therefore immediately moved for a vote on Mr. Wythe's motion for ratification. John Tyler of Charles City County moved to amend the motion by adding Mr. Henry's lists of amendments. . . .

The first vote—the all-important vote—was on Henry's resolution that, previous to ratification, a bill of rights and amendments "ought to be referred by this Convention to the other states in the American confederacy for their consideration." The clerk called the roll. Henry's motion went down to defeat, 88 to 80.

Pendleton then directed the calling of the roll on the motion to approve ratification. All those who, with Madison and Randolph, had voted no on Henry's amendments now voted aye for ratification. With one exception, all those who had previously voted aye with Henry and Mason now voted no. The Constitution was ratified, 89 to 79. A shift of just five votes would have defeated it, but Madison, for all his concern, had been the master of his forces. Madison, "Father of the Constitution," present at its conception in Philadelphia, had also presided as attending physician at its birth.

Two committees now had to be appointed. The first, composed exclusively of Federalists, was charged with preparing a formal statement of ratification. The committee was ready to report immediately, since the Constitution's optimistic supporters had drafted their victory statement even before the final vote. Governor Randolph read the proclamation of ratification. "We the delegates of the people of Virginia," it declared, ". . . *assent to* and *ratify* the Constitution . . . hereby announcing to all those whom it may concern, that the said Constitution is binding upon the said people."

The other group, twenty-man committee, included the prominent spokesmen from both sides. Its task was to report the amendments Virginia would recommend to the new Congress. George Wythe, the committee chairman, presented these recommendations on June 27, the final day of the convention. In addition to the original twenty bill-of-rights provisions, there were now twenty amendments requesting improvements in the new basic law. Antifederalists could thus claim a small victory to salve their wounds.

By its close and hotly contested vote, Virginia had become the tenth, not the ninth, member of the Union. New Hampshire had ratified four days prior to Virginia, although word had not reached Richmond by June 25. It is clear, nonetheless, that the approval of large and influential Virginia cemented the new Union's fate. . . .

2 Limited Government, Civil Liberties, and Civil Rights

The ratification of the Constitution, the adoption of the Bill of Rights, and the occasional addition of new amendments extending civil liberties and civil rights to previously excluded groups reflect Americans' long-standing belief in constitutionalism. Constitutionalism is a commitment to live under, and be governed by, a constitution that defines what authority government has, how this authority is distributed, and who is to exercise this authority (Goldman 1987, 4–6; Shafritz 1988, 134). In essence, constitutionalism is a belief in, and commitment to, the principle of limited government.

It is not an exaggeration to say that this principle is the fundamental one on which our constitutional system of government is built. But as important as this principle is to defining our constitutional system, it is never mentioned anywhere in the Constitution. Rather, the principle is indirectly expressed. Explicit and implied grants and denials of authority to the national government, the creation of separate governing institutions with shared and overlapping authority, the division and sharing of governing authority between the national government and the states, and the stipulation of specific rights belonging to the people are all constitutional expressions of limited government (Patterson 1990, 48–54).

The principle of limited government is commonly characterized as the rule of law rather than the "rule of man." It reflects a belief that government should not be all-powerful and that what powers a government does have should be stated as clearly and precisely as possible. It gives constitutional expression to our belief that individual civil rights and civil liberties shoudl be free from abridgement by the government unless the government's actions are taken in order to further a compelling governmental interest and are accomplished through restrictions that are as narrow as possible (Patterson 1990, 45; Shafritz 1988, 327).

By civil rights and liberties we mean those freedoms and liberties traditionally associated with the first ten amendments and later amendments such as the Fourteenth and Twenty-sixth. Contrary to popular understanding, though, the Constitution does not bestow specific civil rights and liberties upon individuals. Rather, what appears in the Constitution are negative expressions—statements of what actions government cannot take against individuals (Duskin Publishing Group 1991, 45). For example, the Third Amendment prohibits the government from forcing private citizens to quarter soldiers in their homes during times of peace.

Limited government, then, restrains government's ability to tyrannize those in whose name it governs. Nevertheless, throughout our nation's history there have always been elected and appointed public officials who failed to abide by the constitutional limits imposed on them. In his book *Police State: Could It Happen Here?* Jules Archer highlights a number of government transgressions against our civil rights and civil liberties resulting from the failure of elected and appointed officials to adhere to the principle of limited government. For example, the Alien and Sedition Act of 1798 made it illegal to criticize either the Congress or the president publicly in writing or in speech. During the early months of the Civil War, President Lincoln suspended the writ of habeas corpus, something that only Congress has the constitutional authority to do. The Espionage Act and the Sedition Act passed during World War I made it illegal to utter disloyal or abusive language against the U.S. government, its agents, or its flag. Similarly, the political witch hunt carried out by the House Un-American Activities Committee through the late 1940s and the early 1950s greatly endangered civil liberties and civil rights. The same is true of the FBI's surveillance of political dissidents during the 1960s and 1970s (Archer 1977, 139–166).

Government transgressions against our civil liberties and civil rights have occurred in the past, are probably occurring now, and are likely to occur in the future. But this persistent situation should not overshadow the fact that most actions of our national government's decision makers clearly reflect and are constrained by their adherence to, and understanding of, the constitutional principle of limited government. Equally important to remember is that many official actions of government decision makers are aimed at preventing or correcting violations of our civil rights and civil liberties committed by other governmental actors. For example, relying on the enforcement clause of the Fourteenth Amendment, Congress, during the 1960s, passed a series of civil rights statutes aimed at eliminating state-sponsored and state-endorsed discrimination against African Americans and other minorities that had limited their access to public accommodations, employment, housing, and voting.

The actions of Congress aside, most of us view the Supreme Court as the principal guardian of limited government and our civil rights and civil liberties. The Court guards our civil rights and liberties through its power of judicial review—"the power . . . to declare actions of the president, the Congress, or other agencies of government at any level to be . . . unconstitutional" (Shafritz 1988, 304). For example, from the early 1950s through the 1960s, the Supreme Court, under the stewardship of Chief Justice Earl Warren, used its power of judicial review to declare 25 federal and 150 state statutes unconstitutional. Through these actions, the Court "undertook to safeguard civil rights and liberties, promote social welfare, and carefully scrutinize state legislation attempting to restrict Bill of Rights guarantees" (Curry et al. 1989, 135).

Chief Justice Warren Burger, who succeeded Earl Warren, presided over a Court that, in some areas, was even more activist in protecting civil rights and civil liberties than the Warren Court had been. From 1969 through 1984, the Burger Court declared 34 federal and 192 state statutes unconstitutional. In so doing, the Court ventured into such uncharted judicial waters as abortion rights, affirmative action, and busing (Curry et al. 1989, 135). Only the rights of the accused (Amendments IV through VIII) were given less protection by the Burger Court than by its predecessor.

When it functions properly, the Supreme Court may rightly be thought of as a guardian of our civil rights and civil liberties. But we must be aware that, like that of other government decision makers, the Court's behavior is now always consistent. Throughout its existence, the Court has been inconsistent in its protection of a wide variety of individual rights such as freedom of expression and privacy. For example, flag burning is recognized as a constitutionally protected exercise of symbolic expression and is thus protected from government abridgment. Yet other symbolic actions such as draft card burning have been denied similar protection. Also, the Supreme Court has used the right to privacy to protect heterosexual couples from government intrusion into such intimate decisions as whether to use contraceptives or to procreate. Yet the Court routinely fails to extend privacy protection to homosexual couples.

Finally, we must also be aware that in its role as the guardian of limited government, the Supreme Court does not treat all individual rights equally. Four broad categories of rights and liberties are addressed in the Constitution: property rights, political rights (such as freedom of expression or the right to association), due process rights, and equal protection guarantees. The Constitution draws no distinctions among these rights, nor does it rank them. Rather, the text of the Constitution addresses all individual rights as being equal and worthy of equal safeguards against government abridgment.

But the Supreme Court does not treat all rights equally. For example, under what has become known as the preferred freedoms doctrine, government actions alleged to violate First Amendment freedoms are presumed by the Court to be unconstitutional. The government decision makers defending the challenged action then bear the burden of proving that the action was constitutionally permissible. In contrast, property rights are not considered preferred freedoms. Unlike those claiming violation of First Amendment freedoms, individuals alleging that government actions jeopardize property rights bear the burden of proving that the government actions in question are unconstitutional. The government decision makers defending the challenged actions need only establish that the actions taken were reasonably related to government objectives.

The two case studies presented in this chapter illustrate and develop further the above discussion. "The Pursuit of Martin Luther King, Jr." by Kenneth O'Reilly dramatizes J. Edgar Hoover's and the FBI's efforts to both disrupt the civil rights movement of the 1960s and undermine Dr. King's leadership of that movement. As O'Reilly's study shows, the FBI's actions against Dr. King and the movement were motivated by Director Hoover's belief that both communicated ideas that were dangerous to the United States and its survival. "The Pursuit of Martin Luther King, Jr." clearly and strongly reminds us that among our elected and appointed government officials, there will always be those who choose not to act within the limits imposed upon them by the Constitution but instead choose to advance their place and power at the expense of individual rights and liberties. It reminds us that the constitutional principle of limited government is not self-executing—it can only operate if those government officials assigned to live under its constraints believe in it.

"The Courage of Their Convictions" by Peter Irons is the second case study. It tells the story of how one young American's decision to wear a black armband to school to express her opposition to the Vietnam War resulted in a landmark Supreme Court case. In 1965, Mary Beth Tinker was an eight-grade student at Warren Harding Junior High in Des Moines, Iowa. Just two days before her action, the Des Moines school board had banned the wearing of black armbands in all Des Moines schools.

At issue in "The Courage of Their Convictions" is the extent to which the First Amendment guarantee of free speech protects us against government restriction and control of symbolic nonverbal expression. In the course of its discussion of the issue of symbolic expression and the First Amendment, Irons's story of Mary Beth Tinker reminds us that any level or form of government, even a local one like a school board, can transgress our civil rights and civil liberties. It also dramatizes for us that it is the unpopular or unorthodox exercise of civil rights and civil liberties that is most likely to be targeted for government suppression. It further explores the extent to which students enjoy the same level of protection under the Constitution as their parents and other adults.

"The Courage of Their Convictions" is presented in two parts. Part I is a narrative by Irons tracing the events surrounding Mary Beth Tinker's symbolic protest against the Vietnam War and the Supreme Court decision that arose from this protest. In part II, Mary Beth Tinker presents a personal account of this time in her life, her reactions to it, and the impact the events have had on her life. This personal account is important because it reminds us that it is not merely abstract rights and liberties that are harmed by government officials insensitive to constitutional limits imposed on them. Rather, real people are affected, and they may feel the effects of government transgressions against their civil rights and civil liberties throughout their lives.

Suggested Reading

Alderman, Ellen, and Caroline Kennedy. 1991. *In Our Defense.* New York: William Morrow. A popular account of the historical and legal significance of the Bill of Rights told in the context of recent federal court cases that demonstrate the first ten amendments in action.

Barnett, Randy E. 1989. *The Rights Retained by the People.* Fairfax, VA: George Mason University Press. A superb collection of essays on the history and meaning of the Ninth Amendment.

Curtis, Michael Kent. 1986. *No State Shall Abridge: The Fourteenth Amendment and the Bill of Rights.* Durham, NC: Duke University Press. A thorough and thoughtful analysis of the history and meaning of the Fourteenth Amendment and whether its framers intended this amendment to apply the provision of the Bill of Rights to state actions.

Doran, James A., and Henry G. Manne. 1987. *Economic Liberties and the Judiciary.* Fairfax, VA: George Mason University Press. A collection of essays interpreting the Constitution as a charter for limited government and individual rights and drawing attention to a "double standard" concerning economic liberties and civil liberties that has existed in constitutional law for over fifty years.

Halbrook, Stephen P. 1984. *That Every Man Be Armed: The Evolution of a Constitutional Right.* Oakland, CA: The Independent Institute. A historical and philosophical analysis of the Second Amendment that asserts that the right to keep and bear arms is an important private liberty necessary for individuals to be able to protect themselves against crime and potential government infringement of their liberties.

Van Alstyne, William W. 1984. *Interpretations of the First Amendment.* Durham, NC: Duke University Press. An analysis of the factors and considerations surrounding and influencing the various and competing theories about the First Amendment.

The Pursuit of
Martin Luther King, Jr.

Kenneth O'Reilly

As you read this case study, consider the following questions:

1. Why did J. Edgar Hoover and the FBI want to "smash" the civil rights movement?

2. Who did Hoover believe was influencing and giving direction to Dr. Martin Luther King and the civil rights movement?

3. What evidence of communist infiltration into the civil rights movement did the FBI's Domestic Intelligence Division uncover and report to Director Hoover?

4. What was Hoover's reaction to this report?

5. In their efforts to publicly destroy King, what tactics did Hoover and the FBI employ or consider using against him?

6. How did Hoover and the FBI use sexual allegations in the efforts to "smash" Martin Luther King and the civil rights movement?

7. Why was Hoover's obsession with the sexual habits of others so ironic?

8. With what type of civil rights leader did Hoover hope to replace King?

9. Though Hoover opposed both Martin Luther King and the civil rights movement, he did not want the FBI to align itself with every group that also opposed King and the movement. With what types of groups was he unwilling to have the FBI associate?

Abridged with permission of The Free Press, a Division of Macmillan, Inc., from *Racial Matters: The FBI's Secret Files on Black America, 1960–1972,* by Kenneth O'Reilly. Copyright © 1989 by Kenneth O'Reilly.

ON AUGUST 28,1963, J. EDGAR HOOVER AND THE KENNEDYS TURNED THEIR ATTENTION TO MARTIN LUTHER KING, JR., and the 200,000 Americans, black and white, who had gathered around the Lincoln Memorial on the mall in the nation's capital. The civil rights movement came to participate in the March on Washington, the largest of the civil rights demonstrations of the summer of 1963. They came to demand justice, to hold hands and sing freedom songs, to pressure Congress on the Kennedy administration's civil rights bill, and to listen to Dr. King talk about a dream "deeply rooted in the American dream." . . .

The March on Washington convinced Hoover that the civil rights movement would not wither away on its own, that he would have to smash it before it irreparably damaged his America. Before the summer of 1963 ended, the FBI began to tranform what had been a holding action against black demands for justice and equality into a frontal assault on Dr. King and the movement he helped lead. By FBI standards, it was a conventional war. "The director fell back on the cry that had never failed him in the past," Arthur Schlesinger wrote: "The ineluctable threat, evidently undiminished despite all his effort, of Communist infiltration into American institutions." After the March on Washington, FBI officials devoted as much time and energy to the communists-in-the-civil-rights-movement issue as they had once devoted to "the cause"—that is, the McCarthy-era purge of communists and other dissidents from the government and the professions. The director had spent his life destroying communists and their causes, and now he would try to destroy King and his cause.

Hoover's decision in August 1963 caught even his closest aides by surprise. The director saw communism as "secularism on the march," but few of his executives could detect this secularist advance, since Martin Luther King and other black Baptist churchmen were among the primary organizers of the civil rights movement. Every since the sit-ins began in February 1960, the FBI had been predicting a revival of communist activity in the southern black belt. But it never came. When Bull Connor and King faced off in Birmingham, the local FBI office informed the seat of government that no "CP activity" could be found "in connection with these demonstrations and no Communists are known to be participating." . . .

The dearth of communists simply encouraged FBI officials to look harder. On the eve of the March on Washington, a headquarters directive advised twenty-seven field offices to "be extremely alert to data indicating interest, plans, or actual involvement of the [Communist] Party in the current Negro movement." And the FBI devoted its entire Current Intelligence Analysis of August 21 "to the communist plans for the Negro March," distributing at least 149 copies to forty four government agencies. . . .

While the field filed its reports, Hoover requested a general summary of communist attempts to infiltrate the civil rights movement, assigning the task to the Domestic Intelligence Division (Division Five). On August 23, five days before the March on Washington, the Division submitted a sixty-eight page brief that minimized the Red menace. . . .

The closest thing to a Communist party front in the civil rights field, the Southern Conference Educational Fund (SCEF), was active, by the Division Five estimate, in "raising bail funds for those arrested in connection with integration activities, sending food and other relief shipments to depressed southern Negro areas and holding conferences." Of the eleven SCEF officers, the FBI *suspected* only three "of being CP members." . . .

Although Division Five qualified the report before sending it on to Hoover, its conclusion was unambiguous—given the FBI's unwritten rule that it was far more important not to be wrong than it was to be right. "We are right now in this Nation involved in a form of racial revolution," FBI executive Fred J. Baumgardner advised the assistant director in charge of the Domestic Intelligence Division, William C. Sullivan, "and the time has never been so right for exploitation of the Negroes by communist propagandists. The Communist Party in the next five years may fail dismally with the American Negro as it has in the past. On the other hand, it may make prodigious strides and great successes with the American Negroes, to the serious detriment of our national security. Time alone will tell." In the meantime, the communist menace merited little attention.

When Hoover read the report of August 23 he rejected its premise (that communist influence was "infinitesimal") and lectured Division Five chief William Sullivan. "This memo reminds me vividly of those I received when Castro took over Cuba. You contended then that Castro and his cohorts were not Communists and not influenced by Communists. Time alone proved you wrong." The report, Sullivan remembered, "set me at odds with Hoover. . . . A few months went by before he would speak to me. Everything was conducted by exchange of written communications. It was evident that we had to change our ways or we would all be out on the street." . . . The Division had to give Hoover what he wanted, or risk the consequences. . . .

In no position to challenge the director, Sullivan submitted Division Five's apology on August 30: "The Director is correct. We were completely wrong . . . the Communist Party, USA, does wield substantial influence over Negroes which one day could become decisive." He discussed King's "I Have a Dream" speech, labeling it "demagogic," and marked King "as the most dangerous Negro leader of the future in this nation from the standpoint of communism, the Negro and national security." To meet the threat, the FBI must concentrate on "the many Negroes who are fellow-travellers, sympathizers or who aid the Party, knowingly or unknowingly . . .

In Hoover's FBI orthodoxy on matters of policy was sacred. If Sullivan understood this simple fact better than most of the men who became special agents, he did not realize, at the time Division Five prepared the August 23 report, that Hoover was reevaluating previous policy, and that the March on Washington itself would convince him to make the change. "The FBI saw the march, in a sense, as far more important than we did," said Bayard Rustin. "The March terrified them. People in the Congress and the White House were beginning to change their attitude toward us." The movement's explosive growth convinced Hoover that he could no longer contain it through a noninterventionist policy on the law-enforcement front or a relatively passive surveillance policy on the intelligence front. The tactic now would be all-out surveillance (that is, counterintelligence) based on the ongoing operations aimed at the Communist party—specifically, the COMINFIL (communist infiltration) and COINTELPRO (counterintelligence) programs designed to "expose, disrupt, or otherwise neutralize" party members. . . .

Hoover based his case for a more aggressive intervention in the civil rights movement on the contention that communists were manipulating Martin Luther King. Neither the director nor any of his aides considered King an actual member of the Communist party, a charge widely circulated in the white South and among right-wing circles in the Southwest and in California. In the FBI view, King was merely a "security risk," to use one of William Sullivan's more restrained descriptions, because of his associations. At least eight persons, according to the FBI's count, who had helped King and SCLC, particularly during early movement days, were Reds of one sort or another—either former communists or the spiritual, never-had-a-card-kind. Stanley Levison, Clarence Jones, and Hunter Pitts (Jack) O'Dell headed the list, followed by Harry Wachtel, C. T. Vivian, Randolph Blackwell, Lawrence Reddick, and Bayard Rustin. . . .

In reality, there were few ties between the Communist party and the civil rights movement and only one dusty connection (Stanley Levison) serious enough to give reasonable men pause. Though the cry of communist infiltration remained a false (or at least greatly exaggerated) issue, it was impossible to prove or disprove the validity of the FBI's communist-search justification for spying on civil rights groups. There might not be any hard proof one way or the other. . . .

In late September, Hoover finally approved the Division Five request to use "all possible investigative techniques" in its "coverage of communist influence on the Negro." In October, Robert Kennedy approved the director's request to wiretap the phones in King's home in Atlanta and SCLC offices in New York and Atlanta. Two months later, on December 23, representatives from the Atlanta field office and Division Five met at headquarters for nine hours to discuss how best to expose "King for the clerical fraud and Marxist he is." Constrained only by a desire to avoid "embarrassment to the Bureau," Sullivan's groups proposed to infiltrate "King's office" with "colored" agents or perhaps "a good looking female plant," and to utilize "specialized investigative techniques [break-ins, in other words] at the SCLC office." Six days after the Division Five gathering, when *Time* magazine named King its "Man of the Year," Hoover responded: "They had to dig deep in the garbage for this one." Nearly a month later, he described King as "a 'tom cat' with obsessive degenerate sexual urges." The director clearly supported the Division Five proposals. . . .

By expanding its surveillance of the civil rights movement in the wake of the March on Washington, the FBI moved beyond peripheral operations in civil rights areas where the Communist party was thought to be active. From the fall of 1963 onward, FBI officials used counterintelligence tactics to "expose, disrupt, discredit, or otherwise neutralize" the civil rights movement itself. . . .

. . . By targeting King rather than the Communist party, the FBI broadened its assault. King himself, not Levison or some controller in faraway Moscow, was the explicit threat to law and order, and so he was the target of dozens of counterintelligence operations carried out by William Sullivan's Division Five with the cooperation of Cartha DeLoach's Crime Records Division. Crime Records disseminated the embarrassing personal and political information collected through the tap and all those hotel-room bugs not only to the media and King's own wife, but to virtually any individual or organization courted by the movement. The FBI bombarded the White House with data on King, along with select members of Congress—Congressman John Rooney (D., N.Y.), Speaker of the House John McCormack (D., Mass.), and Senator Leverett Saltonstall (R., Mass.), among others. Vice-President Hubert Humphrey, U.S. Information Agency director Edward R. Murrow, Community Relations Service director LeRoy Collins, United Nations representative Adlai Stevenson, and dozens of other government officials, moreover, received oral or written briefings. . . .

In the private sector, FBI officials tried to discredit Dr. King and the movement through leaks to various university administrators, foundation trustees, and labor leaders. In some cases, the Bureau targeted those persons who promised support for the movement. . . . While King was concluding negotiations for a $3 million grant from the Ford Foundation, DeLoach arranged for an ex-agent and current Ford Motor Company employee, John Bugas, to brief Foundation president McGeorge Bundy. In this case the approach failed. When Bundy asked if the FBI was the source of the allegations, DeLoach told Clyde Tolson it was useless. "Bundy is of the pseudo-intellectual, Ivy League group that has little respect for the FBI." Bundy, however, was the exception. Most of the people who greeted Bureau agents bearing dirt on King were considerably more gracious. . . .

Most COINTELPRO schemes attempted to influence public opinion on the un-American nature of the civil rights movement and its leaders in a similar manner. Cartha DeLoach helped arrange an interview in the August 19, 1963, issue of *U.S. News and World Report* featuring S. B. Fuller, a wealthy black businessman and publisher from Chicago, who claimed, as quoted by the FBI, "the current civil rights demonstrations (which are being supported by the Communist Party) do not encourage the Negro to work harder or become more self-reliant." With his advocacy of self-help and modest sixth-grade education, Fuller symbolized black mobility and the efficacy of the American dream. Because "his success gives the lie to the communist contention that the Negro is downtrodden," Hoover ordered DeLoach to circulate the article widely, "particularly with the Negro press," in the wake of the March on Washington. . . .

No matter how sweeping, the FBI's domestic political intelligence activities clearly centered on Dr. King. "King is no good," as Hoover put it back in February 1962. The ferocity of the Bureau's pursuit does suggest a vendetta, an overreaction to a new and potent social force. But King's targeting was quite rational. He was the available man, the most well-known, effective, and charismatic civil rights leader. After the March on Washington, King and the movement were inseparable in the public mind. If King could be damaged, the movement could be damaged. King was vulnerable to a subversion charge . . . King's personal life made him vulnerable on another front. The ease with which the FBI slid from the communist issue to the morality issue indicates that the director and his aides were looking for something—anything—that might work to discredit King. It also paralleled the typical racist belief in the sexual prowess of the black male and the threat to white society that posed. Hoover's fears were deeply personal. . . .

. . . If King could not be ruined by publicity charging him with subversion, perhaps he could be ruined with publicity charging him with adultery. "Hoover was a strict Presbyterian–brought up individual," Crime Records Division agent Lawrence Heim said. "If the Ten Commandments said 'Thou Shalt Not Covet They Neighbor's Wife,' that meant [exactly that]." Years later, after the tragedy in Memphis, the director initially suspected that King's assassin had been a vengeful husband.

Hoover dreamed of destroying Dr. King and replacing him with "a manageable black leader," another former Crime Records agent, Harold Leinbaugh, said. And a few of the more confident FBI officials, William Sullivan included, tried to find others. In January 1964, when Sullivan proposed to remove King from his pedestal, he suggested that the Bureau replace King with the "right kind" of black leader. John F. Malone, the FBI's man in New York, nominated Roy Wilkins. Division Five agents also favored Wilkins ("a man of character"), but in this instance Sullivan overruled his men—offering instead Samuel R. Pierce, Jr., a talented, conservative attorney who joined the Ronald Reagan cabinet seventeen years later as secretary of housing and urban development. Both men, Wilkins and Pierce, were unaware of the plans of their Bureau cheerleaders. . . .

FBI interest in Dr. King as "the 'top alley cat' " accompanied a parallel interest in the sex lives of virtually anyone interested in the subject of racial justice. New York agents tried to find out who the Communist party's top black functionaries were "carrying on" with, while Washington agents worked up a memo on a Civil Rights Division attorney who had gone off on an interracial date. Division Five investigated "the moral character" of Andrew Young and Jesse Jackson and looked into a rumor about Stanley Levison "having a paramour." In the meantime, Hoover discussed the "immoral conditions" within the black family with the ubiquitous David Lawrence, told the House Appropriations Subcommittee that Bayard Rustin (who was in fact homosexual) had once been "convicted for sodomy," and flooded the

White House with memos concerning the "personal behavior" of Community Relations Service workers. "He spread garbage about us," Roger Wilkins charged, "and he spread garbage about everybody in the civil rights movement."

Having documented "the depraved nature and moral looseness" of Dr. King and other black activists, FBI officials' attempts to use the information uncovered met with little success. Sumner Stone said "Hoover was a real prude—he misjudged the morality of the average American." When DeLoach offered transcripts based on the King buggings to a variety of newspaper reporters, columnists, and editors, nobody accepted the offer. Jim Bishop of the Hearst chain even claimed to have seen photographs, snapped by the FBI "through a one-way mirror," of King chasing "White women . . . in motel rooms." "The old man," Bishop concluded, "saw the preacher as a buffoon" and "could barely mention the name without bubbling at the lips." . . .

Hoover's obsession with the sexual habits of Martin Luther King and other civil rights activists posed an irony. The suspicion that the director himself was homosexual followed him for most of his career. Not even the FBI's own agents were quite sure about Hoover, a result of his "strange relationship" with Clyde Tolson, . . . with whom he took all his meals and vacationed over a period of thirty years. "I don't think anybody really knows," Leinbaugh concluded.

Whatever the nature of Hoover's own sexuality, his concern with and condemnation of other people's sexuality was severe, and he was determined to use anything, including sexual inferences, to damage Dr. King and other black activists. "The Negro community" was not much troubled by "a conventional standard of morality," however, and FBI programs designed to discredit movement people by emphasizing "alleged immoral or un-American political inclinations" simply were not working. If anything, the "moral turpitude" label enhanced "the status of these individuals among their peers." Promiscuity, much like "a criminal record or associations with radical groups," was less "a thing of shame to be hidden from public view" than "a badge of honor," sometimes even "a prerequisite to leadership." "Can you imagine anything sillier than somebody starting a rumor that Martin liked women?" asked Charles Evers, the NAACP leader in Mississippi and brother of the slain Medgar Evers. "Now, if he had a hankering for men, that's something else. That's my argument with J. Edgar Hoover. I mean, who's talking about whom? I'd say this to Hoover: You don't have any women anywhere. We might go and check *you* out." . . .

Despite the FBI's all-out attempt to destroy Dr. King, whether as a communist dupe or an adulterer (in order to smear and thereby slow down the black struggle which King helped lead, neither the director nor the men who ran Division Five found themselves completely free from constraints. In standing against the civil rights movement, Hoover's Bureau had to distance itself from other groups that opposed the movement. The FBI could not stand with the Ku Klux Klan, or even such nonviolent resistance groups as the American Flag Committee and its preposterous claim that all civil rights law could be traced to a modest Communist party civil rights initiative known as the Lincoln Project. The FBI investigated the obscure Flag Committee, as well as those southern newspapermen who spread its ideas, on the grounds that they were plotting "to defraud the public." Hoover opposed the black struggle by upbringing, temperament, politics, and bureaucratic instinct, but he would not allow extremists to control or even influence the nature and form of his resistance. . . .

. . . Hoover pursued his opposition to the civil rights movement on safer ground. He sought the safety of a formal alliance not with . . . extreme segregationists, but with the Kennedys, pressing Robert Kennedy to approve an FBI wiretap on King's home phone and SCLC office phones in New York and Atlanta. . . .

The civil rights movement's strategy had always been to force the FBI to choose sides, to turn toward civil rights law and away from the segregationists and the Red menace. "We were not so stupid as not to understand that other Americans who were opposed to what we were doing were also pressuring them," Bayard Rustin said. The FBI's strategy had usually been to avoid a clear-cut choice, a rather predictable strategy regardless of Hoover's own conservatism and fundamental assumptions about the Negro Question. Since the twilight of Reconstruction nearly every American politician with dreams of forging a national constituency had tried to dodge the race issue. The March on Washington, nonetheless, demonstrated that the movement was finally strong enough to force the FBI, and the rest of the federal government as well, to choose sides. . . .

The Courage of
Their Convictions

Peter Irons

As you read this case study, consider the following questions:

1. On what basis did the superintendent of the Des Moines School district and the president of the school board defend the district's ban on the wearing of black armbands?

2. On what basis did opponents of the ban challenge it?

3. What was Federal District Court Judge Roy L. Stephenson's decision pertaining to the constitutionality of the ban on black armbands?

4. Why was the ban on black armbands constitutionally permissible?

5. What decision did Justice Abe Fortas, writing for the Supreme Court majority, make about the constitutionality of the armband ban?

6. What was there about Mary Beth Tinker's childhood that influenced her decision to protest the Vietnam War?

I.

ON THE MORNING OF DECEMBER 16, 1965, MARY BETH TINKER WORE A BLACK ARMBAND TO HER EIGHTH-GRADE CLASSES AT WARREN HARDING Junior High School in Des Moines, Iowa. Her morning classes passed without incident, and she had lunch in the school cafeteria with friends who discussed the armband and topics more typical of conversation among thirteen-year-olds. Mary went from lunch to her algebra class. Before the bell rang, she was summoned to the office of Chester Pratt, the Harding principal. He demanded that Mary remove the armband, and she complied. Pratt did not allow Mary to return to algebra class, but suspended her from school and sent her home for violating a school-board edict which banned armbands from all Des Moines schools.

Mary wore her black armband to school in the American heartland as a symbol of mourning for those who were dying 10,000 miles from Des Moines, in Vietnam. The armband also expressed support for a Christmas truce and cease-fire in Vietnam. Mary's act of symbolic protest put her on the front page of *The Des Moines Register* the next morning. "Wear Black Arm Bands, Two Students Sent Home," the paper reported. Chris Eckhardt, a sophomore at Roosevelt High School, had also been suspended for defying the armband edict. Don Blackman, the Roosevelt vice-principal who suspended Chris, told the *Register* that "no commotion or disturbance" had taken place in the school. The school-board president, Ora Niffenegger, defended the ban on armbands as a "disciplinary measure" against any "disturbing influence" in Des Moines schools. Niffenegger pounded a patriotic drum: "Our country's leaders have decided on a course of action and we should support them." Mary and Chris followed a different drummer and found themselves out of school; they could return when they removed their armbands and rejoined the parade.

That same Thursday night, about twenty-five students and parents met to discuss the armband issue and decide on a response to the suspensions. The meeting was called by Mary's father, Rev. Leonard Tinker, a Methodist minister who worked as peace education director of the American Friends Service Committee regional office in Des Moines. The group issued a statement expressing "deep concern" that students were being "deprived of an important opportunity to participate in this form of expression" about the war. Earlier that day, students had asked the school board for an "emergency meeting" on the ban. Ora Niffenegger refused, saying the issue "wasn't important enough" to warrant review before the next scheduled meeting. Friday morning, three more students were suspended, including Mary's brother John, a tenth-grade student at North High School.

Following the five suspensions, the battle over the armband issue began with moderate words on both sides. Craig Sawyer, a Drake University law professor, spoke for the Iowa Civil Liberties Union in asking the school board to rescind its edict. The Union's statement recognized the need to protect "the educational atmosphere of the school" from disruption, but also recognized "the students' right to freely express themselves" on controversial issues. School superintendent Dwight Davis disavowed any intent to ban the expression of student views on Vietnam: "There should be an opportunity to discuss controversial issues in school," he said. "You have to draw the line somewhere," Davis added. The board drew the line at armbands because they threatened "a disruptive influence at the school." The board's policy had been adopted two days before Mary Tinker was suspended, and the front-page *Register* story about the ban appeared under an editorial cartoon of an American soldier stabbed in the back with a knife that read "Viet Cong Propaganda.". . .

. . . The Des Moines school board . . . met on December 21, but no truce was reached on the armband issue. More than 200 people jammed the meeting room for a two-hour debate. Craig Sawyer, speaking for the Iowa Civil Liberties Union and parents of the five suspended students, asked for their immediate reinstatement and repeal of the armband edict. Board member George Caudill asked Sawyer if he also supported a student's right to wear an armband with a Nazi swastika. "Yes," Sawyer replied, "and the Jewish Star of David and the Cross of the Catholic Church and an armband saying 'Down with the School Board.'"

In the best tradition of American town meetings, the Des Moines school-board debate exposed the roots of the conflict between free expression and public order. One board member, Rev. Robert Keck of St. John's Methodist Church, supported the suspended students. "Controversy is at the heart of education," he said, "and the disturbance of set thinking is the catalyst." Referring to physical attacks on students who wore armbands or black clothing, Rev. Keck said the board had let "the ruffian element dictate educational policy." George Caudill, a pediatric physician, responded that classrooms "should not and cannot be used for demonstrations" on any issue. "Regardless of the type of demonstration," he said, "it will be disruptive to some degree." Speaking from the audience, an elderly citizen asked the board to "maintain law and order in the schools" and recalled his school days: "If we did something wrong, we got the stick" from teachers and parents alike.

Bruce Clark, one of the suspended students, reminded the board that black armbands had been allowed in 1963 to mourn the four black girls killed in a church bombing in Birmingham. Alabama. Lorena Tinker, Mary and John's mother, assured the board that she and her husband had "not encouraged our children to be defiant." Mary and John, and the four other Tinker children, were raised "to be responsible citizens in a democracy," their mother said. "Our children have been raised in a home where we've held certain values. They are, in their way, witnessing to the values we believe in." After one board member moved to postpone any action on the issue, Craig Sawyer burst out, "I am demanding that you decide it. Take a stand! That's what you're here for." The board finally took a stand, voting 4–3 to continue the ban on armbands. Speaking for the Iowa Civil Liberties Union, Sawyer suggested that the board would soon meet Mary Beth Tinker in court. . . .

Following the suspensions in December 1965, the armband issue moved from the classroom to the courtroom. Mary and the other students returned to school after Christmas without their armbands, while the Iowa Civil Liberties Union filed suit in federal court against the Des Moines school board, seeking an injunction against the armband policy. Dan L. Johnston, a twenty-eight-year-old graduate of Drake Law School in Des Moines, represented the students. The board's lawyer was Allan A. Herrick, seventy-year-old partner in one of the city's largest firms, whose practice was centered on defending insurance companies against claimants. The case was assigned to Chief District Judge Roy L. Stephenson, who had been awarded the Bronze and Silver stars during World War II combat duty and who remained in the Iowa National Guard as a Lt. Colonel. An active Republican, Stephenson was named to the federal bench in 1960 by President Eisenhower.

The hearing before Judge Stephenson was brief, and Johnston and Herrick directed their legal arguments solely at the First Amendment and its limits. Mary and John Tinker and Chris Eckhardt each testified, Stephenson wrote in his opinion, "that their purpose in wearing the armbands was to mourn those who had died in the Vietnam war and to support Senator Robert F. Kennedy's proposal that the truce proposed for Christmas Day, 1965, be extended indefinitely." None of the school officials who testified cited any actual disruption of school activities by the armband protest.

Stephenson's opinion, issued on September 1, 1966, made clear his belief that students left their First Amendment rights at the school door. He admitted—citing the Supreme Court's decision in the *Barnette* case of 1943, striking down the school expulsion of Jehovah's Witnesses who refused to join flag-salute ceremonies—that wearing an armband "is a symbolic act and falls within the protection of the first amendment's free speech clause." But he countered that precedent with the Supreme Court's 1951 decision that Communist party leaders presented a "clear and present danger" to American society and that free speech protections "are not absolute."

Judge Stephenson's opinion reached beyond Mary, John, and Chris to put all Vietnam War protesters on trial. He noted that the school-board's armband edict was adopted when "debate over the Vietnam war had become vehement in many localities. A protest march against the war had been recently held in Washington, D.C. A wave of draft card burning incidents protesting the war had swept the country." Stephenson also noted that supporters and opponents of the war "were quite vocal in expressing their views" at the board meeting to debate the armband policy. "It is against this background that the Court must review the reasonableness of the regulation."

Stephenson bowed to the First Amendment in writing that an issue "should never be excluded from the classroom merely because it is controversial." But the board's concern for "the disciplined atmosphere of the classroom" took first prize in this balancing test. Stephenson allowed the "heckler's veto" to prevail over the lack of evidence of any actual classroom disruption. "While the armbands themselves may not be disruptive," he wrote, "the reactions and comments from other students as a result of the armbands would be likely to disturb the disciplined atmosphere required for any classroom." What the judge considered "likely" had not in fact happened, as school officials conceded. But Stephenson considered the armband policy "reasonable" and denied the injunction request.

More than 20,000 Americans died in Vietnam, and many more Vietnamese perished, before the U.S. Supreme Court met to hear arguments in the armband case on November 12, 1968. The federal appeals court in St. Louis had considered the case the previous year, but the judges split evenly and sent the case to Washington without an opinion. The nation had been profoundly shaken during the past two years: Vietnam had driven President Johnson from office; Martin Luther King and Robert Kennedy had fallen from assassins' bullets; Richard Nixon had been elected president with a "secret plan" to end the war. After fifteen years of judicial activism, the Warren Court neared its end: Earl Warren announced his retirement as Chief Justice, but stayed on after Lyndon Johnson failed in a lame-duck move to elevate Justice Abe Fortas to Warren's center seat on the bench. Meanwhile, the war continued as arguments began over Mary Tinker's armband.

Dan Johnston had barely completed his opening statement when Justice Hugo Black fired a barrage of hostile questions at him. Black had misread the trial record and somehow assumed that Mary's armband had disrupted her algebra class. Mary had in fact been called to Principal Pratt's office before the class began. Johnston pointed out that the trial record included "no testimony" by anyone that armbands had disrupted classroom activities. Black, as firm a disciplinarian in schools as he was tolerant of dissent outside them, ignored Johnston's citation to the record. Johnston also noted that school officials had allowed students to wear political buttons and even the German Iron Cross, a symbol to many of the Nazi regime. Schools should tolerate symbolic statements which did not disrupt school activities, Johnston argued. "Marching in the hallway or standing up in the class and making a speech about the war in Vietnam during mathematics class; that kind of thing I think the Court can prohibit."

Allan Herrick took the offensive from the outset of his argument for the Des Moines school board. School officials should not "wait until violence, disorder and disruption break out" before they ban a controversial message. A little latter-day McCarthyism crept into Herrick's argument when he tried to link the Des Moines students with a controversial group which none of them had joined, Students for a Democratic Society. Chris Eckhardt and his mother had attended an antiwar demonstration in Washington "which I am sure this Court is familiar with," Herrick said, referring to the November 1965 march that SDS and many other groups had sponsored. Herrick obviously hoped the justices were also familiar with the violence that erupted in Chicago at the Democratic convention 1968, prompting the indictment of several SDS leaders on riot charges. . . .

Chief Justice Warren argued at the Court's conference on the armband case that school officials had picked out only one message to censor and thus violated the "equal protection" clause of the Fourteenth Amendment. If schools "allowed wearing of Fascist crosses" and political campaign buttons, they could not outlaw Mary Tinker's armband, Warren said. Justice Byron White urged that the decision rest on the First Amendment, agreeing with Dan Johnston that "there's no evidence" of disruption in the classrooms. White's position prevailed and the justice voted 7–2 to reverse Judge Stephenson; only Hugo Black and John Harlan dissented.

Justice Abe Fortas agreed to write the Court's opinion, even though he had voted against hearing the case, which would have upheld Judge Stephenson and the Des Moines school board. This would be the last major First Amendment decision of the Warren Court, issued on February 24, 1969. Looking forward to an uncertain future, Fortas took a long look back at fifty years of Supreme Court precedent and concluded that neither students nor teachers "shed their constitutional rights to freedom of expression or speech at the schoolhouse gate." Fortas adopted Warren's argument that Des Moines school officials had tolerated political buttons and even the Iron Cross, "traditionally a symbol of Nazism." Mary Tinker and four other students had been suspended for "wearing on their sleeve a band of black cloth, not more than two inches wide." Their protest caused "no interference with work and no disorder." With the nation engulfed in an unpopular war, Fortas bluntly stated that schools "may not be enclaves of totalitarianism." His opinion rang with echoes of the *Barnette* opinion of Justice Robert Jackson, who supported the rights of students to express their views during a popular war. . . .

The *Tinker* decision represented the high-water mark of Warren Court rulings in First Amendment cases. After chipping away at rights of student expression for the next two decades, the Supreme Court finally adopted Hugo Black's dissent, ruling in January 1988 that school officials could censor the contents of student newspapers. Justice Byron White, who had grudgingly joined the *Tinker* majority in 1969, wrote in *Hazlewood School District* v. *Kuhlmeier* that students had no right to publish material which was "ungrammatical, poorly written, inadequately researched, vulgar or profane, or unsuitable for immature audiences." White wrote for a 5–4 majority in holding that the principal of Hazlewood East High School in suburban St. Louis acted properly in cutting two articles from the school paper. One dealt with the impact of divorce on students at Hazlewood East; the other described the experiences of three students involving pregnancy. White, now in his seventies, concluded that "the standard articulated in *Tinker* for determining when a school may punish student expression need not also be the standard for determining when a school may refuse to lend its name and resources to the dissemination of student expression.'' White concluded by quoting Black's denial that the Constitution compels officials ''to surrender control of the American public school system to public school students.'' . . .

Writing for the four dissenters, Justice William J. Brennan accused the majority of ''abandoning *Tinker* in this case.'' His prose heated by outrage, Brennan wrote that the lesson of *Tinker* was that teachers and school boards had no ''general warrant to act as 'thought police' stifling discussion of all but state-approved topics and advocacy of all but the official position.'' Brennan concluded on a rueful note: ''The young men and women of Hazlewood East expected a civics lesson, but not the one the Court teaches them today.'' Abortion had replaced armbands as the issue, and another generation of students had replaced Mary Tinker. When her son Lenny reaches high school, he will read these conflicting Supreme Court civics lessons— and decide for himself which best reflected the spirit of the First Amendment.

II.

I was born in Burlington, Iowa, in 1952. My father was a Methodist minister at the time I was born. He was raised in Hudson, New York, but he was making the circuit of small Iowa towns as a Methodist minister. We lived in Burlington, and we lived in Atlantic, Iowa, and eventually when I was about five or six we moved to Des Moines, Iowa. My father was assigned to a fairly big church there, Epworth Methodist Church. My mother was pretty much a housewife at that time. There were six kids in the family, three girls and three boys, and I was the fourth. I had an older sister and two older brothers, and a younger sister and brother. . . .

After we moved to Des Moines, my mother started getting more involved in civil-rights things and my father did, too. I remember there were a lot of civil-rights demonstrations that we all took part in, my parents and all the kids who could hold picket signs. We would go to the courthouse in Des Moines and picket around housing issues and voting rights. This was around the time when the southern civil-rights movement was becoming active and the freedom rides were going on. I remember there was a call by the Southern Christian Leadership

Conference for ministers in the north to come down to the South to witness what was going on there and help protect the freedom riders, because they'd be under less attack if the news was focusing on these northern ministers coming down. So my parents went to Mississippi for a few weeks. . . .

A very important incident happened when I was about ten. It was in about '62, I guess, when my father was removed from the Methodist church. He was not allowed to preach any more, because they were trying to integrate the Epworth Church where he was the minister. We lived in a racially mixed, kind of working-class neighborhood, where Epworth was, on the east side of town. The board of directors of the church was mad at him and gave him all kinds of hell, so he was basically put out of the Methodist church. They kept him as a Methodist minister, technically, but he didn't have anywhere to preach and he couldn't find another church. That was hard on him, because he really enjoyed preaching.

After that, we looked around at different churches. I remember my parents were shopping for churches, going to different ones, and thinking where would they fit in. About a year later, in about '64, he went to work for the Quakers. They took him on as a peace education coordinator for the American Friends Service Committee, which had a regional office in Des Moines. His job was to do a lot of education around a five-state area in the midwest. He'd stop at places, mostly churches, and talk to them about the Vietnam War, which was his job with the Friends. He'd take all kinds of literature and leaflets and movies, to promote the idea of resolving the Vietnam War and having peace in Vietnam.

I used to travel around with my father on his trips. It was kind of fun. I remember going to Kansas with him sometimes. For a treat, he'd take us with him to Chicago once or twice. I guess that affected me as far as the Vietnam War was concerned. And taking part in civil-rights demonstrations with my parents must have affected me personally about what happened to *them* as a result of being involved in integration issues. . . .

After the Vietnam War started to escalate and became controversial, we were going to these various demonstrations and pickets against the war. There was a teen group also that had its own activities. I was kind of a hanger-on because I was a little young. I remember sitting at Bill and Maggie Eckhardt's house one night—their son, Chris, was also involved in our group, along with my older brother, John—and we decided to wear these black armbands to school. I think the idea came nationally from something that Bobby Kennedy started. It was part of a call for a Christmas truce in '65, when there was this tremendous bombing of North Vietnam. . . .

So then we just planned this little thing of wearing these armbands to school. It was moving forward and we didn't think it was going to be that big of a deal. We had no idea it was going to be such a big thing because we were already doing these other little demonstrations and nothing much came of them. All the kids at this meeting went to different schools. The one I went to was Warren Harding Junior High School; I was in eighth grade. . . .

After we had our meeting at the Echkardt's and decided to wear the black armbands, we were all going to do it on the same day. I told this kid at school about it, and the day before we were going to wear the armbands it came up somehow in my algebra class. The teacher got really mad and he said, If anybody in this class wears an armband to school they'll get kicked out of my class. I went back and told the group and the next thing we knew, the school board made this policy against wearing armbands. They had a special meeting and decided that any student who wore an armband would be suspended from school.

The next day I went to school and I wore the armband all morning. The kids were kind of talking, but it was all friendly, nothing hostile. Then I got to my algebra class, right after lunch, and sat down. The teacher came in, and everyone was kind of whispering; they didn't know what was going to happen. Then this guy came to the door of the class and he said, Mary Tinker, you're wanted out here in the hall. Then they called me down to the principal's office.

The girls' counselor was there in the office. She was real nice. She said, Mary, you know we're going to have to suspend you from school unless you take off that armband. Oddly enough, I took it off. I took off the armband because I was intimidated. I was in this office with these people, the principal was there, and they were giving me these threats and I didn't know what was going to happen, so I took it off. The principal was pretty hostile. Then they suspended me anyway. That's the ironic thing about it. There was a moment there where I thought, This is the *end* of it.

The principal sent me home and called my parents. I went home, and everyone was getting a little bit hysterical. It was getting to be a big deal. Everyone was sort of milling around the house. My brother John, who was in the eleventh grade at another school, didn't wear an armband until the next day, and he got suspended right after he got to school. The two little kids in the family, Hope and Paul, were in elementary school. Hope was in the fifth grade and Paul was in the second grade. They wore black armbands too, but nothing happened to them. I don't think the schools thought people would support suspending *little* kids for something like that.

We got suspended about a week before the Christmas holiday started. We were out of school that week, and every day there was a lot of activity. We were going to meetings, discussing this, figuring out what was going on. The school board had a meeting after we were suspended that hundreds of people went to, and there was a lot of argument and coverage in the newspapers and television. We all went there, wearing these armbands, and they decided to maintain their policy.

After the Christmas holiday, we went back to school but we didn't wear armbands. What we did was to wear black clothes every day for a long time, I think until school ended for the year. We wore all black because there was nothing they could do about that, but it was still this statement. It was our way of fighting back. By then, I think some of the kids were thinking, That's just the nutty Tinker kids. But they got used to it real quick.

After all the publicity about what we did, we got a lot of repercussions. People threw red paint at our house, and we got lots of calls. We got all kinds of threats to our family, even death threats. They even threatened my little brothers and sisters, which was *really* sick. People called our house on Christmas Eve and said the house would be blown up by morning. There was a radio talk-show host in Des Moines who was a right-wing war hawk, and he would always start in on our family, the Tinker family. My mother used to listen to this all the time. I couldn't stand to listen to it, but she loved to tune in and see what they were saying. One night he said that if anyone wanted to use a shotgun on my father he would pay for the court costs if anything happened.

I was leaving for school one morning, on my way out the door, and the phone rang and I picked it up. This woman said, Is this Mary Tinker? And I said yes. And she said, I'm going to *kill* you! At that time, I started a policy I still have today; it's a habit. When anyone calls, I always find out who it is before I talk to them, because of that happening that one morning. It's made me a lot more hardened in certain ways, when you learn in a personal way what the repercussions are for doing unpopular things.

It was around that time when the ACLU stepped in and offered to support a lawsuit against the school board. My parents didn't have any money and no one else did—these weren't rich people. My parents were always broke. We had to make these depositions for the court, but I don't remember too much about what happened in court. But we did have to appeal to the circuit court in St. Louis, because the judge in Des Moines dismissed our case.

By the time the Supreme Court decided our case in 1969, we had moved from Des Moines to St. Louis. My father transferred to St. Louis with the AFSC, in the fall of '68. By that time, he was doing a lot of draft counseling. We had just moved to St. Louis. I was a junior in high school by then, sixteen years old. I was new in town, and I didn't know anyone. When you're that age, your friends are so important. I was like a fish out of water; I was kind of scared and shy.

When the Supreme Court decided the case, in our favor, suddenly it was mass hysteria. All these national papers and magazines wrote articles when the case broke. *Time* magazine came and did this whole photo session at the school. They came to my chemistry class; it was really crazy. I was trying to make sense of it all. Where does this all fit in with my personal life? I was trying to make new friends and here I am, this maniac who's all over the news. All the kids were talking about it. I think in a way I just wanted to put it out of my mind. I didn't want to be a big star, because I was a teen-ager. Teen-agers never want to stand out in a crowd. They just want to blend in. It was kind of a rough time when it broke. I was without as much personal support as when it happened, when I had a lot of my own friends around, and my parents' friends. My parents didn't really know anyone here in St. Louis either, outside of the people at the Service Committee.

After I recovered from all the shock when this hit the fan, and not having any friends, we started this little group, and I started being known a little better. Our group was called the Student Mobilization Committee, which was part of the antiwar movement going on in high schools and colleges around the country. It was a peace group, and we worked hand-in-hand with the black student union in the high school, at University City High School. We would go to demonstrations at the colleges and write articles, but I was getting cynical about the armband decision.

I remember being invited to take part in a walk from Columbia, Missouri, to Jefferson City, which is the state capital, because some kids from Columbia were writing an article for a school newspaper about the war, and they were censored—they couldn't write this article. So this huge group of kids and some adults walked about thirty miles, and they invited me to come and speak in Jefferson City when we got to the end of our march. And I said at the rally, Big deal—this armband case really doesn't mean *anything* because you still can't write an article in the paper; you still get ostracized; the war's still going on; these civil-rights cases that are fought through the courts are really just on paper and don't mean that much.

When I got older I became involved in women's rights and black-power groups that were active in St. Louis. Then I started getting real cynical about it. I felt like these legal decisions are really not going to make that much difference. Where it's going to be decided is through political pressure in the streets. I saw the improvements in black rights happening more through people rising up together than these legal decisions. Since then I've changed. I think it's really both that are necessary to change things; it all goes in together.

I didn't go to college when I finished high school. I was getting kind of rebellious about all this professionalism. My parents had lost their jobs; they had this problem with employment—my mother was working on her Ph.D., which wasn't helping her to get employed at all. When she *did* get her Ph.D. she was sort of blacklisted, and she couldn't get a job. I just decided this is not where it's at. I had been raised in kind of a lower-middle-class family; they were professional but they were broke. But they still had these professional values, and I felt like I wanted to be a traitor to my class in terms of these middle-class professional values. . . .

I started out being an apprentice to a piano technician and I learned to repair and tune pianos. From my parents' experience I thought that your job shouldn't be controversial or political at all. That's why I went into piano tuning. I thought, I'll do these political things on the side. In that way, they can never fire me—which through history is actually not true: Millions of trades people have been punished and fired for their political activities and protest. . . .

I liked piano tuning, but I felt like I needed to have another skill, and nursing seemed like a good practical skill. I thought nursing would be closer to what my real heart interests are, which is more trying to support families and make life more decent for them. I got a scholarship from the Veterans Administration and they put me through the last two years of nursing school. Then I had an obligation to work for the VA. I told them on the application, and I really believe it, that it would be a privilege to work with our veterans who have sacrificed part of their lives. And I believe that. I think the veterans should have good services and I am happy to be working in the VA. . . .

Even though I went through a period of being cynical about the armband case, I'm not at all sorry I did it. I'm glad that it all happened. I feel it was a privilege to be part of that whole time period and I'm really proud that we had a part in ending the crazy Vietnam War.

Especially today, when I get to talk to a lot of Vietnam vets and their families, it makes me even more sure that what we did was right and that the war was really a painful mistake. I work with a lot of paraplegics and quadriplegics, and some of them were injured in the Vietnam War. One guy I worked with today was amputated from the trunk down; his spine was shot up in the war. So I don't have any regrets about it at all. I'm proud to have been part of anything that stopped the war.

3 Campaigns and Elections

In our system of representative government, elections hold a cherished and valued place. They are our most basic and fundamental way of consenting to be governed by those to whom we delegate responsibility for governmental decision making. Elections are also our most basic and fundamental way of holding those same persons accountable—of registering support for, or opposition to, elected decision makers.

Campaigns, in turn, are the most basic and fundamental way in which incumbent elected decision makers and their challengers influence our assessments of the current government and its performance. Political campaigns are their means of conveying information to us—information intended to persuade us to elect some candidates and not others. By all estimates, conveying this information is a costly affair.

Take, for instance, the publicly financed 1988 presidential campaign. Jointly, the Bush and Dukakis campaign organizations spent $92 million (Patterson 1990, 456). This figure is an underestimate of the real amount expended during the campaign. It does not take into account the prenomination expenses of the various presidential aspirants. Nor does it include the independent expenditures of interest groups in support of, or in opposition to, one of the candidates (Maisel 1987, 242). For example, the public cost of the 1984 presidential campaign was almost $81 million. But prenomination expenditures were $110 million, and independent expenditures totaled $17 million. From prenomination through the November 1984 election, then, the real cost of the 1984 presidential election was closer to $208 million (Maisel 1987, 242).

Clearly the enormous amount of funds raised and spent in the pursuit of public office underscores the fact that money is a major ingredient of modern election campaigns. In campaigns for the U.S. House of Representatives and Senate, money may even be the most important variable contributing to a candidate's victory or defeat. This is particularly true for those candidates who are challenging incumbent members of Congress. Studies suggest that the most important variable affecting the outcome of congressional campaigns is the amount of money raised and spent by the challengers on their campaigns (Goodwin 1988, 125).

Challengers in congressional campaigns may need as much money as the incumbents, if not more, but they face a much harder time raising campaign funds than do the incumbents (Salmore and Salmore 1989, 74). A study by *Congressional Quarterly* (1982, 666) reports that over 70 percent of all challengers to congressional incumbents claim they have difficulties raising enough money to conduct an effective campaign. In contrast, only 10 percent of congressional incumbents report having problems collecting campaign contributions.

Part of the frustration that challengers in congressional campaigns experience is due to a pattern in interest-group campaign contributions that overwhelmingly favors incumbents. Because incumbents so seldom lose their bids for reelection, contributing more heavily to incumbents is an almost certain way for organized interests to guarantee themselves future political access to members of Congress (Sabato 1985, 78). For example, political action committees, or PACs, account for over 30 percent of all campaign funds raised by House and Senate candidates (Baker 1989, 164; Maisel 1987, 254). These PACs contribute disproportionately to incumbents (Sabato 1985, 73). One study of congressional elections found that over 80 percent of all PAC contributions went to congressional incumbents, regardless of the incumbents' political party. Only 8.6 percent went to the challengers (Baker 1989, 165). This inability to match incumbents' campaign contributions means that challengers simply have less money to spend in their efforts to unseat incumbents (Maisel 1987, 243).

Without a large campaign war chest, challengers cannot afford pollsters, political consultants, media and direct-mail specialists, or the other resources necessary in modern political campaigns for effectively conveying messages to the voters. As a result, congressional elections frequently are characterized by low levels of competition. For example, in the 1986 congressional elections, both the national Democratic and the national Republican parties estimated that only 40 of 435 contests for seats in the House of Representatives were seriously contested. Most of these were in "open-seat" districts where no incumbent candidates were running for reelection. As a result of these conditions, incumbents are overwhelmingly reelected to office. For instance, in the 1986 and 1988 congressional campaigns for the House of Representatives, 98 percent of all incumbents won reelection (Jackson 1990, 5).

For a representative democracy like the United States, the inability of challengers to convey their messages to the electorate and seriously contest elections is problematic. Political campaigns are supposed to be the means by which candidates try to convince us to vote for them and not their opponents. Indeed, in our representative democracy, we depend, in part, on political campaigns for information as to why we should vote for one candidate and not the other (Hershey 1989, 96). All candidates, whether they are incumbents or challengers, try to oblige our need for information by spending heavily to advertise their messages on television and radio and in the newspapers. For example, slightly more than 58 percent of the campaign expenditures in races for the U.S. House of Representatives are for campaign commercials and advertisements in these media (Goldberg and Traugott 1984, 6).

Ideally, as voters we use the information provided through political campaigns to make informed choices among candidates. But this effort is inhibited by the goals of the candidates and their campaigns in providing information. First and foremost among these goals is winning the election (Hershey 1989, 96).

To win, most candidates and their campaigns need a media strategy that conveys information that will convince us to vote for them and not their opponents. In developing a media strategy, candidates must make at least two decisions. First, candidates must decide whether the content of their messages will focus on substance or on image (Sabato 1981, 143). Second, candidates must decide whether the content will be cast in terms of a positive, negative, or comparative message and when it is necessary to respond to their opponents' message (Salmore and Salmore 1989, 145).

In recent years, candidates have been relying increasingly on negative advertising rather than on substantive discussions of the positive aspects of their own candidacies. Through negative advertisements, candidates hope to make themselves look better by making their opponents look worse. Negative advertising dominates contemporary campaigns for a simple reason: It works. In his book *The Rise of Political Consultants*, political scientist Larry Sabato (1981, 145) notes that "[t]he electorate has a better recall of the content of 'image' commercials compared with issue-oriented advertisements.'' Similarly, other studies suggest that although most voters claim to dislike negative campaign advertisements, they nevertheless absorb the information presented in negative advertisements more readily than the information presented in positive advertisements (Salmore and Salmore 1989, 159). An excellent example of this is how quickly Willie Horton became a household name during the 1988 presidential election.

The prevalence of negative campaigning means that those candidates who are attacked must consider how to respond. The failure to respond, or an ineffective response, adds credence to the negative attack and can literally cripple a campaign so seriously that it will never fully recover.

Such was the case with the Dukakis campaign organization during the 1988 presidential campaign. In almost every case in which the Bush campaign launched a negative attack, Dukakis and his principal advisors failed to refute the negative charges effectively. In commenting on Dukakis's failure, political scientist Marjorie Randon Hershey (1989, 86) quotes a senior Bush advisor: ''An election is in part a national tribal ritual, a rite of renewal, and if you don't respond in a way that says you know it, you send a subliminal signal to people that you are really outside the mainstream culture. . . . ''

The two case studies presented in this chapter illustrate the importance of money and media to successful electoral campaigns. Brooks Jackson's ''Money Is What It's All About'' vividly tells the story of an underfinanced challenger's inability to compete effectively against a well-financed incumbent and the inevitable outcome of this circumstance. ''Money Is What It's All About'' tells the story of Republican challenger John Holmes's ill-fated 1986 campaign against Democratic incumbent Fernand St Germain. Congressman St Germain was at that time the powerful chairman of the House Banking Committee. He was also being investigated by both the House Ethics Committee and the U.S. Department of Justice.

The second case study, ''Waving the Bloody Shirt'' by Peter Goldman, Tom Mathews, and the *Newsweek* Special Election Team, is an excellent analysis of the importance of media and a candidate's media strategy. It tells the story of negative campaigning in the 1988 presidential campaign, vividly recounting the effective, yet disturbing, use of negative campaigning by the Bush campaign and the inept way in which the Dukakis campaign responded to it. It dramatizes just how well negative campaigning can work to create negative impressions of one candidate in the minds of the voters. The study also illustrates an important principle of negative campaigning, implied but not really discussed in these introductory comments: When you can't think of anything good to say about yourself, say something bad about your opponent.

Suggested Reading

Alexander, Herbert. 1984. *Financing Politics: Money, Elections, and Political Reforms.* Washington, DC: Congressional Quarterly Press. An examination of the role and influence of campaign contributions and expenditures on elections and government and the reforms designed to control this influence.

Barber, James David. 1980. *The Pulse of Politics: Electing Presidents in the Media Age.* New York: W. W. Norton. An analysis suggesting that a twelve-year cycle of politics as conflict, conscience, and conciliation dominates presidential campaigns.

Fowler, Linda L., and Robert D. McClure. 1989. *Political Ambition: Who Decides to Run for Congress.* New Haven, CT: Yale University Press. An interesting study of why strong challengers to incumbent members of the House of Representatives often choose not to run, thereby helping to promote and sustain the incumbency advantage.

Heard, Alexander. 1991. *Made In America: Improving the Nomination and Election of Presidents.* New York: Harper-Collins. An exploration of how Americans choose their presidents and the consequences that flow from that process.

Maisel, Louis Sandy. 1982. *From Obscurity to Oblivion: Running in the Congressional Primary.* Knoxville, TN: University of Tennessee Press. An examination of the frustration experienced by losing candidates in congressional primaries.

Simon, Paul. 1989. *Winners and Losers.* New York: Continuum. One candidate's perspective on the 1988 presidential campaign.

Money Is What It's All About

Brooks Jackson

As you read this case study, consider the following questions:

1. What is the incumbency advantage?

2. What problems does the incumbency advantage create for challengers?

3. What is the trend in PAC contributions, and how does this trend put challengers at a disadvantage?

4. Why is money so important in today's political campaigns?

5. What is the relationship among money, the media, and challengers' standing in public opinion polls?

6. How does money determine challengers' ability to capitalize on incumbents' electoral vulnerability?

7. What impact does money have on the voters' ability to use elections as a means of registering support for, or opposition to, incumbent officeholders?

THE HEADQUARTERS OF FERNAND ST GERMAIN'S OPPONENT, JOHN HOLMES, WAS IN THE REAR OF A LITTLE SHOPPING PLAZA SEVERAL MILES FROM Providence, under the same roof with a beauty parlor, a butcher shop, and a Chinese restaurant. Grass was growing through the cracks in the asphalt.

It was hard to see any magic political technology at work in the Holmes headquarters one mid-August day in 1986. A big fan pulled humid air through an open back door and blew it into the weeds outside. The unisex toilet in the rear was doubling as a broom closet. There was only one desktop computer capable of communicating with the National Republican Congressional Committee's electronic bulletin board in Washington, and it was inoperative, its keyboard out for repair. In the candidate's private cubicle a tiny air-filtering gadget strained gamely to clear the air of haze from his eight-inch-long cigars. But the little machine, like much else in the Holmes campaign, was overwhelmed by the demands put on it.

Holmes had encountered the challenger's paradox; he couldn't win without spending lots of money, but people wouldn't donate unless they thought he was going to win. Holmes said that even those who did give were telling him, "But, John, money is what it's all about. I'm going to help you out, but he's got a million."

Holmes had raised $114,000 but it was mostly gone. He had bought an early round of TV advertising in May, mainly to boost his rating in a local television-station poll in order to convince potential donors that he could win, so they in turn would give more money. The day-to-day overhead costs of even a modest campaign organization were considerable—rent and furnishings, a political consultant, catering and printing costs for fund-raising events, salaries for a campaign manager, press spokesman, fund-raising aide, and a driver to ferry him to personal appearances around the district. As of June 30, the cutoff date for his most recent disclosure report, he had only $20,139 in the bank and he owed a $4,422 bill for sending appeals for donations.

St Germain's campaign fund meanwhile continued to grow with special-interest checks. The incumbent's donations were running an average of more than $1,000 a day. He was spending for a public-opinion poll and for early television commercials, but still more money was coming in than going out. As of June 30 the total on hand had grown to $747,858.

Business PACs were helping him, not the Republican challenger. St Germain had received more than $210,000 from PACs, nearly all of them run by businesses or trade groups. Meanwhile Holmes received exactly two checks from business PACs, totaling $2,750.

A field representative from the biggest business PAC of all, run by the National Association of Realtors, had visited Holmes a few days earlier. The candidate grew irritated when the PAC man quizzed him about his campaign's secrets: "What do your polls look like? What have you been doing? What about money?"

Holmes said, "What the hell are you asking me these questions for? You've got a major investment in my opponent." The Realtors had given $4,500 to St Germain. "He proceeded to tell me that, number one, oftentimes they make contributions to both incumbents and challengers. Number two, that there was talk around town that Freddy was in real trouble, and they would like to give this particular race a good, hard look." . . . But in the end Holmes got nothing.

St Germain was now officially under investigation by the [House] ethics committee, which began an inquiry on February 5 after months of delay. But that didn't deter the PACs. Merrill Lynch, which was keen on preventing banks from competing with stockbrokers, gave $4,000. The Independent Insurance Agents of America donated $5,000; they wanted to keep banks out of the insurance business. And, not surprisingly, the New York–based banking giant Citicorp sent $5,000, too; it wanted to get *into* the insurance and brokerage businesses. No faction in the turbulent financial-services industry wished to offend the chairman of the Banking Committee by failing to pay tribute.

Some of those who gave loathed St Germain personally. "He's as arrogant and pompous and as expectant a member as there is up there," said one senior official, whose association PAC gave thousands of dollars to his campaign. "He puts the arm on you," complained the head of another trade group that donated thousands. A third lobbyist said he resented having to "kiss the ring" of the chairman, but his group gave anyway. A lobbyist for a major bank said he treated the congressman like "a profit center." All of this, of course, was said behind the chairman's back.

St Germain sought money aggressively. . . .

He was outspending Holmes better than two to one on early television advertising. The challenger was struggling just to introduce himself to voters, half of whom couldn't recall ever hearing his name. One Holmes ad featured his four-year-old son, John A. Holmes III, wearing a tee shirt bearing the words "I'm voting for my daddy, are you?". . .

Holmes had been startled in mid-June when a TV station released a poll showing that despite his advertising, only 25 percent said they would vote for him. He had dropped 5 percentage points since April. Holmes's private polling was showing that only 52 percent recognized his name. Among those who knew him, including many Republicans familiar with his work as state party chairman, Holmes actually seemed to be leading. But after five years in public life, $33,000 worth of advertising, and countless television and newspaper interviews, Holmes was still unknown to half the people he aspired to represent. . . .

Officially, St Germain was near the top of the GOP's list of Democratic incumbents to be defeated. But privately the Republican campaign committee's political director, Ed Goeas, said, "I think Holmes will run a fairly good campaign. But I think that if it's a fairly good campaign with no breaks, St Germain comes in at the end, dumps a bunch of money, and blows us out of the water, and we don't even get 45 percent."

Holmes got no break. He would have been helped had the ethics committee condemned St Germain's honest graft and deception of the voters, but the investigation dragged on past August and into September and it became apparent that the committee would remain silent until after election day. A new and more serious allegation surfaced at the end of August; a lawyer testified in a private lawsuit that his business partner once claimed to have paid $35,000 in bribes to St Germain in connection with federally subsidized apartments. But St Germain and the alleged bribe payer denied the story, which couldn't be substantiated and didn't help Holmes politically.

On the day the bribe story broke, Holmes had only $42,000 in campaign cash in the bank and St Germain had $677,000. Holmes wasn't mailing fund-raising solicitations on time, wasn't scheduling enough money-raising receptions, and wasn't getting anywhere near the amounts needed. From Washington, political director Ed Goeas pressured Holmes to replace his campaign manager with a woman trained at the party's Washington academy for political workers. Fundraising efforts then began to go more smoothly, but there were only a few weeks left.

Polling on both sides indicated that Holmes still had a chance to win if—somehow—he came up with enough money. By mid-September a Republican campaign committee poll showed that 52 percent in

St Germain's district said they favored a "new person" to represent them. St Germain's weakness was remarkable: 37 percent had an unfavorable opinion of him, a dangerously high index of negative feeling toward an incumbent who had represented the district for so long.

But Holmes hadn't been able to buy any television advertising since May, and in mid-September his name was still unfamiliar to nearly two voters of every five. St Germain would win by default unless Holmes could boost his name recognition. In mid-September he began broadcasting a thirty-second commercial that proved to be effective. A Republican campaign committee camera crew recorded Holmes standing before the Capitol saying:

"The future of Rhode Island and our country depends on what goes on in that building behind me. I hope to be working there in January. And if I do, you'll be reading about my legislation, and not my scandals. . . . "

"You may not always agree with me, but you'll *always* be able to trust me."

Holmes found enough money to run the ad for nearly two weeks, often enough so that a typical viewer saw it three times during each week. That was the least that political consultants considered necessary to register any impact on viewers, whose eyes and ears already were assaulted by a clutter of ads for hamburgers, cars, beer, and wine coolers. Some consultants urge candidates to buy their television time in blocks of 600 weekly gross rating points, so that the typical viewer will see the ad six times in a given week. St Germain was buying closer to the 600 level.

. . . Holmes entered the final month with less than $21,000 in the bank. His "trust me" ad was working. A new round of GOP polling showed that more voters had heard of Holmes, and his favorable rating was climbing. St Germain was still polling less than 50 percent. . . .

Holmes was spending an hour in the morning and another hour in the afternoon, every day, calling anyone who might be good for a contribution. It was too little; successful fund-raisers spend much more of their time personally soliciting donations. The campaign staff was getting fund-raising letters out more smoothly, but the mail would gross only about $7,500 in small donations by late October.

Holmes had to raise his money from his own constituents. His staff made a run at the PACs; his new campaign manager, Anna Mary Hoovler, had been a specialist in PAC solicitation at the Republican campaign committee in Washington. She tried to cash in on her old contacts. "We switched gears and began concentrating on PACs for about a week," she said. "By this time I had called up every PAC person I knew, begging." Some business PAC checks came in. . . . A PAC funded by imported-car dealers sent $2,500, showing dissatisfaction with the incumbent's vote for a protectionist trade bill. The American Medical Association, without any banking legislation to worry about, gave $3,500.

But mostly the PACs gave excuses. "They said, 'We don't have a plant in the district,' or 'We're out of money,' or 'What we have left is for debt retirement' [for winners, after the election], or 'We just can't get involved,'" said Hoovler.

In the end, Holmes got barely $40,000 from PACs, including less than $20,000 from business groups. St Germain eventually amassed a PAC total of more than $300,000, predominantly from business interests.

As a liberal Democrat, St Germain could take business PAC money without fear of reproach from consumer groups. He was one of their favorites because he often criticized bankers for charging high interest rates on credit cards and sponsored relatively trivial but crowd-pleasing bills to regulate unpopular commercial practices. In 1986 he was pushing a measure to force banks to credit deposits quickly, trimming the long "holds" they sometimes imposed while waiting for checks to clear. The check-hold problem was of much less import than such matters as the plundering of the savings and loan industry by unscrupulous operators who threatened to bankrupt the federal deposit insurance fund. But consumer groups generally stood by St Germain. . . .

With St Germain monopolizing business money and escaping criticism for it, Holmes faced disaster. His money ran out and his campaign fell silent. . . . . For several crucial days in early October, when the campaign should have been building momentum for the approaching election, Holmes had to withdraw his TV ads.

Holmes sank in the polls while his ads weren't appearing. Republican Gov. Edward DiPrete, polling daily for his own re-election campaign, added to his surveys an extra question asking voters whether they favored St Germain or Holmes. It showed Holmes's support was declining by about one percentage point every twenty-four hours that his commercials were off the air. It was as though his campaign no longer existed.

Holmes resumed advertising with help from Vice President George Bush. His presence enabled the campaign to sell $32,000 in tickets to a reception, although the event netted only $20,000 after paying expenses, including $7,500 for the Vice President's travel. The event was on a Monday and television stations were demanding $18,000 by Thursday to hold the time spots open. Holmes got the check delivered in time and bought another week's worth of television. By this time nearly every available dollar went into TV time.

Holmes couldn't afford to spend $1,500 for a professional coach to help him prepare to debate St Germain on television. But [Rep. Tony) Coelho arranged for the congressman to get media training from Michael Sheehan, a leading Democratic consultant. Sheehan put St Germain through a session at the Democratic campaign committee's television studio in Washington, where he could watch replays of his practice performances. . . .

St Germain's media coaching paid off. He had to agree to at least one televised debate or risk giving Holmes an issue. So he followed a strategy his consultant often urged on incumbents: refusing invitations to debate on commercial television and agreeing instead to a single half-hour debate on a little-watched public television station. He also insisted on a format stacked entirely in his favor; none of the state's knowledgeable political reporters would be present to grill him about embarrassing topics. Media consultant Sheehan had often told clients in Holmes's position, "If there's dirty work to be done, let the press do it." Now the reverse applied. St Germain kept the press away. . . .

St Germain followed his media coach's advice; he smiled like a kindly uncle. He acted the part of a man falsely accused, but suffering his tormentors with patience and grace. He spoke softly and slowly, almost sighing. "Integrity? You bet I've got it," he said.

Holmes, lacking coaching, came off badly. He accused St Germain again and again of lying. "You owe it to the people, sir, to begin telling the truth. . . . Be an honorable man!" He was right; St Germain claimed he was no longer being investigated by the ethics committee when in fact the panel's chairman had said the inquiry was still pending. But Holmes appeared strident and unpleasant, a poor introduction to any voters looking for an embraceable alternative to the incumbent.

The Holmes campaign was all downhill from there. He fired his poll taker, Linda DiVall, and against her advice began airing a boisterous ad ridiculing St Germain's honest graft. It was intended to be hilarious, a send-up of television game shows like *Wheel of Fortune*. In a casino-like setting, a dealer wearing sleeve garters shuffled an odd-looking deck of oversize playing cards while a berserk announcer babbled away excitedly:

"Let's play . . . St Germain Rummy!

"See if you can become a millionaire on a small salary, just like our congressman, Fred St Germain."

The dealer laid out cards with pictures of restaurants on a green felt table.

"Wow!" the announcer gushed. "Just like Freddy, you bought *five* pancake houses with someone else's money! All you have to do is provide a few small favors."

More cards, this time with photos of condominiums.

"Look at this! Condos and houses worth millions! All for just a few small favors.

"Oh-oh!"

A card labeled 'income tax" fell on the table, facedown. But hands reached down and ripped it quickly in half, discarding the pieces.

"Great! You're ignoring it, just like Freddy!"

Combative young staffers at the Republican campaign committee had urged that the ad be aired. But at an early preview Linda DiVall shook her head morosely. "I think very frankly that a spot like this could lose the race," she said. "You could redo the whole ad again, with a touch of humor. But not slapstick. This is amateurish."

When Holmes finally released the commercial, it had pretty much the effect DiVall predicted. St Germain's polling showed it fell flat, and his media handlers were amazed that Holmes kept it on day after day. But Holmes had too little money either to produce a new commercial or to buy the last-minute polling that might have told him that the "Rummy" ad wasn't working.

St Germain's ads ran more frequently and in better-watched time slots. He would have bought even more but several statewide candidates had already purchased all available television time. Instead, St Germain bought radio ads, sending his messages to nearly every car and kitchen in the district. Holmes had nothing to spare for radio, where it was as though St Germain was running without opposition. . . .

Despite the misgivings voters expressed to poll takers, St Germain won re-election easily, crushing Holmes by 57.7 to 42.3 percent. Political professionals faulted Holmes afterward as a candidate weak on personality, saying he gave voters little reason to support him. But St Germain wasn't very personable either. His strength lay in the federal money he had won for his district and in his special-interest campaign funds, which allowed him to dominate a contest fought largely on television and radio. Holmes lost, as nearly all challengers do, for lack of money. . . .

Waving the Bloody Shirt

Peter Goldman
Tom Mathews
With the *Newsweek* Special Election Team

As you read this case study, consider the following questions:

1. How has the decreased role of political parties in elections and the increased role of professional consultants in campaigns contributed to a greater prevalence of negative campaigning and negative advertising?

2. How does the analogy between campaigns and elections and a marketplace serve to justify or rationalize the use of negative campaigning and negative advertising?

3. What marketing techniques are used in campaigns to test for, and find, the best campaign slogans and plan of attack?

4. What role does the "attack ad" play in the modern campaign?

5. Why is it important to respond vigorously to attack ads?

6. What ethical limits, if any, are observed in use of negative advertisements in modern political campaigns?

7. Regarding the use of negative campaigning and negative advertisement, does the end justify the means?

S TU SPENCER WAS ONE OF THE FIRST OF THE MODERN POLITICAL CON-
SULTANTS, THE MEN WHO MADE A RICH BUSINESS OF TELEMARKETING
candidates like Tums or Isuzus. But he was uneasy in the fancified
language of his trade—a euphemistic newspeak in which getting your
guy on Rather or Brokaw was called "earned media" and having him
sling mud when he got there was "comparative campaigning."
Spencer's speech, like his politics, was as subtle as a blackjack, and
the counsel he brought to Bush Inc. when he joined up formally in
New Orleans had less to do with the marketability of their own product than with the weaknesses of the competition. Mike Dukakis was
a mean little prick from Harvard, in Spencer's view, a wise-ass rookie
who didn't know what it was like flying around with a hundred Sam
Donaldsons baying in the back of the plane. You had to get to him,
show him up for what he was. You had to put a knife to his throat
and hold it there for sixty days. If he breaks, Spencer mused, you win.
If he doesn't, you lose—it was as simple as that.

Spencer's formula, more elegantly framed, had already become
the core strategy for Bush's fall campaign—a strategy whose subtext
was that the vice president would have to savage Dukakis because he
was not good enough at the game to win on his own. . . .

The candidate was retrofitted by his managers with a new set of
"values" and with an array of powerful symbols to give them force—a
black rapist, a befouled harbor, an empty electric chair, a revolving-
door prison, and the American flag. Few of the issues or the metaphors
had figured prominently in his past as a public man; in none of his
changing shadings of ideology had he been known, for example, as
a flag-waver, a crime-buster or a battler for the environment. But he
slipped willingly into his new character and was further blessed
with an opponent who seemed not to know how to respond. Dukakis,
Roger Ailes guessed, would on the whole rather talk about auto insurance. . . .

Bush's transformation from pragmatist to ideologue was brilliantly
conceived and greatly aided by the governor's tongue-tied reaction
to it; the vice president became the strong man in the field and Dukakis
the wimp, soft on taxes, criminals, polluters, pornographers and the
Red menace. The blunt-instrument approach to what Bush Inc. chose

to call the Mondaleizing of Mike Dukakis was raw, and his handlers were defensive about it; by late fall, engulfed in bad notices and souring polls, Baker would produce a list of 207 affirmative policy proposals advanced by the vice president in the course of his campaign.

But the politics of incivility remained the dominant tone of his candidacy, and Bush's men had too little faith in him to tone it down, even when his lead over Dukakis was flirting with double digits. You still needed the negative stuff, one of its architects said, to make people afraid of Mike Dukakis; if your own candidate was weak, too much of the kinder-gentler persona he had assumed in New Orleans would only re-create the wimp image and drag him back down again.

The stronger case for the strategy, in the winning-is-everything world of the professional managers, was that it worked so well. As John Sununu, one of its earliest advocates, put it, no sensible campaign repeats a line if it doesn't play the first time, and most of Bush's passed the first-use test. His militance was cynical in a match between two ideologically nondescript men, Mr. Résumé, as one nonaligned Democratic operative put it, against Mr. Position Paper; it required that Bush run against the fugitive murderer Willie Horton as Dukakis's surrogate and that he make the Pledge of Allegiance the leitmotif of his campaign when he himself couldn't dependably remember the words.

The justification, for Bush Inc., was in the marketplace. Aesthetically, one conceded, the flag-and-furlough business was terrible stuff, but it stuck as metaphor because it touched real chords in the electorate—a vein of doubt as to who the governor was and what he did stand for. It was a given, in this view, that the election was about change; the next president would not be Ronald Reagan. The only recourse was to make change look safe in Bush's hands and scary in Dukakis's; they had to use whatever symbols were at hand to make life with the Duke sound dangerous. . . .

Their arsenal was already well stocked and market-tested. The first-wave assault in June was followed by a second in late summer, even more violent. Willie Horton and the flag became the centerpieces of what Bush Inc. chose to call a values agenda, the whole cluster of hot-button issues designed to call Dukakis's sense, his will, his record and even his patriotism into question. The racist and nativist undertones in some of the rhetoric lay in the ear of the listener, so far as Bush's managers were concerned, and were of secondary concern in any case; in a war, only throw-weights counted. The Pledge issue alone, one senior strategist guessed, would be worth a hundred and fifty electoral votes, mainly in the South, but the agenda as a whole had the potential to *destroy* Dukakis.

Gampy Goes Ballistic

The case for going ballistic was further reinforced by the continuing difficulty . . . of finding anything very positive for Bush to say in his own behalf. In the normal course of politics, Teeter's man Fred Steeper mused, you couldn't just give voters a reason to vote against the other guy—you had to give them a reason to vote for *you.* They had a lot of reasons for voting against Dukakis, however removed from the real concerns of the presidency. But as they cranked up in the summer, Bush still hadn't answered the why-me? question that had dogged his campaign from the beginning, and his handlers were still searching for meanings in his candidacy. . . . With the fall campaign almost upon them, they knew only that Bush had to take some kind of strong stand. They didn't know, and would never quite figure out, what he should stand *for.*

The search was not greatly advanced by a . . . series of focus groups . . . in which gatherings of Reagan Democrats were wired with electronic-response meters and shown a series of dummied "news" videos detailing the candidates' positions on various issues. . . .

For the focus groups, Steeper and Sparks commissioned a series of two-to-four-minute scripts in newscast style, each based on one of [several pairs of issues that had been identified previously]. A Las Vegas actor was hired to read them, and the participants were asked to respond by twisting a dial on a scale of zero to one hundred; a stylus recorded their reactions. None of the vice president's positives moved the needle much in his favor; his scores were strongest when he was at his most reactive, coming out against what Dukakis was, or was perceived to be, for. Pro-Bush issues that ought to have been salient weren't. Prosperity, the classic winner for in parties in good times, was a surprising dud. The Reagan Democrats simply didn't recognize it as a description of their own lives, and the P word was whited out of the Republican lexicon, in both ads and fliers. More modest boasts were preferred; Bush's slogan for the fall would be "Experienced Leadership for a Changing World."

What did work were the so-called wedge social issues, the us-against-them hammering on who hated rape and murder most and who loved the flag best. There was in fact little difference between Bush's core values and Dukakis's, both being patriotic and rectitudinous men; Dukakis, in fact, had more to brag about in the falling crime rate on his watch as governor than Bush did in impeding the flood of cocaine on his as Reagan's drug buster. There were, moreover, strong anti-Bush entries on Sparks's ledger, things Dukakis could have used if he had had the skill and imagination; it was considered a wonder . . . that . . . they never saw a Dukakis ad with the Ayatollah's picture in it.

But Dukakis had a way of fighting fire with paper, volumes of it, drawn from casebooks in constitutional law rather than from horn-books on rudimentary political strategy. When he answered at all, his response time was too slow and his cast of mind too legalistic to stand up to what Sparks called . . . "the litany of criticism"—the whole bill of goods about how Dukakis was for everything liberal from abortion to taxes and against everything wholesome from handguns to school prayer to saluting the flag.

The results were sent forward to Bush's propaganidist with EKG-style readouts attached—user-friendly guides to what buttons to push to rouse what emotions among voters. The first reactions were sour, the reflexive response of people who thought themselves artists at politics standing against men who thought they could reduce it to a binary science; it was, Sparks thought, like trying to sell a paint-by-numbers kit to peole lying on their backs getting ready to do the Sistine Chapel ceiling. But when the initial grumbling had subsided, some of the core findings found their way into the ad campaign; several spots used the Litany Effect, cramming three of Dukakis's heresies instead of one into thirty seconds, and the governor's negatives began their steady uphill climb.

The issues involved had little to do with the business of the presidency, but they made effective politics, the beginning of the promised paint job on Dukakis in shadings of libreal pink rather than his preferred managerial gray. "By the time this election is over, Willie Horton will be a household name," Atwater boasted to a meeting of party operatives early in the summer. They were skeptical; one man in his audience wondered whether Lee meant the same Willie Horton who played outfield for the Detroit Tigers. But by fall, Willie the Bad was indeed a national celebrity, his story the stuff of campaign speeches and *Reader's Digest* reprints, his crimes told and retold by his white victims and by Bush's surrogates. In one excess of enthusiasm, a Bush operative said Dukakis had put a hundred million people at risk along the path Horton traveled from Boston to Maryland in his flight from the law. . . .

No single "issue" was quite so devastating to Dukakis. It seemed not to matter that more than forty other states had home-leave programs, too, or that Massachusetts's generous version started under a Republican governor, or that there had been similar horror stories involving furloughed Federal prisoners in the Reagan-Bush years. What counted . . . was that Dukakis was wounded and doing nothing visible to stop the bleeding; the end, in knife-at-the-throat politics, justified the mean. Bush ranged the countryside like a candidate for district attorney, posing, in Dukakis's Boston among other ports of call, with ranks of officers in police blues and khakis. The message was that the governor cared more for criminals than for their victims or for the policemen charged with stopping them; his word to felons, Bush said, was not "Make my day" but "Have a nice weekend."

What Bush couldn't say, Roger Ailes did, eagerly and well, in his advertising campaign. Ailes was in his warrior mode, psyched for battle against an opponent he referred to variously as Shorty for his size, Grapeleaf for his origins, and That Heartless Little Robot for his demeanor. He had gone so far as to consult a psychologist about what made Dukakis tick and had been advised that the governor had the symptoms of a classic narcissist: he was self-absorbed, a guy who believed that only he was right and everyone else was wrong. Smugness in an opponent can be disabling, even paralytic, and the expert opinion only reinforced Ailes's feeling that Shorty could be had.

The means, moreover, were at hand; the attack ad had become to the modern political handler what Flavour-aide had been to Jonestown, a harmless-looking medium for the mass administration of deadly toxins. . . .

It was sometimes forgotten, except by Ailes, that only fourteen of the campaign's thirty-seven spots could be construed as direct attacks on Dukakis. The others were more or less positive, and some were artworks of the "Morning in America" school, soft-focus minifilms splicing bits of kinder-gentler rhetoric with shots of "Gampy" Bush at home hoisting one of his granddaughters joyously into the air. But the negative commercials Ailes made or commissioned, if less numerous and less stylish, were the more potent and more clearly the hallmark of the campaign. The morning-in-Kennebunkport promos became complements to the attack ads; they presented Bush for the most part not as a bold, heroic or even particularly leaderly man but as a candidate for First Uncle, a safe alternative to the swarthy little guy with the ACLU card and the get-out-of-jail-free tickets in his hip pocket.

The negative spots aimed at the jugular rather than the heart, and their superior punch was obvious in the polls; Bush's favorable ratings stayed flat through the fall, the Gampy Tapes notwithstanding, but the picture of Dukakis as a taxer, a polluter and a coddler of criminals was beginning to stick.

There were, of course, limits, though they lay at the far horizons of taste. Ailes's eyes lit at the news that Shorty had long ago allowed his name to go on a bill to clear an old law forbidding "unnatural" sexual acts from the Massachusetts statute books. The measure had not, in fact, been his idea; it came from a constituent, and Dukakis, then a legislator, was obliged by a quirk in the state law to present it for consideration. But it became the subject of some serious discussion and much ribald laughter. . . . "Hey, don't worry, I got the big one in the drawer," Ailes would tell the others on a particularly rough day in the campaign. It opened, he would say, with white letters crawling silently up a black screen: "In 1970, Governor Michael Dukakis introduced legislation in Massachusetts to repeal the ban on sodomy and bestiality." As the last words faded to black, you'd hear a din of moos, baas and other barnyard noises.

That ad—"Bestiality," Ailes called it—never got made. But the jokes continued, and Bush himself joined in one day when his pet dog wandered in on a meeting.

"You're the reason I'm running," the vice president said. "We've got to keep those people away from you."

The Ads That Ate Dukakis

If bestiality was out of bounds, the ethics of negative advertising were otherwise expansively roomy. Its canon for Ailes, as for others of its practitioners in both parties, appeared on inquiry to come down on two cardinal rules. The first was that it work, which usually meant that it had to play on some preexisting feeling about its target; you couldn't make Dukakis into an odd duck if people didn't already suspect he might be one. The second was that it be at least technically accurate. The latter rule was accepted in the business not so much out of respect for truth as out of fear of getting caught; Ailes, for one, was a frank advocate of working right up to that line where fact ends and fiction begins. But he was a bear for documentation, even if it were no more than an ambiguous quote in some newspaper somewhere, and he would, in his own phrase, go completely batshit about demanding it of his subordinates. If you couldn't back your claims with *something*, the press would blow them up on you. Your ad would set off a backlash, and you'd lose the election.

He enforced Ailes's Rules of Order with an iron hand. . . . He had begun by ignoring the high-priced Ad Alley talents who had staffed past Republican campaigns, and did deals instead with smaller agencies around the country, who would, among other virtues, have unformed attitudes about national politics and would be obedient to him. One of his star finds, Dennis Frankenberry, had worked on precisely one political campaign before Bush's, a race for district attorney in Oshkosh, Wisconsin; the candidate was the wife of one of his former commercial clients. . . .

One of Dennis Frankenberry's first and strongest offerings . . . was his Boston Harbor spot, taped from a hired whaler on a suitably gray and drizzly day; the weather gave the polluted waters an even sicklier pallor. Some touches were heightened by editing tricks; an open pipe dribbling wastes into the harbor looked even worse in a slowed-down, stop-frame treatment, with background music of the sort normally associated with the invasion of the killer mutants in sci-fi movies. Some embellishments were dropped; Frankenberry thought better of showing a Dukakis poster floating face up among the flotsam and jetsam, and Ailes vetoed a closing shot of an oil-soaked bird, thinking it rather too much of a bad thing.

But standards of accuracy were less rigorously applied than aesthetics. The ad, at a climactic moment, showed a sign reading DANGER/RADIATION HAZARD/NO SWIMMING. No one . . . questioned it, not until complaints were raised in public that the sign was a leftover from a long-closed Navy submarine facility. Ailes called the producers in.

"You guys didn't fuck around here, did you?" he demanded. "Put something in there that was not in Boston Harbor?"

"I swear to God, Rog," one of them answered, "it's right there. You can see it."

"Are you guys sure?" Ailes pressed. "This is the workhorse right now. We got it on the air. I don't want to have to pull it. I don't want to have to apologize. Get the sonofabitch right."

Right, by Ailes's definition, meant only that such a sign existed in Boston Harbor, not that it necessarily referred to a clear and present danger. It wasn't his job to go find out who put it up when and why; it was enough that the sign was there, and once Ailes was satisfied on that score he relaxed. . . .

Frankenberry's further and deadlier contribution to the First Quadrennial George Bush *Film Noir* Festival was a prison picture, arguably the strongest, frame for frame, since *Cool Hand Luke.* His firm had been assigned one of the litany ads, a three-fer roughing up Dukakis for furloughing murderers, opposing the death penalty and vetoing mandatory sentences for drug dealers. An inspiration struck Frankenberry as he and his two partners sat up brainstorming one evening: the sum of the governor's policies was like installing a revolving door in prison. Great idea, his colleagues said, and Frankenberry ran it up the flagpole to see if anyone on Fifteenth Street saluted. Everyone did, and two days later Frankenberry found himself in Salt Lake City, recruiting extras and scouting the Utah State Prison as a location.

He felt disappointed with the site at first, looking over its clean lines and cyclone fencing; he had hoped for a more *Late Show* look, something with thick walls, high parapets and stir-crazy cons banging the bars with tin cups. But there was not a wide range of choices on the rent-a-joint market, and Frankenberry made do. A revolving door was custom-made at what had once been Donny and Marie Osmond's studio in Provo, and was trucked in for the shoot. A cast of seventy was assembled, some scrubbed-up Mormon youths from Republican headquarters, some homeless men rousted out of the parks in town; they were dressed in prison fatigues and taped in deathly silence, filing in and out through the built-to-order revolving door.

The raw footage alone was powerful, the blank faces of the "convicts" edged with menace. Its passage through the editing room made it even scarier. The work, for once in contemporary television, was *de*colorized, and slowed down, besides, to give it a grainy documentary feel. Doomsday music pulsed in the background. A voice-over said that Dukakis "gave weekend furloughs to first-degree murderers not eligible for parole." The accompanying graphics reported that 268 ESCAPED and MANY ARE STILL AT LARGE. The claims taken singly passed the Ailes test for truth, which could fairly be defined as useful fact. The ad did not find it necessary to explain that the 268 "escapes" had occurred over ten years; that just three of the AWOLs were still at large, as against one-third to one-half who merely had come in late on the day they were due—and that only four of the escapees over that period had in fact been murderers doing life with no parole. . . .

Good George, Bad George

. . . [T]he second objective of the attack strategy, after the dismemberment of Michael Dukakis, was the reconstruction of George Bush into a figure of strong will and fighting faith. He had to be seen doing battle for his values; his road persona accordingly passed through daily and even hourly swings from Mr. Smith going to Washington to Dirty Harry packing a .44 mag.

It was possible, as his handlers discovered, to do too much of a good thing, even swaddling the candidate in the Stars and Stripes. Flags in ever-larger sizes and numbers became the standard decor at his rallies through the summer and the early fall, and so did the ritual recitation of the Pledge, often losing something in Bush's translation; even with practice, he seemed not to know it as well as his audiences did.

Fidelity to the text didn't count. The message did; it was nationalist and nativist, a thinly coded way of suggesting that Dukakis was less than a hundred percent American. But the men on Fifteenth Street ignored its retro-fifties aroma as long as it kept putting points on the scoreboard. It wasn't till the day late in September when Bush carried his campaign to a flag factory in New Jersey that he crossed some invisible threshold of tolerance and taste. "Why do we have to go there?" he had asked at the time. Even he seemed to realize that, as one aide put it, they had gone a flag too far; their reward was a three-network scolding on the news that night for the abject emptiness of their campaign.

But with the passage from summer to fall, the ledgers at Bush Inc. showed all profit for the vice president at small cost, even for his excesses; in the absence of any coherent response from Dukakis, there was no one to call him on them. The flaccidity of the opposition was the source of enduring amazement among Bush's men. . . .

In the vacuum, even Bush's blurry political profile suddenly became a blessing, a clean slate on which he could credibly write anything he chose, and so did the soft-edged personality once called wimpy. Dukakis looked cold and mean, as likable, Ailes gloated, as the kid who puts up his hand in school on Friday afternoon and says, "You forgot to give us our homework." Bush by contrast radiated a kind of awkward amiability, and Peggy Noonan had packaged it for sale in a series of luminous Good George speeches, hymns to compassion and clean water and those thousand mysterious points of light brightening the lives of the afflicted. The man once derided as the Velcro candidate had grown his own coating of Teflon; so long as he spoke softly, it seemed not to matter what he said.

Just in case, his road-company stagehands kept him layered in batting against the reemergence of what one of them called the Silly Factor—the vice president's propensity for tripping over his own tongue. He still got into trouble on those rare occasions when he strayed from his script. . . .

His public appearances were choreographed as carefully as Ronald Reagan's, by some of the same dance masters. His settings were chosen to flatter him on television, usually in sunshine, sometimes in shirt-

sleeves. His performances were stage-managed down to the last spontaneous gesture; an advance man down front would signal him when
to flash a thumbs-up sign, when to fling his arms aloft and when to
start speaking. . . .

There was a schizoid quality to his days on tour, a personality
split between the Good George with "a heart that does not bleed but
feels" and the Bad George re-creating Dukakis as the Brothers Grimm
might have invented an ogre or a troll. But in contrast to the staticky
sounds emitting from Chauncey Street, Bush's message, positive or
negative, was driven home with a rigorous singleness of purpose and
tone. You had to have that kind of discipline, a senior strategist warned,
joining Bush's team in the summer, if you wanted to win—especially,
he added with *this* guy.

Spontaneity was accordingly out . . . and orderliness was in, a
politics of meticulous programming. . . . They began the campaign
with a calendar of "issues of the day" pre-chosen through election
eve, and they met daily to coin the line-of-the-day as well, the sound
bites they hoped would dominate the nightly news and the morning
front pages. . . .

There was a time in late September when a certain lassitude set
in at Bush Inc.—a slump of the sort induced by doing the same thing
too well for too long. Dukakis seemed finally to be getting his act
together, playing to the pinched middle class with programs for college loans, health insurance and prenatal care, while Bush was still out
speaking the dread L word and deriding the "Massachusetts Mirage."
The vice president's lead melted down literally to nothing in Bob
Teeter's polling, and one national survey actually put Dukakis three
points ahead. "We are beginning to lose the war of themes and ideas,"
a young Bush speechwriter, Bob Grady, worried in a memo to the command group. They had, in fact, ben "absolutely themeless" since Labor
Day, he wrote, and were overworking the flag-and-country business
to the point of muddying everything else. "If we do not address this
situation quickly," Grady went on, "we are going to lose the election. . . . The charge that we are a party that has 'run out of ideas'
is sticking."

The memo landed three days before the first debate in Winston-
Salem, North Carolina, a matter of some suspense among Bush's men.
The prospect had reawakened all their bad dreams of what the vice
president might do if left to his own devices; a Bush victory, in their
eyes, meant his surviving ninety minutes without a major howler. That
he might somehow do so was not counted a safe bet. . . ; his people
had, in fact, seriously considered not putting him into the ring at all.

They could not flatly refuse without looking cowardly; their ploy instead was a get a quick proposal on the table for two debates and then walk away, blaming Dukakis, if he demanded more.

To their regret, he didn't, and Bush was stuck with a fight that his own corner men doubted he could win. When they played the traditional game of lowering expectations, their hearts were wholly in it; they saw, among other protective measures, that his speeches were salted with bits of self-deprecating humor—a way, one of them said, of putting the voters on notice that some deep doo-doo would be coming in Winston-Salem and should not be taken too seriously.

The disquiet they felt only redoubled their resolve to shrink Mike Dukakis—to make Bush look big by making the governor look small. Grady's memo stirred some thought at Fifteenth Street, and a few fresh programmatic ideas, most notably a son-of-VISTA youth corps to work among the poor, began appearing in Bush's Good George rhetoric. But the sound of 1988 for most of America was the boom-boom of artillery rounds raining down on Chauncy Street and the answering pop-pop of small-arms fire in the rough direction of George Bush. "Tell George to start talking about the issues," Barry Goldwater chided Dan Quayle in public one day. Bush Inc., in its unconfidence, was too fearful to stop the name-calling, and Bush in his ambition was too malleable to object. He had got where he was by blackguarding his opponent. The question neither he nor his men had addressed was what he was doing to himself.

4 Political Parties

In Chapter 3, we observed that elections are a fundamental way of bestowing continued legitimacy upon our national government and our principal way of holding government officials accountable.

The ability of elections to bestow legitimacy and secure accountability is strengthened by institutions that link the public and government officials politically. Political linkage is "any means by which political leaders act in accordance with the wants, needs, and demands of the public in making government policy" (Luttberg 1974, 3). Political parties are among the premier institutions that provide this political linkage. Interest groups, another important linkage institution, are examined in Chapter 4.

Political parties can be thought of as "coalitions of people organized formally to recruit, nominate, and elect individuals to office and to use elected office to achieve shared policy goals" (Gitelson et al. 1991, 169). This definition suggests that American political parties are large social organizations consisting of people in various roles, with varying responsibilities and patterns of activities (Sorauf 1984, 8). Specifically, our political parties are traditionally considered to be tripartite, or three-part, organizations consisting of a party organization, a party-in-government, and a party-in-the-electorate. Each of these segments is functionally separate, distinct, and largely independent of the others.

The party organization consists of those individuals who hold formal and informal positions within the political party or who regularly participate in the affairs of the party by contributing their time, money, or skills. To be properly understood, a party organization should not be thought of as a single, well-defined entity. Rather, it must be viewed as being composed of local, state, and national party organizations. As this distinction reveals, American political parties are actually "layered organizations" (Jewell and Olson 1988, 81). Each layer is functionally independent of the others and pursues its own goals and objectives, which may or may not be compatible with or complementary to those of the other layers. As our concern in this book is with national politics, we will focus our discussion on the Democratic and Republican national party organizations.

The Democratic and Republican parties are organized around two national committees. These committees consist of prominent individuals from the fifty state parties who are chosen every four years at the national parties' presidential nominating conventions. Prior to their 1992 nominating conventions, the Republican National Committee (RNC) had 162 members, and the Democratic National Committee (DNC) had more than 300.

In practice, the national committees are not the real decision-making bodies of the national parties. Their size alone decreases their ability to be truly deliberative bodies. Also, neither the Republican nor the Democratic party can afford the cost of having its national committee meet for the extended period of time necessary to make it the determining voice in party policy (Patterson 1990, 286).

Instead of the national committees, the national party chairpersons, the administrative staffs they oversee, and a small core of other party leaders run the day-to-day operations of the two parties and make most of the major decisions affecting them. Within this structure, the national chairperson clearly dominates (Sorauf 1984, 117). For example, the RNC chairperson oversees an elaborate structure that includes six other party officials, such as the party treasurer. This organization also includes an impressive administrative structure that includes different units responsible for such activities as direct-mail fund-raising campaigns, issue research, party advertising, political analysis, and general party development (Patterson 1991, 287).

It is worthwhile to have some awareness of the organizational shape of the Democratic and Republican parties. But we should not lose sight of the fact that the national party organizations exist to carry out activities that will lead to the successful recruitment, selection, and election of their parties' candidates. Indeed, to know what the national committees are requires that we know what they actually do (Keefe 1988, 18).

Originally, the national committees functioned primarily to plan for their parties' national nominating conventions, which were held every four years. This is still a principal task today. But, in addition, both national committees provide a range of services to their local and state parties and candidates. For example, under the direction of chairman William Brock (1976–1982), the RNC emphasized the rebuilding of the party's state and local bases, which had been extensively harmed by the Watergate affair. These initial efforts succeeded, and the RNC now provides an array of services to local and state parties and candidates. These include the recruitment and training of candidates, advertisements that promote the benefits of voting Republican and point out perceived Democratic failings, direct financial and in-kind contributions to local and state Republican party candidates, and a variety of technical services such as public opinion polling and voter registration drives (Price 1984, 40–41).

Though active in many of these same areas, the DNC has generally lagged behind the RNC in providing services to local and state parties and candidates. A principal reason for this lag is the poor financial circumstances in which the DNC consistently finds itself. The Democratic party is by nature less affluent than the Republican party. It is, therefore, less able to raise the immense sums of money necessary to be an effective service organization. For example, in 1979–1980 the national Democratic party raised almost $19 million. But this was less than one-sixth of the amount raised by the Republican party (Price 1984, 43).

In contrast to party organization, party-in-government consists of those individuals who are the parties' candidates for public office and who successfully use the party as a vehicle for winning public office. It is a "collection of officeholders who share . . . common values and policy orientations. . . . [I]ts missions [are] to take hold of government, to identify national problems and priorities, and to work for their settlement or achievement" (Keefe 1988, 191).

To take hold of government requires that the party-in-government itself be organized. The Democratic and Republican congressional parties recognize this organizational imperative. Elaborate party organizations exist within each chamber of Congress, allowing their members to pursue common policy goals. In the House of Representatives, the Democratic party-in-government operates through a number of individual party leaders, including the Speaker of the House, the majority party leader, the majority party whip, and the whip organization that serves as a communications link between the party leaders and the Democratic party caucus members. In addition, the Democratic party-in-government in the House of Representatives also relies upon several important party committees, including the Steering and Policy Committee, which is responsible for assigning the party's members in the House to committees and shaping party policy.

For the party-in-government to be effective requires more than organization. Political parties must influence, and to some degree govern, the behavior of those members of Congress elected under their banners. For the majority of members of Congress, party affiliation remains the single most important predictor of how they will vote on legislation that comes to the floor of their chamber. The importance of party is particularly evident on those issues that have a long-standing importance to the political parties and that help to define them to the general public (Keefe 1988, 211–212).

The party-in-the-electorate is the most fluid and least defined segment of either of the major political parties. It has both attitudinal and behavioral components. The party-in-the-electorate consists of those individuals among the voting public who either have a psychological attachment to or identification with a particular party or (with only minor deviation) vote routinely for the candidates of a particular party. By this definition, those who claim to be politically independent (do not identify with any political party) are not part of any party-in-the-electorate.

Two trends within the party-in-the-electorate are worth noting. First, the party-in-the-electorate may be losing its relevance within the larger social organization of American political parties. For the past twenty-five years, dealignment has been shrinking that segment of the voting public belonging to a party-in-the-electorate. Dealignment is the process by which either established voters show weakened and declining partisanship or new voters never acquire partisanship. A dealigned electorate is characterized by greater voter responsiveness and receptiveness to short-term election influences such as the personalities of the candidates (Patterson 1991, 237). For this reason, dealignment can have an effect on government stability, on which party's candidates are elected to office, and on whose shared policy goals are pursued.

The second trend, which is closely related to dealignment, is the increasing evidence that some segments of the voting population are exhibiting a two-tier partisan identification. Prior to the trend toward dealignment, individuals identifying with a particular party would vote for the congressional and presidential candidates of that party. But in this era of the dealigned party-in-the-electorate, voters are more likely to vote for the congressional candidate of one party (who is almost always likely to be the incumbent or of the retired incumbent's party) and the presidential candidate of the other party. This is particularly true of Southern voters, who are now generally congressional Democrats and presidential Republicans. One outcome of two-tier partisanship is divided government, in which the Democratic party retains control of Congress and the Republican party maintains control of the presidency. This division can be the source of policy stalemate and decreases the likelihood that elections will foster accountable government.

As we mentioned, political parties can be thought of as three-part organizations. But we should not overdramatize the distinction among the three parts. The activities of party organization and party-in-government do somewhat reflect their separate status. Recruiting and selecting candidates and contesting elections are activities traditionally associated with party organizations. Organizing the government has usually been the task of the party-in-government. But the lines between these two organizational components of political parties are dissolving. For example, both the Democratic and Republican congressional parties in both chambers of Congress now have their own campaign committees designed to solicit contributions, promote the reelection of their parties' incumbents, and even recruit candidates for House and Senate seats. All of these activities are within the traditional domain of the formal party organization. As we have also seen, the act of organizing government itself requires an elaborate party structure. Thus, it is somewhat misleading to imply that there is only one component of our political parties that can correctly be labeled "party organization."

Nor should we mistakenly think that participation in one part of the social organization of political parties precludes active participation in another. Take, for instance, the case of Congressman Dan Rostenkowski of Chicago, who is the powerful chairman of the House Ways and Means Committee. As such, he is clearly a member of the party-in-government. But the congressman, who cut his political teeth in the rough-and-tumble environment of local Democratic party politics in Chicago, remains a party precinct committeeman there. In this role, Congressman Rostenkowski is clearly a member of the party organization. Finally, as a part of the general voting public, the congressman is also a member of the Democratic party's party-in-the-electorate.

Understanding the multidimensional aspect of the social organization of our political parties is important. But we can gain an even better appreciation for party structure if we remember that the political parties' organizations exist to promote the principal activities our political culture assigns to them. As we observed earlier, our political parties exist to link the public to government officials. As we have seen, they do this by recruiting and selecting candidates, contesting elections, and organizing government. The recruitment and selection of presidential candidates every four years are perhaps the premier activities in which the national Democratic and Republican parties engage. In the past, the state and national party organizations tightly controlled the selection of their parties' candidates. This selection process frequently took place behind closed doors in the proverbial smoke-filled rooms. Today, as a result of a series of ongoing reforms that began in 1972 in the Democratic party, the selection of presidential candidates is a much more visible and open process. It is characterized by weak control by the party organization and extensive control by the party-in-the-electorate and even independents. It is a process in which the parties' presidential candidates are chosen by delegates to the national nominating conventions, delegates who are themselves selected through party caucuses or primary elections.

Caucus literally means "meeting." In the context of presidential nominations, political party caucuses are private meetings of party members, party followers, or candidate enthusiasts. Their purpose is to choose delegates to state or national nominating conventions (Shafritz 1988, 86).

Where party caucuses are used, the selection of delegates to the national nominating conventions is accomplished through a series of meetings. The selection process is likely to begin at the precinct level, where the supporters of the different presidential candidates meet to choose delegates to county or legislative district caucuses. These precinct meetings often take place in such locations as schools, churches, and even private homes. The process continues in the county or legislative district meetings, where delegates are selected to a state party convention. There the delegates to the national nominating conventions are chosen (Jewell and Olson 1988, 263). Though the state conventions ultimately choose the delegates to the national nominating committee, the initial precinct caucus meetings are of fundamental importance because they establish the actual delegate strength of each presidential aspirant in the subsequent district meetings and state conventions (Keefe 1988, 90).

Caucuses allow members of the party-in-the-electorate and independents who are candidate enthusiasts the opportunity to influence the Democratic and Republican parties' nominations for president. But in comparison to participation in presidential primary elections, public participation in presidential caucuses is quite small (Keefe 1988, 90). Today, presidential primaries are the preferred mode of selecting delegates to the national nominating conventions.

Presidential primaries are not all alike. They vary on three important characteristics. First, presidential primaries may be closed to all but those voters who are registered in the political party in whose primary they wish to participate, or they can be open to all registered voters, regardless of party affiliation. Second, presidential primaries may allocate delegates to the national nominating conventions on either a winner-take-all or a proportional basis. Third, presidential primaries can be the means for actually allocating delegates, or they can be mere "beauty contests" in which the voters only record candidate preferences, while the real delegate selection occurs in state conventions.

Presidential primaries and, to a lesser degree, caucuses reduce the national party organizations' control over the selection of their presidential candidates. The truly deliberative national conventions of the nineteenth and early twentieth centuries have given way to ones that largely ratify decisions made earlier in local caucuses and presidential primaries (Edwards and Wayne 1990, 42). But it was, after all, the national party organizations that put forward the changes in delegate selection that led to the proliferation of presidential primaries. It is, therefore, equally within the power of those national party organizations to modify the selection of delegates. The Democratic party has done just that by creating a block of "super delegates." These delegates, who are officially unpledged, are chosen from a group consisting of all Democratic governors, all members of the DNC, four-fifths of the Democratic members of Congress, and a small number of distinguished elected Democratic officials. In a divided convention, these super delegates would supposedly hold the balance of power in determining who would be the party's presidential candidate (Wayne 1988, 96).

The two case studies presented in this chapter highlight the major observations in the above discussion. In "What Is a Democrat? Who the Republicans Are" (two chapters from his book *The Reagan Detour*), Richard Reeves examines the social groupings within both the Democratic and the Republican parties. He does so by telling the story of the delegates attending the 1984 Democratic and Republican national conventions. With this approach, Reeves also identifies the new factions emerging within the two parties and describes the struggle between the old and the new for control of and influence over the parties' futures.

"The Making of a Delegate" by Lucius J. Barker is the second case study. It is Barker's personal account of his participation in the 1984 Democratic presidential caucuses in Missouri which led to his selection as a delegate to the Democratic party's national nominating convention. "The Making of a Delegate" gives a firsthand account of how delegate selection in party caucuses works. It reveals both the politics and the political strategies inherent in this manner of selecting delegates to the parties' national conventions. "The Making of a

Delegate'' further reminds us of just how much of the two parties' selection of presidential candidates is driven by grass-roots politics and the efforts of party footsoldiers like Barker.

Barker's story also underscores the enormous commitment that candidate enthusiasts must have in order to participate in party caucuses. This fact helps us to understand why individual turnout in these caucuses is so much lower than that in presidential primaries. It is simply more costly in terms of time and energy to participate in a party caucus than to vote in a primary. Whether this is an advantage or a disadvantage of selecting convention delegates through caucuses is debatable.

Suggested Reading

Kayden, Xander, and Eddie Mahe, Jr. 1985. *The Party Goes On*. New York: Basic Books. A counterargument to the "party in decline" literature, this book asserts that today's Democratic and Republican parties have experienced political rebirth and have been transformed into new institutions that depend on different resources and perform different tasks than those traditionally assigned to them.

Lurie, Leonard. 1980. *Party Politics: Why We Have Poor Presidents*. New York: Stein and Day. An argument that corrupt behavior has generally characterized presidential politics since the 1840s and that it is the presidential candidate selection process of the Democratic and Republican parties that creates much of this corruption.

Polsby, Nelson W. 1983. *Consequences of Party Reform*. New York: Oxford University Press. A scholarly and insightful analysis of the impact that changes in party rules have had on both the political parties and government.

Riordan, William L. 1963. *Plunkitt of Tammany Hall*. New York: Dutton. Originally published in 1905, this book presents an interesting account of how one of the nation's biggest and most powerful party machines and its boss controlled New York City politics and government.

Wattenberg, Martin P. 1984. *The Decline of American Political Parties, 1952–1980*. Cambridge, MA: Harvard University Press. A mainstream example of the "party in decline" literature, focusing on candidate-centered media campaigns as both the cause and effect of this decline.

Wilson, James Q. 1962. *The Amateur Democrat*. Chicago: University of Chicago Press. A study of the issue-oriented political clubs that first emerged in the Democratic party during the 1950s.

What Is a Democrat?
Who the Republicans Are

Richard Reeves

As you read this case study, consider the following questions:

1. Why is the immigrant experience important for so many Democrats in defining what the Democratic party is?

2. How does the immigrant experience help to define some Democrats' outlook toward the Republican party?

3. Who are the "passionate storytellers" and the "cool neoliberals"?

4. How do the storytellers and the neoliberals illustrate the tension within the Democratic party?

5. What does Reeves mean by the statement that the Republican party is "open to new voters" but not to "new members"?

6. During the Reagan presidency, in what way was the Republican party like an atom?

7. How do the opposing concepts of confrontation and compromise illustrate the tension among competing factions within the Republican party?

8. What is meant by the statement that "people vote Democratic [but] people are Republicans"?

T HE VOICE OF THE GOVERNOR OF OHIO CHOKED AS HE CONGRATULATED THE GOVERNOR OF NEW YORK ON HIS KEYNOTE SPEECH AT THE 1984 Democratic National Convention in San Francisco in July. "My father," Richard Celeste said to Mario Cuomo, "my father—there's a guy named Frank Celeste watching TV right now with tears running down his face."

There were tears, too, in the eyes of the governors, two sons of Italian immigrants who had come to America knowing no people, knowing no English. . . .

An hour later, two other Democratic governors met at a reception. "What did you think of Cuomo's speech?" Bill Clinton of Arkansas asked Richard Lamm of Colorado.

"Terrific," Lamm said. "It galvanized the crowd."

"C'mon," Clinton said. "What did it really say about the issues we're trying to raise?"

"Nothing," Lamm said.

"Passionate statements of what used to be," said Lamm as he left San Francisco. . . . [T]he Governor had been disappointed by the ringing rhetoric of Cuomo, and of Senator Edward Kennedy, Jesse Jackson and . . . Geraldine Ferraro of New York. "They all gave the same speech. We weren't ready to face the issues of the future—like international competition and productivity and confronting organized labor—so we celebrated the past."

The Democrats also celebrated themselves in San Francisco. . . . Conventions are the only place where American political parties actually exist. The nominating conclaves were an American invention. . . . [F]or more than a century the conventions were the accepted mechanisms for choosing national tickets. That function is still the official purpose of the conventions, even though in recent years the real power of nomination, especially in the Democratic Party, has been taken over by voters and elected delegates in state primary elections and caucuses. By 1984, the conventions had evolved into a week-long television show to project the party and its campaigners. And, perhaps more importantly, the conventions were the only chance for party members and outsiders to see who the Democrats are, and who the Republicans are.

Who makes up the Democratic Party? Who are the Republicans? . . .

In San Francisco, the Democratic organism, the party in convention, seemed to rediscover and celebrate itself as the immigrant party. What Cuomo and Celeste and many other Democrats focused on for an energetic week was their party's heritage as the political home and voice of generations of immigrants. . . . The Democrats celebrated themselves, fairly accurately, as the party of the new arrivals of the twentieth century against the Republicans representing an older nation, white Protestant America. Whose America is it?

And whose Democratic Party will it be? . . .

"You can't define the Democratic Party today without beginning with the immigrant experience," said Celeste, whose father came from Italy as a child in 1907, nineteen years before Cuomo's father came as a young man. . . .

"My mother was the first Greek girl to go beyond high school in Haverhill, Massachusetts," said Michael Dukakis, the Democratic Governor of that state, whose father, also of Greek descent, came to the United States from Turkey in 1912. "The historic role of this party is to lift the new people up. If we lose that, we lose everything. This is not going to be the party of exposed brick walls and hanging plants and white wine."

There may be a confrontation coming . . . between Democrats who order Chablis and those whose fathers made their own wine. Some will fit both descriptions and may have to choose sides. For the rhetoric and the mood of San Francisco made it apparent that "neoliberals," or "future-oriented" young politicians like Gary Hart, were not at the heart of the party in 1984. The cooler young leaders who prefer discussing international macroeconomics to quoting Franklin Delano Roosevelt (or their own fathers) were outnumbered and outtalked by Cuomo and Celeste, Ferraro and Senator Edward Kennedy—and by Jesse Jackson. . . .

Feelings of rejection of self or family, now or sometime in the past, was what seemed to be at the heart of the passion of the Democrats in convention. . . .

"We're outsiders—the Republicans keep reminding us of that," said Elizabeth Lara, a twenty-six-year-old Mondale delegate who worked for an oil-exploration company in Houston and is the granddaughter of Mexican immigrants. "People like me have to become Democrats if we're interested in politics. The Republican party is exclusive, a country club that's not open to me. You're supposed to be like them to get in, but I can never be like them."

Neither can people born black—or so an overwhelming majority of American blacks believe. "The Republican Party doesn't really exist for blacks, does it?" said Henry Ficklin, a black thirty-four-year-old Jackson delegate, a public-school teacher and pastor of the Mount Vernon Baptist Church in Macon, Georgia. "For a black, politics is the Democratic Party and the Democratic Party is politics."

The odyssey of Edwina Davis from Bombay, India, to Jacksonville Beach, Florida, and to the convention floor as a Mondale delegate was one of several similar stories I heard on that floor while speakers told their own from the podium. Mrs. Davis, a schoolteacher who married an American merchant seaman in Bombay, came to her new land via Philadelphia International Airport. The first words she heard on American soil were from a teenager at the gate who looked at her, then turned to a friend and said, "Oh, God, not another spic!"

With a group of thirty-one others, she became a United States citizen in Jacksonville on October 16, 1981. Twenty-two people in the group registered to vote that day, eighteen as Democrats. "We knew that the Republicans were the party of the white people," she said. "It's for the fundamentalists and the Moral Majority." . . .

Where you stand politically in the United States often depends on when and where your parents and grandparents landed—on whether your stories are of Plymouth Rock or Ellis Island, Kennedy Airport or the north bank of the Rio Grande. "I'm always shocked when I meet people who don't know when their families got to America," said Carla McDonald, whose mother came to the United States in 1951. "They're the Republicans." . . .

The Democrats in San Francisco obviously believed, in the end, that these are their stories—personally and politically. The excitement of the 1984 convention surprised everyone involved, and most of it came from the passionate interchange between the delegates and their storytellers, Cuomo and Jackson, Kennedy and Ferraro—the immigrant storytellers. In fact, Walter Mondale, whose family, Protestants, came from Norway in 1856, sometimes seemed more than a little discomfited by the passions generated by the later immigrants from warmer places.

The heat was felt by some delegates too. Norman Fletcher, the fifty-year-old chairman of the Democratic Party in Georgia's Seventh Congressional District, who was originally elected as a delegate for Ohio Senator John Glenn, said, "I'm sure this is a more caring party, but it's getting more difficult for me to sit here on the floor. This place is being run by two or three groups—labor and the blacks."

"This just isn't going to go over in the Bible Belt," said Fletcher, a Presbyterian who could not remember when his family came to America. "The newcomers are taking over the party. I'm not sure there's room here for me. Now you know why people like me are moving into the Republican Party at home. There used to be a time when none of us had ever met a Republican."

The politics of the South, the most Protestant region of the country, could almost be described right now as a race between whites deserting the Democratic Party—adding to the white Protestant character of the Republican Party—and blacks registering to vote as Democrats. "I'd call it a settling-out," said David Price, the acting chairman of the North Carolina delegation. "In my state, the Republican Party was a small enclave of white Protestants. Now more and more white conservatives are slipping that way." . . .

So, in some ways, the new tension lines in the Democratic Party were actually extensions of old American lines—the Catholic–Protestant split of American politics was beginning to apply to the South, where the great white Protestant majority also used to be the great Democratic majority. Now those white Protestants were joining their Northern brethren in voting as national Republicans. In fact, the Democratic Party was so diverse, such a fair representation of the entire nation, that all American tensions were reflected when Democrats convened. The young–old tension of the Hart–Mondale contests carried over after the votes were counted. "Yuppies" ("young urban, upwardly mobile professionals," in the jargon of the day) weren't positive they really belonged there, either.

Carla McDonald, an "ethnic yuppie," was thrilled by immigrant stories and references to Catholicism, but she wasn't ready to buy all the politics of the storytellers. She had trouble relating to the dire tales of poverty and modern huddled masses. "The new generation," as she called her peers, seemed convinced that the future is theirs, and they cheered lines like these from Hart's speech to the convention: "The times change and we must change with them. For the worst sin in political affairs is not to be mistaken but to be irrelevant."

"Irrelevant" was a word used by another Hart delegate, Matthew Jones, a twenty-nine-year-old environmental consultant from Fort Collins, Colorado. He was talking about organized labor. "My grandfather was a union man on the railroads, my father began as a union man," said Jones. "I know the unions made working more human, but that purpose has been served. That's over now." . . .

They had all sensed the separation from unions that is near the top of the neoliberal agenda—it's on the Yuppie agenda too. "The young professionals I know are very open to Ronald Reagan," said Jones. "That was the choice for many: Hart or Reagan."

Walking that floor among the Democrats convened, it was not difficult to see the struggles that were coming between the cool neoliberals and the passionate storytellers; Lamm and Hart and Clinton might be in one camp, with Cuomo, Jackson, Celeste and Ferraro in the other. . . . Mayor Cisneros, Senator Bill Bradley of New Jersey and Governor Bob Graham of Florida all talked to me in San Francisco of finding issues that link the proponents of "change" and the champions of "fairness." Bradley, particularly, thought the party could unite diverse constituencies by articulating a range of "workplace/leisure" issues, such as the retraining of workers displaced by automation. "We have to create a work force motivated and anxious to provide what the country needs, greater productivity," he said. "The Republicans will not consider that part of the political process, so they will leave the field open to us, as they did years ago when they did not consider social welfare part of the government process."

Fairness in a changing workplace seemed to be one of the several themes that might unite the younger Democrats who competed for attention at San Francisco. A more flexible, less confrontational American world posture might be another. . . . And both traditional and "neo" liberals were committed strongly to public education as the gateway to both immigrant opportunity and hi-tech futures (while their Republican counterparts pushed tax credits for private-school tuition), and on the idea that working women and women's rights were economic necessities whose time has come. . . .

. . . If the Democrats evolved into a party of immigrants and outsiders, many ethnics, particularly second- and third-generation voters who were economically secure, would almost certainly choose to identify with insiders and the older American heritage. They'll go with the Yankees. They'll go with the winners.

The group most likely to go that way were the young professionals. Ethnicity might have no more hold on many of them than any of the other things that make up contemporary lifestyles. The yuppies could split between the Democratic and Republican parties, perhaps even reconstituting dormant liberal Republicanism. They fit that old mold: culturally liberal, economically conservative. There were a lot of them out there, and a permanent shift to Republicanism by enough of them would change American politics for a long time. It could create real homegrown class politics. But it could happen. Some Democrats might welcome it. . . .

“ “NUESTRA CASA ES SU CASA,” UNITED STATES TREASURER KATHERINE ORTEGA SAID IN THE KEYNOTE ADDRESS OF THE 1984 REPUBLICAN National Convention in Dallas. “Our home is your home”—this party is open.

On the floor below, Barry Jackson, an alternate delegate from Iowa and the co-chairman of the party in Johnson County, wore a red, white and blue button that said, “Republican Mainstream Committee”—the insignia of the small organization of Republicans who identified themselves as “moderates.” A trail of hissing followed him as he walked by other state delegations. “Why don't you just get out of here?” “Go to the Democrats—that's where you belong!” . . .

The Republicans in convention publicly projected word pictures of a land of milk and honey—and television pictures of delegates whose complexions could be described in about the same way. The 2,235 men and women who renominated Reagan in Dallas were almost all white, three-quarters of them were Protestants, their average incomes were $50,000 a year and climbing, and almost every one had been active in the party for at least five years. The Republican Party was open to new voters, but there did not seem to be much room, or warmth, for new members. These folk had stood together for a long time, through the good and the bad, mostly the bad. They were a minority party and proud of it, convinced in their hearts that they were right all along. . . .

“We are committed to ideas, not to men or a man,” said Newt Gingrich, a forty-one-year-old representative from Georgia. “What we do depends on what the Administration does in a second term. We're with Reagan if he's Teddy Roosevelt, against him if he's William Howard Taft.”

“The young hypocrites,” was Senator Dole's characterization of Gingrich and a dozen other conservative young members of Congress who helped write the party's controversial platform, with its provisions pledging to oppose tax increases under any circumstances and the consideration of a return to the gold standard. "They think they can peddle the idea that they've taken over the party. Well, they aren't the Republican Party and they aren't going to be." . . .

That, after the cheers and the balloon drops, was the way Republicans really talked about each other. Senator Mathias was called "a liberal swine" by one member of Maryland's convention contingent, Richard L. Andrews, a member of the state party's central committee. Mathias, along with three other "moderate" senators, was publicly invited to "do us all a favor [and] help the Republican Party by leaving it," by John T. (Terry) Dolan, chairman of the National Conservative Political Action Committee (NICPAC), one of the largest fund-raisers for Republican Congressional candidates. When Vice President Bush questioned such tactics, Dolan responded, "We are the Republican Party. George Bush is not."

What the Republican Party became, ideologically, during the Reagan years might be represented by a line from left to right. . . .

But a more accurate model of the Reagan party, it seemed to me, looked like an atom—a series of concentric circles around an electromagnetic nucleus marked "Ronald Reagan." The President made the Republican Party his party in ways that transcended ideology. The test of position for Republicans was, in general, closeness to the power and person of Ronald Reagan.

The first ring, close to the center but not very wide, was the Reaganites, a small group including the White House staff and Vice President Bush. The next two rings were the orbits of the pragmatists—the "traditionalists" and the "old right." These included most of the party's Congressional leadership—Senators Baker and Dole, House Minority Leader Robert H. Michel of Illinois and his deputy, Representative Lott. Circling them were the "new right," from Jack Kemp to Newt Gingrich, aggressive young conservatives who saw themselves as new populists opposed not only to liberalism but to the country-club elitism of older conservatives. Then there were three wobbly outer orbits. One included the "moderates"—Senators Mathias and Weicker and young Barry Jackson wearing his "Mainstream" button. The other two, spinning and flaring together much of the time, included Phillips and Dolan and another fund-raiser, Richard Viguerie, collectively referred to, unkindly, as "the crazies"; and a companion ring of the "religious right," whose best-known figure was the Reverend Jerry Falwell, leader of the Moral Majority.

Pull out the center, the nucleus of the whirling mass, and the whole thing might implode. And that is exactly what almost every

Republican I talked with in Dallas believed was going to happen. Four years after Ronald Reagan won the Presidency from dispirited and disorganized Democrats, the Republicans who backed him still seemed bound together principally by his magnetism.

"The post-Reagan era begins at midnight on Election Day," said Viguerie in Dallas, echoing the words I had just heard from Newt Gingrich. "It's going to be very rough," said Viguerie, the publisher of *Conservative Digest* magazine. "The bodies will be about six deep if the economy ever turns down . . . the Republican Party could be demolished." . . .

"I know people call us 'crazies,' and the party would love to dismiss us as a minor irritant," Viguerie said. "But you can't ignore people like us. We will make any sacrifice. We are trying to save this country and preserve freedom." . . .

It was not only the so-called "crazies" who talked that way in Dallas. "I believe Western civilization is at stake here," said Newt Gingrich. "Political leadership is the only thing that can save it. I have dedicated my life to doing that." . . .

Even Jack Kemp, whose party stature is higher and whose style is less confrontational, talks about politics and public policy as all-or-nothing affairs. "I'm convinced I'm right about the economy," Kemp said, reviewing his own advocacy of Arthur Laffer's "supply-side" economics. "But if, in a year or two, inflation and unemployment are at or near ten percent, then we will have failed. If the economy goes over a cliff, we're finished. Forget Jack Kemp. Well, I'm willing to take that chance." . . .

Confrontation versus compromise was one of the fault lines of the Republican Party in triumph. The confrontationists—and there were a lot of them in Dallas, from Viguerie on the fringes to Trent Lott near the center of power—had contempt for moderates like Senator Dole. The conservatives looking to fight the good fight liked to say that the traditional goal of older Republicans was to lose as slowly as possible.

"If Dole or anyone else advocates tax increases after the election, yes, dang it, there's going to be some confrontations," said Lott, the forty-three-year-old House minority whip who sometimes tried to act as a bridge between the old and the new right, or between older and younger congressmen. "We're not going that way anymore. The traditional appeal of the Republican Party has not made us the majority. If you keep thinking like a minority, you're going to be a minority." . . .

In fact, there may have been a lost generation of Republican moderates. Senator Mathias, for one, believed that many young men and women who might have become Republicans in the 1960s and the 1970s—some of whom would inevitably have become activists and candidates—were driven away by Vietnam and Watergate. Many, he speculated, became Democrats; many just avoided politics of any kind. . . .

But, if the ideology of the party was exaggerated for a few days, the culture of the Republicanism was represented truly in Dallas. On the floor, a person knew instinctively and instantaneously whether or not he or she belonged. Everyone there knew that"*Nuestra casa es su casa*" was strictly for television.

That bent toward exclusion—and exclusivity—was a principal reason that the Republican Party remained as it had been for almost fifty years, the minority party, claiming the loyalty of something like one-quarter of the electorate. Perhaps Republicans like it that way. People *vote* Democratic; people *are* Republicans. Being a Republican is a cultural statement. . . .

Being a Republican is not taken lightly. It means something. "There is a cultural mind-set," said Gingrich. . . . Republicans share assumptions about proper behavior." That includes the company they keep. . . .

No. Whatever was heard about *nuestra casa es su casa* from the podium, calls to Democrats were for their votes, not their company. The party fully accepts few new members, thank you. . . .

"Our instinctive reaction to newcomers is suspicion," Gingrich said. "Why are you here? Are you really one of us?" The instinctive reaction to Barry Jackson of Iowa when he wore his "Mainstream" button was to say, "Get out. You don't belong." Terry Dolan had the same message for Senators Mathias and Weicker and the rest. "Sure they want to open the party," said Senator Dole, "they want to open it to people who agree with them."

Public agreement—loyalty—has always been a high Republican virtue. . . .

Loyalty. Loyalty to Reagan. Loyalty to America. Right or wrong. "Loyalty is carried almost to tyranny in here," said one of the abstaining delegates, Paul Zimmerman of Pennsylvania. "You get just the whiff of fascism."

What binds Republicans together is that they have been accepted by other Republicans. . . . Patriotism has been what has bound the party together for almost its entire 128-year history. . . .

. . . Our patriotism has always been more self-conscious than tribal. Without a long history, Americans had to invent nationalistic legends. From the beginning, the Republicans proved to be great inventors, telling new generations and new arrivals that being a good American, a real American, was very closely tied to the values of Puritanism and free enterprise. . . .

Weeding out the weaklings was . . . a theme being preached with proprietary love of country in Dallas. "There are two kinds of Americans: the people pulling the wagon and the people looking for a free ride on the wagon," said Phil Gramm, who was elected a United States senator from Texas as a Republican after years of working with House Republicans as a conservative Democrat. "The Republican Party has put together a new majority of the ones doing the pulling," Gramm said, "the people doing the work and paying the taxes, against the ones who want something for nothing from the Federal Government."

Many Republicans have divided the world that way over many, many years. They are, after all, many of them, the descendants of America's Puritans and they have gathered together to make the party that has best embodied Puritan ethics, including the Calvinist notion that earned wealth usually marked a man among God's chosen. . . . That idea, politically reversed, has often made it even tougher to be poor in America. Shirley McKenzie, a Miami real-estate agent who was in Dallas for a meeting of the National Black Republican Council, answered a question about poverty this way: "I'm not interested in talking about poor people. I think the best way I can help poor people is not to be one of them."

That was the right answer in Dallas, among the believers.

The Making of a Delegate

Lucius J. Barker

As you read this case study, consider the following questions:

1. How did Barker's work as a political scientist ultimately lead him to become an enthusiastic supporter of Rev. Jesse Jackson's candidacy for the Democratic party's 1984 presidential nomination?

2. In the caucus proceedings, why was the issue of "viability" important to Jackson's supporters?

3. What coalitions did Jackson's supporters have to form throughout the caucus process in Missouri's second congressional district to achieve viability and guarantee that their candidate would receive at least some delegates to the party's national convention?

4. How does Barker's personal odyssey through the Missouri caucus process highlight the enormous amount of commitment that candidate enthusiasts must have in order to secure delegates for their preferred candidates?

☆☆☆

Some Background Perspectives

A PRIL 18, 1983, WAS THE DATE OF THE FIRST OFFICIAL STEP IN THE MISSOURI CAUCUS SYSTEM FOR THE SELECTION OF DELEGATES TO THE DEMOCRATIC National Convention—city and township caucuses. By that time, of course, I had realized that I could not remain neutral and uninvolved in the Jackson campaign—the scholar-researcher studying and analyzing the Jackson campaign, preserving scholarly objectivity—and had become firmly and openly committed to Jesse Jackson's candidacy. Originally, I planned to do the kind of field-observation research usefully undertaken by scholars in a number of areas. I thought research on Jackson's campaign would both clarify a number of matters in my continuous analysis of black politics and, specifically, unearth information and insights that could prove helpful in revising the 1980 edition of *Black Americans and the Political System.* Accordingly, I set my research plans in motion.

In October 1983 I contacted Jackson's state coordinator in Missouri, attorney Charles Bussey, in order to discuss my research plans and to seek his cooperation. Although I had heard of Bussey, I did not know him. . . . We met at a luncheon at the Washington University–St. Louis Faculty Club—Whittemore House, an elegant old mansion. At the appointed hour, I saw a rather tall, immaculately dressed, youthful black man enter the Faculty Club, and recognizing his inquisitive look, I approached him. . . . Bussey was articulate, obviously sharp, and impressive in appearance—and after our luncheon, I could also say that his representations and comments on behalf of Jackson were equally impressive—well considered and thought out.

. . . I wasted little time in getting down to business. I told Bussey about my work in black politics, in constitutional law and civil liberties, and in American politics generally. I then mentioned my special research interest in the Jackson campaign and my intention to remain detached from the battle. Bussey listened attentively and appreciatively to my plans. In fact, he was most encouraging and indicated that he too would be pleased if black scholars would avail themselves of this opportunity. With my intended role in the Jackson campaign clarified, we then talked about ways in which my research effort could be aided—e.g., making one or two campaign trips with Rev. Jackson, attending meetings of Jackson groups at the state and local levels, setting up interviews with key people—in short, we talked about the research-analyst's central need for access. Bussey assured me that he would help in any way he could. . . .

Some two months passed before I talked to Bussey again. I was gathering background material on the Jackson campaign, making TV appearances, answering questions on radio talk shows, preparing papers for professional conferences and civic meetings—all devoted in one way or another to the Jackson campaign. However, the more I studied and discussed the Jackson campaign, the more difficult I found it to remain neutral, to remain uncommitted and above the battle. My close friends and family, even my two young daughters, were totally involved and openly and strongly supportive of Jackson. I too saw the Jackson effort not just as a political campaign but as the most dramatic holistic strategy that could be developed to remind us all of the unfulfilled objectives of Martin Luther King and the civil rights movement and to warn us that the movement's earlier gains were in danger. . . . By his decision to seek the presidency Jackson obviously became the symbol for the reinvigoration, formulation, and implementation of something very much larger than himself.

Moreover, the Jackson candidacy finally gave me the first realistic opportunity to become an actual delegate to a Democratic National Convention. In this regard, I could not help but reflect on my life as a black person growing up in my small hometown of Franklinton, Louisiana, during the 1930s and 1940s. Not only there, but in the South generally, blacks were not accorded even simple respect and dignity as persons, much less fundamental rights as United States citizens. To think of going as a delegate to a national party convention—to help select a presidential candidate—would have been among the most ultimate of dreams. . . .

The Necessary First Step— The April 18th Township Caucus

. . . [M]y actual presence at the April 18 township caucus depended on whether or not I would attend a long-scheduled, out-of-town professional meeting. I was at the time president of the National

Conference of Black Political Scientists; our national meetings were being held in Washington, D.C., in mid-April, and the preconference meeting of the executive board was scheduled in Washington on Wednesday, April 18. Ordinarily, for a long-established and fully developed organization, a president's attendance at a particular executive council meeting or any other meeting for that matter is relatively unimportant. . . . However, the NCOBPS was still a developing organization, and somehow I thought my presence could be important. Indeed, the potential contributions of NCOBPS to the training and development of future black scholars is for me a matter of very high priority. But I also considered my participation in my local township caucus as a Jackson supporter very important; Missouri's second congressional district, and particularly my home township, was anything but a hotbed of support for Jesse Jackson.

One telephone call to the president-elect of NCOBPS, Professor Huey Perry of Southern University–Baton Rouge, resolved my dilemma. Fortunately, Perry and I were not only close friends but, more important to me, also professional colleagues who attached great importance to the role of NCOBPS. And Perry also saw the Jackson campaign as a crucial development in black politics, one which we should in every way seek to promote and advance. So after discussing agendas and other matters, Perry assured me that I was doing the right thing and that both the executive board and NCOBPS membership generally would understand.

I was glad I could attend my township caucus with my wife and my daughter (a newly registered voter), but I remained somewhat apprehensive about the situation. I considered that the maximum we could do in my particular district was to see that Jackson's name was at least mentioned and placed in nomination; anything more would have been the height of wishful thinking. I knew of no concerted plans or efforts of the Jackson organization for our township, but I could understand why not much effort would be made. My township (Missouri River) is located in the Second Congressional District and includes one of St. Louis's most fashionable west-county suburban areas, Chesterfield. The few Democrats who live in my particular area are not likely to wear Jesse Jackson pins or sport his bumper stickers. . . . Jackson's organization understandably focused attention on those areas that looked more promising. . . .

Once at the caucus I was pleasantly surprised to find that some of my apprehensions about Jackson's chances in my township were more imagined than real. First, I was very much surprised at the unexpected sizeable support for Jackson's candidacy. Everything about past voting patterns and behavior in my township indicated that Jackson would have very few supporters, and even fewer who would turn out. But of the some 340 or so persons in attendance, some 46 persons came forward for Jackson on the initial call for division into individual candidate caucuses. . . . Of course, it was not at all surprising that, with the exception of one or two, blacks in the audience came forward en masse (some 34) to support Jackson.

I was surprised but delighted that this many blacks lived in the Chesterfield area. . . .

But equally as beautiful and surprising, to me and others, is that at least twelve to fourteen whites—young, middle aged, and older—also came forward to join the Jackson caucus. That Jackson could marshall this type of support in Chesterfield was indeed an unexpected but welcome development. . . .

A . . . most important aspect of the meeting was the coming together of the Nuclear Freeze and Jackson forces. To be sure, each group needed the other to become a viable caucus. Under state party rules, in order to be viable (to have the number necessary to be apportioned delegates to the congressional district caucus) a group must have at least 20 percent of the total number of persons in attendance at the caucus. In this instance, with approximately 340 persons present, some 68 persons were needed for a candidate caucus to be viable. Since we Jackson supporters had about two-thirds of that number (48), we needed an additional 20 or more persons to become viable, and as I surveyed the situation, the Nuclear Freeze group, which numbered about 27, was the logical and perhaps only possible group with which we could unite and simultaneously maintain our key positions. . . .

. . . Fortunately, . . . the leader of the Nuclear Freeze group, . . . Carole Hansen, and I, the temporary leader of the Jackson group, developed an immediate good rapport and working relationship. . . .

Of course, the benefits and costs of union were clear to all: of the two delegates allotted to the now viable Jackson caucus, one would come from the original Jackson group and one from the Freeze group. . . . And what especially stands out in my mind is that while Carole Hansen and I were consulting with party leaders about formalities in selecting our two delegates, somehow an informal leadership emerged from our newly combined group, and when Carole and I returned to lay out procedures, an informal consensus over who our delegates to the congressional district should be was already jelling. And that consensus resulted in the selection of Carole Hansen and myself as the two delegates to the district caucus. The added plus, of course, was that Carole was a strong Jackson supporter.

Thus without doubt the story of the Missouri River Township caucus, as one veteran party leader told me, was "you Jackson people—whoever would have dreamed that Jackson would have two delegates (out of nine elected) coming from Chesterfield." . . .

A Delegate Is Selected

On May 22, the next big day in the Missouri caucus system for the selection of delegates to the Democratic National Convention, delegates selected in township and ward caucuses would convene in their respective congressional district conventions, where fifty-one of Missouri's eighty-six national convention delegates would be selected. Preparations for these conventions proceeded at an increasing pace. . . .

Thus soon after our April 18 township caucus, I called Bussey to ask if he had any special plans for coordinating our district to prepare for the May 22 convention. I offered to convene a planning meeting for Jackson delegates from the second district, and Bussey immediately accepted my offer and agreed to attend. Accordingly, I invited our delegates to a meeting at my home in early May. . . .

For me it was one of the most memorable experiences of the campaign. All but one of the some seventeen Jackson delegates from the Second Congressional District attended, along with a few alternates and several other Jackson supporters—all together, about twenty-five persons, about four of whom were white, the rest black. To begin the meeting, each person was asked to say anything he or she wished, and not surprisingly the meeting soon took on the flavor of an old fashioned "testifying" meeting typically held in some black churches. One black woman delegate, for example, gave a particularly moving speech: "I sincerely believe," she said, "that God has really led Reverend Jackson to run in this campaign and to fill the void left by Dr. King." . . .

If nothing else, this meeting convinced me that Jackson's support among blacks was very deep, more than just a matter of voting for him in a caucus or a presidential primary election. . . .

But testimony aside, we had to get down to the politics of the situation. . . . In the Second Congressional District we . . . had to turn out our delegates and to caucus, along with several Freeze delegates who were strongly pro-Jackson, and by secret ballot choose one male and one female candidate for delegate slots. I was designated as the male candidate; and Mickey Thomas was designated as the female candidate from our caucus. . . . In the second district . . . Mondale forces were clearly in control and were expected to win at least four, and conceivably all six, national convention delegate seats at stake. Specifically, Mondale had about 59 of the some 101 delegates elected to attend the Second Congressional District convention; Hart 18, Jackson 17, with some 7 delegates uncommitted. Under the 20 percent rule for a candidate caucus to be viable, Mondale's was at the time the only viable caucus in the second district; both Hart and Jackson had less than 20 percent of the total number of delegates, 101. Thus, the only thing that could prevent Mondale from a landslide was a coalition of Hart and Jackson forces. Of course, Jackson's man in Missouri (Bussey) and Hart's man (Vincent Volpe), and Nuclear Freeze leaders all recognized that to survive and be most effective under the 20 percent rule, it would be necessary to pool delegate resources. And in the end, this happened in my district and in other congressional districts around the state.

However, at least in my district, this union of Hart and Jackson delegates was distasteful to a number of Jackson delegates; I have no idea how the Hart delegates felt, I did not want to know! . . .

What really disturbed many of us, however, was the rumor (later confirmed) that a deal was in the works wherein all seventeen Jackson delegates in the second district were to become part of an expanded Hart caucus. To be sure, we recognized that, since neither Hart nor Jackson had enough delegates to be viable, something would have to give in our district. But we Jackson delegates hoped, with reason, that we could pick up enough Freeze and uncommitted delegates to become viable on our own without Hart. In any case, the situation became so embroiled that on May 21, just one day prior to the congressional district convention, we Jackson delegates held a showdown meeting with Bussey and Hart's state coordinator, Volpe.

This meeting became rather heated and tense as one Jackson delegate after another strongly denounced the impending merger and argued that Jackson delegates were not to be tossed around, that Jackson's campaign was very unlike Hart's, making it difficult for any Jackson delegate to operate under a Hart banner, no matter how perfunctorily or expediently. To be sure, Bussey and Volpe clearly explained how, though Jackson forces would join Hart, it would be for the sole purpose of becoming a viable caucus able to elect two delegates, rather than perhaps one, and that both Hart and Jackson would in fact have one delegate. Otherwise both sides could very well be shut out. . . .

Finally, after the emotions and heat of the meeting subsided, someone suggested what we should have done at the very beginning: add up the cold hard numbers in the second district, including late switches of Freeze delegates and uncommitteds, and look at statewide support for Hart and Jackson to see who would be in the stronger position at the state convention, where other national convention delegates were to be selected. During a brief recess, Hart and Jackson leaders meticulously went over the numbers and, to our relief and surprise, did indeed find that Jackson was not only stronger in the second district but appeared also to have more support in the state overall. Only after such calculations did Hart's coordinator, Volpe, feel that it would probably be more expedient for Hart delegates to join Jackson delegates, although he would have to check before the deal was finalized. This calmed things considerably among Jackson delegates, although some were still not satisfied since Volpe, understandably I thought, left the door somewhat ajar pending appropriate checks. Because of this bit of uncertainty, Ed Harris, chairperson of Jackson's second district delegates, and I (as the prospective Jackson delegate) were asked to serve as liaisons with Volpe, who would call one of us should there have to be a change in our tentative agreement. . . .

Our congressional district caucus, which met at the suburban Parkway East Junior High School, was well attended. Mondale, Hart, and Jackson organizations turned out in full strength with delegates or their alternates all in place well in advance of the 7:30 show time. Throughout Missouri, fifty-one national convention delegates were being selected in such caucuses; six of these delegates were to be selected from our congressional district in this meeting. But with the last-minute merging of Hart and Jackson forces, the outcome was indeed determined before the congressional district convention convened: Jackson's caucus (which now included Hart's delegates) would be able to select two delegates and two alternates, while Mondale forces would be allocated four delegates and four alternates. The real contests of slate-making for these positions had clearly taken place prior to the meeting and formal ratification was all that was left. Even so, all of this pre-planning did little to overcome the interest and excitement that pervaded the meeting hall. Television crews, reporters from the local press, and visitors all turned out to record and witness the proceedings. . . .

After the nomination speeches, as indicated earlier, the selection of delegates was rather pro forma, key decisions having been made prior to the meeting. In the end Mondale won four national convention delegates and the expanded Jackson caucus two, with one pledged to Hart and the other (myself) pledged to Jackson.

It is difficult to express the joyful, appreciative, yet awesome feeling that consumed me upon my formal election as a delegate to the San Francisco convention. What pleased me most was the obvious, openly expressed warmth and support I received from my fellow Jackson delegates. I felt a responsibility to them and to myself to do the best job possible to promote the interests of Reverend Jackson. However, one major contribution, about which I told my fellow delegates all along, would lie in my efforts to capture for the historical record the deeper meaning and implications of the Jackson campaign. . . .

The next step in the delegate selection process, the state convention, was scheduled for June 2 in Columbia, Missouri. Seventeen more delegates were to be selected there. Our state coordinator, Charles Bussey, reminded all of us that each delegate to the congressional district caucus was also a delegate to the upcoming state convention and was expected to attend. Although Columbia was some two hours or more from St. Louis and getting people there could prove a problem, it was important to do so since the 20 percent rule held for the state convention also, and some of the deals worked out between Hart, Jackson, and Freeze people depended on commitments that had to be fulfilled at the state convention.

Fortunately, these commitments were honored. Nonetheless, a few Jackson delegates grumbled about the wheeling and dealing that took place before and at the state convention. In my presence, for example, one Jackson delegate from the Kansas City area complained about the undue influence of ''Bussey and the St. Louis people'' in slate making. Said he to a friend, but loud enough to be heard by others: ''This is the same old smoke-filled-room politics. They're cramming things down our throats.'' This comment stayed with me, for indeed some slate making did take place in smoke-filled rooms; I witnessed some of this and was intrigued by it all. I did wonder whether I too might have felt the same way as the young delegate I heard, had I been in his apparent situation. But I also wondered whether there was any conceivable way for any fairly large political organization to overcome such criticism—i.e., to function effectively without advance planning. I just wondered.

Interest Groups

Like political parties, interest groups are organizations that can provide political linkage. Interest groups are organized collections of individuals who share common goals, objectives, or interests and who organize in order to influence government decision makers. Through this influence, interest groups hope to incorporate their needs into public policy and to secure tangible benefits for their members. For example, interest groups such as the U.S. Chamber of Commerce, the Associated Milk Producers Inc., and the National Small Business Association work to protect and promote the economic well-being of their members. They do this either by opposing government actions harmful to group interests or by supporting and recommending to government decision makers public policies that will advance their members' private economic interests.

In contrast to the tangible economic benefits pursued by some groups, a growing number of interest groups work to secure benefits for nonmembers and the general community. Public interest groups such as Common Cause, the League of Women Voters, and the Environmental Defense Fund seek to influence government decision makers in order to secure "collective goods." Collective goods are any benefits that result from public policies and can be shared equally by all individuals independent of their membership in the group originally seeking the benefits (Berry 1977, 8). Clean air and water, election campaign reforms, and consumer protection legislation are all examples of collective goods.

Interest groups are alternatives to, and competitors with, political parties in providing political linkage. There are some clear advantages associated with having individuals represented by interest groups rather than political parties. One important advantage is that, unlike political parties, interest groups are often "policy maximizers" (Berry 1984, 55). Typically, interest groups care about and focus upon a small number of closely related policy issues. In contrast, to draw enough public support to be electorally competitive, political parties must focus on a large number of often unrelated issues. To win elections, both the Democratic and Republican parties "must dilute many policy stands, take purposely ambiguous stands on others, and generally ignore some [so] as not to offend segments of the population that they need in their coalition" (Berry 1984, 56).

For people who care passionately about some single issue, or only a few related ones, it may be more satisfying and rational to invest time, money, and other resources in supporting a relevant interest group, or groups, rather than either of the two major political parties. Many members of the public appear to be doing exactly that. More and more, we are becoming a nation of people who turn away from political parties and toward interest groups to speak for us in the political process (Berry 1984, 18). Over the past twenty-five years, there has been an advocacy or interest group explosion characterized by the formation of increasing numbers of new interest groups and increasing levels of group participation (Loomis and Cigler 1983, 21). A long list of factors contribute to this advocacy explosion, including rapid social and economic changes, the spread of affluence and education, and advances in communication technologies (Loomis and Cigler 1983, 21). These forces come together to alter established patterns of conflict within our political system, which in turn leads to the formation of new groups that press new demands on government and rival or even replace existing groups for issue dominance.

By linking individuals to their government politically, interest groups perform a number of functions for our political system. First, interest groups offset the disadvantages associated with our constitutionally prescribed geographical representation. At least in theory, members of Congress represent citizens based on where they live, whether in a certain district (for members of the House of Representatives) or state (for senators). Because interest groups link individuals to government decision makers by organizing them based on their economic or noneconomic needs rather than on where they live, some commentators now refer to interest groups as the "third house" of Congress (Botterweck and Hiatt 1990, 133–134).

Closely associated with representation is participation. Interest groups allow people to participate directly in influencing government decision makers and get beyond the limitation inherent in voting.

Elections occur only at two- or four-year intervals, and individual votes get lost in the hundreds of thousands or millions of other votes cast. Interest groups also allow individuals more opportunities for political involvement and a wider array of activities in which to participate than do political parties. These activities range from contributing money to the organization to engaging in its lobbying efforts and, in the case of some groups, to participating in protests, demonstrations, and even civil disobedience. In short, political participation through interest groups is likely to make individuals feel as though they have done more to address and resolve issues important to them (Berry 1984, 7).

Interest groups also seek to shape and influence public opinion and policy making concerning problems and political issues important to them. These efforts are not neutral endeavors. Rather, they are attempts to "try to mold public opinion in the hope that the voters will influence the decision makers at various levels of government to make decisions which are favorable to the interest group in question" (Botterweck and Hiatt 1990, 125). Despite the bias apparent in these efforts to influence public and government opinion, interest groups make a valuable contribution to public and government awareness of problems and issues. They do so by providing the public and elected and appointed officials with information to which they might not otherwise be exposed (Berry 1984, 8).

In carrying out their varied functions, interest groups engage in two broad and closely related activities: electioneering and lobbying. Interest group electioneering centers primarily around providing campaign contributions to candidates and spending independent funds in support of or opposition to candidates. We discussed in Chapter 3 the importance of huge sums of money in our national elections and the impact on candidates, particularly challengers, when they are unable to secure necessary campaign funds. Interest groups are fully aware of the significant role that money plays in contemporary political campaigns. They apply this knowledge by financially supporting candidates with a good chance of being elected. This normally means that in congressional elections interest groups contribute disproportionately to incumbents. In exchange for this financial support, interest groups expect access to the winning candidates.

Political action committees, or PACs, are the vehicles through which interest groups collect and disburse campaign funds. "[A] PAC is either the separated, segregated campaign funds of a sponsoring labor, business, or trade organization, or the campaign fund of a group formed primarily or solely for the purpose of giving money to candidates" (Sabato 1985, 7). Since the early 1970s, the number of connected and unconnected PACs has grown dramatically. In 1974, there were only 608 PACs registered with the Federal Election Commission. By 1988, over 4,200 PACs existed. New corporate, trade association, and non-connected PACs constituted most of this growth. As the number of PACs has grown, so has the amount of money that they contribute to election campaigns. In 1974, PACs contributed $12.5 million to congressional campaigns. By 1988, this amount rose to $148 million, making PACs the largest single identifiable source of campaign contributions (Eagleton 1991, 24–28).

The increases in the number of PACs and in PAC expenditures have generated criticism about the greater role that interest group funding now plays in contemporary political campaigns. Critics allege that PAC money reflects the growing influence of special interests on the policy-making process. Critics also charge that PACs undermine and further erode the traditional role that political parties perform in elections. PAC money makes candidates financially independent of political parties, thereby reducing the parties' control over the candidates running for office under their party labels (Conway 1983, 141; Eagleton 1991, 36). Because so many of them contribute overwhelmingly to incumbents, PACs are further accused of protecting incumbent members of Congress, since strong challengers will not emerge without adequate funds with which to run a competitive campaign (Conway 1983, 139). Finally, critics charge that the influx of large sums of PAC money into the campaign treasuries of so many candidates cannot help but have a corrupting effect on members of Congress (Eagleton 1991, 37).

PAC defenders respond to the critics' charges by asserting that rather than exerting an undue influence in the policy-making process, the proliferating PACs assist in maintaining representative democracy. PAC advocates argue that PACs promote democracy by embodying a broad array of contending political views that might not otherwise be represented (Eagleton 1991, 35). PAC defenders also point out that the decline in the influence of political parties began prior to the advent of PACs, and that PACs and PAC money only allow candidates to "purchase modern campaign technology that substitutes for campaign assistance no longer provided by the political parties" (Conway 1983, 142). PAC defenders also refute the charge that PAC money has a corrupting influence on Congress. They maintain that PAC spending is simply a means by which interest groups seek to maximize their access to members of Congress. They note that this effort, in and of itself, should not be alarming because access to elected officials is "a fundamental element of representative democracy" (Eagleton 1991, 37).

The above discussion suggests that interest group electioneering and PAC spending are intended primarily to gain and maintain access to elected officials. Using this access, interest groups try to influence the decisions made by elected officials. These efforts constitute what is traditionally called lobbying. Through lobbying, interest groups provide government decision makers with information in the hope that it will persuade them to incorporate the groups' perspectives in whatever decisions are made. Lobbying efforts can be directed toward any level or branch of government, but we will restrict our discussion to congressional lobbying.

Congressional lobbying is multidimensional. Direct lobbying is what most of us think of as lobbying. Direct lobbying involves person-to-person contact between interest group lobbyists and the members of Congress they are hoping to influence or congressional staffs. The activities associated with the direct lobbying of Congress are numerous. They range from lobbyists' formally testifying at congressional committee hearings or drafting the actual legislation to be introduced into Congress to engaging in informal contact with members of Congress or their staffs over lunch or cocktails (Gitelson et al. 1991, 219; Greenwald 1977, 69–71).

A variation on direct lobbying is coalition lobbying. Coalition lobbying is the formation of temporary alliances among interest groups for a common direct lobbying effort focusing on a particular issue (Eagleton 1991, 15; Gitelson 1991, 223; Greenwald 1977, 75). Coalition lobbying has at least one advantage over independently pursued direct lobbying. In a coalition, "the pooling of resources . . . permits distribution of the work load to take advantage of each group's special talents, the combining of monetary resources, and the multiplication of possible working contacts" (Greenwald 1977, 75).

Grass-roots lobbying is the third type of lobbying employed by interest groups. Grass-roots lobbying is lobbying by an interest group's rank-and-file members carried out through such tactics as letter-writing or telegram campaigns, personal visits to legislators' offices, or public protests and demonstrations (Gitelson et al. 1991, 224). Interest groups rely on grass-roots lobbying to convince government decision makers that their policy positions have a broad base of public support (Patterson 1990, 327).

Grass-roots lobbying can be particularly beneficial for interest groups having large memberships spread throughout the 50 states and 435 House districts. Memberships of this nature underscore and reinforce the interest groups' potential electoral clout (Greenwald 1977, 73).

It is a political fact of life that members of Congress rarely vote against something that can be defined as promoting the interest of their districts or states. Nor are they likely to vote for something harmful to their constituencies (Eagleton 1991, 16). An interest group can, therefore, use grass-roots lobbying to link its interests with the interests of their states or districts in the minds of members of Congress.

As the above discussion indicates, interest groups can and do play important roles in our political system by representing group members' interests before government decision makers. But interest groups and the political linkage resulting from them are far from perfect. First, all interest groups are not equally able to present their cases to the public and government decision makers for their consideration. Unequal access to resources, especially money and organizational capacity, means that some interest groups are regular losers in pressing their claims, whereas others with greater access to crucial resources habitually win benefits for their members (Loomis and Cigler 1983, 4-5). This imbalance frequently means that the interest groups most successful in representing their members' interests before government decision makers are those representing the wealthier and better-educated segments of our society. Conversely, the poor and the less well-educated, who may have a greater need for government services and benefits, are frequently the least able to present their claims to government decision makers (Botterweck and Hiatt 1990, 135).

Another major criticism of interest groups is that, by definition, the interests of many of these groups may be in direct conflict with the public interest or what a majority of the public would prefer to see as policy (Botterweck and Hiatt 1990, 135). Interest groups, by encouraging government decision makers to advance the private interests of their members, can undermine the public interest. Public policy sensitive to largely private interests "is likely to be flawed because it lacks direction, consistency, and coherence, and ignores long-range considerations" (Everson 1982, 32-33).

Theodore Lowi, in his classic work *The End of Liberalism* (1969), offered what is perhaps the most damning criticism of interest groups. Written over two decades ago, Lowi's assessment of interest group representation still has merit today. It may help to explain why so many individuals are likely to feel cynical about government policies that appear to put private interests above the national good. Lowi maintained that the incorporation of group interests into public policy undermines the legitimacy and authority of our government. Interest group representation is so pervasive in our policy-making process that it "renders government impotent, unable to plan"; weakens government concern for doing what is right; and replaces traditional reliance on formal procedures and the rule of law with informal procedures, bargaining, and compromises (Ornstein and Elder 1978, 16; Lowi 1969, 288–291). Critics of interest group representation, like Lowi, maintain that these and other shortcomings of interest groups inhibit the ability of our government to produce "good public policy"—defined as public policy in the public interest rather than "patch work compromises of the interests of the affected groups" (Everson 1982, 32).

The two case studies presented in this chapter keenly dramatize the basic nature and characteristics of interest groups. They do so by presenting revealing stories about the American Israel Public Affairs Committee (AIPAC). AIPAC is perhaps the most powerful, influential, and successful interest group operating in our political system.

"King of the Hill", by former congressman Paul Findley, presents a general overview and description of the impressive political clout and muscle exercised by AIPAC. Congressman Findley is eminently qualified to write about AIPAC's influence on Capitol Hill. He served in Congress for twenty-two years as a Republican member of the House of Representatives from Illinois. During his long tenure, Congressman Findley served on the House Foreign Affairs Committee. While serving on this committee, he was able to see firsthand the political muscle AIPAC used on his fellow members of the House and Senate, particularly those members with substantial Jewish constituencies.

Congressman Findley also directly experienced AIPAC's political clout as well as that of other Jewish lobbies and PACs. From the middle 1970s until his 1982 campaign for reelection, Findley was critical of the strong pro-Israel bias in U.S. foreign policy toward the Middle East. He advocated a more balanced policy that also recognized the concerns of the Arab countries. He advocated direct talks between the United States and Yassar Arafat and the Palestinian Liberation Organization (PLO). Congressman Findley even went so far as to go to the Middle East and meet privately with the PLO leaders. Despite his interest in a dialogue among all Middle Eastern countries, Congressman Findley demonstrated an otherwise unwavering support for Israel. Still, because of his public criticism of Israel and U.S. Middle East policy, AIPAC and other Jewish interest groups targeted him for electoral defeat. Beginning in 1979, AIPAC and other Jewish lobbies actively worked to defeat Congressman Findley. In 1982, they were finally successful. In the 1982 congressional elections, Findley was narrowly defeated by Democrat Richard Durbin. He was denied reelection by 1,407 votes, less than

1 percent of the total votes cast. During the election campaign, Congressman Findley's alleged support for the PLO was a central issue and AIPAC and other Jewish groups took credit for his defeat.

"The AWACS Battle" by Edwin Tivan, the second case study on interest groups, picks up where "King of the Hill" leaves off. But Tivan's story has a different twist. "The AWACS Battle" is an account of one of AIPAC's few political defeats, thereby reassuring us that powerful interests do not always get their way on Capitol Hill.

AWACS is an acronym for Airborne Warning And Command Systems. These systems represent the state of the art in aerial electronic surveillance. In June 1980, the Carter administration agreed to sell five AWACS planes to Saudi Arabia. Because of the Republican victory in the 1980 presidential campaign, the Carter administration never acted on the president's promise to sell these planes to Saudi Arabia. The outgoing administration was able, however, to convince the incoming Reagan administration of the importance of this sale to United States interests in the Middle East. It therefore became the new administration's responsibility to navigate the AWACS sale through Congress. Its task was made more difficult by intense Jewish and Israeli opposition to the sale. Israel and its supporters in this country feared that Saudi Arabia would use the AWACS planes against Israel. Leading the opposition on Capitol Hill were Thomas Dine and AIPAC. The ensuing battle over the AWACS sale was an important early test of President Reagan's foreign policy leadership. At issue was who would be responsible for the formulation of this country's Middle East policy—the new administration or AIPAC?

Suggested Reading

Berry, Jeffery M. *The Interest Group Society.* Boston: Little Brown. A well-organized introduction to interest group formation, activities, and influence in American politics.

Eismeier, Theodore J., and Philip H. Pollock III. 1988. *Business, Money, and the Rise of Corporate PACs in American Elections.* Westport, CT: Quorum Books. A thoroughly researched examination of the development and workings of corporate PACs and their influence on American politics and government.

McFarland, Andrew S. 1984. *Common Cause: Lobbying in the Public Interest.* Chatham, NJ: Chatham House. An extended case study of one of the nation's best-known public interest pressure groups and how it makes use of today's high-tech lobbying, which now plays a major role in Washington.

Olson, Mancur. 1965. *The Logic of Collective Action.* Cambridge, MA: Harvard University Press. An economic view that challenges the traditional pluralist wisdom that individual group members motivated by self-interest will act rationally and seek to further their common or collective goals.

Paige, Connie. 1983. *The Right to Lifers.* New York: Summit Books. A study of the "right to lifers" as a populist movement with an emphasis on who they are, how they operate, and where they get their money.

Schlozman, Kay Lehman, and John T. Tierney. 1986. *Organized Interests and American Democracy.* New York: Harper & Row. A scholarly study based on original research and analysis that examines the place of organized interests in contemporary American politics.

King of the Hill

Paul Findley

As you read this case study, consider the following questions:

1. What is Congressman Findley's overall assessment of AIPAC's political muscle on Capitol Hill, and what impact does he feel this clout has on congressional behavior?

2. What does Findley mean when he writes about the "ascendancy" of AIPAC's executive director, Thomas A. Dine?

3. How does the ascendancy of Dine in the Washington power structure dramatize AIPAC's influence on Capitol Hill and in the White House?

4. What different types of lobbying does AIPAC employ, and how does AIPAC incorporate these different types of lobbying into its overall efforts to promote Israel's interests?

5. What is the pattern of contributions for pro-Israel PACs?

6. How does the growth in pro-Israel PACs reflect the general trend in PAC development and importance in congressional elections?

7. What significance, if any, should be attached to Dine's comment that because of the political influence of AIPAC and other proIsrael groups and PACs, "American Jews are thus able to form our own foreign policy agenda"?

W ASHINGTON IS A CITY OF ACRONYMS, AND TODAY ONE OF THE BEST-
KNOWN IN CONGRESS IS AIPAC. THE MERE MENTION OF IT BRINGS A
sober, if not furtive look, to the face of anyone on Capitol Hill who
deals with Middle East policy. AIPAC—the American Israel Public
Affairs Committee—is now the preeminent power in Washington
lobbying.

In 1967, as a fourth-term Congressman just named to the House
Foreign Affairs Committee, I had never heard of it. One day, in private
conversation in the committee room, I voiced a brief criticism of Israel's
military attack on Syria. A senior Republican, William S. Broomfield
of Michigan, responded with a smile, "Wait till 'Si' Kenen over at AIPAC
hears what you've said." He was referring to I. L. Kenen, the executive
director of AIPAC, whose name was just as unfamiliar to me as the
organization he headed. I learned later that Broomfield was not joking. AIPAC sometimes finds out what Congressmen say about Middle
East policy even in private conversations, and those who criticize Israel
do so at their political peril.

AIPAC is only a part of the Israeli lobby, but in terms of direct
effect on public policy it is clearly the most important. The organization has deepened and extended its influence in recent years. It is no
overstatement to say that AIPAC has effectively gained control of virtually all of Capitol Hill's action on Middle East policy. Almost without
exception, House and Senate members do its bidding, because most
of them consider AIPAC to be the direct Capitol Hill representative of
a political force that can make or break their chances at election time.

Whether based on fact or fancy, the perception is what counts:
AIPAC means power—raw, intimidating power. Its promotional literature regularly cites a tribute published in *The New York Times:* "The
most powerful, best-run and effective foreign policy interest group in
Washington." A former Congressman, Paul N. "Pete" McCloskey puts
it more directly: Congress is "terrorized" by AIPAC. Other Congressmen
have not been so candid on the public record, but many House and
Senate members privately agree. . . .

In practice, [AIPAC and other Jewish] lobby groups function as
an informal extension of the Israeli government. This was illustrated
when AIPAC helped draft the official statement defending Israel's 1981

bombing of the Iraqi nuclear reactor, then issued it the same hour as Israel's embassy.

No major Jewish organization ever publicly takes issue with positions and policies adopted by Israel. Thomas A. Dine, executive director of AIPAC, spoke warmly of President Reagan's peace plan when it was announced in September 1982, but as soon as Israel rejected the plan, Dine fell silent.

This close coordination sometimes inspires intragovernment humor. "At the State Department we used to predict that if Israel's prime minister should announce that the world is flat, within 24 hours Congress would pass a resolution congratulating him on the discovery," recalls Don Bergus, former ambassador to Sudan and a retired career diplomat.

To Jewish organizations, however, lobbying Washington is serious business, and they look increasingly to AIPAC for leadership. Stephen S. Rosenfeld, deputy editor of *The Washington Post* editorial page, rates AIPAC as "clearly the leading Jewish political force in America today."

AIPAC's charter defines its mission as legislative action, but it now also represents the interests of Israel whenever there is a perceived challenge to that country's interests in the news media, the religious community, on U.S. college campuses—anywhere. Because AIPAC's staff members are paid from contributions by American citizens, they need not register under the Foreign Agents Registration Act. In effect, however, they serve the same function as foreign agents.

Over the years the pro-Israel lobby has thoroughly penetrated this nation's governmental system, and the organization that has made the deepest impact is AIPAC, to whom even the president of the United States turns when he has a vexing political problem related to the Arab-Israeli dispute.

The Ascendancy of Thomas A. Dine

Faced with rising public opposition to the presence of U.S. Marines in Lebanon, President Ronald Reagan in October 1983 sought help from the American Israel Public Affairs Committee. The terrorist bombing which killed more than 200 Marines asleep in their barracks at the Beirut airport was yet to come. Still, four Marines had already died, three by sniper fire, and Congressional concern was rising. Democratic Congressman Sam Stratton of New York, a veteran known for his "hawkish" views, called the Marines "sitting ducks" and predicted heavy casualties. He wanted them out.

Others cited the War Powers Resolution and questioned whether the president had authority to keep forces in a hostile environment such as Beirut for more than 90 days without the express approval of Congress. Some Congressmen began drawing parallels between the Marine presence in Lebanon and the beginnings of the disastrous U.S. experience in Vietnam.

President Reagan objected, as did his predecessors, to the restrictions imposed by the War Powers legislation. If he accepted its terms, he would have to withdraw the forces within 90 days or get Congress to approve an extension. If he insisted that the law did not apply because the situation was not hostile, events might quickly prove him wrong and, regardless, he would have a rebellious Congress on his hands.

He decided to finesse the problem. He asked Congress for legislation letting him keep the existing force of Marines in Lebanon for 18 months. This would please the "strict constructionists" who felt the chief executive must live with the War Powers Resolution. It would suit his own needs, because he was confident that the orderly removal of the Marines would occur within the 18-month period.

Thanks to extraordinary help from an unlikely quarter, Reagan's plan had relatively clear sailing in the House of Representatives. Speaker Thomas P. "Tip" O'Neill, the most prominent elected Democrat in the nation, gave the legislation his strong support. To O'Neill, it was a question of patriotism, and enough Democrats answered his call to assure passage in the Democrat-controlled body.

But the Senate, although controlled by his fellow Republicans, posed a more difficult problem for the president. A "nose count" showed a close vote and probably even defeat. The president decided he needed help and enlisted the cooperation of Thomas A. Dine, the slender, aggressive, . . . young Capitol Hill staff veteran who has headed AIPAC since 1981.

Reagan's appeal to Dine for support on the Marine issue was without precedent. The pending bill contained no money for Israel, and AIPAC and other Israeli lobby groups had kept hands off the Lebanon controversy. Pro-Israeli forces did not want other Americans to blame Israel if the Marines should encounter more trouble. . . . Though AIPAC privately wanted the Marines to stay in Lebanon, under the circumstances its leadership preferred to stay in the background.

The White House call to Dine was exceptional for another reason: Reagan needed help with Senators who were normally his most stalwart supporters. The president was unsure of the votes of twelve Republicans, among them John Warner of Virginia, Dan Quayle of Indiana, William Cohen of Maine and James A. McClure of Idaho. All were generally regarded as "hawkish" on military questions and, except for McClure, strong supporters of Israel. Learning of the presidential plea, one AIPAC staffer said: "If the White House is worried about those votes, the bill is going down."

Despite its reluctance to get involved publicly in the sensitive issue, AIPAC made the calls. Nine of the twelve Senators, including the four mentioned above, voted with the president and helped him win a narrow 54 to 46 victory.

AIPAC's role in the outcome was not noted in most media reports on the dramatic event, but an elated President Reagan called Dine personally to express his thanks. Michael Gale, then handling White House relations with the Jewish community, provided a transcript of the conversation with the suggestion that AIPAC publicize it. AIPAC declined, preferring to maintain its low profile on the issue, so Gale gave the text to Wolf Blitzer of *The Jerusalem Post,* who formerly wrote for AIPAC's *Near East Report.* The *Post* quoted Reagan as saying to Dine, "I just wanted to thank you and all your staff for the great assistance you gave us on the War Powers Act resolution. . . . I know how you mobilized the grassroot organizations to generate support."

"Well, we try to use the telephone," responded Dine. "That's part of our job. And we wanted to do it and will continue to do it. . . . We want to work together, obviously."

Work together they have. The Reagan executive branch established a relationship with AIPAC of unprecedented intimacy. It was not the first time the White House or the State Department had turned to the lobbying group for help. Although these high level approaches are little known even on Capitol Hill, they actually occur every time foreign aid legislation is up for a vote. Whoever controls the White House finds that securing Congressional approval of foreign aid is a challenge and, as the legislation includes economic and military aid to Israel, naturally looks to AIPAC for help. Except for a few humanitarian and church-related organizations, AIPAC serves foreign aid's only domestic constituency.

Without AIPAC, foreign aid legislation would not be approved at the $7 billion-plus level of 1983 and might have difficulty surviving at all. A candid tribute to the lobby came from John K. Wilhelm, the executive director of the presidential commission that made recommendations in late 1983 on the future direction of foreign aid. Briefing a world hunger board at the State Department in January 1984, Wilhelm, a career veteran in the Agency for International Development, said the active support of the pro-Israeli lobby was "vital" to Congressional approval of foreign aid. In the early 1960s when aid to Israel was modest—less than $100 million a year—a foreign-aid bill squeaked through the House of Representatives by a scant five votes. AIPAC was then in its infancy.

AIPAC also crafted the strategy which produced a $510 million increase in 1983 aid for Israel—an increase which was astonishing because it came just after the indiscriminate bombing of Beirut and the failure of Israeli forces to halt the massacre of Palestinian refugees in the Sabra and Shatila refugee camps, events that aroused unprecedented public criticism of Israeli policy.

The administration opposed the increase but was outmaneuvered. By the time Judge William Clark, at the time National Security Adviser to President Reagan, sent an urgent appeal to Republican Senator Mark Hatfield to block the increase, the issue was settled. AIPAC had already locked in support by persuading a majority on the Appropriations Committee that the add-on was a simple question of being for or against Israel. No one wanted to champion the negative side.

AIPAC had already confounded the administration on the House side, where the White House had argued against the increase for budgetary reasons, contending it would be at the expense of other needy countries. This argument was demolished when AIPAC lobbyists presented elaborate data showing how the extra aid to Israel could be accomplished without cutting support for other countries. An AIPAC lobbyist summed up: "The administration lobbyists really didn't do their homework. They didn't have their act together." By 1984 the aid level had risen to over $2 billion a year—all of it in grants with no repayment—and the approval margin was 112.

In February 1983, Secretary of State George Shultz named a "blue ribbon" panel of prominent citizens to recommend changes in the foreign aid program. Of the 42 on the commission, 27 were Senators or House members with primary responsibility for handling foreign aid legislation. The others had prominence in administering foreign aid in years past.

Only one full-time lobbyist was named to the panel: AIPAC's executive director, Thomas A. Dine. It was the first time to my knowledge that a lobbyist had been selected for such a prestigious government assignment, and Dine's selection was particularly surprising because it put him in a close working relationship with the handful of people who formulate and carry out policy on the very matter AIPAC was set up to influence—aid to Israel. . . .

In November, Dine took an even bigger step up the ladder of Washington prestige and influence. He was invited to the White House for a private meeting with National Security Adviser Robert C. McFarlane, President Reagan's closest advisor on day-to-day policy in the Middle East. On the agenda were two foreign policy topics of great sensitivity: the Lebanese situation and the proposal to help Jordan establish a rapid deployment force. Both of these issues, of course, were of vital interest to Israel. Dine's invitation came just a week after he received the President's jubilant phone call.

In January 1984 *Washingtonian* magazine listed Dine among the most influential people in the nation's capital.

Dine's reputation has even stirred Arab capitals. In mid-March 1984 King Hussein of Jordan publicly blamed AIPAC, in part, for the decline in U.S. influence and leadership for peace in the Middle East. He also criticized the inordinate influence of the Israeli lobby on U.S. presidential candidates. He said the candidates had to "appeal for the favors of AIPAC, Zionism and Israel."

One development which especially provoked the king was that, for ten days beginning in mid-March 1984, Dine personally took part in direct foreign policy negotiations with Undersecretary of State Lawrence S. Eagleburger and National Security Adviser McFarlane. During one session, Eagleburger offered to withdraw a widely publicized proposal to sell antiaircraft missiles to Jordan if AIPAC would drop its support of legislation requiring the removal of the U.S. embassy in Israel from Tel Aviv to Jerusalem.

By then, King Hussein's sharp criticism of the United States—and AIPAC—had appeared in U.S. newspapers, and Dine knew it had strengthened Congressional opposition to the sale. At the time Eagleburger made his proposition, AIPAC already had 48 Senators committed in opposition and received pledges from six more the next day. Thus AIPAC was able to kill the sale without cutting a deal on other issues.

After he rejected Eagleburger's offer, Dine promised that AIPAC would cease active opposition to a proposal to help Jordan establish a rapid deployment force and would lobby to work out a compromise on the bill to transfer the U.S. embassy from Tel Aviv to Jerusalem if the administration would take two important steps: first, refuse to sell Stinger antiaircraft missiles to Saudi Arabia, and second, issue a public letter announcing that it would engage in no further indirect communications with the Palestine Liberation Organization. Although the public letter did not appear, the administration backed away from the Stinger sales to both Saudi Arabia and Jordan. . . .

Broadening the Network

To accomplish these feats for Israel . . . AIPAC director Dine utilizes a team of hard-driving, able professionals and keeps them working together smoothly.

He keeps policy lines clear and the troops well-disciplined. AIPAC's role is to support Israel's policies, not to help formulate them, so AIPAC maintains daily telephone communication with the Israeli embassy, and Dine meets personally with embassy officials at least once a week.

Though AIPAC has a staff of only 60—small in comparison to other major U.S. Jewish organizations—it taps the resources of a broad nationwide network of unpaid activists. Annual membership meetings in Washington are a major way to rally the troops. Those attending hear prominent U.S. and Israeli speakers, participate in workshops and seminars, and contribute financially to the cause. The conferences attract top political talent: the Israeli ambassador, senior White House and State Department officials, prominent Senators and House members. . . .

More than 1,200 representatives from 41 states attended AIPAC's 1983 national gathering. . . .

Art Chotin, deputy executive director of AIPAC, reported to the group that during the previous year ten different statewide workshops on political involvement had given the "pro-Israeli community" the "skills they need to have an impact." Ten more were planned for 1984. Chotin illustrated the national impact of these local events by pointing out that a 1982 workshop in New Mexico had helped elect Democrat Jeffrey Bingaman to the Senate. Bingaman, described by Chotin as "a strong pro-Israeli voice in Washington," was among the 100 "pro-Israeli citizens" attending the 1983 affair.

Tightly scheduled workshops, similar to the national conferences, are conducted annually in each of five regions. The "capitals" are Atlanta, Fort Worth, Hollywood, Des Moines and Chicago, and from each a chairperson coordinates all AIPAC regional activities. To help these outreach programs, AIPAC now has full-time staff located in New York, New Jersey and California.

Chotin told the conference that during the 1982 Congressional elections, 300 candidates "came to visit AIPAC" to explain their positions on "foreign aid, arms sales to Arab nations, and the general nature of U.S.–Arab relations."

Ties with other interest groups are carefully cultivated. Christian outreach was announced as AIPAC's newest national program, and Merrie White, a "born-again Christian," was introduced as the director of relations with the Christian community. According to Chotin, the goal was nothing less than to "bring that community into AIPAC." He noted the presence of 50 Christians representing 35 states as evidence of progress already made toward this end. . . .

AIPAC's coast-to-coast outreach is enhanced by its speaking program. Its officers, staff members and representatives filled over 900 dates in 1982 alone. Receptions are held in scores of smaller cities. "Parlor briefings" in the homes of Jewish leaders nationally help raise money to supplement revenue from membership dues. Social events on Capitol Hill help spread the word to the thousands of high school and college students who work as interns in the offices of Senators and Congressmen or in committee offices. . . .

Another group of potentially influential—but often overlooked—Washington functionaries that AIPAC tries to influence is made up of Congressional staffers. AIPAC works with Israeli universities who arrange expense-paid tours for staff members who occupy key positions. These annual trips are called the Hal Rosenthal program, named for a staff aide to former Republican Senator Jacob Javits who was gunned down by a Palestinian terrorist on the first such trip. By 1984 over 50 Congressional staffers had participated. . . .

AIPAC's outreach program is buttressed by a steady stream of publications. In addition to "Action Alerts" and the weekly *Near East Report,* it issues position papers and monographs designed to answer, or often discredit, critics, and advance Israel's objectives.

The most controversial publication of all is an "enemies list" issued as a "first edition" in the spring of 1983. A handsomely printed 154-page paperback entitled *The Campaign to Discredit Israel,* it provides a "directory of the actors": 21 organizations and 39 individuals AIPAC identified as inimical to Israeli interests.

Included are such distinguished public servants as former Undersecretary of State George W. Ball, retired ambassadors Talcott Seelye, Andrew Killgore, John C. West and James Akins, and former Senator

James Abourezk. There are also five Jewish dissenters and several scholars on the list.

Seemingly unaware of the AIPAC project, the Anti-Defamation League of B'nai B'rith almost simultaneously issued its own "enemies list": *Pro-Arab Propaganda in America: Vehicles and Voices.* It too is identified as a "first edition," and lists 31 organizations and 34 individuals. These books are nothing more than blacklists, reminiscent of the worst tactics of the McCarthy era.

A similar "enemies list" is employed in AIPAC's extensive program at colleges and universities. . . .

"They Get the Word Out Fast"

Through "Action Alert" mailings AIPAC keeps more than one thousand Jewish leaders throughout the United States informed on current issues. An "alert" usually demands action to meet a legislative challenge on Capitol Hill, requesting a telephone call, telegram or, if need be, a personal visit to a reluctant Congressman.

The network can have almost instantaneous effect. One day I whispered to a colleague in the Foreign Affairs Committee I might offer an amendment to a pending bill cutting aid to Israel. Within 30 minutes two other Congressmen came to me with worried looks, reporting they had just had calls from citizens in their home districts who were concerned about my amendment. . . .

This activism is carried out by an elaborate system of officers, committees and councils which give AIPAC a ready, intimate system for political activity from coast to coast. Its nineteen officers meet once a month to confer with Dine on organization and management. Each of its five vice-presidents can expect eventually to serve a term as president. A large executive committee totaling 132 members is invited to Washington every three months for briefings. A national council lists over 200 names. These subgroups include the leadership of most major U.S. Jewish organizations. . . .

Lobbyists for AIPAC have almost instant access to House and Senate members and feel free to call them at their homes in the evening. Republican Congressman Douglas Bereuter of Nebraska, an exception, will receive no lobbyists, AIPAC or otherwise, but the doors are wide open to AIPAC lobbyists at the offices of almost all other Congressmen. A Congressional aide explained why:

Professionalism is one reason. They know what they are doing, get to the point and leave. They are often a useful source of information. They are reliable and friendly. But most important of all, they are seen by Congressmen as having direct and powerful ties to important constituents.

The result is a remarkable cooperation and rapport between lobbyist and legislator. Encountered in a Capitol corridor one day, an AIPAC lobbyist said, "Tomorrow I will try to see five members of the House. I called this morning and confirmed every appointment, and I have no doubt I will get in promptly." Two days later, even he seemed somewhat awed by AIPAC's clout. He reported, "I made all five. I went right in to see each of them. There was no waiting. Our access is amazing."

This experience contrasts sharply with the experience of most other lobbyists on Capitol Hill. One veteran lobbyist reflected with envy on the access AIPAC enjoys: "If I can actually see two Congressmen or Senators in one long day, it's been a good one."

Despite its denials, AIPAC keeps close records on each House and Senator member. Unlike other lobbies, which keep track only of a few "key" issues voted on the House or Senate floor, AIPAC takes note of other activities, too—votes in committees, co-sponsorship of bills, signing of letters and even whether speeches are made. "That's depth!" exclaims an admiring Capitol Hill staff member. . . .

"I Cleared It with AIPAC"

Until his defeat in an upset on November 6, 1984, Congressman Clarence D. "Doc" Long, a 74-year-old Democrat of Maryland, exemplified the strong ties between AIPAC and Capitol Hill. He delivered for Israel as chairman of the House Appropriations Subcommittee which handles aid to Israel.

The tall, gray-haired, former economics professor at Johns Hopkins University trumpeted his support: "AIPAC made my district their number one interest." AIPAC supported Long for a good reason: He held the gavel when questions about funding Israeli aid come up. The lobby wanted him to keep it. Chairmanships normally are decided by seniority, and next in line after Long is David Obey of Wisconsin, who earned lobby disfavor in 1976 by offering an amendment to cut aid to Israel by $200 million. "Doc" Long never had any misgivings about aid to Israel and helped his colleagues defeat Obey's amendment, 342 to 32. . . .

In September 1983, Long led a battle to get U.S. Marines out of Lebanon. He proposed an amendment which would have cut funding for the operation in 60 days. John Hall, a reporter who knew Long's close ties with the lobby, asked Long, "Are you sure this amendment won't get you in trouble?" Without hesitation, the Congressman replied: "I cleared it with AIPAC." He was not joking. Though this was not the first Congressional proposal to be cleared in advance with the Israeli lobby, it was the first time the clearance had been specifically acknowledged in the public record. The proposal to cut aid to Lebanon provoked a lively debate but, opposed by such leaders as Speaker "Tip" O'Neill and Lee Hamilton of Indiana, chairman of the Subcommittee on Europe and the Middle East, the measure failed, 274–153.

Although heavily supported by pro-Israeli interests—18 pro-Israel political action committees chipped in $31,250 for Long's 1982 re-election campaign—Long denies a personal linkage:

> Nobody has to give me money to make me vote for aid to Israel. I've been doing that for 20 years, most of the time without contributions.

The money and votes Israel's supporters provided to Long's candidacy were insufficient in 1984. Although pro-Israel PACs gave him $155,000—four times the amount that went to any other House candidate—Long lost by 5,727 votes, less than three percent of those cast. A factor in his defeat was advertising sponsored by people prominent in the National Association of Arab Americans which attacked Long for his uncritical support of Israel's demands. . . .

Beyond AIPAC to the PACs

AIPAC differs from most lobbies, in that it avoids endorsing candidates publicly and does not raise or spend money directly in partisan campaigns. Campaign involvement is left officially to pro-Israel political action committees (PACs). Over 3,000 PACs are registered under federal law, and almost all are directly affiliated with special-interest lobbies. There are 75 PACs which focus on support for Israel, though none lists an affiliation with AIPAC or any other Jewish organization.

Prior to 1979, pro-Israeli financial support to candidates and party organizations came entirely from individuals. Some of these individuals focused heavily on an Ohio Congressional race in 1976, the candidacy of Mary Rose Oakar, who was to become the first person of Syrian ancestry elected to Congress. A popular member of the Cleveland city council, she confronted a field of twelve male Democrats and an avalanche of Jewish money in the primary election race. Pro-Israeli interests selected State Senator Tony Celebreze, regarded as a "comer" in Ohio politics, as the candidate with the best chance to nudge her from the nomination.

During the campaign Dennis Heffernan, a fundraiser for Celebreze, was asked by a surprised and uneasy colleague to explain why more than thirty "Jewish-appearing" names were each recorded as donating $1,000.

"What's going on here?" he asked, wondering aloud if his friend Celebreze had "caved in" to a special interest. He asked bluntly: "Is Tony selling himself out, or is this money given in a worthy cause?" Heffernan responded, "Well, is Israel a worthy cause?"

Oakar found the focus by pro-Israel forces "upsetting." She explained, "I hadn't said a word about the Middle East, so it had to be because of my ethnic background. My father served in World War II and my brother in the Army later, but you would think we were less American."

The money helped Celebreze defeat the other eleven men, but Oakar won the nomination. Noting the district was overwhelmingly Democratic, the pro-Israel group sensed a hopeless situation and made no fight against Oakar in the fall or in subsequent elections.

The prominence of "Jewish-appearing" names in the Ohio race may have been a factor in encouraging Jews nationally to organize the first pro-Israel political action committees in 1979. By 1982 they had mushroomed to a total of thirty-one. Pro-Israel PACs contributed more than $1.8 million dollars to 268 different election campaigns during the 1981–82 Federal Election Commission reporting cycle, putting them in the highest political spending range. By mid-August 1984, the list had increased to 75 PACs, and they had accumulated $4.25 million for the 1984 federal elections.

None of them carried a name or other information which disclosed its pro-Israeli interest, nor did any list an affiliation with AIPAC or other pro-Israeli or Jewish organization. Each chose to obscure its pro-Israel character by using a bland title, like the "Committee for 18," "Arizona Politically Interested Citizens," "Joint Action Committee for

Political Affairs," or the "Government Action Committee." Yet all are totally committed to one thing: Israel.

"No one is trying to hide anything," protests Mark Siegel, director of the pro-Israeli National Bipartisan Political Action Committee and a former White House liaison with the Jewish community. He insists that the bland names were chosen because "There are those in the political process who would use the percentage of Jewish money [in a given race] as a negative."

Norman Silverman, who helped to found the Denver-based Committee for 18, is more explicit, saying the name selection became "an emotional issue." Some of the organizers, mainly younger people, wanted Jewish identity plainly set forth in the name. "Others," Silverman noted, "said they didn't want to be a member if we did that."

Whatever their names, pro-Israel PACs enlarge the opportunities for individual supporters of Israel to back candidates. An individual may contribute up to $5,000 to a political action committee but only $1,000 to a candidate in each election. PACs, in turn, may contribute $5,000 to a candidate in each election. Individuals often contribute the $1,000 limit directly to a candidate and also the $5,000 limit to a PAC supporting the same candidate. *The Wall Street Journal,* reviewing the growth of pro-Israel PACs in August 1983 reported that Lawrence and Barbara Weinberg of Beverly Hills, California, gave $20,000 to the Citizens Organized Political Action Committee, based in Los Angeles, over a period that encompassed both the primary and general elections in 1982 and gave $2,000 to Democrat Richard J. Durbin, the man who defeated me in 1982. The PAC also contributed $5,000 to Durbin. That kind of generosity is not ignored by your average politician.

The largest pro-Israel PAC is the National Political Action Committee (NatPAC), headquartered in New York with Marvin Josephson, head of a theatrical and literary talent agency, as chairman. Its Washington-based executive director is Richard Altman, who previously worked as political director of AIPAC. It draws money heavily from the entertainment industry and got off to a fast start in 1982 when Woody Allen signed its first nationwide fund-raising appeal. *The National Journal* rates it as the nation's largest non-labor, non-business political action committee.

In 1982, NatPAC raised $1.04 million and spent $547,500 on 109 candidates for Congress. It gave the $5,000 legal limit to each of 31 Senate candidates. Twenty-eight of these were elected. On the House side, 57 of the 73 candidates it supported won. In the wake of those successes, NatPAC ran a full-page advertisement in *The New York Times* inviting further support and declaring that it was "helping to elect officials in all fifty states who realize that Israel's survival is vital to our own." . . .

Executive director Richard Altman calls NatPAC a "grassroots movement." By late 1983 he had signed up over 20,000 members, with his goal for 1984 set at 100,000. NatPAC strives for "ecumenical fund-raising," he says, noting the presence of Methodist Bob Hope among the one hundred prominent Americans listed as charter members.

He is candid: "Money makes the political engine run. To elect a friend, you have to pay for it—and we're not the only ones who know that."

Altman declares that participating in PACs "is quintessentially both American and Jewish, as an expression of our involvement in political life."

Small PACs sometimes focus on candidates far from their locales. Robert B. Golder, a Philadelphia businessman, organized the Delaware Valley Political Action Committee (Del-Val PAC) in 1981, recruited 160 members, and dispensed $58,000 to 32 widely scattered candidates. Twenty-eight of them won. Golder explains that his goal is to elect pro-Israel Congressmen "in faraway places who don't have Jewish constituencies." For example, his PAC sent $1,500 to Jeffrey Bingaman, the Democrat elected to the Senate in 1982 from New Mexico. In late 1983 it sent $5,000 to Tom Corcoran, the unsuccessful challenger of Republican Senator Charles Percy of Illinois. A 12-person executive committee decides where the money is spent.

A San Francisco-based PAC concentrates on contests outside California. Melvin Swig, who is chairman of the Bay Area Citizens Political Action Committee, says: "There are enough people locally who do enough for their constituency. We look for areas that have less Jewish visibility than others, places where there are fewer Jews." . . .

Golder, Swig and other PAC leaders receive guidance from AIPAC, which keeps them up to date on votes cast and statements made by Senate and House members as well as positions taken on the Middle East by candidates seeking office for the first time.

AIPAC sometimes drops all pretense at staying apart from fund raising. For instance, a pro-Israel political action committee was organized in Virginia in 1983 during a workshop sponsored by AIPAC. . . .

A lobby veteran who is now engaged fulltime in fund-raising worries about appearances. AIPAC's former executive director, Morris J. Amitay, feels that smaller local PACs are best and fears that large well-publicized national PACs may create the impression that Jews exercise too much political power. He operates the relatively small Washington Political Action Committee, which dispensed $89,075 in 158 races during the 1982 campaigns.

Too much or not, Jewish influence in fund raising is widely recognized. In August 1983 the *Wall Street Journal* reported,

> Several ranking Congressmen—most of whom wouldn't comment on the record for this story—say they believe the political effect of Jewish PAC money is greater than that of other major lobbies because it is skillfully focused on one foreign policy issue.

Focused it is. The pro-Israel PACs concentrate exclusively on federal elections and focus heavily on Senate races and on House members who occupy key foreign policy assignments.

PAC leader Mark Siegel says the PACs concentrate on the Senate, because it is the "real battleground" on questions of foreign policy. In 1982, they invested $966,695 in Senate races, with $355,550 going to key House contests.

Guided by AIPAC, PACs choose their targets with care. When Lynn Adelman, a Jewish state senator in Wisconsin, in 1982 mounted the first primary election challenge that Democrat Clement J. Zablocki had experienced in thirty years, AIPAC recommended against an all-out effort. AIPAC was unhappy with Zablocki's record, but did not consider him a problem; furthermore, it concluded that Adelman could not win. Adelman received only $9,350 from thirteen pro-Israel political action committees. The contest made national news, because Zablocki was chairman of the House Foreign Affairs Committee, through which all Israeli aid measures must go. . . . Despite AIPAC's low-key recommendation, a letter soliciting funds for Adelman cited two "gains" if Zablocki lost: "Adelman's election not only means a friend of Israel in Congress, but also that the House Foreign Affairs Committee will have a friend of Israel as its new chairman," referring to Dante Fascell of Florida, the Democrat who was next in line to succeed Zablocki. Zablocki was re-elected by a two-to-one margin.

Meanwhile, Fascell, the "other friend" cited in the fund-raising appeal, was receiving strong support from pro-Israel PACs in his successful campaign for re-election in a Florida district that includes part of Miami. Twenty-two of these PACs provided Fascell with a total of $43,250, the second highest amount to a House candidate that year. These funds helped him survive a challenge by a former television newsman. . . .

Despite the dramatic growth of these PACs—a development that has occurred entirely since 1979—most of the contributions to candidates still come directly from individual pro-Israel activists. . . .

After the 1982 election—a year before he was elected chairman of the Foreign Affairs Committee after the sudden death of Zablocki—Fascell remarked:

> The whole trouble with campaign finances is the hue and cry that you've been bought. If you need the money, are you going to get it from your enemy? No, you're going to get it from your friend.

"Our Own Foreign Policy Agenda"

Much of the American Israel Public Affairs Committee's work in 1982 centered on expanding grassroots support, enlarging outreach programs to the college and Christian communities, and helping pro-Israel political action committees sharpen their skills. These efforts were largely aimed at increasing the lobby's influence in the Senate. AIPAC wanted no repetition of its failure to block the 1981 AWACS sale to Saudi Arabia.

One way in which AIPAC increases the number of its Senate friends is illustrated by its interventions in a critical race in Missouri. AIPAC stood by a friend and won. Republican Senator John C. Danforth, an ordained Episcopal minister, was opposed for re-election by a Jewish Democrat, Harriett Woods. In the closely fought contest, the non-Jewish Danforth found that an unblemished record of cooperation brought him AIPAC support even against a Jewish challenger. The help was crucial, as Danforth won by less than one percent of the vote.

AIPAC also weighed in heavily in Maine, helping to pull off the upset victory of Democratic Senator George Mitchell over Republican Congressman David Emery. The *Almanac of American Politics* rated Mitchell "the Democratic Senator universally regarded as having the least chance for re-election." He had never won an election. Defeated for governor by an independent candidate in 1974, he was appointed to fill the Senate vacancy caused when Senator Edmund Muskie resigned in 1980 to become President Carter's Secretary of State.

Encouraged by AIPAC, 27 pro-Israeli political action committees, all based outside Maine, contributed $77,400 to Mitchell's campaign. With this help Mitchell, who has Lebanese ancestry, fooled the professionals and won handily. In a post-election phone call to AIPAC director Thomas A. Dine, Mitchell promised: "I will remember you."

In another example, Republican Senator David Durenberger of Minnesota received for his 1982 re-election bid $57,000 from 20 pro-Israeli political action committees, with $10,000 of this total coming from the Citizens Organized PAC in California. This PAC contributed $5,000 during a breakfast meeting four months after he voted against the sale of AWACS planes to Saudi Arabia, and added $5,000 more by election day. . . .

In close races, lobby interests sometimes play it safe by supporting both sides. In the 1980 Senate race in Idaho, for example, pro-Israeli activists contributed to their stalwart friend, Democrat Frank Church, chairman of the Senate Foreign Relations Committee, but also gave to his challenger, Republican Congressman Steven D. Symms.

One reason for the dual support was the expected vote in the Senate the next year on the AWACS sale to Saudi Arabia—during the campaign both Symms and Church were listed as opposing it. With the race expected to be close, the lobby believed it had a friend in each candidate and helped both.

Symms defeated Church by a razor-thin margin; but the investment in Symms by pro-Israel interests did not pay off. By the time the new Senator faced the AWACS vote he had changed his mind. His vote approving the AWACS sale helped to give AIPAC one of its rare legislative setbacks. . . .

Because favored candidates need more money than PAC sources provide, AIPAC also helps by providing lists for direct mail fundraising. The appeal can be hard-hitting. An example is the literature mailed in early 1984 on behalf of Republican Senator Rudy Boschwitz of Minnesota. Fellow Republican Lowell Weicker wrote the introductory letter, citing him as a "friend of Israel in danger." He noted Boschwitz's key position as a chairman of the subcommittee "that determines the level of aid our country gives to Israel," and praised his efforts to block military sales to Saudi Arabia. The appeal included tributes by Senator Bob Packwood and Wolf Blitzer, Washington correspondent for *The Jerusalem Post.*

AIPAC has convinced Congress that it represents practically all Jews who vote. Columnist Nat Hentoff reported this assessment in the New York *Village Voice* in June 1983 after a delegation of eighteen dissenting rabbis had scoured Capitol Hill trying to convince Congressmen that some Jews oppose Israeli policies. The rabbis reported that several Congressmen said they shared their views but were afraid to act. Hentoff concluded: "The only Jewish constituency that's real to them [Congressmen] is the one that AIPAC and other spokesmen for the Jewish establishment tell them about."

An Ohio Congressman speaks of AIPAC with both awe and concern:

> AIPAC is the most influential lobby on Capitol Hill. They are relentless. They know what they're doing. They have the people for financial resources. They've got a lot going for them. Their basic underlying cause is one that most Americans sympathize with.

> But what distresses me is the inability of American policy-makers, because of the influence of AIPAC, to distinguish between our national interest and Israel's national interest. When these converge—wonderful! But they don't always converge.

After the 1982 elections, Thomas A. Dine summed up the significance of AIPAC's achievements: "Because of that, American Jews are thus able to form our own foreign policy agenda."

Later, when he reviewed the 1984 election results, Dine credited Jewish money, not votes: "Early money, middle money, late money." He claimed credit for defeating Republican Senators Charles Percy of Illinois and Roger Jepson of Iowa and Democratic Senator Walter Huddleston of Kentucky, all of whom incurred AIPAC wrath by voting for the sale of AWACS planes to Saudi Arabia.

Dine said these successes "defined Jewish political power for the rest of this century."

The AWACS Battle

Edwin Tivnan

As you read this case study, consider the following questions:

1. Prior to the Reagan administration's formal announcement of the AWACs sale, how did AIPAC and its friends in Congress work to discourage the administration from going through with the sale?

2. How did Thomas A. Dine use the potential damage the AWACS sale would inflict on President Reagan's popularity as an argument against the sale of these planes to Saudi Arabia?

3. How did the proponents of the AWACS sale enlist the support of other groups that would benefit from it to counterattack AIPAC's opposition?

4. How did President Reagan use his professional reputation, his public popularity, and the powers of the presidency to counteract AIPAC's intense congressional lobbying?

B Y THE TIME RONALD REAGAN WAS ELECTED PRESIDENT IN 1980, JEWS HAD BEEN LOBBYING IN THE U.S. ON BEHALF OF THE ZIONIST STATE FOR THIRTY-five years. Both the Presidents' Conference and AIPAC had been operating as full-fledged pro-Israel pressure groups since 1954, though mainly in obscurity. Most Americans still knew very little about the "Jewish lobby," and Jewish leaders preferred to keep it that way, ever concerned about charges of "dual loyalty" and spurts of anti-Semitism. . . . AIPAC, however, was famous on Capitol Hill, or notorious, depending on one's opinions about the Middle East, or about Morris Amitay, the lobby's swashbuckling director.

Amitay's eye-for-an-eye tactics . . . not only offended many politicians who considered themselves long-time friends of Israel, but also concerned other Washington operatives of national Jewish organizations who saw their own good relationships with politicians and their staffs being poisoned by Amitay's overenthusiasm. . . .

Amitay insists he had never intended to stay on as long as he did and had already informed the AIPAC board [in 1978] of his plans to leave. "I felt I had succeeded in changing AIPAC and after years of government service and lobbying, it was time for me to go out and make some money for my family," he says. Split over Amitay's leadership, "confrontational" style, and autocratic tendencies, the AIPAC board accepted his resignation and looked for a new leader.

Their choice, was, eventually, Thomas A. Dine, a Senate aide with a master's degree in Southeast Asian history and no experience in Jewish organizations. When Dine took over as director of Washington's fabled pro-Israel lobby in October 1980, many of his old colleagues on the Hill were stunned. "I didn't even know Tom was Jewish," recalled one legislative aide who had known Dine for almost a decade. . . .

. . . [Tom Dine] took over as director of AIPAC in October 1980, and two months later, during the December transition period between Carter's departure and Ronald Reagan's entry into the White House, AIPAC got the word that there would be another attempt to sell arms to the Saudis. The package would be additional gear for the F-15 fighter planes the Carter Administration had sold in 1978 plus five airborne warning and command systems (AWACS), the state of the art in aerial electronic surveillance. Arms sales can be blocked only if a majority of both houses of Congress disapproves. . . .

The first hint of the Saudi sale had come in June 1980 when the Carter Administration announced that it was seriously considering a Saudi request for missiles, bomb racks, and fuel pods that would give the F-15s the Saudis had already ordered more lift and longer range. The Saudis were also interested in buying KC-135 tankers, which could refuel the F-15s in midair, and "airborne warning and command systems" aircraft, also known as AWACS, for directing the F-15s in combat. During the F-15 sale, the President had promised that the planes would not be equipped in such a way as to be a threat to Israel, but the new gear would more than double the fighter planes' range to a thousand miles. . . .

And then Ronald Reagan was elected President. Jimmy Carter may have returned to Plains, Georgia, his political career a memory, but the AWACS package remained alive and well in Washington. "We heard about it during the transition period," Tom Dine recalled. "Brzezinski and Brown finagled it after the election. It's a perfect time, and once you get it going, it's hard to stop something like that."

The outgoing Carterites convinced the incoming Reaganites that it was important—to U.S. interests in the Middle East and to the Presidency—to keep their promise to the Saudis; Carter was willing to take the heat. The details of the package were delegated to a State and Defense interdepartmental committee headed by the Pentagon's undersecretary for policy, Fred Iklè. The Reagan Administration was quickly divided on the issue: Secretary of Defense Caspar Weinberger favored the sale, and thought he could get it through Congress; Secretary of State Alexander Haig, whose own presidential ambitions were no secret, was worried about the domestic political consequences of arming the Saudis.

Haig's political instincts were right, and his intelligence probably better. AIPAC had begun building opposition to the Saudi sale on Capitol Hill in December, and refined its strategy in January for what looked like a long fight. . . .

. . . And if anyone doubted the issue was heating up, the same week, Tom Dine's old boss, Senator Edward Kennedy publicly warned that the additional equipment would disrupt the balance of power in the Middle East as well as violate Carter's pledge not to allow the F-15s to become an offensive threat to Israel. . . . The next day most of the members of the Senate Foreign Relations Committee signed a letter to Reagan also contending that the F-15 gear violated the Carter promise. AIPAC was on the job.

Dine had already paid a visit to the Administration's new counsel, Edwin Meese. . . . Candidly (and arrogantly from the White House's point of view), Dine informed Meese that the American Jewish community was prepared to "fight all the way." The man from AIPAC explained a "scenario" of intense opposition from American Jews and their "friends" in Congress. The results, Dine noted, "would not be in the best interests of anybody." Dine emphasized to Meese the firm belief of the Jewish community and other Middle East observers that the Saudi regime was hardly the most stable in the region; he also reminded the White House aide of the Phoenix missile systems and F-15s that had been sold to America's friend the Shah of Iran, only to end up in the hands of America's sworn enemy the Ayatollah Khomeini. . . .

The Administration did not flinch. Reagan was still riding the top of his November mandate, and, like every new President, relishing his power. The President also, it seemed, was not giving the AWACS matter his top priority. The details of the deal were being worked on in the Pentagon and State Department interdepartmental committee. And before long it looked as though Secretary Weinberger, a fan of the sale, would be more persuasive than Haig, who was not crazy about it. By the middle of the spring, the President made it known that he was committed to the sale. Reagan's national security adviser, Richard Allen, had taken over directing the fight on Capitol Hill. While Allen may have been a close friend of the President's, he was not making friends in the Senate. "Allen seemed to have a talent for pissing people off over on the Hill," reported one observer who was rooting for the AWACS deal. . . .

In early February, Dine had done a vote count in the Senate, and the numbers looked good. . . . AIPAC knew it owned the House, if only on partisan grounds, with the Democratic majority eager to keep a Republican President in line. In the Senate, California's Alan Cranston, a loyal Israel supporter with presidential ambitions, and Oregon's Robert Packwood were collecting the names of opponents of the sale. Packwood, chairman of the Senate's Commerce, Science, and Transportation Committee, also held the influential post of chairman of the Republican Senate Campaign Committee. He had been laboring heroically to lure to the GOP the kind of generous support that wealthy Jews had bestowed traditionally on the Democrats, and with some success. Packwood now recognized that if the AWACS deal passed the Senate, checkbooks might very well close shut.

Meantime, AIPAC made sure that Jews were well informed about what was happening in Washington. Phone calls to Jewish "community relations councils" around the country alerted local leaders to AIPAC's needs. Letters, calls, and telegrams to members of Congress followed. Information on the capacities of F-15s with and without the proposed enhancements, the risks of AWACS to Israeli security, the instability of the Saudi regime contrasted to the stability of Israel—"the only Democracy in the Middle East"—poured into the offices of members of Congress.

Fred Dutton, the Saudi lobbyist, was no happier about how the Administration was handling things than Tom Dine, for different reasons. He watched in horror as Iklè's interdepartmental committee and then Richard Allen antagonized the very people on Capitol Hill whom the Saudis would need in order to win. . . .

Dutton was in favor of matching AIPAC's efforts with a major Saudi offensive of his own, though he recognized that by March, as the Reagan Administration was preparing to go public with a formal announcement of the Saudi sale, AIPAC had been rounding up opposition for almost five months. His main opposition came from his clients. The Saudis were reluctant to push for a confrontation. After all, two American Presidents had made promises. What else did a small nation sitting on billions of dollars of oil need? In the desert monarchy of Saudi Arabia, the head man delivered. But, as Fred Dutton has said often, "The Saudis do not really understand the limitations of the U.S. Presidency." . . .

On March 6, the White House announced that the U.S. would sell to the Saudis air-to-air missiles and fuel tanks for the F-15s. The Administration, however, rejected the Saudi request for bomb racks that would have made the fighter planes more effective against targets on the ground. To diffuse Israeli opposition, Reagan offered Israel an additional $600 million in military credits over the next two years. The White House also hinted the U.S. would relax restrictions on Israel's efforts to sell its new Kfir fighter plane abroad. (The Kfir had a U.S. engine, and the Israelis needed U.S. approval to export any planes.) . . .

On March 18, Secretary of State Haig testified before the House Foreign Affairs Committee on a wide range of foreign-policy issues, particularly the increased vulnerability of the U.S. and its allies to international terrorism and the Soviet tilt to "an imperial foreign policy," a trend that Haig described as "most alarming." Discussing the Middle East, Haig told the House committee that it was "fundamentally important to begin to develop a consensus of strategic concerns throughout the region among Arab and Jew and to be sure that the overriding danger of Soviet inroads is not overlooked." The next day, before the Senate Foreign Relations Committee, Haig stressed again the need for "a strategic consensus" in the Middle East. The secretary of state proposed that the U.S. route to peace was strengthening regional states like Israel, Egypt, Saudi Arabia, Jordan, Turkey, and Pakistan through military, economic, and political cooperation and assistance. . . .

The President's personal attention to the difficult matter of getting the Saudi sale through Congress was diverted by an event out of Ronald Reagan's control. On March 30, 1981, Reagan was shot in the chest by a young assassin named John W. Hinckley, Jr. The President apparently issued the go-ahead for adding the five AWACS planes to the Saudi package from his bed in George Washington University Hospital. "His aides gave it to him to sign, and he did," claims Dine. . . .

In the first week of April . . . after reports of the AWACS add-on had surfaced in the newspapers, Tom Dine paid a visit to Howard Baker, who was preparing to visit the Middle East during the upcoming Easter recess. Dine reiterated essentially what he had told Meese a few months before, though the evidence was by then much more obvious. The AIPAC director beseeched the majority leader to consider the consequences of a battle over the AWACS sale in Congress, and assured him that "we are going all out." The Administration would have to respond in kind to the opposition on Capitol Hill. "They may win," Dine conceded to the majority leader. "But in the end they would lose." The lobbyist warned that the press would wallow in the controversy and "dissect the Administration and find it in disarray—because almost by definition every new Administration is in disarray." Reagan, whose popularity was now at an all-time high due to his courageous (and good-humored) recovery from Hinckley's bullet, certainly did not need that kind of bad publicity—especially amid concern over how fit the seventy-year-old President would be when he returned to work.

Baker listened, commiserated—he was not looking forward to the inevitable fight either—and pointed out to Dine that it was his job as majority leader to push the President's legislation through the Senate. Dine asked that the Administration postpone its final decision to bring the issue to a vote, "so that they at least be able to understand fully what they were doing." One of Dine's main arguments was that before the White House started changing U.S. policy in the Middle East, the President ought to have a Middle East policy.

Dine left the Baker meeting without anything more satisfying than the possibility of more time to build his case in the Senate. AIPAC had already decided not to bother lobbying the House very strenuously; Dine did not want the Saudi sale to be seen as a partisan issue. It was in AIPAC's interest—in the short term and long term—that arming the

Saudis be seen as a threat to Israel. Even if AIPAC lost—and Tom Dine knew that no President had ever lost an arms-sale vote—he recognize the propaganda potential of a heavily armed Saudi Arabia.

On April 18, the State Department disclosed that the Administration had tried to persuade the Saudis to settle for the F-15 gear and postpone the AWACS purchase. The Saudis rejected any compromise intended to help ease Israel's fears. The Administration formally announced its decision to go ahead with the Saudi deal on April 21.

Baker returned to Washington after Easter and advised Secretary Haig to postpone submitting the arms package to Congress for a vote until after the Israeli elections scheduled for June 30. Should the President try to submit the package to Congress for a vote before then, he would lose, in Baker's opinion. . . . Baker . . . knew that polls in Israel showed Begin's Labor opposition leading, and he was hoping that a new prime minister might be more reasonable about the new American President's desire to establish closer ties with the Saudis. Perhaps the prime minister would even be so kind as to help cool the enthusiasm of Israel's friends on Capitol Hill for giving the President a beating when the deal came to a vote. . . .

Baker, like Tom Dine, was trying to buy some time. He believed that the Saudi deal was necessary and in the best interests of the U.S. in the Middle East, but he was just not sure whether he'd be able to peel off enough senators who had already signed on with Packwood and Cranston (and thus AIPAC) to carry the vote.

Neither the White House nor the State Department had made Baker's job any easier. . . . Internal bickering within the Administration over the direction of policy between Haig, U.N. Representative Jeane Kirkpatrick, and Reagan confidant (and foreign-policy novice) Judge William Clark, along with differences of opinion between Haig and Weinberger, diverted attention from the importance of the AWACS fight. The Administration, of course, had other priorities, particularly on the domestic front where Reagan was eager to push through economic measures to cut the budget and bring down inflation. Nevertheless, the Saudi arms package was the President's first foreign-policy initiative, and, at the moment, it looked as if he was heading for a major embarrassment. . . .

So when the job fell to good Indian Howard Baker, he told his own staff, ''I don't take something on to lose, but, boy, we've got big trouble here.'' He also informed the White House that he required a total commitment to winning. James Baker, Reagan's chief political adviser and legislative liaison, took over the day-to-day coordination of the AWACS fight, working closely with Howard Baker and the Saudis. The signal went out to members of Congress that the President himself was lobbying this one, and he wouldn't take kindly to losing. . . .

On August 24, the Reagan Administration formally notified Congress of its decision to sell $8.5 billion worth of arms to the Saudis—five AWACS, ground stations to support them, and for the F-15s, 1,177 Sidewinder air-to-air missiles, fuel tanks, and six KC-707 tanker planes.

There was no immediate reaction to the announcement from Begin, who had beaten his Labor opponent, Shimon Peres, again in a close election. But Begin had other matters to attend to. The day of the AWACS announcement in Washington, Begin was beginning a two-day summit meeting with Egyptian President Anwar Sadat, during which they decided to resume talks in September about Palestinian self-rule. . . .

Israel, however, could afford to remain silent about the AWACS announcement. AIPAC and the lobby's supporters in Congress were on the case. The head count looked good. On September 17, Senator Packwood produced the names of half the Senate—fifty senators—as cosponsors of a resolution opposing the sale. The Administration, finally, recognized what was at stake; the gloves came off as the two Bakers set out to counterpunch that total down to a winning number for their side. Dutton stayed away from the Hill—he had not even registered for the right to lobby Congress—and spent his time keeping the Bakers informed on Saudi negotiations and which senators were on the fence or leaning toward the President. Dutton preferred to leave the arm twisting to James Baker and his aides. The Saudis, led by Prince Bandar, a politically savvy young fighter pilot and son of the Saudi defense minister, mounted a widespread campaign to persuade American corporations that the sale was not only in U.S. interests but in their economic interests too.

The presidents of Boeing and United Technologies generated thousands of letters and telegrams supporting the sale from scores of corporations and executives around the country to members of Congress. Mobil Oil, according to one report, spent "more than a half million dollars on a media blitz," running a series of full-page ads in at least twenty-six newspapers. . . . American corporations may have thrown themselves into lobbying for the sale, but they certainly needed little prodding from the Saudis. Boeing, the main contractor for the AWACS planes, had billions at stake; United Technologies reportedly had about $100 million riding on the success of the sale. And, as one of the Mobil newspaper ads pointed out, "Saudi Arabia is far more than oil—it means trade for America, jobs for Americans, and strength for the dollar." . . .

Supporters of the sale began poking holes in AIPAC's headcount. "We did our own poll, contacting people who had allegedly committed [to opposing the sale] and discovered a large number who said they had not committed or were waiting though they were sympathetic to American Jewish opposition," recalled Ron Cathell, spokesman for the National Association of Arab Americans. "We were quite surprised because we really believed the AIPAC numbers, until we found weak spots or overexaggeration or misrepresentations." . . .

By mid-September, things had begun to take a turn for the better for the Administration. . . .

There was some anti-AIPAC sentiment too. AIPAC had been lobbying against the sale for ten months. Dine had kept his promises to Ed Meese and Howard Baker. But now some prominent Jews expressed concern that AIPAC might have done its job too well. As one put it: "We've done enough. If we lose, we lose; if we win, we really lose." Dine argued that they were falling into the "Reagan or Begin?" trap, while he . . . contended the AWACS fight was a classic struggle between Congress and the executive branch over the direction of foreign policy. Still, few Jewish leaders shared Dine's passion for political science; they were eager to protect Israel and the American Jewish community, and AIPAC's success on the Hill, in their opinion, was provoking a backlash. . . .

Dine had enough pressure on him on Capitol Hill. Meese and National Security Adviser Allen had appealed to all Republican senators to support the President. Haig claimed the list of opponents was "replete with soft spots." He could tick off a dozen senators who were "ready to reconsider," he said.

On September 22, the Administration staged a separate press briefing to clarify "misunderstandings" about the alleged threat of the AWACS to Israeli security. National Security Adviser Richard Allen informed reporters that the planes were incapable of collecting photographic intelligence or pinpointing ground targets. Nor would the Saudis be up to coordinating an all-out multination Arab air attack on Israel because they would lack the sophisticated battle command equipment carried by the AWACS used by the U.S. and NATO forces. According to Allen, these AWACS would not even carry electronic countermeasure devices; the Israelis could jam their radar. The Saudis had already agreed not to fly the AWACS over Syria or Jordan. . . .

To those involved in the AWACS battle, and many watching on the sidelines, it seemed as if the business of government in Washington had stalled while the White House and Congress focused only on the sale of five airplanes to Saudi Arabia. And, in a sense, they were right. As one Senate aide later put it: "If the deal did not go through—if there was not enough support for Ronald Reagan's first foreign-policy initiative— there was no doubt that the Administration would have not been able to regain any standing in the foreign-policy community for the remainder of the term." AWACS was worth some undivided attention.

On October 1, Ronald Reagan laid his reputation on the line. His Administration finally submitted its formal notice, in writing, to Congress of its proposed sale of arms to Saudi Arabia. Congress had thirty days to veto the proposal. Having racked up some success on the diplomatic front with concessions from the Saudis, the White House was now prepared to devote the month to winning a majority of the Senate.

The President had already called for reinforcements. A few weeks before, one Republican senator attending a dinner was summoned from the table by "a call from the White House." Ex-President Ford was on the line, and on behalf of the current President, he bluntly asked, "Are we going to let the Jewish lobby run American foreign policy?" Obviously shaken by the call, the senator returned to his table—at a dinner for Jewish leaders. . . . Yet Ford was simply (and carelessly) reflecting the anxiety at the White House. In a televised announcement of the sale, the President himself sent out the same message to Israel, though in less inflammatory words. In a sure shot at Israeli opposition and American Jewish lobbying efforts, Reagan bluntly declared: "It is not the business of other nations to make American foreign policy." Reagan said he was determined to defend Saudi oil fields against "anyone" who threatened them. Three days later, former President Nixon attacked the "intense opposition [of] the Begin government and parts of the American Jewish community" for interfering with the White House's aims to benefit the nation. A defeat of the AWACS sale, he argued, would be "a Pyrrhic victory" that would cause "serious embarrassment to Reagan, at home and abroad." A week later, Jimmy Carter called for support of his former opponent, warning of "the danger of a third worldwide oil shock."

On October 14, the House, as expected, voted overwhelmingly against the sale—301 to 111. The next day the Senate Foreign Relations Committee endorsed a resolution disapproving the Saudi deal by nine to eight. Senator Rudy Boschwitz, a Republican from Minnesota and a staunch friend of Israel, joined the eight Democrats on the committee. Two other Republicans whose positions had been up in the air—Maryland's Charles Mathias, Jr., and S. I. Hayakawa of California—supported the President. A third Republican, South Dakota's Larry Pressler, who had signed the September 17 resolution opposing the sale, switched after a phone call from the President that came in the middle of the debate preceding the vote. Howard Baker announced that ''the momentum'' was now with the President. Baker also reported that the full Senate would not vote on the measure until later in the month. Reagan was scheduled to attend an international conference of developing nations the next week, and the Senate felt it inappropriate to vote while he was out of town. The postponement would also be ''convenient to members of the Senate.'' Indeed, Baker could use the time.

Throughout September and October, Baker had coordinated an intense lobbying effort on behalf of the AWACS deal. Baker himself collared senators he thought he might be able to persuade; James Baker canvassed the Senate Office Building, trying to win over others. In several cases, Howard Baker invited a senator to his office, where he *and* James Baker would lean on him. They also decided which senators required a visit with the President, and Howard Baker would, as one observer put it, ''march him down to the White House.'' A Baker aide recalled that ''at one time or another, probably half to two-thirds of the Senate went to the White House to discuss the AWACS proposal, either in small groups of two or three or individually.'' . . .

''They used all the tools available to them to run this thing through,'' recalls an aide to Howard Baker. Senator Dennis DeConcini, an Arizona Democrat, charged that someone ''close'' to the President had promised him Reagan would not campaign against him in 1982 if he voted for the sale. (DeConcini eventually voted against it.) Iowa's Charles Grassley claimed he had been promised his choice for a U.S. attorney for Iowa would be ''expedited'' if he voted ''right.'' (And ''right'' Grassley eventually did vote.) Senator John Glenn attacked such tactics as ''political bribery'' and ''abhorrent.'' (He eventually sided with AIPAC.)

The vote now seemed up for grabs. AIPAC was trying to hold its lead, and in the final weeks sent a copy of the novel *Holocaust* to each member of the Senate. (One AIPAC staffer flying out of Washington noticed a fellow passenger, a Republican senator, reading the book intently.) The lobby was not above some horse trading of its own. Unlike the President, AIPAC really did not have to stress what would happen if a senator voted for the sale. Some were still suffering the ire of Jewish constituents for voting for sale of the F-15s to the Saudis in 1978. As

Packwood and others who preferred to run with some Jewish contributions in their campaign chests well knew, AIPAC could shut off the tap as easily as it turned it on. . . .

For eleven months the AWACS debate had belonged to AIPAC. October was the President's month. "In my 19 years up here, I have never seen such 180-degree turns on the part of so many senators," Senator Edward Kennedy told a reporter the day of the vote. All along the way, the White House had been looking for a key Democrat to go along with them. After trying unsuccessfully with several senators, they finally found their man in Oklahoma's David Boren, a former governor who confided in Dine that he believed a chief executive had to keep the promises of his predecessor.

But the coup de grâce was winning over Iowa Republican Roger Jepsen forty-eight hours before the vote. Jepsen, a first-term senator who would not be up for re-election until 1984, had always been a vigorous supporter of Israel in the Senate. He was one of the first senators to oppose the AWACS sale publicly. . . . The day before the vote, Jepsen announced, in tears, that he had decided to vote for the sale.

What had happened? "We just beat his brains out," a White House aide explained in a two-page article on the AWACS battle and Jepsen in the Des Moines *Register.* "We stood him up in front of an open grave and told him he could jump in if he wanted to." The same day eight "uncommitteds"—four from each party—endorsed the sale.

Baker went into the vote hopeful but cautious. For the first time as majority leader, he kept a written tab of the roll call, making sure the vote was going according to plan. One Baker aide involved in the AWACS fight on a day-to-day basis recalled years later, "We were at the finish line ahead, but we still didn't know if we'd cross it a winner. It was a tough fight, believe me." Just before the vote began, Tom Dine was standing outside the Senate Chamber in a group that included Virginia senator John Warner, who had been active in rounding up votes for the President. Dine was overheard asking Warner, as he headed into the chamber, "John, isn't there anything I can tell you that will change your mind?" Warner replied: "Tom, you've done an excellent job. You really did your homework. But today is not your day."

The Senate approved the AWACS sale 52 to 48. . . .

6

The Media

Reality, like beauty, is in the eye of the beholder. For most Americans, the media are the conveyors of political reality. Political reality is "the fundamental ideas people have about what the world of politics is really like" (Ranney 1983, 6). Since most of us experience little, if any, government or politics firsthand, we depend upon television, radio, newspapers, and magazines to inform us about them. Media, therefore, control what we know, think, and discuss about government and politics. They shape for us a particular view of political reality; one that would be difficult for us to challenge or refute, if we were so inclined (Patterson and McClure 1976, 74–75).

The public image of Vice-President Dan Quayle is a good example of media-fostered political reality. Since his selection by George Bush to be the 1988 Republican candidate for vice-president, Quayle's public image and reputation have been of someone who is intellectually shallow and immature. This negative image has been fostered and encouraged by the media (and assisted by the vice-president's own public gaffes). Quayle's public image has made many of the American people uncomfortable with the vice-president and fearful about the possibility of his becoming president.

Media influence over the public's uneasiness about Vice-President Quayle's fitness to succeed to the presidency was clearly apparent in May 1991 when President Bush was hospitalized for an erratic heartbeat. An article in the *Washington Post* entitled "The No. 2 Man Is Still Seen as a Poor Second" noted that "[p]resident Bush's erratically beating heart sent political shudders through the body politic as Americans confronted the possibility that ace golfer and malapropist *nonpareil* Dan Quayle could become president" (Morin 1991, 37). The article concluded that in light of heightened concern over Bush's health, the "Quayle factor" was likely to be a more serious issue in the 1992 election than it was in 1988.

The way in which the media have reported on and portrayed Dan Quayle raises questions about how they portray political reality to the American public and their overall ability to convey this reality accurately. Many reporters, journalists, editors, and television news producers would have us believe that the media are mirrors reflecting what is really going on in the world around us (Ranney 1983, 18) and that the view of political reality presented to us is an accurate one based upon the media's objective reporting of the facts (Patterson 1990, 345). Much of the political reality presented by the media is objective—or at least as objective as people are capable of being. It is less likely, though, that the media genuinely reflect all that goes on around us. Rather, the media present selected slices of political reality (Ranney 1983, 19).

One important reason why the media cannot present a complete and accurate portrayal of political reality is that political news competes with human interest stories, advertisements, editorials, commercials, and entertainment programming. Political news generally loses this contest. The average daily newspaper is 68 percent advertisements and only 38 percent news and other stories. The typical thirty-minute television news program contains only about twenty-two minutes of news, much of which consists of human interest stories, sports, and weather (Gitelson et al. 1991, 238).

The limited space allotted for news means that media must make choices about what slices of political reality to present to their readers, listeners, and viewers. They must have some criteria for measuring what is newsworthy. Media are first and foremost businesses. Therefore, the decision criteria used to make choices about what news items to present are likely to be largely unrelated to the political significance of the news stories selected. Rather, the choice of what political news to include in daily papers, weekly news magazines, or nightly network or local television news programs is likely to be driven largely by the economics of audience appeal (Graber 1980, 63).

In her book *Mass Media and American Politics,* Doris Graber (1980, 63–65) describes five main criteria of newsworthiness on which the media regularly rely, all of which, to some extent, emphasize whether the news item is likely to titillate the readers, viewers, or listeners. First, political news stories must have a high impact on the audience, in that the people exposed to the story must find it relevant to their own lives. In this regard, stories about public anxieties over a possible Quayle presidency are more newsworthy than stories about the assassination of a distant world leader. Second, political news stories filled with violence, conflict, scandal, or disaster are newsworthy because of their ability to excite audiences. Based upon this criterion, the media found the alleged marital infidelity and draft evasion of presidential wannabe Governor Bill Clinton of Arkansas to be politically newsworthy in 1992.

A third criterion of newsworthiness is whether the political news involves situations that many persons are concerned about and familiar with or situations that involve well-known political persons.

Fourth, political news must also be current or unusual. For example, shortly after the near meltdown in 1979 at the Three Mile Island nuclear power plant, every major print and electronic news agency had reporters on the scene (Patterson 1990, 355).

Finally, a criterion important for local rather than national media is that political news must be "close to home." It must have an impact on local people and communities or at least appear to do so. News coverage of Operations Desert Shield and Desert Storm illustrated how national and international political news can be made more newsworthy by local media if it is given a local spin. Throughout the Persian Gulf conflict, local television and radio news programs and local newspapers easily found the local angle. They flooded their viewers, listeners, and readers with "local" Desert Shield and Desert Storm stories. Stories about local reservists preparing to go to war, the impact of the military call-up on their families and employers, and community support for the war could be found in every local media outlet. Even the local television stations' meteorologists were not immune, as their weather reports began to include information and forecasts on weather conditions in Saudi Arabia.

A sixth criterion can be added to the above list. To be newsworthy, political news must concern events that can be covered by the media at a cost that editors, news directors, and reporters consider reasonable. Limited staffs and budgets and media owners' concerns for profit mean that reporters do not have the resources to engage in extensive investigative reporting or travel. Also, news gathering involves personal costs above and beyond the hard dollar cost of reporting a story— personal costs such as the disruption of a reporter's day-to-day life and established routines (Press and VerBurg 1988, 71).

Because of these economic and personal costs, members of the media generally prefer "easy-to-gather" political news that does not disrupt established routines or require much extra effort (Press and VerBurg 1988, 77). In their pursuit of this kind of political news, reporters and journalists rely almost exclusively on interviewing and rarely, if ever, on substantive research into the stories they are covering (Gitelson et al. 1991, 239). This preference for interviewing means that to collect easy-to-gather news, most members of the media rely heavily on official sources such as White House and congressional staff (Press and VerBurg 1988, 77). For example, the president's press secretary is usually the only on-the-record source for most reporters assigned to cover the White House (Patterson 1988, 167). The media also depend heavily on the unofficial Washington sources, "whistleblowers" and "leaks."

The media's preference for easy-to-gather news encourages persons both in and out of government who seek media coverage to create easy-to-report-on events that bring attention to stories that would not otherwise be newsworthy. Events such as the president's touring the site of a recent natural disaster, public protests outside of the Supreme Court building opposing a Court decision, or almost any campaign rally or related activity fall into this category. These pseudo–news events, or "medialities," are particularly important for television news, since they provide good video opportunities. Most television news programs generally welcome these staged news items. They are easy to report and allow a studio to avoid using more costly news-gathering methods that would be needed if these "medialities" were not available (Ranney 1983, 23).

All six of the decision criteria for newsworthiness affect the media's conveying of political reality. But the preference for easy-to-gather news is particularly interesting because it underscores the close and mutually beneficial relationship between those who report political news and those who make it. It denotes an uneasy but necessary alliance between government and the media and captures an important political reality: Media, particularly reporters and journalists, need politicians, and politicians, in turn, need the media.

In their book *American Politicians and Journalists,* Charles Press and Kenneth VerBurg (1988, 15–18) argue that reporters use politicians to advance their own journalistic careers. Being on good terms with established politicians increases the likelihood that reporters will have access to good stories, which can enhance their professional reputations. Politicians, likewise, use the media to advance their own ambitions, favorite policies, or other pet projects and to create a favorable public image of themselves among their constituencies. They endeavor to create such an image by trying to manage political news, control the story content and interpretation of such news, make the information provided to the media seem special, and engage in damage control, or "spin control," on fast-breaking news stories (Press and VerBurg 1988, 105–138).

The two case studies presented in this chapter underscore many of the above observations. "Was the Press Any Match for All the President's Men?" by Scott Armstrong, former *Washington Post* reporter and founder of the National Security Archive, presents an analysis of the media's coverage of the Iran-contra affair. In telling this story, Armstrong examines just how well the press performs its self-appointed role of watchdog for the American public. Taking a somewhat atypical stance on the power and influence of the media, Armstrong argues that the press is less prepared to perform the watchdog role than it is usually presumed to be. He notes that being a watchdog should entail knowledge and pursuit of constitutional questions. But he concludes that the media lack a basic competency in constitutional areas. Lacking this competency, the media regularly take the position that political stories invoking basic constitutional questions are too complex and difficult to present to the American people. Rather, the media usually cede the investigation of constitutional issues to other major institutions (Armstrong 1990, 35).

The second case study, "Making Laws and Making News" by Timothy Cook, illustrates how politicians need the media and how in the process of acquiring media attention they create easy-to-gather news. In particular, "Making Laws and Making News" details the media strategy used in 1985 by Congressman Don J. Pease to try to win renewal of the Federal Supplemental Compensation (FSC) program in Congress. The program provided eight to fourteen additional weeks of unemployment compensation to workers who had exhausted their basic twenty-six weeks of state unemployment compensation.

Suggested Reading

Broder, Davis S. 1987. *Behind the Front Page: A Candid Look at How the News Is Made*. New York: Simon and Schuster. An assessment of the Washington press corps by one of the nation's leading political reporters.

Grossman, Michael Baruch, and Martha Joynt Kumar. 1981. *Portraying the President.* Baltimore: Johns Hopkins University Press. An examination of the relationship between the president's White House staff and the Washington press corps.

Halberstam, David. 1979. *The Powers That Be.* New York: Alfred A. Knopf. The story of how the *New York Times,* the *Washington Post,* the *Los Angeles Times,* and the CBS television network became rich and powerful and changed forever the shape of American politics and political reporting.

Hess, Stephen. 1984. *The Government/Press Connection.* Washington, DC: Brookings Institution. An examination of the personnel and operations of government press offices.

Lamb, Brian, and the staff of C-SPAN. 1988. *C-SPAN: America's Town Hall.* Washington, DC: Acropolis Books. One hundred and four true stories of people whose lives have been changed through the news and information they received through the Cable-Satellite Public Affairs Network (C-SPAN), a nonprofit news and information network funded by the cable television industry.

Patterson, Thomas E., and Robert D. McClure. 1976. *The Unseeing Eye.* New York: Putnam. An interesting and insightful analysis of television's coverage of presidential campaigns.

Was the Press Any Match for All the President's Men?

Scott Armstrong

As you read this case study, consider the following questions:

1. In reviewing the various "chapters" of the Iran-contra affair, what conclusions does Armstrong draw about the media's overall coverage of the scandal?

2. In "chapter one" of the Iran-contra affair, how did "the best tradition of a free press" manifest itself?

3. Why does Armstrong say that during "chapter one" of the Iran-contra affair, while Oliver North and William Casey "were keeping track of the press, the press lost track of itself"?

4. In "chapter two" of the Iran-contra affair, how did the media exercise a "new-found discipline"?

5. In "chapter three" of the Iran-contra affair, what was the principal question that the media began to ask regarding President Reagan's participation in the scandal?

6. How did its coverage of the House and Senate Iran-contra hearings reveal the media at both their best and their worst?

7. In pursuing questions surrounding Vice-President Bush's involvement in and knowledge of the arms-for-hostages deal with Iran, what important "slipups" on the vice-president's part did CBS evening news anchor Dan Rather fail to pick up on?

From the *Columbia Journalism Review*, May/June, 1990. Reprinted by permission.

8. What was the general impact of the 1988 presidential campaign on the media's coverage of Vice-President Bush's knowledge of and participation in the arms-for-hostages deal with Iran?

9. How can the media's coverage of Oliver North's trial be characterized?

10. In the Iran-contra affair, why did the media largely fail in "holding the various branches of the government accountable [to] the Constitution?"

NOW THAT THE LATEST CHAPTER OF THE IRAN-CONTRA AFFAIR, THE TRIAL OF JOHN POINDEXTER, HAS DRAWN TO A CLOSE, SEVERAL QUESTIONS haunt me. I am left wondering if that's all there is—or will there be a final chapter, one that puts the pieces together? I sometimes wonder if, should new revelations emerge—about George Bush's role in covert and illegal support for the contras, for example—the press would even bother to cover the story. And if it did, would the story get the hit-or-miss attention given to chapter one—the covert operations while they were still covert?

Or would the press bring to the story the same tenacity it displayed early on in chapter two, which began with Attorney General Edwin Meese's stunning announcement of the diversion of Iran arms-sales profits to the contras and closed with the Tower commission's exoneration of the president—innocent by virtue of a staff coup?

Or would the coverage become as passive as it was throughout chapter three, months of congressional hearings

• which sidestepped the issue of a government that had gone off the books (covert operations masterminded by U.S. officials, funded by Saudi Arabia, and implemented by Israel);

• which bypassed fundamental constitutional questions—questions raised by evidence of the diversion of American taxpayer funds to foreign coffers as part of an elaborate scheme designed to garner congressionally forbidden support for the contras;

• and which sidetracked the entire affair into attempts to answer such secondary questions as, Did Ronald Reagan know and approve of the diversion of Iran arms-sales profits to the contras?

Or would the press lose its nerve at key moments, as it did in chapter four—the 1988 presidential campaign? (Is it not astonishing that after the campaign we seemed to know less about Bush's involvement than we knew a year before?)

Or, worst of all, would new revelations be viewed with the myopia that vitiated chapter five—the Oliver North trial and aftermath? Where was the press, for instance, when North's attorneys and the independent counsel agreed that the Reagan-Bush administration had engaged in a series of quid pro quos—economic and military aid to Central American countries in return for military assistance to the contras? At the time, sources close to the investigation said these acts (particularly the misuse of congressionally appropriated funds) were of such magnitude that they should be addressed through articles of impeachment.

As one of the major political scandals of the twentieth century melts into a formless puddle on the floor, I find I am not alone in posing these questions. The band of reporters who have followed the Iran-contra story from the beginning worry that many of their colleagues, not to mention the public, still don't understand what lay at the center of the scandal. Let's take one last look at what we learned about the Iran-contra affair and about the strengths and weaknesses of our collective journalistic performance.

Chapter One: 1981–1986
The Pieces of the Puzzle

The best traditions of a free press were frequently manifest during the five years of reporting between the start of U.S. aid to the contras and the administration's November 1986 acknowledgement of the Iran-contra affair. Journalists abroad—both American and foreign—kept close track of the contra story. Reporters from *Newsweek, The Washington Post, The Miami Herald,* and the *Los Angeles Times* traveled with the contras and observed them in their base camps. *The Washington Post* and *The New York Times* vied to report on the

presidential findings that authorized covert actions against the Sandinistas, competing to provide either the first revelation or the definitive
follow-up, often correcting the others' account. David Ignatius and
David Rogers of *The Wall Street Journal* provided excellent detail, with
several stories about the contras' covert activities and the support they
received from the CIA.

During this time it became increasingly clear that Congress had
let intelligence oversight become a double entendre. Upset that it had
been misled by CIA Director William Casey, Congress sought ways to
constrain his enthusiasm for covert actions, sometimes by leaking information about those actions. In a further attempt to assert itself, Congress in October 1984 passed the second in a series of what became
known as the Bolan amendments—meant to keep the CIA from running a proxy war in Nicaragua. But before Boland II was even enacted,
Casey and his colleagues took covert action off the books, beyond the
reach of Congress. The now-infamous "enterprise," run by Richard
Secord and Albert Hakim at the direction of Oliver North, was quietly
under way.

While major news outlets reported on the post-Boland II assistance
to the contras provided by the Honduran and El Salvadoran governments—the quids—and on the beefed-up American money, arms, and
military support which those governments received—the quos—the
possible link between the two was left unexplored.

By mid-1985, a few reporters were already on the trail of Oliver
North. Alfonso Chardy of *The Miami Herald* and Robert Parry and
Brian Barger of The Associated Press were in hot pursuit. On August 8,
1985, as Congress was lifting the total ban on aid to the contras, allowing humanitarian aid, *The New York Times* ran a piece by Joel Brinkley
and Shirley Christian which stated that an unidentified "military officer who is a member of the National Security Council" had been
providing military advice to the contras. Despite some confusion in
the article (North was a member of the NSC *staff,* not of the NSC itself),
it showed a clear grasp of North's involvement. Three days later, Joanne
Omang of *The Washington Post* for the first time identified North by
name as the NSC point of contact with the contras. The *Post* article
and a subsequent *New York Times* piece revealed that North's name
had been withheld from earlier stories at the request of the White
House, which had claimed that publishing the name would endanger
North's life.

While a few reporters joined Parry and Barger in tracking North
throughout Central America, exotic-sounding theories about an

elaborate private arms network seemed to scare away the very papers—
The New York Times, The Wall Street Journal, The Washington Post—
that had earlier exposed the complicated exploits of CIA renegade
Edwin Wilson, who had used some of the same personnel that would
turn up in the Iran-contra arms network. By and large, news organizations pulled back from reporting on that network, focusing instead
on Washington fund-raising for the contras and on contra propaganda
efforts in the United States and Europe.

As for the Iranian end of this story, the press showed an ability
to pick up pieces but less skill at putting them together. For example,
dozens of stories made it clear that the government of Israel was selling arms to Iran; several of them even included claims by Israeli officials
that the sales had been approved by the Reagan administration, which
continued to proclaim its opposition to such sales.

There were two notable exceptions to the press's failure to ferret
out the arms-for-hostages swap. On July 11, 1985, John Wallach, foreign
editor for the Hearst Newspapers, reported that the U.S. and Iran had
exchanged secret messages in "a mutual desire to improve relations."
In September of that year, Wallach revealed other details of the U.S.-
Iran relationship and, on November 3, 1986, wrote that the U.S. had
been involved in "secret negotiations with Iran" since July 1985.
Wallach's articles, published in various cities but not in New York or
Washington, went largely unnoticed.

Then there was the case of Jack Anderson's resourceful younger
partner, Dale Van Atta. By December 1985, Van Atta had assembled
facts for a story about how the U.S. had allowed Israel to ship American
arms to Iran in return for release of the American hostages. By February 24, 1986, the reporter had confirmed the details in an interview
with President Reagan. Withholding explicit references to the deal at
the president's request, Van Atta published glimpses of the arrangement beginning in April 1986. On June 29 he wrote that "secret negotiations over arms supply and release of American hostages have involved
members of the National Security Council and a former official of the
CIA." On August 11, the Anderson-Van Atta column took the story a
step further, stating, "the United States and its Western allies continue
to conduct secret talks and cut secret deals with Iran while . . . Khomeini's terrorist lackeys control the fate of three surviving American
hostages—and several Europeans."

Unfortunately, because Washington journalists take Anderson's
column with a grain of salt, and because they failed to link Van Atta's
stories with other reports—such as Wallach's—they found it easy to

dismiss his revelations. Moreover, most Washington reporters never saw a key element of Van Atta's work on Iran in 1985 and 1986, because *The Washington Post* consistently cut all but the first reference the column made to the death by torture of one hostage, the CIA's station chief in Lebanon, William Buckley. William Casey and others at the CIA had told the *Post*'s Bob Woodward—incorrectly—that Buckley might still be alive, and that stories about him could get him killed.

The sad lesson implicit in those five years of sporadically spectacular reporting is that the press corps does not read itself. There was no institutional memory. Breakthroughs by star reporters passed largely unnoticed by peers until months or years after they were first published or aired.

They were not unnoticed by the Reagan administration, however. Thanks to the inadvertent preservation of Oliver North's memos and electronic mail, on the so-called PROF system, the Iran-contra record is now replete with examples of the White House tracking which reporters were making what advances on the story, even reporters from the foreign press. Often the White House was able to keep Iran-contra revelations from resonating simply by denying and trying to discredit stories by such reporters as Wallach, Van Atta, the AP's Parry, and *The Miami Herald*'s Chardy.

As it happens, the Iran-contra affair took shape during the first decade in which electronic databases were generally available in newsrooms. A systematic search of the major electronic databases— Nexis and Dialogue—would have produced most major pieces of the story. If reporters had taken advantage of the electronic age to build on each other's work, more attention could have been focused not on *whether* arms had been sent to Iran, for example, but *why*; not on *if* the contras had been illegally resupplied after the Boland cutoff, but on *how* they were being resupplied and what that meant.

Thus, while North, Casey, and their colleagues were keeping track of the press, the press lost track of itself.

Chapter Two: November 1986–March 1987
Meese and Tower Tell 'All'

On October 5, 1986, a Sandinista surface-to-air missile crew brought down on Nicaraguan soil a plane involved in the contra resupply network, snaring numerous documents and Eugene Hasenfus, an American mercenary. Reporters began connecting their earlier reporting with the information that suddenly poured out of Central America. Privately funded public interest groups, such as the Coalition for a New Foreign and Military Policy, the International Center for Development Policy, the Washington Office on Latin America, the Christic Institute, and my own National Security Archive, provided the interpretive threads needed to link Hasenfus to the Reagan White House and its private support network. On a more practical level, they kept the story alive by supplying reporters with new details: phone numbers from the logbooks found in the downed plane and phone records from a safe house in San Salvador that, along with Hasenfus's confession, linked and relinked players in the private contra support system to the governments of Honduras and El Salvador, and, ultimately, to the White House.

Among those closely watching these developments was Manucher Ghorbanifar, a middleman in the 1985–1986 arms-for-hostages transactions, who insisted he still had not been fully paid for his part in the deal. Ghorbanifar, through intermediaries, warned Casey that if he wasn't paid he would reveal aspects of the deal in the courts. Subsequently, a leak to the Lebanese publication *al-Shiraa* resulted in a November 3, 1986, story about American officials visiting Iran to discuss trading arms for hostages.

The Hasenfus and *al-Shiraa* stories galvanized the press. Already aware that there was considerably more than had been admitted to the government's role in the resupply flights on which Hasenfus had been a crew member, reporters gave little credence to a series of White House denials of a scheme to swap arms for hostages. As the pressure built, President Reagan conceded U.S. involvement in the transfer of arms to Iran, but denied any arms-for-hostages deal. Congress summoned Casey and Poindexter to clarify the unreconciled details and the two men lied to the Senate and House intelligence committees. As their versions began to leak out, the press compared details of their testimony with what was independently verifiable. As Attorney General Meese would later testify, this was precisely what he had feared the most—the press hammering out the details against the anvil of congressional inquiries, the unraveling of two years of misstatements, including Reagan's, and, thus, possible impeachment of the president. To make matters worse, Secretary of State George Shultz was threatening to go to the Hill and tell more of the truth than his colleagues. Reagan put Meese in charge of damage control.

On November 25, in a dramatic nationally televised press conference, Meese gave the emerging scandal its name when he revealed that some of the proceeds from the sales of arms to Iran had been used to buy arms for the contras. He went on to lay out the principal cover story—namely, that the Israelis had sold the arms and diverted the funds, and that within the American government only Oliver North was involved with contra aid. The press swarmed over Meese's account, picking apart every inconsistency. Meanwhile, in what Reagan said was an effort to get at the truth of the affair, he appointed his own commission, headed by former senator John Tower.

During the three months in which Washington waited for the Tower commission to issue its report, it was open season on Oliver North. Despite the free-wheeling environment, however, the press collectively exercised a new-found discipline: stories in one paper corrected and built upon stories in another. The contours of North's activities in official and off-the-books covert operations began to emerge. Ghorbanifar, Secord, Secord's Iranian partner Albert Hakim, and Adnan Khashoggi, the Saudi arms dealer responsible for financing much of the arms-for-hostages deal with Iran, became household names. The methods by which North had been able to tap a private funding network of rich conservatives, as well as the propaganda network he had set up with State Department funds, were revealed. The involvement of the Israelis in a variety of American intelligence activities was documented. Even the identities of the contras' secret funders, including Saudi Arabia, began to surface.

Then, on February 26, 1987, the Tower commission delivered its version of the scandal, complete with a guide to villains and victims. The nearly 300-page report depicted a clandestine coup d'etat carried out by Casey, McFarlane, Poindexter, and North. The president, the vice-president, Secretary of State Shultz, and Secretary of Defense Caspar Weinberger were all exonerated. Chief of Staff Don Regan was chided for the "chaos that descended upon the White House."

The report served the press well in at least one respect. Many reporters could comment openly on what only a few had pointed out over the previous six years: the president of the United States seemed utterly removed from the day-to-day flow of events: TOWER COMMISSION EXPOSES NAKED EMPEROR! Suddenly, sources who had been denying the obvious joined sources who had been trying to explain it away. The press printed the obligatory "but it is the president who determines the policy direction of the administration" alongside portraits of a disengaged and nearly irresponsible president.

Chapter Three: March 1987–November 1987 . . . What Didn't Reagan Know and When Didn't He Know It?

As members of Congress readied themselves for the joint House and Senate hearings on the Iran-contra affair, the press began posing an Iran-contra version of the famous Watergate question: What did the president know and when did he know it? (The newly arrived presidential chief of staff, Howard Baker, happened to be the very senator who had originally posed that question as a softball for Richard Nixon.) The new question was: Did the president know of the diversion of monies from the Iran arms deal to the contras? And to this Baker and his aides felt they had an answer that would hold up under challenge.

Although the Tower commission version had minimized the president's knowledge, a skeptical press seemed to determine that the most extraordinary story it could write was one that proved that the president knew not only about both parts of the Iran-contra story but about the connection between the two. Pundits joined investigative reporters in marshalling "evidence" that this president would or would not have known about such a level of detail as the diversion of funds to the contras. White House sources were suddenly willing to talk about Reagan's detachment and about the departed senior staff members who had supposedly kept things from him—Regan, McFarlane, and Poindexter.

What had been an informed and effective corps of journalists, independently pursuing the story in the preceding months, mysteriously gravitated toward this one question. Reporters who had covered other aspects of the scandal were forced off the front page.

The Iran-contra hearings themselves, which began in May, 1987, yielded the best and the worst of reporting. In cities that get Pacifica radio, aficionados of the hearings reprogrammed the first button on their car radio to get Larry Bensky's unparalleled coverage. Extraordinarily knowledgeable on his own, Bensky regularly turned to other journalists and experts to provide context. National Public Radio, public television, and a handful of print sources provided coherent daily commentary; the bulk of the coverage of the hearings was undistinguished.

The media paid little or no attention to how the committee's inquiry had been structured. Congress was not about to examine its own role in the affair—its endless waffling over contra policy, its failure to provide oversight of intelligence activities, and the desire of many of its members to protect Israel and Saudi Arabia from embarrassment. The committee, for its part, ignored the natural chronology of the tale, starting in the middle with the most contentious of all witnesses, Richard Secord. This made a coherent exposition of the events impossible. If the storyline of the Iran-contra affair was going to be laid out intelligibly it would be up to the press to do so.

Instead, reporters concentrated on who was scoring more public relations points on any given day—the witnesses or the committee members and their counsel. Finally, when Republican members of the committees began to convert the hearings into a debate over the meaning of the Boland amendments, the crowd of investigative reporters that had been pursuing the story the previous fall dwindled quickly to a small band (Bob Woodward, Walter Pincus, Joseph Pichirallo, and Dan Morgan at *The Washington Post*; Robert Parry, who had moved to *Newsweek*; Doyle McManus and Michael Wines at the *Los Angeles Times*; Roy Gutman and Knute Royce of *Newsday;* Steven Emerson of *U.S. News & World Report*; Stephen Engelberg and Jeffrey Gerth of *The New York Times*; James Ridgeway of *The Village Voice*; Karen Burnes of ABC News; Frank Greve of *The Philadelphia Inquirer*; David Corn and Jeff Morley of *The Nation*; David Rogers of *The Wall Street Journal*; and Miguel Acoca of *The San Francisco Examiner*). Sifting through new leads uncovered by the hearings, they occasionally linked up the new with the old. But once again most of their colleagues allowed themselves to be distracted, this time by the hearings' grand finale—the trumpeting of George Shultz's outraged innocence.

There had been indications of Shultz's involvement in the most constitutionally troubling portion of the scandal—the use of congressionally appropriated funds to get other countries to do what the U.S. government could not legally do. But the committee had ears only for Shultz's impassioned denunciation of the NSC staff. And the press seemed to join committee members in a bipartisan salute to Shultz's unsullied integrity.

The committee's final report came out on November 17. Its gist was that there was evidence of egregious abuses of power by members of the Reagan administration. But doing something about them seemed to be a job for the independent counsel. For its part the press, having blamed everything once again on the National Security Council staff, seemed ready to take a break. Thank God, every wrap-up article seemed to sigh, George Shultz and Caspar Weinberger would be left to operate the government.

Chapter Four: The 1988 Campaign
Iran-Contra Becomes a Partisan Issue

In 1988, George Bush, formerly a member of an administration loosely under investigation, became a presidential candidate under direct scrutiny. Yet, remarkably, despite the fact that the committee's report offered a wealth of facts and leads, only a few of the most expert reporters felt confident enough to take on the issue of Bush's role in the affair. Among them were Bob Woodward, Walter Pincus, and David Hoffman, who in the January 7, 1988, *Washington Post* catalogued Bush's entanglement down to his being in the room when Reagan signed the Bible that would be delivered as a gift to the Iranians.

Other close looks were taken by Malcolm Byrne and Jeff Nason in *The Nation* and Judy Woodruff in a *MacNeil/Lehrer NewsHour* segment (in which I was interviewed, along with Lee Atwater). These were criticized by the Bush campaign staff as partisan. But the ultimate charge of partisanship was yet to come. This was, of course, Dan Rather's interview with candidate Bush.

CBS producer Howard Rosenberg was, along with ABC news consultant Frank Snepp, one of the most aggressive television journalists to pursue the Iran-contra story. It was Rosenberg who, after staking out Oliver North's suburban house morning after morning, had wondered how North was able to afford an expensive remote-control security gate. His reporting on that detail ultimately led to a criminal charge against North for having accepted a gratuity—one of the few charges on which the lieutenant colonel was subsequently convicted.

For the Rather interview, Rosenberg and fellow CBS producer Martin Koughan prepared a taped piece reviewing Bush's activities, highlighting claims that he had been "out of the loop" on Iran-contra and that he was "never involved in directing, coordinating, or approving military aid to the contras." It pointed out that Donald Gregg, Bush's national security adviser and a veteran CIA agent, had lied about his involvement in covert Central America policy.

Then came the interview, which was live at Bush's insistence. Bush came out aggressively, eating up air time by answering unasked questions. Rather maneuvered back to the key question: What role had Bush played in facilitating the arms-for-hostages transactions with Iran? The lead-in piece had made it clear that during a trip to Israel in late July 1986, Bush had met with Israeli counterterrorism chief Amiram Nir. The piece pointed out that according to the notes of Bush's aide,

Craig Fuller, which first surfaced in the Tower commission report, Nir had told Bush that the arms trade was "an effort to get the hostages out . . . the whole package for a fixed price. . . . " Moreover, since he sat in on at least fifteen Oval office briefings of the president on the arms-for-hostages deal, it was logical to conclude that Bush could not be as ill-informed, even uninformed, about the deal as he professed to be.

Early in the interview, Bush tripped up on a key detail: he claimed that the staff memo summarizing his meeting with Nir showed that the arms-sales deal was an Israeli plan. In fact, the memo makes it clear that it was primarily an American initiative. Rather failed to pick up on this. He had been forewarned by one of his producers about Bush's next move, but still seemed flustered when Bush asked the anchorman how he would like it if "I judged your career by the seven minutes you walked off a set in New York?"—a reference to Rather's having left minutes of dead air at the beginning of a newscast a few months earlier.

Seconds later, Bush said he had gone along with the arms sale because he wanted to get one particular hostage, CIA station chief William Buckley, "out of there, before he was killed." Yet the record was clear that by the summer of 1985 the CIA and the White House believed that Buckley was dead; by fall they knew it. Again, Rather missed the significance of the slip. He also failed to follow up on the fact that the day after Bush met with Nir a new shipment of arms, which had been on hold, was suddenly approved by the president. And he did not pick up on Bush's claim that he never had an "operational role" in the deal—a curious defense given the fact that Bush had long claimed to have known nothing at all about the deal before December 1986, and that if he *had* learned of it, he would have opposed it.

The next day the press played the story as a major confrontation but paid scant attention to the substance of the interview. Bush was portrayed as a clear victor over the aggressive anchorman. A few days before, it had looked as if George Bush had both feet locked in concrete. Who could imagine a presidential campaign in which a determined press corps would not wrestle a presidential candidate to the mat to get some clear answers? And if the press corps could not, surely the emerging Democratic candidate would. Who could imagine *not* pursuing such a thing?

Encouraged by this p.r. victory, the Bush team resorted to the strategy of simply asserting that any questions about Bush or his role were essentially partisan. During a presidential campaign this strategy succeeded as it might not have otherwise. The Bush team stonewalled. Apart from David Hoffman's work in *The Washington Post,* the press did not make a serious effort at examining the vice-president's role in the affair.

During earlier stages of Iran-contra, the press had sought the interpretive assistance of public interest organizations. Now, with few exceptions, it eschewed similar help. The "Secret Team" theory offered by the Christic Institute had proven useful when the institute was identifying—largely accurately—the network of individuals that North and Richard Secord had employed in their various operations. Less useful were the imaginative interpretations subsequently offered by the institute, making North, Secord, et al. part of a cabal that had grown out of World War II espionage, that financed itself with Southeast Asian drug smuggling, and that maintained elaborate secret facilities throughout the world.

Similarly, the "October Surprise" theory, most conspicuously proffered by former White House aide Barbara Honegger, initially asked a useful question: Given that some individuals connected with the 1980 Reagan campaign had made contact with Iranian representatives, and given that the Iranians held on to the hostages in the occupied U.S. Embassy until Carter's loss was assured, did the Reagan team promise to provide arms to Iran in return for delaying the hostage release? But a subsequent and more elaborate version of the October Surprise scenario was so poorly documented that the date of an alleged George Bush secret rendezvous kept changing as each old date was disproved by campaign film footage, newspaper clips, and schedules.

Afraid to be associated with these increasingly wild theories, most of the press backed off. By the time of the presidential conventions, reporters began to also shut out virtually *any* coherent interpretation of the Iran-contra affair. Without pegs on which to hang new facts, editors fell back to retrospectives about Bush's involvement in the scandal. Each new version was more watered-down than its predecessor.

The perversely protective rules of campaign coverage were taking effect: any story about Bush's involvement in the Iran-contra affair would have to contain increasingly serious charges as the election grew nearer. By the last week in October no story short of a confession by Bush would have been able to find its way into the media.

On November 30, 1988, the most likely vehicle for reporting on Bush's involvement in the Iran arms deal—Amiram Nir, who served as the point of contact with Israeli intelligence for both George Bush and Oliver North—was killed in a Mexican plane crash. Thereafter, even investigative reporters seemed to lose interest in the already well-documented set of facts about Bush's involvement.

Chapter Five: February 1989–May 1989
A Twice-Told Tale Puts the Press to Sleep

The North trial, which got under way on February 21, 1989, was covered by scores of reporters gathered for a spectacle. Some were familiar with the Iran-contra story, others were skilled at covering trials; few were both. The Iran-contra aficionados tended to judge evidence as new or significant not in terms of its role in proving the case against North but on the basis of whether it advanced the overall Iran-contra story. But the way this trial unfolded defied the easy advancement of the plot. The prosecutors and the jurors had to be untainted by the immunized testimony provided in the earlier hearings. This meant that much of the early part of the trial was a recapitulation of details the public had already heard. Coverage fell off quickly.

By the time the newsworthy disclosures came, the trial reporters had taken over. The news came in the form of defense exhibits, particularly a stipulation between North's lawyers and the federal prosecutors. This summary of classified documents demonstrated that people at the highest levels of government, including then Vice-President Bush, had entered into quid-pro-quo deals with Honduras, El Salvador, Costa Rica, and other countries. Here was Oliver North's own defense attorney asserting that monies appropriated by Congress for one purpose had been used by the executive branch for another purpose—to support the contras—without Congress's knowledge. A series of potentially impeachable acts had been allegedly committed with the knowledge and approval of a former president and the participation of a former vice-president who was now president.

The networks and papers gave the story a one-day run, and that was more or less the end of it. Even news organizations that had provided excellent trial coverage up to that point—National Public Radio, *MacNeil/Lehrer*—seemed oblivious to the significance of the revelations. Legal specialists, such as Tim O'Brien of ABC and Nina Totenberg of NPR, fixed on the color at the expense of the political and foreign policy implications. *The New York Times* seemed to downplay the trial, as it had the hearings.

Prosecutors and defense attorneys alike complimented the *Post*'s George Lardner, Jr., for accurately capturing the subtleties of the struggle over what classified information could be used and for connecting trial testimony to the Iran-contra narrative. Walter Pincus, David Hoffman, and Joe Pichirallo of the *Post* fleshed out the story of the various quid pro quos. Again, Pacifica's Larry Bensky provided ememplary daily wrap-ups.

After the verdict had been delivered on May 4, 1989—North was found guilty on three minor charges, including receiving gratuities— reporters got another chance to sum up. Few could handle the sweep of information. *The Washington Post* and CBS, already accused by the White House press office of overplaying the significance of the North trial's revelations about Bush, began to understate the same information in their summary stories. Other organizations, including *The New York Times,* tended to confine any meaningful post-verdict analysis to their op-ed pages. At ABC, the story was consigned to *Nightline,* whose reporter Brit Hume considered the Iran-contra story to be, as he told me off-camera, "a nonstory." The publication that did comprehend the constitutional ramifications of the North trial is one not found on every corner newsstand. It was left to Theodore Draper in *The New York Review of Books* to put the trial in perspective.

Chapter Six
Who Will Guard the Constitution?

While the North trial should have provided all the fuel that was necessary to keep the journalistic inquiry running, the press seemed to lose interest, perking up briefly only when some key Iran-contra players were nominated for high-level posts in the new administration. When Donald Gregg, Bush's choice to be U.S. ambassador to South Korea, was being considered, a few news organizations highlighted the implausibility of some of Gregg's explanations about his former boss's activities. (At one point, Gregg maintained that a career White House secretary must have written "resupply of the contras" on a Bush meeting agenda when Gregg had told her the meeting was devoted to "resupply of the copters." Not contras in Nicaragua, but helicopters in El Salvador, Gregg claimed, was the subject of the gathering.)

Neither of the other two presidential appointees who would have been aware of the circumstances of the quid pro quos pinned down in the North trial—Richard Armitage (nominated as Secretary of the Army, he later withdrew) and John Negroponte (ambassador to Mexico)— were seriously examined by the press. The congressional committees dealing with these confirmations, as well as other committees dealing with appropriations for Central America, began to examine the loose ends of Iran-contra but soon determined that there was insufficient public interest to warrant sustained public scrutiny.

Since the North trial I have talked to more than a dozen of the reporters who have methodically tried to connect the dots to fill in the Iran-contra picture. Almost to a person, these journalists expressed frustration with three groups of players. The first two—the independent counsel and the joint congressional committee—were faulted for not pursuing the most obvious trails of evidence: the violations of law that occurred as the Reagan administration gave American assistance to third countries in return for acts and favors which Congress had either forbidden or would have forbidden had it known of them. These reporters rejected the independent counsel's position that his authority extended only to clear-cut criminal prosecutions and that such matters as the quid pro quos and off-the-books government activities were subjects for impeachment inquiries. Similarly, they were dismayed by Congress's unwillingness to seriously confront the violations of the Constitution, particularly since Congress generally explained its inaction by saying it could not justify moving further given the lack of general public or even press interest.

But their strongest complaints were reserved for their peers—those editors and colleagues who treated the subject of constitutional violations as academic or, worse, as trivial, precisely because Congress had not responded with outrage.

As we have seen, one lesson of the Iran-contra affair is that reporters should pay considerably greater attention to each other's reporting. The more significant lesson, I believe, is that in a constitutional democracy the press is responsible for holding the various branches of government accountable under the Constitution. In covering this scandal, the press largely failed to do so. Why?

Fatigue and boredom were certainly factors. So was the relationship between the press and the Congress. When Congress fails to act as an anvil, the hammer of the press flails harmlessly in the air. "If neither house of Congress cares, why should we?" went the typical Washington journalist's refrain.

The fervor with which serious journalists pursued Watergate was missing. For a time, that story was pursued by only a handful of journalists, but once evidence of serious constitutional violations was revealed by prosecutors, the rest of the media began to follow every trail, incrementally and relentlessly, until the story was told. This was not so in Iran-contra. Here, the press seemed to share, rather than challenge, Congress's willingness to pass the buck.

The . . . Poindexter trial provides a perfect epilogue. Once again, fundamental constitutional questions raised by the trial were virtually ignored by the media.

A highlight was the videotaped testimony of Ronald Reagan. Yes, the former president said, he did recall the 1984 meeting at which George Bush brought up the subject of third-country assistance and admonished all present that such aid would be permissible "provided that you didn't offer a favor or quid pro quo to someone in return for their helping the [contras]." Reagan made it clear that he understood Bush's point. "[We] must not make any promise of something we would do for them in return for that. . . . No, we couldn't—we couldn't offer a quid pro quo."

Minutes later, however, Reagan said that in early 1985, faced with "a possibility that Honduras was maybe going to back away from supporting the contras," his national security advisers "agreed that we should make an approach to the Hondurans which emphasizes our commitment to their sovereignty and provides incentives for them to persist in aiding the Freedom Fighters." Reagan went on to testify about his personal involvement in this and one other quid-pro-quo chain.

These admissions would have brought impeachment to the lips of journalists in the late fall of 1986. Yet *The New York Times,* for example, barely touched on the remarks in the next day's story and failed to include them in seventy-three inches of excerpts.

Elsewhere in his testimony, Reagan framed the legal and constitutional criteria by which he apparently expects to be judged. Repeatedly the former president said that he had told his aides not to break the law and that he had never authorized them to lie to Congress. At the same time, he said he saw nothing wrong with Poindexter's statements to the congressional committees—statements which were clearly false, lies for which Poindexter was convicted in April. Listening to these two seemingly contradictory positions over and over again, it finally struck me that Reagan seems to perceive Congress as a debating forum in which the laws are merely the winning propositions, subject to further debate, rather than the body that is the source of the nation's laws within a constitutional system. Oddly, this also seems to be the view of many reporters, whose contempt for Congress is exceeded only by their own uncertainty about where constitutional responsibilities lie.

If there is one area in which reporters in America should feel compelled to carry on without the peg of an official investigation it is when **fundamental constitutional separation-of-powers principles** appear to have been violated. It would be unreasonable to expect reporters to lace their stories with references to the Constitution. But it does not seem unreasonable that allegations of constitutional breaches should motivate journalists to pursue their investigations to the very end. Were not the allegations of executive quid pro quos outlined by the cumulative evidence precisely this type of deliberate and knowing breach of Congress's power of the purse? Were not the actions that took national security off the books violations of other congressional prerogatives? Do not secret agreements between the U.S. and foreign powers constitute a form of unratified treaty? Are these not, taken singly, more than sufficient reason to keep alive full-scale inquiries in the major newsrooms across America? Taken together, do not these allegations amount to a newsworthy alteration of our constitutional system?

The managing editor of one major metropolitan daily refuses—like the late Supreme Court Justice John M. Harlan—to vote in any election for fear someone may ascribe to him a partisan motive. While I don't agree that journalists lose their franchise on election day, I can comprehend the position. What I cannot comprehend is the corollary belief that seems to have gained credence throughout the Iran-contra affair—that the media must cede constitutional questions to virtually any other major institution in our society. Have newspaper and broadcast editors declared stories that invoke basic constitutional questions too complex, too tough to handle? Is clarifying the facts surrounding those questions necessarily partisan? Have news organizations come to believe that they cannot fairly report on the government if they have to take a stand on what our Constitution means?

Making Laws
and Making News

Timothy E. Cook

As you read this case study, consider the following questions:

1. What actions did Congressman Pease and his staff take to make congressional renewal of the FSC program newsworthy?

2. Was the congressman successful?

3. How did the media's attention to the FSC program change as the deadline for its expiration grew closer?

4. Why did the approaching expiration date change the media's interest in this program?

5. Why did Pease use a spatula during a speech at a rally for unemployed workers to try to secure media attention?

6. Why was House Speaker Tip O'Neill better able than Pease to direct media attention toward the FSC?

7. What was the impact of O'Neill's actions on media coverage of the FSC?

8. What impact did increased media interest in the FSC program have on Pease's leadership on this issue?

W HEN HOUSE MEMBERS TURN FROM FOCUSING ON THEIR DISTRICTS
TO TAKING ACCOUNT OF NATIONAL ISSUES THAT INTEREST THEM, IT
becomes the business of their press secretaries to help make sure that
these issues become concerns for the national legislature. This means
that press secretaries' interests turn toward the national media. What
the newsmagazines, newspapers of record, and broadcast networks
can help to do is to set the congressional agenda—the unwritten but
influential list of problems that are generally considered to be important and worth some sort of action—and, not coincidentally, to boost
a member's career in the process. . . .

Setting an agenda is especially valuable as a form of persuasion.
It determines both what issues will be addressed or neglected and how
they will be treated. . . .

Yet the agenda, for all its power, does not guarantee any particular
result. Raising an issue's prominence, often through exploiting one
aspect of it, is necessary but not sufficient to enact a member's proposal. A case study I report here, on the 1985 attempt to renew the
Federal Supplemental Compensation (FSC) program, illustrates the advantages and potential pitfalls of influencing policy by agenda setting.
To pressure politicians who would have preferred to do nothing, FSC's
proponents had to resort to calling attention to the program in a way
to which the media would respond. A particular image of the problem became widespread in the news, but it was resolvable by responses
different from the solution originally set forth. The pitfall for House
members is that media strategies can work to call attention to their
issues without ensuring the successes they seek. . . .

Selling the Issue . . .

The possibilities and limitations of using publicity to set the congressional agenda come more clearly into focus with an action that
accomplished some but not all of its goals: the 1985 attempt to renew an
expiring unemployment compensation program. Federal Supplemental

Compensation (FSC) was created during the 1982 recession when the unemployment rate was the highest it had been since World War II. The program provided at least eight and as many as fourteen additional weeks of federal benefits for those who had exhausted their basic twenty-six weeks of state unemployment benefits. When I signed on as congressional fellow in the office of Representative Don J. Pease in December 1984 to review his press operations and suggest possibilities for a more concerted media strategy, his preoccupation was the expiration of the FSC program on March 31, 1985.

In 1984 Pease won his fifth term as the Democrat representing the Thirteenth District of Ohio, just west of Cleveland and centered on Lorain County, a steel region that had double-digit unemployment. In the wake of Ronald Reagan's reelection in 1984, the rising budget deficit, and an America that seemed to be turning to the right, Pease was skeptical of the chances for keeping FSC alive. Nor was he convinced that the program was the best it could be: its benefits were available regardless of the health of the local economy. Still, he concluded that promoting its renewal was essential, if only to keep the issue of unemployment before Congress and the public so that future consideration of job training legislation and continued support for retraining workers displaced by foreign competition would be made easier.

Unemployment was a problem that had not gone away. The economy was on an upswing nationally, but in many pockets the recovery had not arrived. Although the unemployment rate had declined since 1982, it was still historically high, not even counting so-called discouraged workers, who had stopped looking for jobs, and those working part-time because they could not find full-time jobs, all of whom were excluded from Bureau of Labor Statistics calculations. Total employment may have increased, but many of the new jobs were in the service economy; not only did they pay less but they were less secure in the event of another downturn.

Expiration of FSC would mean that thousands of workers would be immediately dropped from public assistance and left with virtually no other source of government help. In the patchwork of unemployment insurance programs, the combined federal and state extended benefits program of assistance to the long-term unemployed went into effect only when it was triggered by the state unemployment rate. At the start of 1985 these benefits were in effect only in Alaska and Puerto Rico. . . . In the Ninety-eighth Congress Pease had introduced a bill with William Clinger of Pennsylvania to combine the FSC and extended benefits programs into a single program with less restrictive eligibility requirements. The proposal, however, was not high on the agenda of the Ways and Means Committee, whose primary concern at the start of the Ninety-ninth Congress was what (if anything) to do about tax reform. Any consideration of unemployment would have to begin with the impending expiration of FSC, but if the program were extended for even a short time, the committee might be pressured to consider the Pease-Clinger bill and other proposals.

Toward the end of 1984 Pease held a series of meetings with his staff to consider establishing a media strategy to keep the unemployment problem before the public. He was initially apprehensive about going public. He had been slowly gaining influence in the House through his membership on Ways and Means and by his position as a regional whip. In addition, as he reminded his staff, "I'm known for a commonsense approach, reasonableness, an unthreatening style; I'm concerned that quotable statements will infringe on that." And indeed, press accounts had described him as "hard-working and mild-mannered" or "the bespectacled Pease, who resembles a professor more than a crusader." But Pease did have strengths that could support an outside strategy. In particular, his years as editor-publisher of the *Oberlin News-Tribune* had given him a knack for editorializing in what his staff called "Peasese"—clear language and short, punchy sentences and paragraphs. And unlike many members, he continued to write his own weekly columns and op-ed pieces. Thus a staff consensus emerged: an outside strategy indeed, but instead of relying on glib quotability, its core would be "facts and logic."

Unemployment was an appropriate issue for a media strategy. Not only was it germane to his district, but Pease had acquired considerable expertise on the subject from two terms on the subcommittee of Ways and Means that dealt with public assistance and unemployment compensation. He had also cochaired, with Clinger, a task force on unemployment insurance with the Northeast-Midwest Congressional Coalition, a Rust Belt caucus. Unemployment was a sporadically recurring problem likely to reappear on the political agenda. It was thus a way for Pease to get his name known so that he could promote related issues with which he was concerned. Moreover, the path was clear. There were no competing congressional authorities on unemployment. No one but Pease had both the position and the desire to pursue the issue: even members of the small Public Assistance Subcommittee had turned to other interests. Finally, a problem such as unemployment could be part of a manageable strategy because opportunities for publicity could be anticipated well in advance. If press releases were timed regularly, reporters would begin looking for them. One such opportunity would occur the first Friday of each month when the Bureau of Labor Statistics released the previous month's unemployment statistics. Another would come after the Commerce Department released the monthly trade deficit figures, when Pease could use his position on the Ways and Means Subcommittee on Trade to dramatize how many jobs were lost with each increase in the deficit.

Setting the Strategy

At the beginning of 1985 the staff collaborated on an initial press release set to go out on January 9 when BLS would announce the December unemployment figures. Actually, two releases were prepared—one if the figures went up, one if they went down or stayed the same—and redrafted by Pease. The release asserted that the unemployment rate was stuck around 7 percent, a historically high level, and even that percentage was a low estimate, given the increasing duration of unemployment and the number of discouraged workers. I picked up the figures—up one-tenth of 1 percent—at the Labor Department on the way to Capitol Hill in the morning, called up the appropriate draft from the computer, filled in the gaps, and mimeographed the release. While the press secretary made her usual contact with the Washington reporters from Ohio papers, I took copies to the House and Senate press galleries and then dropped more off with reporters on the labor beat in various bureaus.

This activity produced mixed results. The national media ignored Pease's statements, but the Washington bureau chief for the *Cleveland Plain Dealer,* who had long suspected that the unemployment statistics were incomplete, was inspired to interview Pease on the telephone and write a story using the December figures as the peg. The story made the top of the front page. But whether or not it stimulated publicity, the release drove home the message that Pease was working hard on unemployment issues. This reputation was furthered by his January 29 op-ed piece, written with Clinger, in the *Wall Street Journal* on the need to reform the patchwork unemployment system before, not during, an economic downturn. Following the Commerce Department's January 30 announcement of the record $88 million trade deficit in 1984, Pease's press release calculated that 2.2 million jobs were created overseas that would have otherwise been created in the United States, a detail picked up at the end of *The Washington Post*'s front-page trade deficit story. The story identified Pease as a "congressional trade specialist," which won, to his surprise, congratulations from several colleagues.

Still, the strategy would not have gone far had there been no vehicle to promote. In the Ninety-eighth Congress, Pease and Fortney "Pete" Stark had introduced a bill to renew FSC for eighteen months; it could easily be dusted off and reintroduced, which it was, on January 31, followed on February 7 by a reintroduction of the Pease-Clinger Bill to merge FSC and extended benefits.

The Public Assistance Subcommittee was slow to react, however. First, Harold Ford had to be reelected chair and the composition of the subcommittee decided. Then hearings were delayed, presumably because Ford was deferring to Ways and Means Chair Dan Rostenkowski's unwillingness to waste time on legislation that he thought could not be passed. Many junior Democrats thought pushing a bill could make an important political point, possibly by passing the buck to the Republican Senate, which would have the distasteful choice of concurring with it or killing it. Rostenkowski disagreed. He saw no point in what he thought "an empty exercise."

Given doubts among both Democrats and Republicans about the value of FSC, merely holding hearings would not have ensured that the legislation would move out of subcommittee. But hearings were necessary to push the process to its next stage and to certify unemployment as an issue of continuing importance. While Rostenkowski considered hearings as the first step on a slippery slope, other party leaders might have been more amenable to them, if only to allow members to take credit for doing *something* to save unemployment benefits. At this stage, therefore, adopting an inside strategy still held possibilities. One afternoon as they rode a downward elevator in the Capitol, Pease and a key ally, Sander Levin, were speculating on whether Speaker O'Neill could be induced to intercede and mediate disagreements over how to handle the legislation. As a staffer recounted it, Pease said, "Well, why don't we go right back upstairs and make an appointment?" and pushed the "up" button to ascend to the Speaker's office. A few days later, O'Neill met with Pease, Levin, Ford, and Rostenkowski. When Pease suggested expediting hearings, O'Neill asked Rostenkowski if it could be done. Grumblingly and grudgingly, the chair of Ways and Means agreed.

Once the hearings were announced on February 12, Pease's staff sent a media kit to those reporters who had already received the unemployment and trade press releases and to others in Washington.

In effect, Pease was attempting to reinvest his previous publicity to get back more, so the kit included the *Wall Street Journal* op-ed piece, the *Plain Dealer* front-page story, and a profile in the *Akron Beacon-Journal,* as well as previous press releases. In a cover letter Pease called attention to the upcoming hearings and reinforced two interlocked themes—the continuing importance of his issue and his accessibility to the press. . . .

Hearings Inside, Press Conferences Outside

The hearings, which began on February 20, occasioned little attention from reporters. Held in an obscure basement meeting room in the Rayburn House Office Building, they had a small audience of labor lobbyists, staffers for other members of Congress, and a smattering of regional reporters for news outlets in the districts of members who were on the subcommittee or were slated to testify. Few witnesses were of any prominence. Indeed, the Reagan administration's desire to play down its opposition to extending FSC was indicated by the emissary it sent, a deputy assistant secretary of labor. Republican members of the subcommittee were absent; only the ranking minority member, Carroll Campbell, attended any of the hearings. But this very lack of competition from other representatives would reinforce Pease's role as spokesperson for unemployment issues.

The hearings ended on February 26. Rostenkowski apparently considered O'Neill's request satisfied. With no sign that the Ways and Means chair would encourage Ford to report out a bill, Pease's aides again turned to the outside strategy to keep FSC renewal moving. The press had now begun to contact Pease's office rather than the other way around. During the hearings a reporter from *Congressional Quarterly Weekly Report* wrote a two-page story on the expiration of the program, complete with a photograph of Pease and a quotation in boldface. Another journalist, from the "MacNeil-Lehrer News Hour," suggested the possibility (never realized) of a broadcast comparing the plight of the farmers—then receiving extraordinary attention in the news—with that of unemployed workers.

But with the legislation stalled, attention to FSC would have petered out if a new publicity vehicle were not available. Fortunately, a coalition of labor organizations allied with religious and civil rights groups and known as the Full Employment Action Council (FEAC) was preparing its own report, one that would estimate much higher unemployment because it counted discouraged workers and those forced to work part-time. This report was to be released on March 8, the same day as the BLS February unemployment figures. Having witnessed Pease's efforts, FEAC staff asked if he would introduce the report at a Capitol Hill press conference following the BLS presentation before the Joint Economic Committee. The effort made sense from both sides: the FEAC needed to legitimize their report in Congress, and Pease needed new data to emphasize the persistence of seriously high rates of unemployment.

Still, seeking further publicity meant challenging Rostenkowski's opposition to the proposal. By now, however, Pease was ready to move, even if he did range beyond his usual quiet methods. In a staff meeting held to decide whether to accept FEAC's invitation, he concluded,

> I'm not eager to criticize the Democratic leadership but this can accomplish the same purposes. We must sound the alarm: it's March 8; the program expires in twenty-three days; the House is not in session for thirteen days; the decision is to be made by the House leadership within the next few days . . . If the leadership is going to make the right decision, people must be in contact with O'Neill, Rostenkowski, and the like. . . . Otherwise, all the pressure will be off until the next recession.

Pease agreed to hold the press conference, and both his office and the FEAC sent out media advisories, but reporters only stopped at the Joint Economic Committee hearings and few showed up at the conference (Pease gamely termed the conference a "good exercise"). The FEAC report was, however, finally noticed in a few short paragraphs in *Congressional Quarterly,* which picked up his quip that "Workers are moving from the assembly line to the burger line," a one-liner drafted to dramatize the shift from manufacturing to service jobs. And with the March 31 deadline approaching, reporters had begun to pay at least passing attention to the demise of FSC and the prospect that some 325,000 unemployed workers would be kicked off the public rolls. Such a story made better news than the complexities of the statistics that estimated the extent of unemployment. It was clear-cut, dramatic, and the direction of the action could be anticipated early enough for reporters to be in the right place at the right time.

Using the Deadline

The expiration of FSC began to seem the only news peg that could call attention to unemployment. Pease agreed that it had to be exploited. FEAC also decided to push the outside strategy one step further. Taking a page from the farmers who were then pouring into Washington, it invited unemployed workers from across the country to rally on the morning of March 20 and to lobby members in the afternoon. On March 14 Pease, joined by Sander Levin, sent a letter to House colleagues that proclaimed in inch-high capital letters, "325,000 UNEMPLOYED WORKERS WILL LOSE THEIR BENEFITS MARCH 31." The letter announced the rally, which would "call attention to the imminent demise of FSC," and invited the members to "*Please* join us in urging the majority and minority leadership, and the President, to expedite extension of FSC."

Although Pease had decided to pressure the leadership, there were pitfalls. One day in early March when members of his staff skimmed the newswires, they were surprised to find him mentioned in investigative reporter Jack Anderson's column that was set to run the next day. Initial pleasure at seeing Anderson decry the forthcoming FSC cutoff and praise Pease's labor to save the program turned to dismay when the columnist blamed Majority Leader Jim Wright for dragging his feet on the issue. I had been the source for an Anderson staff member on some of the FSC information, but no one in the office had ever considered Wright an obstacle. The publication of such an accusation, especially if it appeared that Pease's office was the source, could compromise working relations with the leadership. Fortunately, the next day's *Washington Post* ran the column without any references to FSC at all.

As the March 20 rally approached, there was some movement among the party leadership, which suggested that applying both inside and outside pressure was paying off. Shortly before the rally, Levin's office received a call from one of O'Neill's aides: "Rostenkowski's unwilling to support a bill that will not get anywhere. He's the prototypical legislator. But you should know that O'Neill doesn't feel that way." In effect, the Speaker was indicating his readiness to pressure Rostenkowski. To join in the outside strategy was one possibility, and since President Reagan had not yet committed himself, O'Neill was prepared to send a letter asking where he stood. The Speaker's aide asked Levin's and Pease's staffs to submit a draft to him as quickly as possible.

The letter was a perfect way to placate those such as Rostenkowski who wished to avoid passing a law just to incur a veto. It first addressed the deadline: "In 11 days, the Federal Supplemental Compensation program will expire. . . . Unless you and the Congress can agree on terms for extending FSC, over a quarter million people will be instantaneously cut off." However, echoing Rostenkowski the letter concluded, "I am prepared to bring legislation extending FSC to the floor of the House, but it should not be an empty exercise. . . . Mr. President, where do you stand?" Regardless of how Reagan responded, the publicity would call attention to the expiration and protect those favoring renewal from being accused of advocating an irresponsible political act. As luck would have it, Reagan was readying for a rare press conference on the evening of March 21; O'Neill was scheduled to release his letter that morning.

In the meantime, though, the unemployed workers would come to Washington. FEAC asked a number of representatives and senators to speak at the rally on the steps of the Labor Department. Pease accepted the invitation. Remembering his quip about workers staying employed only by transferring "from the assembly line to the burger line," one staff member suggested, possibly tongue in cheek, that Pease show up with a spatula. The idea took off. For one thing, television cameras might be present, and the visual symbolism might make a good news clip. No one was sure if the normally staid Pease could bring it off, but everyone agreed it was worth a try. The day of the rally, the press secretary brought a spatula from home, and Pease set out for the Labor Department. The crowd was small, but it was spirited and compact enough to give the impression that it was larger. When his turn came up, Pease vigorously deplored official Washington's callousness toward unemployed workers: "If you want to know the truth, the Reagan administration acts as if you don't even exist." Then, raising the spatula in his right hand, he shouted, "Do you know what this is? *This* is a burger flipper. *This* is the Reagan administration's answer to unemployment. And *you* can flip burgers all day, and *your spouse* can flip burgers all day, and you *still* won't get above the poverty line!" As far as the staff could tell, the idea had seemed to work. Television cameras whirred as the representative wielded the spatula. A Baltimore *Sun* reporter who had been at the rally phoned for further details, as did a reporter from a medium-sized Pennsylvania paper who had taken the story from the wires and cited Pease's earlier comments in *Congressional Quarterly.*

The network evening news programs ignored the story, however, and the next morning neither the *New York Times* nor the *Washington Post* mentioned it. The staff's one consolation was a color photograph in the Baltimore *Sun,* although the caption neglected to explain why Pease was waving the spatula. The regional wires had noted his logic, but most news organizations had paid far less attention to the unemployed workers' rally than they had to the farmers' protest several weeks before. That would begin to change; the same morning in his daily Speaker's briefing, O'Neill released the letter to the president.

Bringing in the Big Guns

O'Neill read the letter, updated to invite the president to state his position on "any variety of extension that you could support," and added, "I hope that some media person will ask the president about FSC tonight." This attempt to set the journalists' agenda met with resistance, however. Reporters were more interested in asking O'Neill about the MX missile—in particular, the controversy over Les Aspin, the new chair of the Armed Services Committee, who was beginning to support additions to the missile force. I counted five questions on MX before the Speaker steered the discussion back to FSC and Reagan's responsibility: "It's my understanding that the Senate won't take it up. It's my understanding that the president is locked in concrete. I'm appealing to his decency. Hundreds of thousands of people will be without benefits. Here is a window for compromise." When a reporter asked, "If it was so important, why have you waited?" O'Neill replied, "I was waiting for a signal from the president."

O'Neill's letter got the action that the unemployed workers' rally could not. For the first time a reporter from the *New York Times* contacted Pease's office about the status of FSC. And in his press conference Reagan did have to address the issue. Like O'Neill's letter, the question for the president used the peg of the deadline and the prospect of 340,000 Americans losing unemployment benefits: "Are you going to let this happen or do you plan to take some action to extend the program?" Reagan's response was, in part, "We believe that it is time. It has been extended, you know, for quite some time through the emergency of the recession." After noting that 300,000 people were going back to work and emphasizing the need for job training, he concluded, "we don't believe that we should continue with this program indefinitely."

The answer was imprecise; nobody was favoring an indefinite renewal of FSC. But the tone was clear. Even a solution, mentioned by O'Neill, to allow those on the rolls before March 31 to receive the full amount to which they were entitled—a "wind-down" of FSC rather than an abrupt termination—could be vetoed. Nothing in Reagan's answer was likely to push Rostenkowski to schedule markups.

Still, there was some good news. FSC had become newsworthy. More reporters from national outlets such as CBS radio and local outlets outside Ohio were calling Pease's office. An op-ed piece by the representative on "the new unemployment" that had been turned down by the *Washington Post* was now slated by the *Los Angeles Times* for its Sunday "Outlook" section. And on another front, Representative James Oberstar had been lining up support to force a Democratic Caucus meeting on FSC; Rostenkowski was informed on Friday that the fifty signatures required were in hand. Pease told his staff that he had requested Rostenkowski to "hang loose," suggesting that there might be substantial support in the caucus for a program that was less costly than the eighteen-month extension originally proposed.

The following Monday Speaker O'Neill, Majority Leader Jim Wright, Majority Whip Thomas Foley, Caucus Chair Richard Gephardt, and several members from high-unemployment districts (Pease, Levin, Oberstar, and John Murtha) attended a meeting to consider options and strategies. Rostenkowski was notable by his absence. The caucus was expected to support renewal for six months or less, with an expression of commitment to some sort of reform by the end of that period. A six-month extension was deemed possible only with a reduction of the number of benefit weeks available. Otherwise, two months was probably the maximum, given fiscal constraints. Pease was willing to accept these limitations if they were linked to consideration of his bill to reform and combine FSC and extended benefits. But for any of this to occur, the subcommittee and committee had to act, and time was running out.

The outside strategy had not yet run its course: Pease's op-ed piece appeared in the *Los Angeles Times* on March 24, and he accepted an invitation to be a guest on a C-SPAN call-in show on March 27. But with the Republican Senate awaiting House action before doing anything of its own, it was time to change tactics. The unemployment issue now became painted as the first confrontation in the Ninety-ninth Congress between the Democrat-controlled House and President Reagan over "fairness." On March 27 the Democratic Caucus meeting called by Oberstar urged Ways and Means to report out a bill that would extend FSC for three months. During that time, Congress would overhaul the FSC and extended benefits programs to target them at areas with high unemployment. . . . Although some influential Republicans, such as Minority Leader Robert Michel and Silvio Conte, ranking minority member of the House Appropriations Committee, were on record as favoring an extension of FSC, Democratic leaders specified that the issue would show that, in Gephardt's words, "As Democrats, we need to clearly articulate to the country our priorities as opposed to the President." Now that the unemployment issue was on the agenda, partisan position taking was de rigueur.

This shift in tactics was not without its costs. When his staff opened the *Washington Post* the next morning, they were chagrined to find that Oberstar and Gephardt had held a press conference after the caucus that had received prominent treatment, complete with a photo of the two, but no mention of Pease or his proposal. Although Pease was not shut out of the *New York Times* account, his squatter's rights to the issue had expired, and his role as its chief spokesperson was being challenged. Bringing in allies is a sign that an issue is becoming prominent, but allies can also dilute the power of the authoritative source.

Inside Ways and Means

The pressure of publicity was ultimately successful in persuading Rostenkowski to accede to the requests of party leaders and caucuses. Late on March 27 a legislative schedule was assembled. The subcommittee would mark up a proposal the next day; the full Ways and Means Committee would vote on it the following Tuesday, April 2. Under an accelerated timetable, it would report a proposal to the floor before the scheduled Easter recess was to begin on April 5 and in time to get the checks to the unemployed the second week of the month. That afternoon, committee staff met with aides of the majority members. One committee staff member noted the importance of the outside strategy: "Events have overtaken [Rostenkowski]. Many events have occurred outside the committee to really push this." He added that solving the cutoff problem by a phaseout in place would not satisfy the House leadership or the Democratic Caucus, but Robert Packwood, chair of the Senate Finance Committee, had told Rostenkowski such a proposal would be "all I could live with and the White House could live with." If the House committee passed a more ambitious measure, some Republicans threatened to invoke a three-day delay for allowing expression of dissenting views that would push action past the recess unless the rule was suspended by a two-thirds majority. Even if the bill passed both houses, the president might veto it while Congress was in recess. A three-month extension was now the most that could be hoped for, and none of the conditions made it propitious to consider reform. . . .

The impending expiration had raised the issue to the agenda without dictating a given response. Moreover, support in the subcommittee was uncertain. When the Democratic members caucused before the subcommittee markup on March 28, Pease found only two sure votes—his and Stark's—for an extension. Ford would vote with the majority. Barbara Kennelly was noncommittal. Robert Matsui saw it as "a program patched together late at night." Neither Kennelly nor Matsui thought that extension would improve chances for the reforms or job training provisions they both supported.

When the subcommittee was called to order, the possibility of an extension beyond a phaseout-in-place seemed dim. Had the only question been safeguarding the benefits of those already on the rolls, the outcome in subcommittee might have turned out differently, particularly since Campbell held the proxies of his two absent Republican colleagues. But through a tactical error Campbell changed the alignments by altering the image of what they were voting on. He said noncommittally that he would be inclined to support reform "rather shortly" but "wouldn't burden the Senate in the last hours." Raising the partisan stakes, he then said anything beyond a phaseout would simply be vetoed by the president. Matsui exploded. Angered by Reagan's recent defiant Clint Eastwood tone toward Congress, he stormed at Campbell, "Maybe we could have a little fun here if we want. Let him veto something we pass. We could always tell Reagan to make *our* day." Sensing the opportunity if not the necessity for a compromise among the majority, Ford called a recess. When the members returned, they approved, on a party-line vote, a three-month extension of FSC that cut the number of weeks of eligibility. The Pease-

Clinger reforms were not included in the bill, but they were approved as a separate bill to be considered by full committee later.

Pease's office continued to receive calls from newspapers asking for updates on the status of FSC. Saturday's *Los Angeles Times* ran a front page article focusing on "a growing army of jobless persons who are falling outside the safety net of government unemployment compensation," with references to the Washington rally and Pease's fight. But by now, Pease had stepped back from the outside strategy. Though the FEAC had arranged a press conference with leaders of the National Unemployment Network, he decided to pass up the opportunity and instead attempt to use inside tactics to get some form of extension passed and keep the Pease-Clinger reform alive. Rostenkowski's support was still doubtful as long as Packwood would not go beyond supporting a phaseout, and any opposition from Rostenkowski might provide cover for other Democrats. But the extent of Republican support was unclear, since many hailed from districts still hard hit by high unemployment.

When the full Ways and Means Committee met on April 2, Ford introduced the proposal to extend FSC for three months. Campbell promptly presented an amendment to eliminate the extension in favor of a phaseout in place, arguing that to support anything except his amendment would result in stalemate or in veto, and either could deny further benefits from reaching those already on the rolls. In one stroke he turned the deadline against Pease and, by implying that the Reagan administration was opposed to any extension, even a phaseout in place, took the high moral ground. Although the first Democrats to speak urged that the amendment be defeated, the ranking minority member, John Duncan, responded simply: "To vote against the Campbell amendment is to vote against any relief." Conservative Democrats agreed, and Rostenkowski, last to speak, went with Campbell: "It's a question of getting a bill signed or a subcommittee extending false hope. . . . This committee ought to do what's doable."

Realizing that the game was up, Ford proposed to extend FSC for thirty days, but the motion was voted down 19–17. Campbell's amendment was then adopted 20–16. Eight Democrats voted for the phaseout in place; only one Republican, Richard Schulze of Pennsylvania, voted against it. Some staff argued against reporting this bill to the floor, anticipating that the drama of workers being thrown off the rolls at once would attract more attention and do more in the long run to reassert unemployment as a worthy issue. But in the spotlight, facing the deadline, and wishing to do something, the committee voted unanimously to send the amended bill to the House floor. Late that afternoon, the House approved the phaseout by a unanimous voice vote; the Senate followed suit the next day after defeating efforts at extension and reform, with Packwood using the same arguments as Campbell. Reagan signed the bill into law on Good Friday, April 5.

After the Ways and Means vote, Pease wearily mused, "It was amazing to get seventeen members against the chairman. . . . It went farther than I ever thought it would without our efforts. Our reputation, for what it's worth, is enhanced. There's some pleasure in that." But with the end of the FSC battle, unemployment became old news, and reporters went on to other things. A few stories appeared just after the phaseout vote, but after that joblessness was mentioned only when BLS released the monthly statistics.

Enacting the phaseout was also the end of the Ninety-ninth Congress's concern for unemployment insurance, though Pease did win a victory in 1986 in the renewal of trade adjustment assistance. His legislative director had hoped that Campbell would be willing to join a bipartisan proposal to reform the mechanism of providing extended benefits, but nothing came of it before Campbell began running for governor of South Carolina. As Pease suspected, once the FSC issue was off the agenda, pressure to reform the unemployment insurance program was off as well.

Congressional Agendas and Media Agendas

Turning to the press to promote an issue has become more attractive as setting an agenda in Washington has become more complex. The spotlight not only draws attention but also obliges politicians to respond in some way. Thus in the case of FSC, publicity helped an issue shoulder onto the agenda when powerful House members would have preferred that nothing be done.

Media strategies to promote one issue also make members more effective in selling other issues and accomplishing other legislative tasks. Pease used his office's systematic contact with reporters to link his name to one issue; he could emerge as spokesperson on other problems. Whatever reputation he had built could only help in taking further advantage of media attention and making use of inside opportunities. After all, what members do to attract attention so they can set an issue on the agenda is not fundamentally different from what they do to

create a reputation within the House. It requires surveying the opportunities within their committees, noting the appropriate niches, and
developing an expertise that will win respect in Washington and votes
back home. The inside rules play well in winning outside publicity.

But for setting an agenda, only some problems and positions are
newsworthy and therefore useful. Pease's success was partial, and his
difficulty in calling attention to unemployment shows how political
entrepreneurs must adapt to the needs of the press. Because unemployment rates had become old news by 1985, reporters often did not respond to his determined publicity efforts until he took advantage of
the drama inherent in the approaching expiration of the FSC program.
But his emphasis on this news peg undercut his earlier emphasis on
the true gravity of the situation and his concern that workers would
be recycled into insecure service jobs. More important, raising the question of what to do about those who were about to lose their benefits
may have placed the issue on the political agenda, but it invited
remedies Pease found less effective than his own. Successfully setting
an agenda through a press strategy does not guarantee that favored solutions will become the frontrunners.

Of course, the failure to get FSC renewed was shaped by the wake
of Reagan's reelection victory, fiscal constraints that discouraged new
spending, the lack of an agreed-upon, readily available alternative to
a phaseout, the partisan division of Congress into a Democratic House
and a Republican Senate, and the presence of other, seemingly more
tractable, national problems. These factors probably affected the final
legislative product more than media strategy or coverage. But such influences came into play only after the press had emphasized the im-
minence of the expiration and implicitly pressured Congress to respond.

The journey of FSC legislation in 1985 provides one model of
how to build a legislative strategy. Press strategies call attention to the
importance of an issue, to a member's position on the issue, and to
his or her qualifications to address the issue, but they will fall short
of success unless some kind of institutional action—subcommittee hearings, markups, floor resolutions—provides a peg for further coverage.
If institutional action grinds to a halt, sponsors may have to keep the
momentum going by enlisting the support of colleagues or others who
can attract attention without threatening the member's reputation for
being the authoritative source. Such attention can force further institutional actions that will confirm the newsworthiness of the topic, and
so on.

But this cycle relies on the news media's willingness to report
on the issue, and that assistance comes with a price: the issue has to

satisfy journalistic criteria of importance and interest. Problems that are complex, have no distinct sides, seem to affect few people, or lack an easily grasped "there oughta be a law" solution are harder to promote. Legislators who wish to weld media strategies to legislative strategies may either have to find matters that meet journalists' standards or package difficult issues and proposed policies in such a way that they seem simpler and more clear-cut than they are.

7 Congress

The framers of the Constitution expected Congress to be the first and superior branch of government, with the president and federal judiciary exercising sufficient checks over the legislature to prevent congressional tyranny. In "Federalist Paper 51," James Madison succinctly expressed the framers' intention: "In republican government, the legislative authority necessarily predominates" (Rossiter 1961, 322). Throughout much of the nineteenth and early twentieth centuries, Congress was indeed the first branch of government. But the contemporary Congress is not as dominant as its nineteenth-century predecessor. Since the 1930s, the presidency has generally eclipsed Congress and dominated the American political system. (See Chapter 8.)

In addition to losing its preeminent position within the national government, Congress also regularly seems unable or unwilling to address effectively such pressing public problems as the national debt, enormous budget deficits, the savings and loan debacle, inadequate access to health care, and homelessness. The common public perception of Congress is of a "broken branch; an institution incapable of effective action" (Gitelson et al. 1991, 255). There is a paradox of sorts in the public's perception of Congress. As a governing institution, Congress is perceived to be ineffective and to have failed to address pressing public problems. But members of the public do not see their own representatives and senators as contributing to Congress's overall ineffectiveness. Rather, they strongly approve of how their own representatives and senators are doing their jobs (Davidson and Oleszek 1985, 161).

This paradox exists because there are really two Congresses. Each corresponds to one of the two principal functions of the legislative branch. Under the Constitution, Congress exists as both a lawmaking institution and a representative assembly in which individual members articulate and advance the interests of their districts and states (Davidson and Oleszek 1985, 7). When the public expresses dissatisfaction with Congress as an institution, it is largely dissatisfied with Congress's handling of its lawmaking function. On the other hand, public approval of individual members of Congress is largely based on how these members are perceived to perform their representative function.

The public's contrasting opinions about Congress and its members reflect a difference in emphasis between lawmaking and representation. Lawmaking is concerned with providing solutions to public problems that affect the general community. For Congress, the general community is the nation, and lawmaking is supposed to reflect the national interest. In contrast, representation is responsiveness to local interests. Responding to constituents' individual requests is one way members of Congress represent their districts or states. This constituency service can be as simple as procuring a U.S. flag that has flown above the Capitol dome for a local Boy Scout troop or acting as ombudsmen between their constituents and the federal bureaucracy to ensure that the constituents receive important government benefits (such as social security checks). Members of Congress are also expected to respond to the economic needs of their districts or states. A member of Congress with a high approval rating is likely to be one who has "brought home the bacon"—who has delivered economic benefits and other government largesse to the people back home. Finally, members of Congress are supposed to be responsive to the policy preferences of their constituencies.

The lawmaking and representative functions frequently conflict with one another. Focusing on one function lessens the chances of exercising the other (Vogler 1988, 25). Members of Congress routinely find that what is in the best interest of the nation does not always coincide with the interests of their districts or states. The reverse is equally true.

Caught between the two functions pulling them in conflicting directions, members of Congress must regularly choose which interests to promote. Subsidies for tobacco farmers offer a good example of the conflict between representation (local interests) and lawmaking (the national interest). For over twenty-five years, smoking has been recognized as a major cause of heart disease and cancer. More recent scientific studies have established the harmful effects of secondhand smoke on nonsmokers. Despite the national interest in reducing the public's risk of heart disease and cancer, senators and representatives from certain states are still successful in securing subsidies for their tobacco-farming constituents. Why are they successful?

One explanation seems to be that there is a recognition among members of Congress that distributive policies are good politics. Such policies allow them to bestow tangible benefits upon their constituents regardless of the fact that these benefits lack national relevance. Since all members need to deliver something to their districts or states or prevent some entrenched benefit from being removed, members of Congress are reluctant to vote against each other's "pork barrel" policies for fear that their own will also be challenged. As one member of Congress observed, "Hey, if I don't get mine, you're not going to get yours in Iowa or Washington State or anyplace else" (Davidson and Oleszek 1985, 413). Also, sometimes a decision that is clearly good for the nation, such as a decision to discontinue tobacco subsidies, can permanently damage or even cripple districts' or states' economies.

The dual obligations of lawmaking and representation pull Congress as an institution in opposing directions in much the same way they pull individual members. To be simultaneously a lawmaking institution and a representative assembly requires an organizational structure that can accommodate the tension between the two functions. For members of Congress to pursue their representative functions, a fragmented, or decentralized, organization is required. But lawmaking requires an integrated, or centralized, organization. The U.S. Congress is both (Ripley 1988, 3–19).

Political parties and party leadership are the most centralizing and integrating organizational forces in Congress. Party leadership can often ensure that lawmaking and the national interest take precedence over representation. Party leaders are charged with a number of responsibilities. They assist in making committee assignments, assign bills to committees, and schedule floor action on upcoming legislation. They are also expected to promote party unity, publicize the party's policy positions and achievements, and provide campaign assistance to candidates who are party members (Davidson and Oleszek 1985, 188–192; Ripley 1988, 210–213). The majority party in each chamber of Congress has the added responsibility of selecting that chamber's official leaders and establishing its operating rules and procedures. For example, because it has generally had a numerical advantage in the House of Representatives, the Democratic party has selected the Speaker of the House. (The speakership is an unusual position in that it is both constitutionally prescribed and partisan.) Similarly, all committee chairpersons are selected from the Democratic party.

The central task of party leadership, particularly majority party leadership, is to achieve the policy and program goals of the party (Ripley 1988, 212). The constant demands of the representative function make this integrative task difficult to perform. To be successful requires that party leaders delicately balance and weave together their formal and informal responsibilities and maximize the resources available to them. For example, the Speaker of the House, as the leader of the Democratic party, has three formal powers that are of assistance in coordinating and advancing the party's policy positions. First, the Speaker of the House controls much of the Democratic party whip organization. The whip organization has two functions: to provide information to the party leaders, particularly head counts on impending legislation, and to assist in executing party policy by convincing members to vote with the party and the party leadership. The whip organization consists of the majority party whip, the chief deputy whip, and a number of deputy, at-large, and assistant whips. The majority party whip is an elected position. The assistant whips are chosen by regions. The Speaker, in consultation with the majority leaders and the majority whip, appoints the chief deputy whip, the deputy whips, and the at-large whips. This appointive power gives the Speaker an important cadre of faithful lieutenants and a way of rewarding party members for their loyalty.

Second, the Speaker is responsible for appointing a block of members to the Democratic Steering and Policy Committee. The Steering and Policy Committee is responsible for assigning Democratic members to major committees such as the Agriculture Committee or the Appropriations Committee. By appointing loyal followers to the Steering and Policy Committee, the Speaker can increase his influence over committee assignments and, therefore, his influence over the policy-making committees.

Third, the Speaker is able to control the procedure by which legislation is debated through his appointments to the House Rules Committee. The Rules Committee has the mundane-sounding task of determining the parliamentary procedures under which particular bills will be discussed. Control over parliamentary procedures is important, though, because application of these rules determines whether it is easy or difficult to pass proposed legislation. The rules govern such things as the length of debate, the type of amendments that can be offered, and whether the legislation will be voted on as a whole or in parts. By appointing loyal party members to the Rules Committee, the Speaker can use this committee to promote legislation that he and the party leadership favor and defeat legislation to which they are opposed.

Party leadership is amazingly successful in influencing members to vote the party's position. In fact, party affiliation is the principal predictor of how members of Congress are likely to vote on legislation that comes before them (Vogler 1988, 125). But, as might be expected in an institution that is both a lawmaking body and a representative assembly, party leaders compete against other agents for the attention of their members. For example, party leaders will be better able to influence their party's members in Congress when the issue has low visibility and little importance to the members' constituents or when the party's position and the opinions of the members' constituents coincide (Ripley 1988, 221).

Like political parties and party leadership, committees and subcommittees also promote lawmaking. Lawmaking must be somewhat decentralized if Congress is to be able to pass legislation addressing serious public problems (Kelman 1987, 46). Congress decentralizes lawmaking authority to committees and subcommittees so that individual members can develop expertise in specific policy areas— expertise on which the whole membership can then rely. No member of Congress can reasonably be expected to be an expert in all areas. The committee and subcommittee system, therefore, represents a division of labor necessary for Congress to carry out its general lawmaking function.

At the same time that it facilitates lawmaking by fostering expertise and specialization, the committee and subcommittee system also promotes representation and fragments legislative decision making, thereby making the task of the party leaders that much more difficult. Committee assignments are one aspect of the committee and subcommittee system that can promote local interests over the national interest. One motivation for seeking a particular committee assignment is the relevance of the committees' subject matter to the member's district or state. Members of Congress are naturally attracted to committees that allow them to protect district or state interests and to perform constituency service. For example, members of Congress with rural constituencies gravitate to the two committees dealing with agriculture, whereas members with urban constituencies tend to be found on such committees as the Senate Labor and Human Resources Committee and the House Education and Labor Committee. Attraction to constituency-related committees is particularly evident among junior members of Congress who still need to secure support for reelection (Smith and Deering 1984, 84).

The representative function is a legitimate motivation for seeking particular committee assignments. But this motive contributes to the possibility that local interests rather than the nation's interests are likely to be the driving force behind much of the legislation produced by Congress. If a majority of members of a committee initially sought assignment to it because of the committee's constituency link, public policy emanating from the committee is likely to be heavily influenced by and slanted toward local interests. For example, local, not national, interests explain why members of the House and Senate Armed Services Committees rarely see a new military weapons system that they do not like or a military installation that needs to be closed. Members of these two committees almost always have major defense contractors or military bases in their districts or states. Local interests, therefore, dictate their fondness for new weapons systems and their continued support of possibly unnecessary military installations.

In addition to advancing the representative function, the extensive use of committees and subcommittees frustrates the lawmaking function by diffusing legislative decision making and leadership responsibilities. There are more than 250 subcommittees in Congress. Of the 535 members of the House and Senate, over 200—approximately 37 percent—are chairpersons of a committee or subcommittee. Even more remarkable is the fact that all 200 chairpersons are from the majority party, that is, the Democratic party. In the 1989–1990 session of Congress, majority party control of committees and subcommittees meant that of the 317 Democrats then in Congress, 63 percent held committee or subcommittee chairs. All of these chairpersons oversee fixed and specific policy jurisdictions, control their own budgets, and hire their own staffs. In short, these chairpersons reign over 200 "little kingdoms."

The large number of chairpersons means that party leaders find it necessary to work with an ever increasing number of members in their attempts to centralize and coordinate Congress's lawmaking responsibilities. Prior to the 1970s, when the proliferation in the number of chairpersons began, party leaders had to work with and coordinate the activities of only a few powerful chairpersons and leaders of state delegations. These individuals could normally be counted on to deliver the votes of their committees or their state delegations. Today, however, members who are chairpersons are also potentially independent leaders who can use their positions to pursue policy positions different from those of the party leadership (Davidson and Oleszek 1985, 199).

The rules and procedures by which Congress conducts its business also promote both lawmaking and representation. In Congress, rules and procedures for doing business "provide stability, legitimize decisions, divide responsibilities, reduce conflict, and distribute power'' (Oleszek 1989, 5). For example, the flow of legislation through each chamber of Congress is established by that chamber's rules. Similarly, committee jurisdiction and the ratio of majority to minority committee members are also fixed by rules. House and Senate floor debate on legislation is fixed by rules. For example, in the House a bill that has been approved by the relevant standing committee is likely to be assigned one of four rules governing debate: open, closed, modified, or waiver of points of order. Open rules means that any relevant or germane amendments can be proposed during floor debate. Closed rules prohibit any amendments to the proposed legislation except those from the committee recommending the bill. Modified rules allow only certain parts of legislation to be amended. Waivers are used to set aside technical rules of the House that would otherwise prevent a bill from coming to the floor for debate (Davidson and Oleszek 1985, 271).

As previously noted, these rules and procedures have political implications. They are politically important because they define how the debate on legislation will proceed. The structure of debate, in turn, helps to determine whether a bill will pass or be defeated (Davidson and Oleszek 1985, 271–273). For this reason, an effective party leader such as the Speaker of the House can use his control and influence over rules to increase the degree of centralized party control. But individual members of Congress who develop a proficiency for congressional rules can use this skill to thwart majority preference, delay it, or extract some modification or compromise that may further their own policy positions or take into consideration the local interests of their constituents (Oleszek 1989, 9).

The Senate rule regarding debate is a good example of the power individual members of Congress can exercise if they are intimately familiar with their chamber's rules and procedures. Unlimited debate is both the rule and a tradition in the Senate. Filibusters evolved out of the Senate's reluctance to limit debate. A filibuster is most commonly thought of as a nonstop speech—an attempt to talk a bill to death. But a filibuster frequently involves other parliamentary rules and procedures such as quorum calls, motions to reconsider, and motions to divide the question (Oleszek 1989, 220). Through a filibuster, participating senators hope to defeat, delay, or modify legislation to which they are opposed. A filibuster can also be used to hold one senatorial action hostage in order to gain passage of some unrelated piece of legislation. For example, in 1985, farm bloc senators filibustered against the confirmation of Ed Meese as Attorney General in an attempt to gain support for certain agriculture legislation that the Reagan administration was opposing (Duskin Publishing Group 1991, 117).

Filibusters clearly obstruct the Senate from conducting its business, and prior to 1917 the Senate had no way of ending filibusters other than relying on the participating senators' willingness to do so. In that year, the Senate approved its first cloture, or debate-ending, rule. Today, a filibuster can be ended on a three-fifths vote of the entire Senate membership. If a cloture vote passes, each senator is then limited to one hour of floor time.

Ironically, the Senate cloture rule has given rise to a new tactic: the post-cloture filibuster. Under Senate rules, any amendment to pending legislation introduced prior to cloture can still be called up and voted on once cloture is invoked. Filibustering senators with the foresight to do so can extend post-cloture debate well beyond the hundred-hour limit by introducing a large number of amendments to the offending legislation before cloture is invoked (Oleszek 1989, 226). For example, in 1977 Senators James G. Abourezk of South Dakota and Howard Metzenbaum of Ohio engaged in a post-cloture filibuster over legislation to deregulate natural gas by introducing 508 amendments to the bill prior to cloture being invoked.

In highlighting the themes presented in these introductory comments, the two case studies in this chapter pay particular attention to the tension between lawmaking and representation. "The Ambition and the Power" by John M. Barry, the first case study, examines how former Speaker of the House Jim Wright used the institutional resources available to him to centralize as much legislative authority as possible into the speakership. Through his efforts, Wright hoped to enable the House of Representatives to govern the nation in the way the framers of the Constitution envisioned it would. Had alleged ethics violations not forced Wright to resign from the House after a mere two years of tenure as Speaker, it is quite possible that he would have become the most powerful Speaker of the House in the nation's history. With his vision of the speakership, it is equally likely that Wright would have rivaled presidents for preeminence in policy making.

"Filibuster" by former South Dakota Senator James G. Abourezk is the second case study. This is the story of the 1977 filibuster and post-cloture filibuster by Senators Abourezk and Metzenbaum against natural gas deregulation legislation. "Filibuster" underscores how individual members of Congress who know the rules and procedures of their chamber well can influence public policy even when they are in the minority.

Suggested Reading

Baker, Ross K. 1989. *House and Senate.* New York: W. W. Norton. A discussion of the differences between the House of Representatives and the Senate that describes members' mutual suspicion of one another.

Bisnow, Mark. 1990. *In the Shadow of the Dome.* New York: William Morrow. A chronicle by a congressional aide that underscores the enormous power that staff members have over both public policy and the members of Congress whom they are hired to serve.

Fenno, Richard F., Jr. 1991. *The Emergence of a Senate Leader: Pete Domenici and the Reagan Budget.* Washington, DC: Congressional Quarterly Press. An in-depth case study of how Senator Domenici's leadership of the Senate Budget Committee affected his political fortune and career in his home state of New Mexico.

_____. 1978. *Home Style: House Members in Their Districts.* Boston: Little, Brown. A truly classic study of congressional politics focusing on how members of the House of Representatives explain their Washington activities to their constituencies back in their districts.

Fisher, Louis. 1987. *The Politics of Shared Power.* Washington, DC: Congressional Quarterly Press. An insightful study of the Madisonian separation of powers that explores how this constitutional principle actually works in the give-and-take between Congress and the president.

O'Neill, Thomas P. 1987. *Man of the House.* New York: Random House. The personal political memoirs of the former Speaker of the House of Representatives, which dramatize the political truism that all politics is local.

The Ambition and the Power

John M. Barry

As you read this case study, consider the following questions:

1. What is the significance of Jim Wright's decision to let "action, not talk" define his speakership?

2. Why did Wright need to build an internal political machine capable of dominating the inner workings of the House of Representatives?

3. What three House organizations did Wright maneuver to control as he went about building his political machine?

4. Why were each of those organizations important to Wright's overall plan to govern the nation from the House?

5. In his effort to gain control over the House Rules Committee, what did Wright do to remind the members of this committee that they were his appointees?

6. What problem did Wright face in his attempt to gain control over the House Democratic whip organization, and how did he overcome this problem?

7. In gaining control over the whip organization, what message did Wright send to Democratic whip Tony Coelho?

8. Why was control of the Democratic Steering and Policy Committee important to Wright?

9. How did Wright's approach toward the Steering and Policy Committee differ from that of his predecessor?

A^{CTION, NOT TALK, WOULD DEFINE HIS SPEAKERSHIP; BY ACTING HE WOULD} DEFINE THE AGENDA, FORCE OTHERS TO REACT TO HIM, EXERCISE POWER. Even before the 1986 election returned control of the Senate to the Democrats, Wright was preparing immediate, decisive action for the next, the 100th, Congress to take. He wanted a definitive, quick victory over the administration to signal to the press, the public, and the White House itself that a new era had begun. So he talked with Jim Howard, chairman of the Public Works and Transportation Committee, about having a major bill ready for floor action within forty-eight hours of the House's convening.

Such action would be unprecedented. . . . Each new Congress usually takes weeks to organize itself as members get new committee and subcommittee assignments, staff changes jobs, and agendas are redefined. Legislation which does not become law in one Congress must start all over, often with an entirely new series of hearings and "markups," the committee sessions in which bills are actually written. So it takes weeks before any significant legislation reaches the floor. Asking Howard to report out a bill immediately infringed on his and his entire committee's prerogatives. Most chairmen would react angrily, refusing to be bullied.

But Wright had picked his man carefully. Wright had been the first colleague Howard had met when he arrived in Congress twenty-two years earlier when Wright, in a red vest and with a southern accent, had come over to him at a reception and introduced himself. Howard, from New Jersey, had wondered, "Who the hell is this?" But they had hit if off, and had also served on Public Works together until Wright became majority leader. Even though Howard ran perhaps the most bipartisan committee in Congress and his Republicans might not like being used as pawns in a battle against their President, Howard agreed to Wright's request. . . .

Even as Wright was talking to Howard, he was also wooing Robert C. Byrd, who would soon reassume his post as Senate majority leader and who, like Wright in the House although not with the same power, controlled the Senate floor schedule. Byrd and O'Neill had gotten along poorly, and all but their most formal and pro forma communications had occurred at the staff level. As a result, House and

Senate Democrats had rarely acted in concert. Wright would work to improve that. . . .

Wright had to work with him, . . . and treated him with deference and courtesy. . . . As a courtesy, Wright called on Byrd to discuss his plans, and then extended another courtesy. The Democratic Party was given equal time each year to respond to the President's State of the Union speech. This year Wright controlled that time. . . . Wright had decided to respond himself and now graciously offered to share the time with Byrd. Byrd accepted. Already he and Wright were getting along better, much better, than had he and O'Neill.

Byrd was also enthusiastic about Wright's idea of a quick start, to demonstrate that the Democrats were in command and could govern the country. They agreed to talk often and hold regular meetings between the joint—both House and Senate—Democratic leadership. . . .

In essence, Wright wanted to govern the country from the House. That required overawing the Senate and confronting and defeating the White House. Such ambition soared so high as to seem almost laughable. And yet he intended to succeed, by transforming the House into a disciplined weapon, a phalanx which he could hurl at his enemies. To do that, he had to change the way the House had operated for three-quarters of a century, ever since 1910. Back then, Speaker Joe Cannon, a Republican, had tremendous powers, among them the power to appoint all chairmen and all members of committees, which gave him dictatorial control over the House. His rigid dictatorship became a national issue while he mocked his opponents, declaring, "Behold Mr. Cannon, the Beelzebub of Congress! Gaze on this noble form! Me, the Beelzebub! Me! The Czar!" The House finally rose against its czar, stripped the speakership of power to appoint members to committees— giving it to Ways and Means—created the seniority system, made chairmen kings, and allowed Rayburn later to say, "You can control the floor without being Speaker."

But chairmen soon became the target of wrath. Rayburn's personal force had kept them somewhat in check and responsive to the Caucus, but he died in 1961. His successors John McCormack and Carl Albert could not control them, and junior members grew restive. Simultaneously, party discipline was breaking down; junior members increasingly owed their elections not to party machinery but to their own fundraising and their abilities to communicate on television. . . . Pressure for reform intensified and reform came, gradually at first, explosively in 1974 with the dismantling of the formal seniority system.

The most obvious result of the reforms was the decentralization of power. Over one hundred relatively junior members won new powers as subcommittee chairmen, and each one tried to expand his or her authority. Jurisdictional overlap made legislating unruly and complex. Members who lacked any formal power base learned to influence policy through the media. . . .

Yet the same reforms that seemed to atomize power also vastly strengthened the Speaker's hand. The revolt had been not against the Speaker, but against chairmen. . . . The Speaker gained the power to appoint Rules Committee members, to set deadlines for committees to report out legislation—so chairmen could not block his will and the will of the Caucus—and other procedural weapons. Ways and Means lost the power to make members' committee assignments; that went to the Democratic Steering and Policy Committee, and the Speaker dominated that committee. Carl Albert did not even try to avail himself of his new powers. O'Neill was much, much stronger, but under him the House still ran loosely. The nuts and bolts of the place rattled; O'Neill had not turned the screws. Wright intended to bring the power of the speakership full circle; he would turn the screws. That required building an internal political machine which would dominate the inner workings of the House. . . .

The key to controlling members lies in form and structure; through form and structure, one can control substance. The most important element of form is procedure; of structure, the whip organization. Parliamentary procedure is dry, technical, and mundane; but, like the coils of a rope, it can constrain or even strangle. Procedure is part of the minutiae of politics which the press and public do not understand; the insiders understand. John Dingell, a creature of the institution who came to Washington when he was five years old with his congressman father, then worked as a page, then inherited his father's seat, once told the Rules Committee, "If I let you write substance and you let me write procedure, I'll screw you every time."

Procedure is the primary shield against power, whether for individuals against the state in the due process clause of the Constitution, or for minorities in Congress. The Constitution stipulates that the House and Senate will write their own "rules," their own procedures, and the two bodies are radically different. . . .

The floor of the House is controlled by the Speaker, who has the power of recognition—he may even ask, "For what purpose does the gentleman rise?" Depending on the answer, he may recognize the member or not. But even more crucial are the standing rules of the House and the House Rules Committee.

In each Congress, the two most partisan votes are the first two: the first elects the Speaker and the second adopts a set of standing rules—each party offers a nominee for Speaker and a package of standing rules—and both will govern the House for two years. For example, according to the Democrat-written rules for the 100th Congress, although Republicans controlled 41 percent of House seats, Democrats hold a two-thirds-plus-one advantage, nine Democrats to four Republicans, on the Rules Committee. Since the 1974 reforms, the Speaker has had the power to appoint personally, with Caucus approval, all Democrats on Rules. And Rules writes a specific rule covering floor handling of almost every piece of major legislation.

The rule for the bill dictates several things, most important being which different parts of a package, if any, will be voted on separately and what amendments can be offered. The House . . . first debates and votes on the rule for a bill, and only later on the bill itself. Because of the constitutional mandate that the House write its own rules, House rules take precedence over the law, even over the Constitution itself. In procedure lies power.

Process. Suppose there are two bills. One is very, very popular; the other is somewhat unpopular. Suppose the Speaker has Rules link the two bills together, and only allows members one vote—they either take both bills or reject both bills. The unpopular bills passes. *Process.* The rules of the House require a committee to have a quorum before voting out legislation, but suppose less than a quorum attends a certain meeting, suppose hardly any Republicans, and the committee votes out a bill anyway, and the Speaker has the Rules Committee waive the standing rules of the House. *Process.* Suppose a law—the law of the land, something the House itself has passed, the Senate has passed, the President has signed into law; *this is the law*—requires the House to allow a vote on a certain issue. Suppose the Speaker asks the Rules Committee to write a House rule that voids the law. *The rule takes precedence over the law.* Procedure is power.

When Wright took over from O'Neill, all the Democrats on Rules were returning, including chairman Claude Pepper. Several had served on the committee for all of O'Neill's ten years as Speaker; some had served even longer. Wright didn't care about their seniority. Nor did personalities interest him. But power did, having them heed him did. A few came to see him privately to assure him of loyalty and ask to be reappointed. Wright wanted that little investiture ceremony; they would ask, and he would grant. But he wanted them to ask. Not all of them did. "Some of them had got to thinking they were on Rules through the divine right of kings," Wright said. "That was a little foolish. I just wanted them to remember they were the Speaker's appointees.''

He delayed telling them he would reappoint them, until some began to wonder. Rules was one of three ''exclusive'' committees, meaning that members served only on it. Anyone removed and placed on other committees would start dead-last in seniority would go from being one of nine members on one of the most important committees in Congress to number twenty-five or thirty in seniority on a lesser one. Finally, a few days before the organizing Caucus in which Wright would formally name Rules members, he hosted a luncheon for committee Democrats. He explained that he intended to use the committee as a tool, and sometimes they would have to obey the leadership. Then he said, ''I assume you all want to be reappointed.''

There was a still moment. They would not forget again whose appointees they were.

The Rules Committee gave Wright control over the form of legislation on the floor. He needed control over structure as well, beginning with the leadership. This was more delicate. He did not appoint the majority leader or the whip. They were elected. . . . And being elected meant that the majority leader and whip had their own constituencies.

Still, Thomas S. Foley, the majority leader from Spokane, Washington, was loyal. He had, unopposed, stepped up to majority leader from the whip job, but he still owed Wright for it; Wright had made the phone call after the 1980 election telling him he would be appointed whip. That had taken guts on Wright's and O'Neill's part: Foley had been reelected with only 51 percent of the vote, which could have made it difficult for him to side with the leadership on tough issues. Foley appreciated the vote of confidence and had proven his loyalty over the years. He was not the kind of man to rock the boat anyway. . . .

Tony Coelho, the newly elected whip from California, was different. He understood loyalty well enough and said, ''There's only one leader.'' But he also said, ''I'm a political entrepreneur.'' Coelho did not wait for something to happen; he made it happen. Few members— few people—had his intensity. . . .

Foley had been the last appointed whip. Coelho was the first elected one. The difference was stark: Coelho owed the membership for his job, and Foley owed Wright. It mattered because the whip headed a powerful organization, the only real organization inside the Congress.

The whip organization had two jobs: to provide intelligence by counting votes, and to execute policy by convincing members to vote with the leadership. The organization included a chief deputy whip, ten deputy whips—just four years earlier there had been only four, but O'Neill had doubled that number as a concession to insurgents and Wright added two more—twenty-two whips elected by region, and forty-five at-large whips. They met every Thursday morning in H-324, the big townhouse two-storied room across from the House chamber, whose second floor was used for Steering and Policy staff. Between forty and sixty members would show up at a given meeting; the leadership sat at the front of the room, the members facing them in rows like in a lecture hall. The organization was designed to reach into every crevice of the Caucus, and even, delicately, to some Republicans.

The whip meetings began in 1969 at Rostenkowski's suggestion to undermine, not enhance, the Speaker's power. Rostenkowski's idea was to go over the legislative schedule for the following week with a handful of members. Colleagues who wanted to know what was happening had to come to them on the floor. "We became an exclusive group of guys," Rostenkowski said. At the time, he was Caucus chairman and talked whip Hale Boggs, who was running for majority leader, into holding the meetings. Back then, Boggs's wife, Lindy, got up at four-thirty in the morning to bake pastries for them. Much was discussed besides the schedule. Speaker John McCormack was not invited and did not attend.

Wright would not allow any such undermining of his authority; he intended to control this organization himself, to burn into everyone's mind that, make no mistake, *he* was king, that *he*, Wright, held power now, that *he*, Wright, was the one who made the decisions. And those in the House who wanted to share in his power had to· recognize that fact.

The chief deputy whip was now the most senior slot appointed by the Speaker. With it went an office in the Capitol, prominence in Washington, and a step onto the leadership ladder which could lead to bigger steps. The choice would also send an important signal from Wright to the membership. O'Neill asked him to keep alive the Boston-Austin connection, the fifty-year history of a leadership team including both Massachusetts and an oil state, by naming Brian Donnelly, from Dorchester, a working-class Boston area. Donnelly served on Ways and Means and was as savvy and tough a politician as there was in the House. . . .

Another candidate was Steny Hoyer. Forty-eight years old, Hoyer, along with Coelho and Richard Gephardt, had led the group of House insurgents seeking internal changes after the 1984 election, but he had simultaneously worked to maintain relations with O'Neill and Wright. He had gone out of his way to do that. A Wright aide said, "Steny carried water for Wright for two years." He worked hard, particularly in organizing the Democratic Congressional Dinner, which would bring in $2.3 million in early 1987. . . . Hoyer had even opposed electing the whip, preferring to keep the position an appointive one, and believed in a strong speakership. Coelho urged Wright to name Hoyer. . . .

But Hoyer was not already active as a deputy whip. Wright wanted to promote from within that organization. He was determined to let members know that being part of the organization meant work, but that unlike under O'Neill, who played personal favorites, work would be rewarded. And the *Baltimore Sun* printed a story saying Hoyer was the choice. That annoyed Wright, made him wonder if someone was trying to use the press to make something happen. Finally, Wright's aide John Mack weighed in. Mack liked Hoyer, liked him a lot, and Mack and Coelho were close friends—close enough that some people worried that Mack's loyalties were split. They were wrong; Mack served Wright first. When Wright and Mack sat down to talk over the appointment, Mack warned, "Members are going to see Steny as Coelho's man, not yours." *Coelho's man, not yours.* Then Mack suggested David Bonior.

Bonior? Bonior was no one's man, but everyone respected him. Bearded—one of the very few in Congress—divorced, a former Big Ten quarterback at Iowa, Bonior had a deceptively laid-back quality that made him easy to talk to. Yet underneath the surface affability lay a toughness. Elected in 1976, he had repeatedly risked his political life back home by voting against antibusing legislation, and had supported tax increases even though a state senator in his district had been recalled for that reason. He served on the Rules Committee, and a Speaker can never have too many friends on Rules. Bonior was the right age, just forty-two, a Vietnam veteran, and came from Michigan. The Midwest had no representation in the leadership. Bonior was also a deputy whip already. More than that, he had run the Democrats' efforts to kill funding of the Nicaraguan contras. He had lost on the issue, but had run the operation so well—orchestrating the media and lobbying by outside groups—that Coelho planned to model all his whip task forces on Bonior's approach.

Bonior also had his own constituency in the House, his own loyalists. He had assembled them in preparation for running for Caucus chairman in case a vacancy occurred there. (It didn't.) His constituency was precisely where Wright was weakest, among younger members and liberals opposed to Reagan's Central America policy. . . .

The relationship between Bonior and Wright was part of the weave in the House fabric. Over the years members cross paths over and over; those criss-crossed pathways form a web. Wright had talked to Bonior. Would he be a team-player? *Yes,* Bonior replied excitedly. *Yes.*

Wright did not tell Coelho of his choice. It was no accident. He also neither consulted nor informed Coelho about the selection of the ten deputy whips. Californian Norman Mineta, a longtime Wright ally, was named a deputy and, assuming Coelho had also argued for him, thanked him.

"Help you?" Coelho exclaimed. "The first I've known about it is what you just told me. Do you know who any of the others are?"

Mineta told him that Bonior—*Bonior?!*—was chief deputy whip. Coelho looked stunned for a moment. The appointment was bad enough, but to find out this way? He turned on his heel and stormed away.

Coelho might be the whip, but the whip organization belonged to Wright. Coelho might manage the organization, but only as a delegatee. A final indignity came after the Caucus elected Coelho whip; while members were still applauding, interrupting the applause, killing it, was the announcement of the ten deputy whips. Coelho thought bitterly, *They could at least have waited for the applause to end.*

Lastly, Wright took control of the Democratic Steering and Policy Committee. Members joked that it neither steered nor set policy. But it did make committee assignments (subject to virtually automatic Caucus confirmation) to all the "standing" committees of the House except Rules. Committee assignments could determine members' political future, whether they enjoyed or hated their daily routine, even whether they won reelection. If a member wanted Foreign Affairs because he thought himself a statesman, he went to Steering and Policy. If he wanted Appropriations or Ways and Means because of their power, he went to Steering and Policy. If he wanted Armed Services because of a navy base in his district, he went to Steering and Policy. Thirty-one members sit on Steering and Policy; the Speaker chairs it, and the entire leadership plus the chairman of the Appropriations, Budget, Rules, and Ways and Means committees automatically have seats. Eight other members are appointed by the Speaker; another twelve are elected by region. A committee assignment requires an absolute majority of sixteen votes no matter how many members attend a meeting. . . .

. . . O'Neill had dissipated his control of Steering and Policy by letting factions among House Democrats—freshmen, blacks, women— choose one of their own to fill several of the eight Speaker-appointed seats. Not Wright. Instead of allowing the freshmen to elect their representative, Wright named a Texan, Jim Chapman, who had actually won a special election eighteen months earlier and was beginning his second term. To the traditional black seat, Wright named Harold Ford, a member of Ways and Means. Wright also named Brian Donnelly, also on Ways and Means. . . .

Wright asked Jack Brooks, the dean of the Texas delegation, to run for election from his region, knowing he would win and be loyal. And there was Energy and Commerce chairman John Dingell. . . . Just two years earlier, in O'Neill's last term, Dingell had asked O'Neill to name him to Steering and Policy to give him a strong voice in who was named to his committee. O'Neill refused. Dingell asked Wright for one of the Speaker-appointed seats, promised his support, and guaranteed that the member elected from his region would support Wright as well. "That's two loyal seats instead of one," Dingell said. In return, Dingell would have Wright's support when it came to naming members to Energy and Commerce. It was a deal.

Steering and Policy belonged to Wright. . . .

Wright was finally ready to move.

Filibuster

James G. Abourezk

As you read this case study, consider the following questions:

1. Why did Senators Abourezk and Metzenbaum believe it was necessary to filibuster the natural gas deregulation legislation?

2. In taking full advantage of the Senate rules, how did the two senators prepare for and guarantee that there would be a post-cloture filibuster?

3. What was their filibuster strategy? For example, what is a "chaser," and how did the two senators employ one?

4. Why were both supporters and opponents of the filibuster outraged by Vice-President Mondale's and Majority Leader Byrd's heavy-handed way of crushing it?

5. After ending their filibuster, how did Senators Abourezk and Metzenbaum try to influence the final passage of the natural gas deregulation legislation?

6. How did Senator Abourezk's support for the Panama Canal treaty enter into this new strategy?

7. Ultimately, what was the only satisfaction that the two senators were able to derive from their filibuster?

A FTER ALL THE YEARS OF FILIBUSTERING BY SOUTHERN SENATORS IN AN EFFORT TO STOP THE PASSAGE OF CIVIL RIGHTS LEGISLATION, AND AFTER all the filibustering by Alabama Senator Jim Allen against progressive anti-trust bills, I found it interesting that no one ever tried to change the rules on filibustering until after I began using the filibuster to take the side of the consumer. The new rules, passed by the Senate after I left in January 1979, make it virtually impossible to conduct the kind of filibuster that I staged in 1977. . . .

Permit me to explain what a post-cloture filibuster is. Unlike the House of Representatives, the Senate allows unlimited talking time on legislation, that is, unless all the senators agree to limit the duration of a debate. When such an agreement is reached, the amount of time set for debate depends on the number of senators who want to take part and how long each wishes to speak. But when no time limit is set, the debate can go on as long as there is a U.S. senator left standing and still able to draw a breath. Apart from an agreement to limit debate time, the only way to prevent a talk-a-thon, or a filibuster, is for the Senate to vote on a cloture motion. Simply stated, cloture is the Senate's way of telling verbose senators to shut up. If a cloture motion passes, each senator is then limited to a maximum of one hour of debate on the bill in question. In 1976, however, a loophole existed in the rules that provided a way for senators, after cloture was voted, to circumvent the one-hour time limit. If any amendments were introduced before the cloture vote, each one could be called up and voted on *after* cloture without being counted against the allotted one hour of time. This dizzying phenomenon is called the post-cloture filibuster. . . .

The rules also specified that once cloture was voted there must be unanimous agreement of the senators on the floor in order to raise any other issue. This meant, of course, that a senator could, simply by objecting, prevent anything other than the bill under debate from being acted upon. All this, I soon found out, was what the textbooks defined as power. . . .

Senator Howard Metzenbaum of Ohio asked me to help him filibuster the natural gas deregulation bill [in 1977]. I imagine that he had a couple of different reasons for asking me. I was against deregulation, as he was, but unlike him, I was familiar with the Senate rules, knowledge of which is absolutely essential to keeping a filibuster going. Unwittingly I had been preparing for something like this for a long time. My training as a civil engineer, my total immersion in litigation as a trial lawyer, and the experience I had acquired fighting against three separate . . . filibusters gave me, so to speak, a triple whammy of expertise and discipline, suitable for manipulating the Senate rules into a heavyweight delaying strategy.

The effort to deregulate gas prices has an interesting history. The federal government instituted regulation of natural gas prices in the 1930s to prevent price gouging by an industry that had a near monopoly both on the supply and the transmission of natural gas. Deregulation, long sought after by the natural gas industry in an effort to increase their profits, ultimately passed both houses of Congress in 1956, and, but for a major scandal that year, it would have been signed into law by President Eisenhower. During the debate on final passage, Republican Senator Francis Case of South Dakota rose on the Senate floor and disclosed to the world that the Superior Oil Company had offered him a $2,500 bribe in exchange for his support of the legislation. Incredibly, despite the scandal created by Case's disclosure, the bill passed the Senate. But President Eisenhower correctly decided that the smell of foul play was too overpowering, so he vetoed it.

Deregulation was never mentioned again until 1973, when oil shortages gave the oil and gas industry the courage to renew their campaign. Deregulation almost passed then, and it came close again in 1975. By 1977, the industry had picked up so much support that when the Energy Committee split on a nine-to-nine tie vote on the deregulation amendment, it retaliated by manufacturing an artificial fuel shortage. The natural gas industry understood that deregulation would pass if they could frighten the public and the Congress. Ordinarily a tie vote means defeat, but Senator Henry M. "Scoop" Jackson, chairman of the Energy Committee, announced that he would send the bill to the floor anyway. Our informal count indicated that it would pass if the entire Senate were to vote on it. This made a filibuster necessary to delay the final vote until either the pro-gas senators grew tired, or until we could change enough votes to defeat it.

I knew that the whole affair would not be easy. It would be a major undertaking, and I wasn't overly anxious to begin, knowing that I couldn't quit until it was over. The filibuster would require my total concentration to the exclusion of everything else—specifically other legislation and family life. . . .

I told Metzenbaum that both of us had to be ready for the immense peer pressure that would be placed on us during the filibuster.

I knew all too well what Senator Byrd would do to try to stop us. The constant roll calls and late night sessions would cause most senators to complain about missing dinner engagements, evenings with their families, speaking trips outside of Washington, and so forth. They would exert heavy pressure on us to abandon it, but I told Metzenbaum that we had to resolve from the beginning to resist the efforts to stop us. A half-hearted filibuster, I told him, was worse than none at all.

Howard and I knew there would be a cloture motion, and we knew that we would not be able to defeat it. So I asked Bethany Weidener, the energy expert on my staff, to work with Metzenbaum's staff to prepare amendments to be introduced. Bethany had worked in the field of energy for only a few years since I recruited her from the Institute for Policy Studies, but she learned so quickly and so well that her advice was much sought after on Capitol Hill. In addition to the storehouse of knowledge that she had accumulated, she was quite brilliant in formulating public energy policy. Metzenbaum and I introduced exactly 508 amendments prior to the cloture vote, giving us the right to call them up and have them voted on after cloture was voted. Cloture was voted after the second day, and the dance began. We called up amendments, demanded a roll call vote on each one, demanded a vote on either a motion to reconsider the original vote or a motion to table, and demanded a quorum call each time the floor was emptied of senators. Everyone was harassed by this process, but it was our only weapon.

As I had predicted to Metzenbaum, the pressure to stop the post-cloture filibuster started coming in hot and heavy. Senator Warren Magnuson of Washington complained that, at least, in a regular filibuster, you were able to learn something. But in this one, he said, all you could do was sleep. After a few days into the filibuster, Texas Senator John Tower sat down beside me and said, ''Abourezk, someday when I decide not to run again, I think I'll start acting like a prick, too.'' I responded with a great big knowing smile.

I assigned Maine Senator Bill Hathaway the job of ''chaser,'' making certain that there was never a quorum of senators on the floor. If I could keep enough senators off the floor, I would be able to demand a quorum call, then a vote on requiring the sergeant-at-arms to round up senators, then a vote to table this motion, then a vote to reconsider the motion to table. Because I was not debating, and because the votes were not charged against the one hour of time allotted to me, under the post-cloture rules, chasing a quorum off the floor was a valuable tool. To this end, Bill Hathaway read from a tome in the most boring voice he could muster each time there were too many senators on the floor. It would not take him more than thirty seconds of reading to literally empty the Senate. And each time he did, I would call for another quorum count.

Before the filibuster began, George McGovern had introduced a lengthy amendment proposing the creation of a government energy corporation. It was a piece of legislation that I supported, but it also presented, for me, a wonderful opportunity to advance the filibuster. Using an obscure parliamentary technique, I called up McGovern's amendment, then asked for a roll call vote on it. Once the senate agreed to the vote, I demanded that the chair divide the amendment into separate parts, which, under the rules, was considered divisible. The parliamentarian looked at the amendment, then groaned as he advised the presiding officer that it had to be divided into over twenty sections. Because a roll call vote had been ordered on the entire amendment, *each section would now require a separate roll call vote.*

We were in control of the Senate floor for thirteen days, during which time President Jimmy Carter, who started out on our side, switched positions to oppose us and to favor deregulation. For me it was a lesson in duplicity at the highest levels of government.

Early in the filibuster, I had asked Frank Moore, Carter's congressional liaison, if the president would make a statement opposing deregulation. He agreed to propose the idea. We never received a direct confirmation from Moore, but a couple of days later Carter made the statement that we had asked for during a speech that he made in Virginia on behalf of Henry Howell, the Democratic candidate for governor.

Subsequently we gave Frank Moore a list of senators whose support for deregulation was soft, and asked that Carter trundle them up to the White House to convince them to vote with us. The White House staff kept hauling these senators in, but Carter changed not one vote. I later learned from one of the senators that he never really tried. Instead of applying heat to the wavering politicians, Carter made each visit into a social event. But I didn't know this then, and I was perplexed by Carter's failure to get results.

There was no question, however, that all of Carter's people— Frank Moore, Dan Tate, and Fritz Mondale—were against deregulation. On the tenth day of the filibuster, Metzenbaum and I met with Mondale late in the evening in the Capitol office of the Senate's sergeant-at-arms, Nordy Hoffman. We explained to Mondale that Carter was not having much luck switching votes and that we needed his advice and assistance. Metzenbaum suggested that, because we seemed to be getting nowhere, the Administration ought to help us find a way to end the filibuster without making it look as though we had caved in. Mondale told us that Schlesinger was the expert on the matter, and that he would ask him to come to the Hill to talk to us.

The next morning, Saturday, Secretary of Energy James Schlesinger came up to the Senate. We met in the vice-president's office just off the Senate floor. . . .

Metzenbaum told Schlesinger that there was not much use in continuing the filibuster, because nobody was changing his vote. I agreed that we would probably have to give up the struggle, but I thought that we should hang in a bit longer. A test vote taken the night before showed that we needed to switch only a couple of votes to defeat deregulation. I told Schlesinger that I was convinced he and Carter could swing the votes if they made one more big push. We ended the meeting and returned to the Senate floor. . . .

On Sunday, as I later learned, Majority Leader Byrd and Senator Russell Long met privately to devise a plan to crush the filibuster. As the meeting was described to me by a staffer who sat in, both were violently angry, and Russell Long spent part of the time mimicking me objecting to the parliamentary maneuvers that they were planning. The two apparently called President Carter at the White House to demand his cooperation. Although no one witnessed the call, it must have taken place, because that was the point when Carter totally switched positions, coming out against the filibuster virtually overnight, and without notifying those of us trying to stop deregulation.

On Monday morning, as we prepared for the Senate session to start, Metzenbaum told me that he had heard a rumor that Carter was sending Mondale to the Senate to help crush the filibuster. Mondale and I had been good friends all through my time in the Senate. I had helped him out in his brief presidential campaign in 1974, and we had been political allies on a number of issues when he was in the Senate. I was unable to imagine that Mondale would be willing to do anything adverse to our cause, because I knew that he agreed with our position on natural gas. My optimism—or naivete, depending on your point of view—did not last long.

Earlier that morning, I had bumped into Schlesinger and his entourage coming out of Byrd's office, but I had smelled nothing fishy then. When Mondale entered the Senate chamber and took the presiding officer's chair, I approached him and said, "Fritz, someone told me that you're up here to stick the knife into us. Would you do that?"

Mondale instantly tightened up. "Jim, you can depend on me to do the right thing," he blurted out as his face turned a bright red.

There was no mistaking his reaction. A deal had been made and he was part of it. Then Bob Byrd rose and began calling up my amendments, one by one, and, one by one Mondale ruled them out of order.

I was on my feet, shouting objections to the procedure and asking for a parliamentary ruling on Mondale's actions. When my requests were ignored, I asked for a vote of the Senate to appeal his rulings. Each time I made a request it was arbitrarily denied by Mondale, or worse, he would refuse to recognize me at all.

Pandemonium broke loose on the Senate floor. Everyone began shouting in protest against Mondale's heavy-handed rulings. Even senators who opposed both the filibuster and my position on natural gas were angered, rising to denounce the actions of Byrd and Mondale. To them it was a question of principle. They saw a threat to the system of fairness on which Senate procedure is based. Then, in the midst of the pandemonium something both strange and funny happened.

Majority leader Byrd asked for recognition from the chair, and was advised that he had already used the hour allotted to him. In order to speak further he had to get the unanimous consent of the Senate, a request that was ordinarily granted. But when he made the request, Senator John Culver objected. Suddenly Byrd spun around and loosened all of his pent-up anger directly at Culver. He said nothing about either Metzenbaum or me, who had been the burrs under his saddle for the thirteen-day filibuster, but, looking straight at Culver, he spoke passionately about all the times he had "carried the spear" for the liberals, expressing total resentment at the mistreatment now being meted out to him by those he had helped. Then he broke into tears, a spontaneous act that succeeded, unwittingly, in bringing temporary quiet to the Senate floor.

After a time, I rose, got recognition, and called Jimmy Carter a liar. What I actually said was that during my entire adult life I knew that governments lied, but I had never thought that Jimmy Carter would like. I was playing on one of the themes of Carter's campaign for the presidency in 1976, when he repeatedly vowed that he would never tell a lie to the American people. Senator Jim Allen walked over to me, and demanded—privately—that I apologize to the president. I told him that I refused to do so until the president first apologized for stabbing me in the back. . . .

A few minutes later I called together the small band of Democratic senators who had supported the filibuster, asking for advice on our next move. Surprisingly, we still had at our disposal more than 300 of the original 508 amendments that we had introduced at the beginning of the filibuster. With that many amendments it was possible to keep the filibuster going for the rest of the year, but because Carter was no longer even pretending to switch votes, there seemed to be no advantage in doing so.

Ted Kennedy pulled me off to the side and suggested that we end the filibuster, but that we put the blame for the whole affair at Carter's feet. . . . Given our anger at Carter and Mondale for what we saw as their treachery, it seemed like a reasonable thing to do. So Metzenbaum and I called a quick press conference at which we described what had happened. . . .

Our filibuster ended in late 1977. At the beginning of 1978, the House-Senate Conference Committee was unable to iron out the differences between the two gas deregulation bills they were working on. Metzenbaum and I were members of the Conference Committee and we compounded the difficulty by using every opportunity to prevent agreement by the committee members. The Carter-Schlesinger response to the committee's failure to produce a unified bill was to cut a deal with Republicans on the committee and those Democrats who supported deregulation. To that end they invited committee members to the White House for secret meetings in an effort to build a consensus. Of course, Metzenbaum and I were excluded from the meetings. We were outraged, but we were unable to stop the meetings, which I was convinced were illegal.

But I soon discovered another lever I could pull—my vote on the Panama Canal Treaty. Getting the treaty ratified by the Senate was a major centerpiece of Carter's foreign policy. Although I had previously announced my support for the treaty, I decided to use my vote, which at that point happened to be the crucial 67th, as a bargaining chip to stop Carter and Schlesinger from completing their effort to deregulate natural gas.

During the days leading up to the canal treaty vote, I told Dan Tate, Carter's man in the Senate, that I intended to withhold my vote until Schlesinger stopped holding the secret Conference Committee meetings in the White House. What Schlesinger and Carter were trying to do was to get an agreement from a majority of conferees, then present it as a *fait accompli* to the rest of us, preventing a public debate on the question. I knew that if the meetings were held in public, those in opposition . . . could probably defeat the bill.

At a few minutes after six on the day that I informed Dan Tate of my decision to vote against the treaty, Jimmy Carter called. His voice was soft, betraying none of the tension that he must have felt, knowing that his greatest potential foreign policy achievement could go down the tubes if he failed to convince me to vote with him.

"Jim, I hear you're upset with me," he said.

Carter had always encouraged people to use his first name, but I was angry enough to be fiercely formal. "I am *Mr. President*," I said. "In fact, I'm so upset that when I woke up at three-thirty this morning . . . I couldn't get back to sleep. And the longer I lay there, the madder I got about the secret meetings that you and Schlesinger are sponsoring at the White House. Finally, at five this morning, I got up and wrote a speech denouncing the meetings and announcing my intention to vote against the treaty next Tuesday."

I was totally unprepared for Carter's response. "Now Jim," he said, "if you ever have trouble sleeping at night like that again, just call me up. You can always talk to me if something like this is bothering you."

Suddenly my anger dissipated and I heard myself laughing, almost uncontrollably.

"No, no, I'm serious," Carter shouted over my laughter.

"That's a great line," I said, while he protested again that he was not joking. I suddenly realized that he was genuinely sincere about it.

The events that followed resembled fraternity rush week. Carter phoned me a great deal, pleading with me to vote yes. He called everyone I knew in politics asking them to try and to get me to change my vote—Ted Kennedy, John Culver, Fred and LaDonna Harris, Saudi Arabian Prince Bandar, among others.

I had always intended to vote for the treaty. To do otherwise would have violated a lifetime of principle and belief. To me, the United States was an occupying power in the Panama Canal Zone. It was my conviction that sovereignty over the canal belonged to the Panamanians. But I also felt strongly about stopping the deregulation of natural gas and the astronomical price increases that I knew would come with it.

I couldn't express my true feelings about the canal treaty publicly, at least not until I had wrung out the concessions on the natural gas legislation that I wanted from the Administration. When everything else failed, Carter tried another tack. I had told Carter at one point that I wanted his commitment that he would stop holding secret meetings. He had indicated that stopping them was no problem for him, and that he would send Energy Secretary Schlesinger to me to discuss the matter.

Schlesinger appeared in my office in all his arrogant splendor, reminding me of a prisoner of war about to make a statement with a guard's gun in his back. He told me that the president had ordered him to come to see me. "That's all he told you?" I asked, "Nothing about the meetings in the White House?"

"That's all," Schlesinger replied.

"Goodbye, Mr. Secretary," I said, absolutely flabbergasted.

It was clear that Carter intended to do nothing about the Conference Committee, and that he probably perceived, correctly, that I would be unable to vote against the treaty. At the time of the vote, I supported it, it passed, and the Conference Committee reached agreement on a deregulation bill later in the year. The only satisfaction that Metzenbaum and I derived was the knowledge that the filibuster delayed deregulation and the increase in gas prices for over a year. . . .

8 The President

Whereas the framers expected that Congress would be the first branch of government, they had no such expectations about the presidency. Though they sought an independent chief executive able to curb legislative excesses, the framers did not necessarily want that official to be strong enough to usurp authority properly belonging to Congress, the people's branch of government (Nachmias and Rosenbloom 1980, 71). Accordingly, the framers assigned to the president an array of fairly unimpressive constitutional powers.

Most of the president's constitutional authority is executive or ministerial in nature. A principal constitutional charge to the president is to "take care that the laws be faithfully executed" (Article II). Beyond this basic executive authority, the president's constitutional powers are relatively constrained. For example, the president's constitutionally recognized ability to participate in lawmaking is extremely limited. Under Article II, the president has the power to call special sessions of Congress, to adjourn Congress when the House and Senate are unable to determine a time for adjournment, to provide the Congress with information on the "state of the union," and to make legislative recommendations. A president's only major lawmaking power is outlined in Article I, which provides qualified presidential veto power over legislation passed by Congress.

The constitutional presidency, then, is a fairly limited and restricted office, and it remained so throughout the late eighteenth, nineteenth, and early twentieth centuries. Most presidential scholars agree that during this extended period only Andrew Jackson (1829–1837), James Polk (1845–1849), Abraham Lincoln (1861–1865), Theodore Roosevelt (1901–1909), and Woodrow Wilson (1913–1921) were strong presidents who competed effectively with Congress for control over policy making (Milkis and Nelson 1990, 121–235). But beginning with the presidency of Franklin D. Roosevelt in 1932, presidents have come to exercise a great deal of influence over policy making. Today, this influence extends far beyond the limited constitutional authority the framers originally assigned to the presidency. This transformation, though, was not the result of any formal amending of the Constitution. To the contrary, the only constitutional changes concerning presidents have centered on their selection, their tenure in office, and the presidential succession.

How do we account for the great political influence exhibited by contemporary presidents? This development occurred largely through extra-constitutional or informal means. For example, the approach to the presidency taken by the men who have held the office since 1932 is one factor contributing to the growth in presidential influence. These men have generally viewed the presidency as a stewardship—that is, presidents must be strong and assertive in their efforts to govern the nation, and their powers are limited only by expressed constitutional or statutory prohibitions. What is not expressly forbidden, then, is expressly implied. In contrast, nineteenth- and early twentieth-century presidents (with the exception of Jackson, Polk, Lincoln, Theodore Roosevelt, and Wilson) subscribed to a "Whig" theory of the presidency. This theory of presidential power — the direct opposite of the stewardship approach—stresses that presidents are constrained in their actions unless there is an expressed constitutional or statutory grant of authority to act.

The expansion of government activities has also assisted the dramatic growth of presidential influence. Since the beginning of the twentieth century, and particularly since the 1930s, the national government simply has come to do more than it did in the nineteenth century. For example, prior to 1932, the public did not expect the national government, especially presidents, to respond to changes in economic conditions. Depression and recession were accepted as natural events, characteristic of capitalism and a free market. But since the Great Depression of the 1930s, both the public and Congress expect presidents to propose ways to guard against economic disasters and respond to changing economic conditions (Cronin 1980, 91–92).

Congress has also contributed to the growth in presidential influence by transferring or delegating significant portions of its legislative authority to the president. A notable example of this is the Budget and Accounting Act of 1921. Prior to this act, there was no presidential budget as we know it today. Instead, agencies would submit their budget requests directly to the appropriations committees in Congress. The Budget and Accounting Act of 1921 changed this practice by requiring presidents to prepare and submit to Congress a single budget for the national government (Shafritz 1988, 67). In passing the law, Congress, in effect, transferred to the president a substantial portion of its constitutionally assigned responsibility and obligation for appropriating public money. Though Congress was still responsible for shaping and passing appropriations legislation, the content of that legislation was greatly influenced by presidential requests found in the proposed federal budgets. In this regard, the Budget and Accounting Act of 1921 enhanced presidents' legislative influence by giving them control of national spending priorities.

The advent of the electronic media, particularly television, further transformed presidential influence. Both radio and television have helped to make the presidency a truly national office, to a degree that could not have been envisioned by the framers of the Constitution. Television's constant coverage of all facets of the presidency, ranging from important policy initiatives to the president's health, makes those who occupy this office the Paul Bunyans of national politics and the center of Americans' political universe.

Through its preoccupation with the presidency, television provides presidents with a near monopoly on press coverage. For example, presidents are the primary focus of 57 percent of network news stories about one of the three branches of government, whereas the Congress and the Supreme Court are the primary focus of only 35 percent and 8 percent of these stories, respectively (Patterson 1990, 501). This preoccupation, in turn, diminishes the perceived political role and importance of other important government decision makers, particularly congressional leaders such as the Speaker of the House or the Senate majority leader. In contrast to their nineteenth-century counterparts, today's congressional leaders are overshadowed by the media attention given to presidents, even though Congress in fact possesses greater constitutional responsibility for policy making (Cronin 1980, 99–100).

These and other factors cause the public and Congress to expect the president to be the nation's chief policy maker (Edwards and Wayne 1990, 11). These expectations translate into the potential for presidential influence. But since this presidential influence over policy making is supported by limited constitutional authority, every president since Franklin D. Roosevelt has had to rely heavily upon informal resources in order to fill the expected extra-constitutional role of chief policy maker. The principal informal resource at a president's disposal is the power of persuasion. The essence of a president's power to persuade is convincing individuals "that what he wants of them is what their own appraisal of their own responsibilities requires them to do" (Neustadt 1990, 40).

In persuading other government decision makers to do their bidding, presidents enjoy natural bargaining advantages. In particular, they are able to draw upon the inherent status associated with being president and the formal authority of the office (Neustadt 1990, 30). Unfortunately for most new presidents, it is difficult to seize these advantages quickly upon taking office. Most new presidents are actually "deeply ignorant about the job to which [they] have . . . been elected." They need "a period of orientation and learning, which may take as long as eighteen months" (Hess 1988, 12).

Part of this orientation and learning must include developing ways of enhancing one's persuasive power and the natural advantages associated with it. In particular, all presidents need to find ways of securing and maintaining a high level of public prestige (Neustadt 1990, 73–90). In its simplest form, the president's public prestige is somewhat analogous to his public approval rating. Its contribution to maintaining the persuasive power of the presidency should not be underestimated. For as long as presidents retain a high level of public approval, other government decision makers and members of the "Washington community" cannot easily ignore presidential efforts at persuasion (Edwards and Wayne 1990, 102; Patterson 1990, 449).

A high level of public approval does not occur naturally. It must be manufactured and cultivated. To this end, all recent presidents have depended upon a media strategy and media advisors to boost their public approval ratings. There is no single best media strategy for all presidents, however. In the hope of sustaining a high level of public approval, each president is packaged and marketed to accentuate his strengths and to deflect attention from his weaknesses. For example, if a president is known to perform poorly at press conferences, this form of interaction with the media is minimized.

Although no one media strategy will work well for all presidents, there are some basic ingredients likely to be found in almost all efforts to heighten a president's public approval. Perhaps the most fundamental principle underlying presidential media strategies is the recognition that "the essence of political communication is control of subject matter and format," a control that should never be surrendered (Seib 1987, 105). And, because most members of the public get their news from television, a second important principle of presidential media strategies is to focus on controlling the visual portrayal rather than the written portrayal. In this age of video, the public appears to retain images better than it does the printed or spoken word. Individuals also tend to believe what they see with their eyes more readily than what they hear with their ears.

In controlling the visual portrayal of the president, successful media strategies also emphasize style over substance. Media advisors contrive ways of making the president appear presidential. Summit meetings, trips to foreign countries, and receptions for foreign dignitaries are useful in pursuing this end. These activities have the added advantage of portraying presidents in action (Cronin 1980, 105, 111). Similarly, presidential media strategies emphasize and embrace symbols that make the public feel good about itself (Miroff 1990, 294). In recent years, and especially since the Gulf War, patriotism and the flag have become excellent symbols for presidents to embrace regularly.

Presidential media strategies also accent those characteristics that most sharply contrast with those of the president's immediate predecessor and for which this predecessor received the greatest criticism (Miroff 1990, 293). Strategies aim to make the president the bearer of "good news" about the nation but to keep him as far away as possible from "bad news" (Cronin 1980, 112). News that is likely to be controversial or create a negative impression of the president is announced as late as possible. The preferred time for announcing unpleasant news is late Friday afternoon, when it is too late for the announcement to make the evening network news and thus there is a chance of its dying out over the weekend.

Finally, presidential media strategies must provide for "spin control" (Fallows 1990, 321). Spin control is a technique that gained prominence during the Reagan administration because of President Reagan's habit of inducing "self-inflicted wounds" whenever he gave off-the-cuff, impromptu remarks. Specifically, spin control is the process by which members of the administration serve as a "shovel brigade," cleaning up after presidential or administration errors, misstatements, or other actions that have the potential of damaging the president's public approval. After such incidents, "spin doctors" try to contain, deflect, and minimize potentially embarrassing or politically damaging media portrayals of the president (Shafritz 1988, 511).

With the rise of media advisors, media strategies, and a small army of presidential staff engaged in media relations, it is no surprise that many of the public activities in which presidents now routinely engage are undertaken almost exclusively for their probable impact on presidential popularity. The substantive policy impact of these activities or their relationship to other presidential responsibilities is often secondary, if even relevant at all (Miroff 1990, 290). Indeed, this constant preoccupation with public approval suggests that the conscious cultivation of a high public approval rating is one of the most distinctive characteristics of the contemporary presidency (Miroff 1990, 289).

As important as a high level of public approval is for maintaining presidential influence and persuasive power, it is not the only ingredient. Presidents must also be concerned about the Washington community's assessment of their professional reputation. Presidents perceived by the Washington community as not having persuasive skills will see their influence and power to persuade decline precipitously (Neustadt 1990, 50–72). An increasingly important aspect of this professional reputation is the managerial skill and leadership presidents exercise over the Executive Office of the President and especially their immediate White House staffs.

Prior to the late 1930s, managerial abilities were of little consequence. Until Franklin D. Roosevelt was elected, presidential involvement in domestic and economic policy was minimal. Accordingly, presidents did not have large White House staffs to manage and oversee. For the first seventy years, Congress did not even authorize any secretarial help for the president. Presidents were expected to write their own speeches and answer their own correspondence. When presidents did employ assistants, they did so at their own expense. In fact, it was not until 1857 that Congress finally authorized a personal secretary or assistant for the president (Burke 1990, 385; Edwards and Wayne 1990, 173). In 1939, largely at the insistence of the Roosevelt administration, Congress created an Executive Office of the President, thus marking the beginning of the modern institutional presidency.

The modern institutional presidency is characterized by the presence of a large staff that assists and aids the president in carrying out his constitutional and extra-constitutional obligations. For example, half a century ago Franklin D. Roosevelt's White House staff consisted of about forty people. These assistants were largely generalists who carried out a variety of different and often unrelated assignments for the president (Hess 1988, 225). In comparison, President Bush employs a White House staff of almost six hundred individuals with such specialized titles and functions as "special assistant to the president for communications" and "deputy assistant to the president for agricultural trade and food assistance" (Burke 1990, 387).

This proliferation of staff over the past fifty years largely reflects the increased demands placed upon presidents and the enormous political influence they have come to exercise (Hell 1988, 225–226). In turn, this growth in staff has aided the trend toward the concentration of national policy making in the presidency. The institutional presidency better enables presidents to protect and promote those areas of public policy most important to them (Burke 1990, 393). In particular, it provides presidents with independent and reliable advice on which to base their decisions (Nachmias and Rosenbloom 1980, 92).

But the institutional presidency in fact gives presidents a double-edged sword. Because of the demands and expectations placed on them, contemporary presidents become heavily dependent upon a bloated bureaucratized staff for advice and assistance in decision making. Yet there is no guarantee that staff members will faithfully serve their president and act in the latter's best interest. For this reason, then, all contemporary presidents are faced with the recurring problem of finding ways to ensure that the aides and assistants upon whom they so heavily depend will serve their interests and do so in a manner that is constitutional, statutorily correct, and not politically embarrassing (Patterson 1990, 483).

The need to accentuate the advantages of the institutional presidency while avoiding and minimizing its pitfalls has given rise to the need to be a good manager capable of providing managerial leadership to presidential staff. For this reason, the managerial skills of contemporary presidents also become an important component of their professional reputations. Unfortunately, most contemporary presidents seem to lack the managerial skills necessary for administering the modern institutional presidency. Most presidents are actually "atrocious administrators" (Hess 1988, 221).

Despite their lack of native managerial skills, all contemporary presidents must find some way to administer their institutional presidency. The managerial styles of most contemporary presidents reflect some variation on either the "pyramid" or the "hub" approach. The pyramid approach is analogous to the hierarchical structure found in most large businesses and corporations. With the hub approach, presidents avoid this hierarchical arrangement and instead place themselves in the center of a presidency with power and authority flowing from them in every direction, as if along the spokes of a wheel (Patterson 1990, 481–482).

Admittedly, there is no ideal or perfect approach to managing the institutional presidency (Edwards and Wayne 1990, 192). Nevertheless, all contemporary presidents must stay actively engaged in such management or be prepared to suffer consequences (Edwards and Wayne 1990, 199–200). Presidents must be ready to engage in a "hands-on" rather than a "no-hands" management style or risk staff actions that are likely to be detrimental to their professional reputation and public prestige.

Though presidents need a hands-on management style, they must also be careful not to become too involved in the day-to-day operating affairs of the institutional presidency. Rather, presidents must learn where to apply their managerial leadership. In his well-received book *Organizing the Presidency,* political scientist Stephen Hess (1988, 227–228) notes some of the more crucial areas in which presidents should exercise managerial leadership. According to Hess, presidents should be actively involved in the development of national security policy, the development of domestic policy initiatives, the preparation of the annual federal budget, the selection of noncareer presidential appointees to the numerous federal executive branch departments and agencies, the resolution of conflicts between executive branch departments, and the oversight of the executive branch in order to uncover corruption and abuses among the presidential staff and throughout the federal bureaucracy.

The two case studies presented in this chapter illustrate many of the above themes. "Scripting the Video Presidency" by Hedrick Smith is an excellent and informative account of the media strategy employed by the Reagan administration to boost and maintain President Ronald Reagan's already high level of public approval. It describes how Reagan's media advisors successfully controlled and manipulated the media's public portrayal of him. Particularly revealing is just how "scripted" the entire Reagan presidency was and how, in many respects, Ronald Reagan really did "act" his way through his eight years in the Oval office.

"The Carter Years" by former Speaker of the House Thomas "Tip" O'Neill is the second case study. In this story, O'Neill assesses the presidency of Jimmy Carter. He focuses particularly on Carter's inability or unwillingness to learn how Washington politics works. As Speaker O'Neill correctly points out, this lack of understanding was a major reason why President Carter was generally unable to sustain effective presidential leadership.

Suggested Reading

Donovan, Hedley, 1985. *Roosevelt to Reagan: A Reporter's Encounter with Nine Presidents.* New York: Harper & Row. Remembrances of personal encounters with nine of the modern presidents, including examinations of their character, evaluation of their presidential tenure, and an assessment of their place in history.

Haas, Lawrence, 1990. *Running on Empty: Bush, Congress, and the Politics of a Bankrupt Government.* Homewood, IL: Business One Irwin. A critical examination of President Bush's and Congress's handling of the federal deficit that analyzes why both Congress and the president have settled for short-term fixes rather than long-term solutions and how the deficit has generally sapped the political will of both branches of government.

Hodgson, Godfrey, 1980. *All Things to All Men: The False Promise of the American Presidency from Franklin D. Roosevelt to Ronald Reagan.* New York: Simon and Schuster. An exploration of the myth of the modern presidency, examining how and why most modern presidents have been much less effective than the nation expects its presidents to be.

Kernell, Samuel. 1986. *Going Public: New Strategies for Presidential Leadership.* Washington, DC: Congressional Quarterly Press. An examination of how recent presidents have sought to promote themselves and their policies in Washington, DC by appealing directly to the American public for support.

Neustadt, Richard E. 1990. *Presidential Power and the Modern Presidents.* New York: Free Press. An updated and expanded edition of the classic work on the limitations of presidential power.

Robinson, Donald L. 1987. *"To the Best of My Ability": The Presidency and the Constitution.* New York: W. W. Norton. A study of the "constitutional presidency" with recommendations for reforms.

Scripting the Video Presidency

Hedrick Smith

As you read this case study, consider the following questions:

1. According to Hedrick Smith, how does television portray politics?

2. Though all recent presidents have relied on television to boost public approval and support, what made the Reagan administration's media strategy so markedly different?

3. What does Smith mean when he equates the Reagan administration's media strategy with jujitsu?

4. During Reagan's presidency, what was the significance of "the story line of the day"?

5. In what way does the Reagan administration's media strategy illustrate that focusing upon the visual portrayal of the president is superior to emphasizing the printed or verbal portrayal?

6. How did Ronald Reagan's media advisors use the "pageantry of the presidency" to make him look presidential?

7. Why did Reagan's media advisors feel it was necessary to take an "arms-length" strategy toward the press?

8. Ultimately, how was Reagan the "victim" of the public image that his media advisors created for him, and what lessons does this suggest for future presidents?

From *The Power Game: How Washington Works,* by Hedrick Smith. Reprinted by permission of Random House, Inc.

NO PRESIDENCY HAS BEEN MORE IMAGE CONSCIOUS OR IMAGE
DRIVEN THAN THAT OF RONALD REAGAN. DURING THE
Reagan era, Washington began calling itself "Hollywood East," exulting
in celebrity politics. As the nation's first chief executive with a long
show-business background, Reagan exploited his acting skills to the
fullest. His choreographers played to those strengths as they staged
his presidency. Reagan never seemed more at home as president than
when performing: standing before an audience or landing on a former
battlefield in Normandy or Korea to personify the nation's strength
and determination. Reagan has loved the role of president, especially
the ceremonial role, and he has played to the emotions of his countrymen in an almost-endless string of televised performances. For millions,
the Reagan years became a political home movie.

Quite obviously, image making or political public relations was
not invented by Reagan, though it reached new peaks of sophistica-
tion in the Reagan era. . . .

Once in office, all modern presidents have enlisted the power
of the tube to try to increase their bargaining leverage with Congress;
they "go public" to sell their policies by demonstrating that public
opinion is with them. . . . But no president has used television more
than Reagan to promote his personal popularity as well as his policies,
and then to use his popularity as a club with Congress to pass his programs. In Reagan's hands, the presidency became the terrain of the
permanent campaign. . . .

On television, politics becomes seen and presented as cinema:
a series of narrative episodes about political personalities, not an
abstract running debate on policy. To the mass audience, issues are
secondary. The mass audience focuses on the hero, with whom it identifies unless he does something so outrageous that it falls out of sympathy with him. Television feels driven to dramatize the news, to give
it plot, theme, and continuity in order to make it comprehensible to
a mass audience. Television needs action and drama. It needs to boil
down complexities. It needs identifiable characters. Hence the focus
on personality, preferably one personality. . . .

In what amounts to the running soap opera of politics, television needs a leading man, and the president fits the bill. As Austin

Ranney, a political scientist at the University of California in Berkeley, observed, the public can follow the news only when the confusing tumble of daily developments becomes episodes in an ongoing story. The presidency becomes a TV serial; the president, his family, his aides and cohorts become recognizable characters in the play—known and familiar, heroes and villains. Special episodes draw attention: "Ronald Reagan Goes to Peking," "Nancy Reagan Says No to Drugs," "Ollie North Sells Arms to Khomeini." . . .

Reagan's approach is ideal for the television age. His political actions are cinematic. Both he and his political choreographers have played to the public's need for a clear plot line. The Reagan team recognized that the public and Congress can focus on only one major development or one major story at a time. In the presidential TV serial, each episode replaces the last one; most are almost instantly forgotten. Each sequence of events is treated like a minidrama, with beginning, middle, and end. . . . When American Marines were shot at and bombed in Lebanon in late 1983, the nation shared their daily ordeal, but when the Marines were pulled out in February 1984, that show was over. Never mind the long-run policy consequences in the Middle East. . . . The episodes were over; on to the next episode. For an incumbent president, this is a brilliant strategy. Problems do not accumulate, and that makes a president such as Reagan seem invincible: the Teflon image. . . .

What made Reagan's image-game politics distinctive were not only the president's formidable personal talents and salesman's instincts, but the conscious decision of his strategists to *make television the organizing framework* for the president, to an unprecedented degree. . . .

"I can't think of a single meeting I was at for more than an hour when someone didn't say, 'How will this play in the media?'" confessed Lee Atwater, a senior White House political strategist. "Cabinet officers got run out of office because the White House couldn't manage the story in the media. You got it all the time. Major decisions were influenced by the media." . . .

Media Jujitsu: Controlling the Stage

Quite obviously, the television networks (and the press in general) have power—however disorganized—to play havoc with the agenda games of presidents by crystallizing issues that the White House would rather ignore. As Reagan took office, many conservatives felt that the media had gained the upper hand. . .

As the Reagan team took over the White House in 1981, it saw battling the press as political jujitsu. The trick in jujitsu is to take your adversary's force and turn it to your own advantage by clever maneuver. In media strategy, the goal is to use the power of television to enhance the president's power, not to let it break him. The most basic rule of the image game is to control the stage, according to David Gergen, Reagan's first White House communications director. Rather than let the press fix the news priorities and batter the president, Gergen said, the White House intended to set not only the political agenda for Congress but also the television agenda for the networks. . . .

In its image-game strategy, the Reagan White House operated by a . . . P.R. script built around the "story line of the day." The imperative is to pick the main public relations message each day and frame it just the way White House strategists want it to appear in the short bites on the evening television news, in headlines, and in the lead paragraph of news-agency stories. The president does many things each day, and only a portion of his actions are made public. Getting the proper bit on TV requires organizing the public portions of the president's day—the portions that will be filmed or reported—to dramatize the story line or central message. Otherwise the press and TV apply their news judgment, their filter. The trick for White House video managers is to get their story line through the press filter in its purest form. Nothing is left to chance. The public may think it is witnessing spontaneous remarks or actions, but the Reagan White House rule was that no matter how spontaneous a presidential utterance might appear, it was to be scripted in advance. As an actor used to making things look ad-libbed, Reagan was ideal for "scripted spontaneity." . . .

. . . At their eight-fifteen morning strategy meeting, Jim Baker, Ed Meese, and Mike Deaver would decide on the day's story line; they would pass the word to Gergen and press spokesman Larry Speakes. The broad lines of the Reagan presidency are familiar: The president wants less government, more money for defense, military aid for Nicaraguan rebels; the president will veto the congressional budget . . . ; the president will accept a tax increase only "as a last resort" . . . .

. . . Often the official story line is directed at shaping how reporters cast White House stories. For example, when the White House was putting together the Reagan antidrug package in September 1986, Larry Speakes scolded reporters for highlighting mandatory drug testing for about one million federal employees. The mandatory tests had stirred up a hornet's nest. Speakes wanted testing played down as "just one part of a six-part package," to reduce public resistance to Reagan's plan. . . .

Putting Spin on the Story Line

Setting the story line is the easy part; selling it and protecting it are much harder, especially when the president is prone to trip over carefully crafted media strategies with a loose tongue, as Reagan often did. Three things can trash the White House story line: hotter, competitive news from elsewhere; independent-minded White House reporters who refuse to buy the White House slant on presidential news; and self-inflicted wounds—the administration's own snafus. . . .

The most lethal threat to the Reagan image game was loose talk in the White House, especially from the president. For getting the networks to do your bidding requires enormous internal discipline to hold the focus. The established story line was often upstaged by stories of internal feuding, or more likely, slips of the presidential tongue.

Reagan became famous for stepping on his own policy line with ad-libs. That is why his staff carefully plotted, coached, and rehearsed his statements and restricted his press conferences. In May 1986, for example, Reagan spoke to a visiting group about his budget priorities. But answering a question, he remarked that hunger in America was caused not by lack of money or food-distribution problems, but by a ''lack of knowledge'' among the poor about where to obtain help. His budget push got lost; his comments about the ignorance of hungry people became the headline, making Reagan look callous. . . .

What is probably Reagan's most costly blooper came in August 1984, during a microphone test for one of his Saturday radio broadcasts. Instead of the standard 5-4-3-2-1, the president, intending a joke and thinking he was speaking in private, said: ''My fellow Americans, I am pleased to tell you I just signed legislation which outlaws Russia forever. The bombing begins in five minutes.'' Network technical crews heard his remarks and the story quickly got into print. The Allies erupted, and it took an energetic diplomatic campaign to calm them. The episode also cost Reagan with American voters; his private polls showed a dip of several points, shrinking Reagan's lead over Mondale to its narrowest margin in the 1984 campaign. . . .

The Visual Beats the Verbal

In the image game, the essence is not words, but pictures. . . . The visual wins over the verbal; the eye predominates over the ear; sight beats sound. As one Reagan official laughingly said to me, ''What are you going to believe, the facts or your eyes?''. .

Lesley Stahl of CBS, a top network reporter proud of her critical independence, told me how this point was driven home to her after airing a very tough commentary on the 1984 campaign. It was a four-and-a-half-minute piece that ran on October 4, during the campaign homestretch, analyzing how Reagan strategists used video forays "to create amnesia" about Reagan's political record. Her piece was so blunt about Reagan's techniques, Stahl told me, that she braced for a violent reaction from Reagan's video managers. . . .

Stahl's producers created a montage of Reagan video vignettes to illustrate her piece: Reagan cutting the ribbon at an old-folks home; greeting handicapped athletes in wheelchairs; giving a hug to Olympic gold-medal winner Mary Lou Retton; touring a cave saved by an environmental project; receiving a birthday cake and a kiss from Nancy; pumping iron and tossing a football with his Secret Service guards; mingling with black inner-city children and white kids in the suburbs; relaxing on his ranch in faded jeans; talking with midwestern farmers in an open field; paying tribute at Normandy to American G.I.'s who had died in the World War II landing in Europe; bathing in a sea of jubilant, flag-waving Reagan partisans while red-white-and-blue balloons floated toward the sky.

"I thought it was the single toughest piece I had ever done on Reagan," Stahl said, recalling her apprehension about the White House reaction. "The piece aired, and my phone rang. It was a senior White House official and I thought, 'I keep telling people that they've never yelled at me, but here it comes.'

"And the voice said, 'Great piece.'

"I said, 'What?'

"And he said, '*Great piece!*'

"I said, 'Did you listen to what I said?'

"He said, 'Lesley, when you're showing four and a half minutes of great pictures of Ronald Reagan, no one listens to what you say. Don't you know that the pictures are overriding your message because they conflict with your message? The public sees those pictures and they block your message. They didn't even hear what you said. So, in our minds, it was a four-and-a-half-minute free ad for the Ronald Reagan campaign for reelection.' . . . "

The Storybook Presidency

Reagan's video managers created a storybook presidency, using the pageantry of presidential travel to hook the networks and captivate the popular imagination. They projected Reagan as the living symbol of nationhood. And there was a payoff for policy: The more Reagan wrapped himself in the flag, the harder it became for mere mortal politicians to challenge him, the more impossible he was to defeat come reelection, the more worthy he seemed of trust and latitude on policy. . . .

Reagan's video managers embellished the pageantry of the White House and lured the TV networks into partnership by staging irresistible visuals. Their goal was to imbed Reagan in public consciousness as the personification of the nation. They made dream productions impossible to edit by timing Reagan's most dramatic comings and goings for live coverage in prime time or for the morning news shows.

One rule of the image game is to attract viewers by taking them on trips. With Bill Henkel, the chief of advance (trip preparation), Deaver produced a Michener presidency which, like James Michener's immensely popular novels about Hawaii, Poland, Spain, or Texas, plunged a nation of viewers into new worlds and took them on glossy adventures that outdid *National Geographic.* Often the policy purpose seemed secondary to the travelogue. President Reagan not only went for business at economic summits in London, Tokyo, and Venice, but he took highly photogenic journeys to Versailles, Bali, Normandy's beaches, the Korean demilitarized zone, the Great Wall of China— all great box office staged by Deaver, Henkel, and Company. . . .

Reagan's trip to the demilitarized zone in Korea in 1984 was a prime example. Deaver and Henkel wanted to place Reagan at the most exposed American bunker, Guardpost Collier, peering into North Korea—evoking John F. Kennedy's standing at the Berlin Wall in June 1963. But the Secret Service tried to veto that photogenic moment, fearing for the president's safety from North Korean sharpshooters or infiltrators. After days of haggling, Henkel got the Army to string thirty thousand yards of camouflage netting from specially erected telephone poles to protect Reagan. And to get the most dramatic camera shots, Henkel made the Army build camera platforms on the exposed hill just beyond Guardpost Collier, so photographers could snap Reagan surrounded by sandbags. Another camera platform was behind Reagan for the most celebrated video shot: looking over the president's shoulder as he raised binoculars toward North Korea. This was Reagan at the front—echoes of General Douglas MacArthur.

Again, to heighten the drama, Henkel wanted Guardpost Collier's sandbags low enough—waist-high—for a clear picture of Reagan in Army parka and flak jacket. The Secret Service wanted sandbags virtually up to Reagan's neck; Henkel compromised on four inches above Reagan's belly button. As if staging a play, Henkel's team put down red tapes showing Reagan precisely where to stand for the memorable picture. "This was it, the commander in chief on the front line against Communism," Henkel said. "It was a Ronald Reagan statement on American strength and resolve." It was also textbook image game—one picture carried the message. . . .

Arm's-Length Strategy vs. the Press

In 1980, as the Reagan team approached Washington, it was of two minds about the press. One approach was to charm and co-opt the press and make it a vehicle for spreading the Reagan line. But a second, mistrustful strain gained voice in a memorandum entitled "The Imperial Media," written by Robert Entman, a Duke University professor. It was part of a study produced for candidate Reagan by the Institute for Contemporary Studies in San Francisco, a think tank with links to Meese and Weinberger. Entman's advice was to hold the press at arm's length and make it accept the role of merely reporting the "what" of presidential policy and not probe for the "why" and "how." His memo cautioned against "personal mingling between press officers, other White House staff, and journalists." The White House press office, except for the top man, Entman said, should be kept "in the dark about the politics of White House decision-making" to reduce leaks on inside debates. The memo advocated taking several steps to "tame White House-beat reporting" by decreasing reporters' expectations of full access to officials.

The Reagan team pursued both strategies: the charm offensive and arm's-length stonewalling. Reagan has been shielded from the press far more than other modern presidents. In his first term, Reagan held only twenty-six press conferences—fewer than any other modern four-year president and less than half Jimmy Carter's fifty-eight. His media managers cut the size, access, and rules for press pools—the small, rotating groups of photographers and reporters who cover the president on most events—with the result that White House regulars have had less daily access to Reagan than to his predecessors. Impromptu question-and-answer sessions were curtailed. . . .

When it has come to making government officials available for television appearances, the Reagan team has applied the squeeze to protect its story line. I know TV correspondents who have scrapped stories because the White House barred senior officials from appearing, and the stories seemed unbalanced without government spokesmen. When top officials do appear, the White House imposes conditions. The networks will ask for one official: The White House, like a Hollywood studio doling out stars, will provide someone else, or demand *unequal* time. Connecticut's Senator Chris Dodd, a Democratic critic of Reagan's Central American policy, told me that when he appeared on ABC's *This Week with David Brinkley* in 1984, the White House price for producing a spokesman was to sandwich Dodd—with the smallest time segment—between its spokesman and former Secretary of State Henry Kissinger, who pushed the Reagan line. Major cabinet officers like Secretary Shultz set their own terms. Lesley Stahl said she could not get Shultz on CBS's *Face the Nation* unless she guaranteed Shultz two thirds of the airtime and promised that no unfriendly foreign spokesman would appear. . . .

The Reagan team was expert, moreover, at distancing the president from bad news. In any White House, the president announces good news and others—preferably other agencies—handle bad news. That's how the power game is played. Frequently, Reagan has appeared suddenly in the pressroom for "mini" briefings with bright economic news to announce and quickly ducked out, leaving aides to handle tough questions. In September 1986, Reagan personally announced the Soviet release of American reporter Nicholas Daniloff and left it to Shultz to break the bad news that in an undeclared swap, Gennady Zakharov, a Soviet accused of spying, had been let go by the United States.

But the most valuable defensive gambit for negative news is dumping it on Friday afternoon after four P.M. That gives the networks little time to work the story, and it relegates the news to Saturday newspapers, which are lightly read. It also increases chances the story will die over the weekend. Late release means that the first stories have an administration spin because reporters lack time to get balancing comment. Moreover, the main editorials and columns for the Sunday papers have usually been written by Friday afternoon. So odds are good that the bad news will not get heavy weekend comment and will look stale by Monday.

At times, the strategy has been extremely successful. In 1984, the White House picked March 30—after the president had flown off to his California ranch and the White House press plane was landing in Santa Barbara—to dump the news that American Marines were being pulled out of Lebanon. For all Reagan's grand declarations about the importance of the Marines to the entire American position in the Middle East, their withdrawal merited only a brief printed statement from the press office, handed to reporters late afternoon Pacific time. It was too late for Eastern prime-time network news; comment was light. By clever press agentry, Reagan limited the political scar. . . .

Oddly for a politician who projects ease in public, Reagan's most defensive area has been the press conference. . . .

. . . [F]or Reagan, who has trouble with details and even some essentials of policy, a press conference is an obstacle course, a minefield to be gingerly negotiated. His aides held their breath every time he met the press. They viewed each encounter as a bad gamble. "The problem is you're playing roulette at a press conference," one top Reagan lieutenant lamented to me. "With Reagan, he's either right on or he's off, way off. There's no middle ground." . . .

To reduce the risks, Reagan's handlers ran him through major dress rehearsals for each press conference and interview. Nixon, Ford, and Carter used to get briefing books two or three days in advance, defining policy and anticipating questions, but Reagan's prepping was more rigorous. After boning up, Reagan would spend whole afternoons doing dry runs in the White House family theatre with his staff. Two panels of aides would fire questions, one on domestic topics and the other on national security issues. Senior aides would critique Reagan's answers, suggesting where precision or vagueness would serve him better. . . .

Sometimes, he would fool his staff. "Reagan treated the pre-briefs [rehearsals] as a chance for a stand-up comic routine, and then the staff was never quite sure whether he was going to use what he said in the real press conference," one official told me.

One such case—with real backlash—occurred in October 1983, during Senate debate of a national holiday for Martin Luther King, Jr. Senator Jesse Helms opposed it, arguing that King's associations "strongly suggest that King harbored a strong sympathy for the Communist Party and its goals." Helms called on the FBI to open its "raw files" on King, sealed until the year 2027. Civil rights leaders were furious and Senate Republican leaders wanted to get rid of the issue.

During a press conference rehearsal, one aide asked Reagan, "Do you think Martin Luther King was a Communist?"

"Well, we'll know in thirty-five years, won't we?" Reagan shot back.

Everyone laughed, assuming it was a gag. But when Reagan repeated the gag line at the press conference, his aides were stunned. The implication that Reagan shared Helms's suspicions caused Reagan such political embarrassment that he had to apologize to Coretta King. . . .

Access Control . . .

It is remarkable that Reagan's flow of bloopers has not been more costly politically. To limit the risk of his disrupting the story line, his political handlers imposed tight restrictions on press access to Reagan. For example, President Carter had made it a practice on Friday afternoons to take reporters' questions just before helicoptering to Camp David for the weekend. Reagan tried that initially, but after some flubs, his staff cut the time down and later had the helicopter pilot turn on the motors to drown out questions. That gave Reagan's imagemakers what they wanted: a television picture of the Reagans and a wave from the president, but no risky dialogue.

Within the White House, access to Reagan was cut. For years, a small pool of reporters would accompany cameramen into the Oval Office for "a photo opportunity," to see the president meet foreign leaders, congressional delegations, and various groups. That gave reporters a chance to ask about breaking news. In that setting, Reagan would talk off the cuff, often to the dismay of his handlers. In late 1981, Larry Speakes issued an edict: "Look, no more questions in the photo ops. If you feel you can't abide by it, you don't have to go in." According to Sam Donaldson of ABC, the TV correspondents replied: "Then no cameras. You don't want us in there, we're not going to send our cameras." The White House, always angling for camera coverage, backed down; but in early 1982, Deaver laid down the law to network bureau chiefs, imposing what became known as the "Deaver rule": no questions in photo ops. The networks tried holding out their cameras, but after ten days, White House hardball prevailed.

Those strict guidelines marked a significant change. They created distance between regular White House reporters and the president. "I've covered city hall and the state house, I've covered Capitol Hill, and one of the things that's most useful, most important, and also most stimulating about the job is your engagement with the main player, not just the staff," remarked NBC's Chris Wallace. "In Boston, you'd sit around in the mayor's office with him late in the afternoon or go off to dinner and engage with him. You had a sense of who the man is, what he's thinking, what's his mood now. We don't have any of that with Ronald Reagan. There is no intellectual engagement at all."

"I never see Reagan very much in relation to the times I saw Carter," echoed Donaldson. "I would see Jimmy Carter almost every working day of his presidency. With Reagan, cameras always get in. It's reporters they don't want there.''

The Reagan team's arm's-length strategy—shutting out reporters—reached a climax with the American invasion of Grenada on October 25, 1983. The administration barred print, radio, and television reporters during the early days of the operation, breaking military precedent and rejecting a long tradition of front-line press coverage dating back to the Civil War. Reporters had gone into combat with American troops in the Spanish-American War, World War I, World War II, Korea, Vietnam, Lebanon in 1956, and more than twenty Caribbean expeditions.

But what was fresh in mind to Reagan's imagemakers was the British handling of the Falklands Islands War in 1982. The Thatcher government had barred live broadcasting from the Royal Navy's task force. Still photographs of burning British warships were blocked by censors. Television films had to be shipped to London by boat or plane, a process that took weeks; the war was nearly over before the British people saw scenes of their warships being blown up or heard emotional interviews with survivors. The aim of the news blackout was quite clear: Prime Minister Thatcher and her cabinet colleagues asserted that it would have been hard to sustain popular support if the British public had been exposed to nightly TV coverage.

On Grenada, the White House and Pentagon said they had refused to let American reporters on the beaches out of concern for their safety, though they let French and Latin American reporters cover the combat. When American newsmen tried to get to Grenada on commercial boats, American military planes threatened to fire on them. Four American reporters were held on a Navy ship for several days, forbidden to transmit stories, while the Pentagon set up its own news service, distributing reports with serious omissions and inaccuracies. The administration seemed to want a news monopoly until it could shape public attitudes. . . .

Death of a Salesman

The administration's success in manipulating the media in the first term and the 1984 campaign bred an overconfidence in Reagan's second-term inner circle that hastened its undoing. For Reagan's first-term popularity and success had ridden in part on avoiding excessive power plays or quickly repairing the damage when his administration got caught off base. On Nicaragua, Casey at the CIA repeatedly overreached and then banked on Shultz and others, who had credibility with Congress, to bail him out, and bail out Reagan, too. But under Don Regan, Bud McFarlane, and John Poindexter, the second-term White House team became more willful, and more secretive—a formula for political disaster. . . .

Within the month after disclosure in early November 1986 of the Iranian operation, Reagan's extraordinary public standing plummeted— from sixty-seven-percent to forty-six-percent approval in *The New York Times*/CBS News poll. Sizable majorities who had taken Reagan's word on so many other things distrusted his disclaimer that he had not known about the diversion to the Nicaraguan *contras* of millions of dollars from profits made on the American arms sales to Iran. The political debacle was compounded by Chief of Staff Don Regan's crass boast that image-game manipulation could dispose of the Iranian affair, just as White House P.R. had sloughed off three earlier setbacks: the Libyan "disinformation" controversy, the collapse of the Reykjavík summit, and the Republican loss of the Senate in the 1986 elections.

"Some of us are like a shovel brigade that follow a parade down Main Street cleaning up," Don Regan told Bernie Weinraub, White House correspondent for *The New York Times*. "We took Reykjavík and turned what was really a sour situation into something that turned out pretty well. Who was it that took this disinformation thing and managed to turn it? Who was it took on this loss in the Senate and pointed out a few facts and managed to pull that? I don't say we'll be able to do it four times in a row. But here we go again and we're trying."

Three months later, the president pushed Don Regan's shovel brigade out the White House door.

But the president had fabricated his own catastrophe. He had violated the cardinal rule of the image game: acting contrary to the image he had developed for himself. He was a victim of his own effective salesmanship. As president, Reagan had cast himself as a firm and unflinching foe of precisely what he was now caught doing— dealing with a terrorist state. Reagan had built the arguments against such double-dealing with Iran. He had castigated Carter harshly for pragmatism and patience in negotiating the release of earlier American Embassy hostages in Iran—a course Reagan derided as weakness.

Reagan's fall from grace was so swift and sharp precisely because so much of his popular appeal had ridden on image: his image of steadfastness, his image as a man of principle, his image of uncompromising refusal to deal with the devil. Suddenly he was none of those in reality. Public disapproval fell hard on Reagan when he was exposed as willing to traffic in arms with Ayatollah Khomeini's closest henchmen to buy freedom for three American hostages, because Reagan's actions did violence to the image he had created. . . .

. . . [I]n the Iranian quagmire, he lost credibility with millions of people. He had risked his most precious political asset for a single highly dubious strand of policy. For a long time, Reagan had stretched the truth on his Nicaraguan policy, officially pretending to Congress that his goals were limited and only belatedly admitting that his real objective was to force the Sandinistas to "say uncle" and give up power. And he had lived the fiction that his administration had not instigated the arming of the *contras* during the congressional ban on such action. But never before had Reagan been caught so baldly in a policy lie—saying one thing publicly about Iran and doing the opposite in private. Reagan violated a basic rule of the image game. The story line has to match reality, or come far closer than Reagan did, or the image game is mere gloss. After Iran, nothing else Reagan pushed would sell as well as it had before. . . .

The Carter Years

Thomas (Tip) O'Neill

As you read this case study, consider the following questions:

1. What qualities contributed to Jimmy Carter's winning both the 1976 Democratic presidential nomination and the presidency and suggested that he would probably be an effective president?

2. In his meeting with Speaker Tip O'Neill shortly after being elected president but before actually taking office, what did Carter say to make O'Neill suspect that getting elected might end up being Carter's greatest achievement as president?

3. How did Carter's Southern manner and style complicate O'Neill's working relationship with the president?

4. What is O'Neill's assessment of Carter's White House staff?

5. In what way did Carter's White House staff affect his ability to provide effective presidential leadership?

6. According to O'Neill, what was Carter's "political style" as president and in what ways did it hinder his ability to be an effective president?

7. How did President Carter's "political style" affect his ability to move his energy package through Congress?

8. In what ways does the story of Carter's energy package suggest that effective presidential leadership is likely to depend, at least in part, on the presidents's having friends and supporters in Congress, particularly among congressional leadership?

WHEN IT CAME TO UNDERSTANDING THE ISSUES OF THE DAY, JIMMY CARTER WAS THE SMARTEST PUBLIC OFFICIAL I'VE EVER KNOWN. THE range and extent of his knowledge were astounding; he could speak with authority about energy, the nuclear issue, space travel, the Middle East, Latin America, human rights, American history, and just about any other topic that came up. Time after time, and without using notes, he would tick off the arguments on both sides of a question. His mind was exceptionally well developed, and it was open, too. He was always willing to listen and to learn.

With one exception. When it came to the politics of Washington, D.C., he never really understood how the system worked. And although this was out of character for Jimmy Carter, he didn't want to learn about it, either. . . .

The first time I can remember hearing Jimmy Carter's name was in 1972, on my way back from the Democratic National Convention in Miami. . . .

Flying back from the 1972 convention, I had a long talk with Bob Strauss, the treasurer and future chairman of the Democratic National Committee, and Senator Henry Jackson of Washington. . . .

In the plane, Jackson, Strauss, and I discussed some of the upcoming congressional races, as well as the Democratic Congressional Campaign Committee, of which I was still chairman. Then Strauss turned to me. "I've been meaning to ask you," he said. "Do you have anybody out there who can be the top man in our speakers' bureau?"

"Not really," I replied. "I usually go out myself to speak for our candidates."

"Well, I've got a guy who'll go *anywhere*," said Strauss. "His name is Jimmy Carter and he's the governor of Georgia. He wants to be president, and he's willing to speak wherever you need him."

That sounded fine to me, so I signed up Carter, who delivered just as Strauss promised. Over the next couple of years, Jimmy Carter did a great deal of speaking for the party—much of it in remote areas for candidates who didn't have a prayer. Along the way, however, he got to meet thousands of Democratic activists, especially in small cities and rural towns. . . .

It wasn't until January 10, 1975, when I was majority leader, that I finally met Jimmy Carter. I was in a conference with my staff when Eleanor Kelley, my personal secretary, stuck her head in and said, "There's a gentleman in with Leo who'd like to meet you. He says he's running for president."

"That's nice," I said. "What's his name?"

"Jimmy Carter."

It took me a moment to remember who that was. I knew, of course, that Carter hadn't done all that speaking for Democrats around the country merely out of the goodness of his heart. Still, the idea that this Georgia peanut farmer, a complete unknown, saw himself as a serious candidate for the highest office in the world struck me as pretty farfetched.

I was still smiling when Jimmy Carter strode into my office, full of confidence and vigor. I began by thanking him for all the trips he had made on behalf of Democratic candidates, and for hiking into the hinterlands to help the party. Carter listened graciously as I spoke.

Then he got to the point, which was that he was dead serious about becoming the nominee for president at the 1976 Democratic convention in New York. "At the moment," he acknowledged, "I'm only one-half of one percent in the polls. But by the time we get to Madison Square Garden, I'll have this thing wrapped up. I know you're boosting [Senator] Ted Kennedy, but Kennedy won't be running because of Chappaquiddick. Neither will [Hubert] Humphrey. He's got his own problems, and he's still in debt from 1968. [Senator Henry] Jackson has the support of the Jews because of his positions on Israel and Soviet emigration, but his political base isn't broad enough, and he'll drop out after three or four primaries. [Congressman Morris] Udall may run, but he doesn't have a chance. As I look at it, there's only one man who can beat me, and that's [Senator] Walter Mondale. But he's not running." . . .

After dismissing just about all his potential opponents in less than a minute, Carter made an astonishing prediction: "Mr. Majority Leader," he said, "I'm telling you right now that I'm going to be nominated on the first ballot, and that in November of next year I'll be elected president of the United States."

I thought that was impossible, but Jimmy Carter hit it right on the nose. He ran a great campaign, which was made easier by the fact that in 1976 there were no other strong Democratic candidates. I was supporting Udall, who came in second in New Hampshire . . . but behind Jimmy Carter, who finished with 28.4 percent of the Democratic vote, well ahead of Udall's 22.7 percent. After Carter continued winning primaries—including Illinois, Wisconsin, Pennsylvania, Indiana, Michigan, and Ohio—he soon became the uncontested front-runner. . . .

But luck was only part of Carter's winning formula, and luck alone can't explain his success. He won because he did everything right in pursuing the nomination. That's what impressed me so deeply about him—that he set himself so high a goal and didn't stop working until he reached it. Although I barely knew him, I was terribly excited when Jimmy Carter was elected. Here, I thought, was a guy who knew how to get things done.

What I hadn't realized, and what almost nobody in Washington knew at the time, was that Carter's greatest political achievement was already behind him. He got himself elected as an outsider, but once he got to Washington, he had to deal with other national politicians. . . .

After he won the election, but before he took office, Jimmy Carter came to see me again. This time we met in the Speaker's office. Our meeting was scheduled as a routine and largely ceremonial affair, in which the president-elect paid a courtesy call to the new Speaker. On such an occasion, I thought it would be fitting to tell my visitor a little about how the legislative process worked. In view of Carter's remarks during the campaign, when he ran against Washington, I wanted to make sure he fully understood the difference between rhetoric and reality. But when I tried to explain how important it was for the president to work closely with Congress, he didn't seem to understand. As governor of Georgia, he had run into certain problems with the state legislature, and he assured me that if he didn't get his way with Congress, he wouldn't hesitate to do what he had done back home—which was to go over the heads of the representatives by appealing directly to the voters.

"Hell, Mr. President," I said, "you're making a big mistake. You don't mean to tell me that you're comparing the House and the Senate with the Georgia legislature? The Congress of the United States includes some of the most talented and knowledgeable lawmakers in the world. Some of them have been here for years, because the people at home have such faith in them.

"As for the younger members, you better watch out. Many of them got here by running against the Washington establishment, just like you did. A lot of the Democrats ran ahead of you in the election, and believe me, next time they won't hesitate to run *against* you." . . .

Although Carter and I came from vastly different backgrounds, we grew to appreciate each other. This took time, however, and required some adjustments on both sides. When Carter's peple came north to Washington, they just didn't understand Irish or Jewish politicians, or the nuances of city politics. The southerner is a different breed from the other pols I've known: he's a sweet talker who can skin you alive with his charm. In the North, politics is far more blunt and rambunctious. Whereas the northerner enjoys conflicts and will actually seek them out, the southerner does his best to avoid political quarrels and skirmishes.

This might explain why it took me so long to understand Carter's manner—to realize, for example, that his silence on a particular topic didn't necessarily mean acquiescence. . . .

. . . I'd give him my views, and he'd say, "I understand, I appreciate that," and I'd leave the White House under the mistaken impression that we were in agreement. A few days later, however, he would say something that made me realize that his views and mine were actually very different. Jimmy Carter was so polite and gracious that he was often reluctant to express open disagreement. This took some getting used to, as I was accustomed to dealing with politicians who told you straight out when they thought you were wrong. . . .

The first time Millie and I visited the Carters in the White House, we had barely sat down to dinner when the president wanted to hear all about James Michael Curley. Then he asked about some of the other political leaders I have known. I told a few stories, including one about a frank exchange between President Jack Kennedy and Speaker Sam Rayburn. Kennedy had wanted to know the terrible things that members of Congress were saying about him, and Mr. Sam dutifully went down the list, starting with the complaint that Kennedy had forgotten his early supporters.

"They won't say that about me," said Jimmy Carter with a grin. "I've brought all of mine up here with me."

That was true enough, but it was nothing to laugh about. After eight years of Republican rule, Jimmy Carter rode into town like a knight on a white horse. But while the gentleman leading the charge was capable, too many of the troops he brought with him were amateurs. They didn't know much about Washington, but that didn't prevent them from being arrogant.

Too many of Carter's people—especially Hamilton Jordan, the president's top aide—came to Washington with a chip on their shoulder and never changed. They failed to understand that the presidency didn't operate in a vacuum, that Congress was fundamentally different from the Georgia legislature, and that we intended to be full partners in the legislative process.

. . . Carter's people assumed that because they had succeeded in capturing the White House, they had Washington all figured out. . . .

. . . [D]uring the Carter years, congressional Democrats often had the feeling that the White House was actually working against us. Once, when the city of Boston applied for a government grant for some new roads, I called the Carter people to try to speed it along. Instead of assisting me, however, they did everything possible to block my way. When it came to helping out my district, I actually received more cooperation from Reagan's staff than from Carter's. . . .

I must have told Carter about his inadequate staff a dozen times or more, but he never acted on my complaints. . . .

It was the greatest frustration of my career: we had a chance to accomplish so much, but the White House simply wouldn't cooperate. . . .

One member of the White House staff whom I did respect was Stuart Eizenstat, who was responsible for preparing domestic legislative proposals and for keeping an eye on the various bills being considered by Congress. I had great admiration for Stu's abilities, and the members of Congress certainly appreciated him. But we always had the feeling that he wasn't fully accepted into Carter's inner circle. . . .

From Carter's own perspective, his key staff member was Hamilton Jordan. In an ideal world, the president's top aide and the Speaker of the House work hand in hand to carry out the legislative goals of the administration. But in the real world of the Carter administration, we barely spoke to each other. . . .

To Jordan and his pals on the White House staff, Tip O'Neill represented the old way of doing things, which was precisely what their candidate had run against. I could live with that, because I took it for granted that their anti-Washington talk was merely campaign rhetoric that would fade away after the election. But I was wrong. They really believed these things. . . .

All things considered, I expected a more liberal President Carter than we got. He was progressive on foreign affairs and human rights, but on economic issues he was still a lot more conservative than I was. It was Reagan who promised to get government off our backs, but it was actually the Carter administration that initiated deregulation in banking, railroads, trucking, airlines, and oil.

And it was Carter who alerted the country to the problems of the federal deficit, back when it was only a fraction of what it grew to be under Reagan. . . . Carter was able to cut the deficit from $79 billion in 1976 to $27 billion in 1979. By the standards of the Reagan era . . . this was practically a balanced budget.

. . . He [Carter] believed . . . that the modern presidency has become overly imperial. Carter's moral zeal was admirable, but morality and intelligence are not enough in politics. You also need a third ingredient—political style—and this, as I say, is what Carter lacked in Washington.

With the best of intentions, Carter went too far in his attempt to portray himself and the administration as "just plain folks." . . . To make the presidency appear more accessible, he banned the playing of "Hail to the Chief" by the Marine Corps Band. . . .

What Carter failed to understand is that the American people love kings and queens and royal families. They *want* a magisterial air in the White House, which explains why the Kennedys and the Reagans were far more popular than the four first families who came in between. The fact is that most people prefer a little pomp in their presidents.

Of Carter's various misguided attempts to cut down on "frills," the worst move of all was his decision to get rid of the *Sequoia,* the presidential yacht. Eisenhower used to have congressmen and senators down for a drink on that boat, and so did Johnson and Kennedy. More than any of the other trappings of power, the *Sequoia* provided a unique opportunity for the president to spend a relaxed couple of hours socializing and talking business with small groups of legislators in a serene and friendly environment. In such a setting, Jimmy Carter could have been enormously persuasive. He and Rosalynn were charming and gracious hosts, and if somebody had only arranged a few evenings on that yacht with the right people, the president could have accomplished far more on Capitol Hill than he actually did. . . .

Ultimately, a president is judged by the legislation he initiates, and this is where Carter's political problems came home to roost. The first legislative item on his agenda—and by far the most important—was energy. . . .

The energy problem had been with us since 1973, when the oil embargo following the Arab-Israeli war threw us into a panic. Four years later, we had done nothing to solve this problem, which was steadily growing worse. At the time of the embargo, for example, we were importing one-third of our oil. In 1977, when Carter came in, we were importing *half* our oil—approximately nine million barrels a day. It was amazing, but we were the only developed nation without an energy policy.

It was clear to the president that our available supplies of gas and oil would not last forever. It was also clear that it was dangerous for us to be so reliant on foreign sources of energy—as we learned all too well during the subsequent crisis with Iran. Fortunately, the solution was equally clear: we had to find ways to conserve more energy, generate more domestic production, and discover alternative sources of new energy. . . .

On February 2, 1977, less than a month after he was inaugurated, Jimmy Carter gave his first speech about energy. To drive the message home, he wore a cardigan sweater and spoke from the White House library, in front of a fireplace. . . .

That night, the president spoke about the importance of energy conservation. The words of his speech were terrific, but Jimmy Carter was never very effective as a communicator. People were amused by the sight of their president in a sweater, but it wasn't enough to get them to change their behavior. . . .

The president tried again in his address to the nation on April 18, when he referred to the energy crisis as "the moral equivalent of war," and "the greatest challenge our country will face in our lifetime."

After the speech, I went up to congratulate him. "That was a fine address, Mr. President," I said. "Now here's a list of members you should call to keep the pressure on, because we'll need their votes."

"No," he replied, "I described the problem to the American people in a rational way. I'm sure they'll realize that I'm right."

I could have slugged him. Did he still think he was dealing with the Georgia legislature?

"Look," I said, trying to control my frustration. "This is politics we're talking about here, not physics. We need you to push this bill through."

"It's *not* politics," he replied. "Not to me. It's simply the right thing, the rational thing. It's what needs to be done."

He was right in theory but wrong in practice. It was true that his energy plan was a rational response to a real crisis. But the president just didn't understand how to motivate Congress. The textbooks all say that Congress reflects the will of the people, and, over time, that's true. But it doesn't happen overnight. Sometimes the people are slow to catch on, and Congress has to take the lead.

The way the president goes to Congress is not always by going to the people. It's also by communicating directly with the members.

The energy package that was sent over by the Carter White House was so enormous and complex that I took one look at it and groaned. What the president and his staff failed to understand was that their legislation would be taken up by as many as *seventeen* different committees and subcommittees of the House, and that each of these committees included members who opposed certain parts of the package. I shuddered to think what would be left of the bill when it was all over—assuming we managed to get any of it through.

Forget it, I thought, as I leafed through the five volumes of legislation, each one the size of a telephone directory. This bill was going to pit one region of the country against another. A representative from Maine or New Hampshire would certainly see things very differently than his colleagues from Texas, Oklahoma, or Louisiana would.

And that was just the tip of the iceberg. . . .

Everyone knows the old saying that politics is the art of the possible, but this one looked hopeless to me. And under the existing structure of congressional committees, there really *was* no way.

Unless, of course, we changed the existing structure. . . .

The only way to score on this play was to make an end run around the existing committees of jurisdiction, and the only way to do *that* was to create a whole new committee just for this bill. I checked with Bill Brown, the House parliamentarian, who said that although it was a little unorthodox, there was no reason it couldn't be done. . . .

On the other hand, the relevant House committees and their chairmen would be furious if we simply ignored them. So we worked out a compromise—that the new committee would not be empowered to initiate legislation. Instead, we took the bill, divided it up, and sent it to the respective committees of jurisdiction, including Interstate and Foreign Commerce, Ways and Means, and the Subcommittee on Energy and Power. The package would then come back to the ad hoc committee, which had the right to suggest amendments. . . .

As soon as I named the [members of the ad hoc committee], I called in all the Democrats. "You've got to move fast," I told them, "and I'll be biting your ass to make sure you keep going. Remember, I selected you people from over a hundred and fifty applicants. My reputation, our party's reputation, and the reputation of the Congress are all tied up with this legislation. You've got to get it out.

"Now I realize that each of you is opposed to some part of this bill. And I appreciate how much you're concerned about its effect on your own region. Believe me, nobody understands that better than I do. But this is an emergency, and you've got to think in terms of the national interest."

As the package moved forward, President Carter kept coming up with new ideas. We'd get part of the bill taken care of, and then he'd issue another recommendation. Carter was a great idea man, but he didn't always appreciate the difficult process of moving a bill through the House. Even with the new structure, it was a mighty struggle.

The final vote came on August 5, 1977, less than four months after the process had begun, when the president's energy package passed the House by a vote of 244 to 177. The bill succeeded for a number of reasons, but one key element was that I had managed to put the right people together to work it all out.

Unfortunately, the energy bill ran into big problems in the Senate, where two of the most influential Democrats, Russell Long of Louisiana and Henry Jackson of Washington, had strong differences of opinion, not only with the White House, but also with each other. It took more than a year before it was finally passed by the Senate, where it was watered down considerably, thanks to aggressive lobbying on the part of the auto and oil industries. The president wasn't too pleased about the bill he finally got, but as I told him more than once, he was damn lucky to have one at all. . . .

[M]y first run-in with Carter's White House staff took place the day before the president was inaugurated. So I suppose it's fitting that our last feud came on election day, 1980, as Jimmy Carter was being defeated by Ronald Reagan. Here, too, the problem concerned the White House's lack of regard for Congress—only this time it was not merely symbolic.

On November 4, by seven-thirty in the evening, the television networks were projecting a Reagan victory. A few minutes later, Frank Moore called to ask me to join the president as he made his concession speech.

"Don't let him concede *now*," I said. "It could cost us some seats."

My mind was on the western states, where the polls would remain open for another two hours. . . .

Because the western states still had three hours left to vote, I begged Frank Moore not to let the president concede so early. A few minutes later, he called back to tell me the decision had already been made. I was livid. The President had nothing to gain by giving up now, while some of our guys were still involved in tough fights. As it turned out, James Corman from Van Nuys, California, lost his seat by only a few hundred votes; if the president hadn't conceded early, Jim would have won. . . .

. . . [T]o this day I'm angry at the Carter people for allowing the president to make an early concession. I really lost my temper that night. "You guys came in like a bunch of jerks," I told Frank Moore, although I used a more colorful expression, "and I see you're going out the same way."

In his memoirs, Carter acknowledged that his early concession may have been a mistake. But he didn't want to come off as a bad loser, as Reagan's victory was already painfully clear. Looking back, it's hard to blame him, for how often in our history has an incumbent president been defeated so decisively?

I miss Jimmy Carter. With his intelligence and energy, and his tremendous moral strength, he could have been a great leader. But talent isn't enough, and raw power won't do it either. As Carter found out the hard way, even the president of the United States needs all the help he can get.

9 The Bureaucracy

The federal bureaucracy is the part of American national government that is hardest to understand. This obscurity arises from a number of factors. First, the extensiveness of what the federal bureaucracy does affects our understanding of it. The federal bureaucracy is involved in too many diverse and unrelated activities—ranging from AIDS research conducted by the Centers for Disease Control to mail delivery by the U.S. Postal Service—to permit any simple explanation of what it is or does.

Second, our understanding of the bureaucracy is hindered by the derogatory image we as citizens have of it. The word "bureaucracy" conjures up an image of a "red-tape-bound set of civil servants, inefficient, negative, bored, impolite, and unhelpful to citizens seeking services" and information from government (Fesler and Kettl 1991, 3).

Third, our understanding of the federal bureaucracy is impaired by our tendency to speak and think about it as if it were one enormous, monolithic structure. But the federal bureaucracy is actually a conglomeration of many bureaucracies that include the fourteen executive, or cabinet, departments, a multitude of independent executive branch agencies (such as the Peace Corps and the Environmental Protection Agency), a number of independent regulatory commissions (such as the Interstate Commerce Commission and the Federal Trade Commission), various government corporations (such as the Tennessee Valley Authority and the Federal Deposit Insurance Corporation), and literally hundreds of small boards, foundations, endowments, and special presidential commissions.

To understand what the federal bureaucracy is, we must first overcome our misconceptions of it. We can begin by defining what public or government bureaucracies are. Public bureaucracies are complex organizations created by law, vested with the legal authority to implement government programs, and staffed with political appointees in upper managerial positions and permanent career civil servants in lower-level positions. Government bureaucracies possess certain characteristics similar to those of other bureaucracies, such as large corporations. Government bureaucracies are usually hierarchies. There is a ranking of roles and a system of status that provide for an identifiable chain of command. In theory, information flows upward to those with higher rank within the organization. Command and direction flow downward to subordinates. In addition, public bureaucracies are normally characterized by a division of labor emphasizing specialization and expertise. Government bureaucracies also rely a great deal on formal written communication, or what is derogatorily called "red tape." Taken together, these characteristics are intended to promote rational and efficient decision making by government bureaucracies on matters that fall within their assigned responsibility.

It is the responsibility of the various federal bureaucracies to implement the public policies formulated and adopted by Congress and the authoritative directives of presidents and the federal courts. The very presence of federal bureaucracies testifies to the fact that government policies are not self-implementing. All of them must be put into effect by some organizational structure or bureaucracy.

Implementation is a multidimensional process. It involves a number of different functions such as initiating and developing public policy, delivering government services and benefits, making rules and regulations affecting the private economic and social behavior of individuals, deciding whether private citizens and groups have complied with federal laws and regulations or have been improperly awarded or denied government services and benefits, and evaluating programs to determine whether they are having their intended impact (Patterson 1990, 521–524). To carry out these functions, the federal bureaucracies must engage in a variety of activities, including acquiring resources such as the personnel necessary for implementing public policies, interpreting the often vague and broad language in statutes and authoritative directives, creating divisions within themselves to be responsible for particular policies, establishing procedures by which these divisions are to carry out their responsibilities, and extending benefits to the individuals or groups whom the policies are designed to assist (Ripley and Franklin 1986, 4–5).

The above discussion may suggest that implementation is a dry, mechanical, objective, and nonpolitical process. Indeed, from the late

1880s through the 1930s, leading scholars in public administration described a politics-administration dichotomy and expressed the belief that politics and administration could be and were separate, distinct actions. The dichotomy made politics the realm of legislators and chief executives; administration belonged to bureaucracies (Fesler and Kettl 1991, 14–15). Today, however, no one seriously maintains that politics and administration are separate. Rather, politics and administration are recognized as inevitably and inseparably linked (Shafritz 1988, 422). Similarly, public bureaucracies are recognized as political actors deeply involved in the exercise of political power. As political actors, those within the federal bureaucracies draw political power from several internal and external sources. Those sources include the bureaucrats' subject matter expertise, grants of discretionary authority by Congress, the constituencies served by the policies the bureaucracies implement, and the bureaucrats' longevity in office (Gitelson et al. 1991, 341–344; Ripley and Franklin 1988, 45–50).

An additional source of political power is a general lack of attention on the part of Congress and presidents to the implementation of public policies. Congress's participation in implementation is commonly called legislative oversight. Political scientist Joel Aberbach defines legislative oversight as "congressional review of the actions of federal departments, agencies, and commissions, and of the programs and policies they administer, including review that takes place during program and policy implementation as well as afterward" (1990, 2). Aberbach contends that in recent years congressional oversight of implementation, particularly formal hearings, has increased (Aberbach 1990, 19–47). Despite this increase, most members of Congress are rarely involved in overseeing how bureaucratic power is exercised. This is so because effective oversight is often a time-consuming, tedious activity that offers few if any political rewards. In particular, legislative oversight rarely, if ever, advances the fundamental goals of most members of Congress—reelection, constituency service, and institutional influence. In short, there are few political incentives to encourage congressional review of implementation. For most members of Congress, overseeing how bureaucracies exercise political power lacks relevance to the other aspects of their congressional careers (Bowers 1990, 56). This lack of relevance, in turn, increases the political power exercised by the federal bureaucracies.

For most contemporary presidents, how the federal bureaucracies implement public policy has also been a low priority. (The Reagan administration is an exception to this general pattern.) This lack of attention occurs despite the president's constitutional obligation to see that the laws are faithfully executed. It is particularly evident for domestic policy. Presidents give the implementation of domestic policy low priority for several reasons. First, paying attention to domestic policy implementation leaves less time for other, competing presidential obligations and responsibilities. Second, contemporary presidents generally have been more interested in foreign policy and feel better able to make an impact in that area than on domestic policy. Third, as with members of Congress, for the president there are few political incentives to focus on implementation. Focusing on the formulation and passage of legislation is always more politically visible and gratifying than focusing on the nitty-gritty of implementation. Presidents also are aware that they will receive little credit if public policies are implemented effectively because it is difficult to attribute successful implementation to any one individual (Edwards and Wayne 1990, 251).

The political power exercised by the federal bureaucracies is problematic for our constitutional democracy. Bureaucratic power combines and concentrates legislative, executive, and judicial authority in the federal bureaucracies. In so doing, bureaucratic power brings together what the framers of the Constitution intended to keep somewhat apart through the separation of powers. In particular, they sought to separate the different government authorities to prevent tyrannical government. As James Madison noted in "Federalist Paper 47," "the accumulation of all powers, legislative, executive, and judicial, in the same hands, whether of one, a few, or many . . . may justly be pronounced the very definition of tyranny" (Rossiter 1961, 324). To prevent a form of bureaucratic tyranny from evolving, the federal bureaucracies must be made to exercise their political power in a responsible manner. Getting bureaucracies to behave responsibly means finding ways of getting them to do well the things they ought to do and to refrain from doing what they ought not to do (Powell 1967, 8).

One way to promote responsible bureaucratic behavior is to hold the federal bureaucracies accountable to the three constitutionally recognized branches for their actions. Congress, presidents, and the federal judiciary need to oversee how the federal bureaucracies exercise their political power. But as we have already indicated, most members of Congress and most contemporary presidents have paid little attention to the implementation of public policies, even though this is the sphere of activity in which the political power of federal bureaucracies is likely to be strongest. Despite the general trend away from overseeing implementation, both the Congress and the president have available to them numerous ways to conduct oversight, if they so desire. Though the efforts of both branches of government are equally important, these introductory comments will focus on presidential means for promoting responsible bureaucracy.

In Chapter 8, we observed that contemporary presidents need to provide managerial leadership to the White House staff. The same is true for the federal bureaucracies. To make the federal bureaucracies responsible and accountable for the executive power they exercise, all contemporary presidents need an administrative strategy through which to provide presidential leadership. This strategy is an important way to guarantee that the federal bureaucracies respond to and follow presidential directives. The appointment of cabinet and subcabinet positions is one important ingredient of this administrative strategy.

The cabinet secretaries, the various assistant and deputy secretaries, and a select number of individuals from the senior executive service are the president's front-line troops and "eyes and ears" in the various federal bureaucracies. These individuals, all of whom are presidential appointees, establish the general policies for the various executive departments and oversee their daily operation. By taking seriously the task of appointing cabinet and subcabinent positions, presidents can make the federal bureaucracies more accountable to them. In his often-cited book *The Administrative Presidency*, political scientist Richard Nathan observes that in appointing individuals to these positions, presidents should recognize and accept that "political executives should be just what the name indicates—*political and executive*;" that the management of the federal bureaucracies "*can and should* be performed by partisans" (1983, 7). To promote the partisan management of the federal bureaucracies and thereby increase their accountability, presidents can consciously select presidential partisans— that is, people who hold the same policy views they do—for cabinet secretariats and subcabinet positions. Once these presidential partisans are in office, presidents can promote their continuing loyalty and partisan management of the bureaucracies by motivating them to pay attention to agency operations and administrative processes (Nathan 1983, 88; Waterman 1989, 22).

Appointing presidential partisans to cabinet and subcabinet positions may be easier said than done. Filling these positions is a truly enormous task. In his insightful book *The Ring of Power*, Bradley Patterson (1988, 240) notes that filling these cabinet and subcabinet positions requires six specific tasks: (1) job descriptions need to be prepared for each position to be filled; (2) candidates for each position need to be identified and recruited; (3) final candidates must be selected and cleared by the FBI; (4) once they are inaugurated, presidents need to open up additional noncareer positions in the federal bureaucracies;

(5) new appointees must be oriented to the national government and the "Washington community"; and (6) the performance of presidential appointees must be continually evaluated.

If all of these tasks are successfully completed, there is still no guarantee that the presidential partisans appointed to cabinet and subcabinet positions can make the federal bureaucracies accountable to the president (Waterman 1989, 30). But one thing is certain. Without a willingness on the part of contemporary presidents to administer and control bureaucratic power, this power is likely to grow and the federal bureaucracies will compete with, challenge, and possibly undermine presidential policy intentions and directives.

The two case studies presented in this chapter illustrate the power, accountability, and oversight of federal bureaucracies. "An Aborted Regulation" by Robert Reinhold is the first case study. It tells the story of the Food and Drug Administration's (FDA) ill-fated attempt to require druggists to provide consumers with basic information about prescription drugs. In telling this story, Reinhold examines rulemaking, an important administrative activity that is the functional equivalent of lawmaking. Through this discussion, "An Aborted Regulation" highlights external controls on the exercise of bureaucratic power and strongly suggests that federal bureaucracies may exercise less political power and be more responsive than they are commonly perceived to be.

The second case study, "Staffing Reagan's *Titanic*," is by former Secretary of Education Terrel Bell (from his book *The Thirteenth Man*). Bell gives a personal account of how he struggled against President Reagan's administrative strategy affecting the Department of Education. This story underscores the role cabinet and subcabinet appointments play in presidential management and oversight of the federal bureaucracies.

Suggested Reading

Kaufman, Herbert. 1981. *The Administrative Behavior of Federal Bureau Chiefs*. Washington, DC: Brookings Institution. An analysis of six bureau chiefs from various federal executive branch departments or agencies that describes their primary activities and how they go about exercising bureaucratic power.

Lewis, Eugene. 1984. *Public Entrepreneurship: Toward a Theory of Bureaucratic Political Power.* Bloomington, IN: Indiana University Press. An insightful and original study of the organizational lives of Hyman Rickover, J. Edgar Hoover, and Robert Moses with an emphasis on how the personal character and style of principal agency administrators can determine organizational behavior.

Rasnor, Dina. 1985. *The Pentagon Underground.* New York: Times Books. A compelling story of "whistle-blowers" and other hidden patriots fighting against deceit, fraud, and corruption in the U.S. Defense Department.

Rohr, John A. 1986. *To Run a Constitution: The Legitimacy of the Administrative State.* Lawrence, KS: University of Kansas Press. A generally successful attempt to build a normative theory of public administration and bureaucratic power that is grounded in the Constitution.

Rubin, Irene S. 1985. *Shrinking the Federal Government.* New York: Longman. Five interesting case studies of federal agencies that analyze the Reagan administration's first-term efforts to promote bureaucratic responsibility through cutbacks in important resources on which the federal bureaucracy depends.

Wilson, James Q. 1989. *Bureaucracy: What Government Agencies Do and Why They Do It.* New York: Basic Books. An in-depth study of what government agencies do, why they behave as they do, and how they might be made more effective.

An Aborted Regulation

Robert Reinhold

As you read this case study, consider the following questions:

1. What is the general responsibility of the FDA?

2. How do its broad responsibilities make the FDA a "powerful but embattled agency"?

3. On what statutory authority was the FDA acting when it decided to issue regulations requiring patient package inserts?

4. What kind of political and economic issues were raised by the proposed regulations?

5. What was the public reaction to the proposed regulations?

6. How did groups such as the American Pharmaceutical Association "assault" the rules about package inserts?

7. What action did the Carter White House and Congress take against the regulations?

8. What impact did presidential and congressional involvement have on the proposed regulations, and how did this involvement affect the final version of the regulations?

9. Why and how did the Reagan administration reopen the seemingly resolved issue of patient package inserts?

10. What was the outcome of the Reagan administration's interest in these regulations?

From *American Politics and Public Policy: Seven Case Studies,* Allan P. Sindler (Ed.). Copyright © 1982 by CQ Press. Reprinted by permission.

•   •   •   THIS IS THE STORY OF HOW ONE NEW REGULATION WAS HAMMERED OUT. IF IT IS AT ALL TYPICAL, IT DOES NOT SUPPORT the widespread notion of an overbearing federal bureaucracy, heedless of anything but its own petty interests. If anything, the process of writing this regulation was excruciatingly slow, a process marked by vacillation and uncertainty on the part of the agency as it tried to steer its way through three administrations and several agency directors, as well as changing moods in Congress and the electorate. The final product bore little resemblance to its original proposal. However, the story of how this regulation was shaped, pounded, twisted, and squeezed is not one of misdeeds or backroom dealing. Rather it is the sometimes dull—but highly important—story of how government really works, how different interest groups bring their power and information to bear on the process, how federal agencies respond to changing political realities.

The issue in question here concerns the efforts of the Food and Drug Administration to require that druggists hand out little flyers to buyers of prescription drugs to give patients some basic layman's information on how best to use the drug and to warn of its dangers. The notion was first pushed by consumer groups at a time when they held greater sway than they do today. As simple and desirable as the notion of providing patients with more information about their treatment might sound at first blush, the proposal raised a host of complex objections on the part of doctors, pharmacists, drugstore owners, and others. They argued—persuasively in the view of two administrations—that the priorities of "consumer" organizations were not necessarily identical with the "public interest" taken in the larger context of who is to pay for implementing the regulation.

Ultimately the agency was forced to retreat from its original proposal, which would have compelled that patient information inserts—known as "patient package inserts" or "PPIs" to the trade—be dispensed with as many as 375 drugs comprising nearly all prescriptions and refills ordered in this country. The final rule—issued in the waning days of the Carter administration in 1980—applied to only 10 drugs and drug classes covering only 16 percent of all prescriptions.

Even that was too much for the incoming Reagan administration. Riding into power on a promise to reduce the regulatory burden, the administration quickly ordered a temporary delay in implementing the rule early in 1981, and then ultimately decided to drop it altogether a year later, expressing the hope that better results could be achieved through voluntary efforts by industry and doctors.

Thus nearly a decade of work went for naught. Still, the agency won a victory of sorts, in that it forced druggists, doctors, drug makers, and others to think about an issue they had long avoided and take "voluntary" steps toward achieving what the agency wanted. Despite the official "failure" of the PPI rule, this study illustrates how an active bureaucratic organization, taking its often vague instructions from Congress, affects public policy. That the rule was eventually defeated, in the long run, is not as important as the process by which it evolved. . . .

The Background

As any consumer who has ever purchased a prescription drug knows, the container in which it comes has almost no information on the label other than instructions on how many times a day to take it and perhaps a little sticker warning against combining it with alcohol consumption. Consumer activists have long argued that because many drugs are extremely hazardous the patient has a right to know more about what he or she is taking. Ironically, over-the-counter drugs have long included little folded-up inserts on their proper use while ostensibly more potent prescription drugs have not, the rationale being that the doctor's oral instructions to the patient when writing a prescription were sufficient. But evidence has been mounting for some years that doctors often do not supply adequate information, that they are sometimes ignorant of the latest studies about drugs, and that patients easily forget what they are told.

For these and other reasons the FDA began in 1974 to investigate the issue, with a view toward new rules requiring inserts with prescription drugs. Soon after, in 1975, a coalition of consumer groups, led by the Center for Law and Social Policy in Washington, entered the picture. The center was one of a number of the many so-called "public interest" organizations that began to spring up with the rise of consumer, women's, and other movements in the 1960s. . . .

The consumer groups petitioned the FDA to require warnings on drugs that posed dangers to pregnant and nursing women, drugs such as tranquilizers that involve serious hazards, and those that have been overprescribed and have caused untoward side effects. Both the petition and the drug agency's thinking reflected an evolving medical consensus that patients should play a greater role in their own care and that doctors were prescribing too many drugs. Thus the process of writing a new regulation was begun.

FDA: Powerful but Embattled Agency

The Food and Drug Administration is a curious animal, powerful yet vulnerable in many ways, frequently derided by both industry and consumer groups. It is charged, in general, with protecting the public against unsafe and ineffective drugs, and against hazardous foods, food additives, and cosmetics. Often its decisions have major financial effects on certain industries, and thus it is as much a political as a scientific agency. Its authority under law is strong and it is widely feared among drug and food makers. In 1982, for example, it began requiring makers of infant formula to test the nutritional quality of their products throughout the manufacturing process after one firm's product was found deficient in an essential infant nutrient; nearly three million cans were ordered recalled. And when it began to make noises about requiring makers of processed foods to list sodium content on their labels, to help people on low-salt diets, companies such as Campbell's Soup began to market a low-sodium line and label its regular products as a means of warding off more draconian regulation. For all that, the FDA has had uneven relations with Congress and it has often been politically naive. Its scientific competence has often been questioned. Nevertheless, with every new case of botulism poisoning or a failed drug, Congress invests the agency with new authority.

The agency, in this case, was not acting to implement a new law. Rather it was moving on what it believed was its statutory authority under a series of existing laws dating back to 1906. In that year, the Pure Food and Drug Act began the government's efforts to control fraudulent and deceptive drug claims. The FDA's early regulatory actions were aimed at nostrums such as "Sporty Days Invigorator," claimed to cure "male weakness," and a headache remedy called "Curforhedake Brane-Fude." The Food, Drug and Cosmetic Act of

1938 (with subsequent amendments) significantly strengthened the FDA's hand, but the agency's regulations over the years chose to exempt prescription drugs from the usual labeling requirements as long as the manufacturer provided detailed information to physicians. Under the law, the FDA's power was limited to drug makers and druggists and it had no authority to order doctors to do anything. Thus its efforts to promote patient education had to be worked through that route.

As it began the PPI project in 1974, the FDA felt it already had the authority to order the inserts under laws that authorized it to prohibit the "misbranding" of drugs. A drug was considered misbranded, under law, it if failed to "reveal facts that are material in light of representations made in the labeling or material with respect to consequences that may result from the use of the product under customary or usual conditions of use," in the FDA's words. In fact, the FDA, using this argument, had already ordered PPIs in a few isolated instances. . . .

While the stated purpose of PPIs—to enhance the safe and effective use of drugs—could hardly be disputed, the issue raised other troubling concerns. On the one hand, it seemed like a straightforward way of informing patients of the risks and benefits of the drugs they take. But some doctors said it represented an insidious indirect means of increasing government control over the practice of medicine and an unwarranted interference with the doctor-patient relationship. . . .

A full-scale PPI program . . . raised the possibility of significantly altering the practice of medicine and pharmacy in the United States. In 1976, the Department of Health, Education and Welfare (HEW) reported that about 42 percent of all office visits to doctors ended with the patient leaving with a prescription to fill. A national prescription audit conducted in 1977 for the pharmaceutical industry found that American doctors wrote 1.4 billion new and refill prescriptions annually. Very important questions were being raised, then, about whether all these prescriptions were really needed, whether doctors were telling their patients all they needed to know about the drugs, whether doctors themselves knew all they needed to know about the drugs, and whether patients were complying with their regimens.

Beyond all these philosophical issues, money also played a role. While proponents believed the PPIs would ultimately save billions in unnecessary medical costs and consumer expenses, detractors argued that the rule would cost hundreds of millions to implement without any compelling proof that it would have any substantial beneficial effect.

It was no wonder, then, that this seemingly innocuous proposal struck some raw nerves.

Evolution of the Regulation

It was against this backdrop that the FDA's Patient Prescription Drug Labeling Project wrestled with the problem. The project was headed by an affable young psychologist from Brooklyn, Louis Morris, who had come to the agency after taking a Ph.D. at Tulane, where he studied the placebo effects of drugs on patients. He was soon to learn that the hardball world of Washington politics bore little resemblance to the polite academic world of science and objective facts.

On November 7, 1975, the FDA published one of those turgid gray notices in the *Federal Register* saying that it was considering requiring PPIs generally, and inviting comments. It received more than 1,000—from consumers, doctors, druggists, and professional organizations. It also commissioned studies of the issue and sponsored conferences and symposia in conjunction with the American Medical Association (AMA) and the Pharmaceutical Manufacturers Association (PMA). It reviewed all the scientific literature on the value of PPIs. All of this was necessary to meet any later challenge claiming that the agency had not given full consideration to the implications of its actions. But even before the agency made up its mind on a full-blown program, trouble began brewing when it issued an estrogen PPI rule in 1978. Morris explained in an interview:

> That started to bring out a lot of the professionals against PPIs. The estrogen insert was frightening to people—it stressed the risks, and it was very difficult to read. It was a fear-inducing document, written by doctors at the FDA. Estrogen sales were cut in half. That's what we wanted. But unfortunately the message in the insert was one of fear. We could have written it a lot clearer.

Despite this harbinger of trouble, the FDA plunged ahead. . . .

Thus on Friday, July 6, 1979, a dry notice appeared in the *Federal Register* announcing a "proposed rule." The rule would have required inserts for 375 of the most widely prescribed of the 5,000 prescription drugs on the market. It proposed to phase in the plan over several years, starting with about 50 to 75 drugs and drug classes the first year. . . . The notice stated:

> This action is being taken because the FDA believes that prescription drug labeling that is directed to patients will promote the safe and effective use of prescription drug products and that patients have a right to know about the benefits, risks, and directions for use of the products.

Further, the proposal stated, "It became obvious to FDA that physicians had neither the time nor the facilities to investigate carefully each product to determine its proper uses" and that the information drug companies were already compelled to provide to doctors and pharmacists "did not affect the information required to be given to patients, which remained minimal."

Finally, brushing aside the numerous objections, the proposal declared: "FDA has now determined that new information demonstrates that for the safe and effective use of prescription drug products more information about products must also be provided to patients."

The rule would have required drug makers to prepare and distribute through pharmacies a leaflet written in nontechnical and nonpromotional language. It would list, among other things, the proper uses of the drug, circumstances under which it should not be used, and possible side effects. It would have to be given to all drug buyers, except those deemed legally incompetent, whose primary language was not English, or who were blind, whose doctors directed the insert withheld, patients in emergency treatment, and institutionalized persons.

Response and Reaction

The response was not entirely what the FDA might have hoped for. "The response was very emotional," recalls Morris. "The industry and other opponents really got together. They say it was a major issue. I learned a lot of politics. At the time I felt paranoid, but that's the way things are done. I was very depressed—we took a lot of grief." The trade press began to be sprinkled with damaging items about the FDA. Druggist groups, doctors, drug makers, and others began to write letters to members of Congress. The proposal elicited about 1,300 written comments, not all of them unfavorable, and other reactions were expressed at hearings held in three cities.

In all these preliminaries, required before a regulation takes effect, the FDA may have been its own worst enemy. Given the antiregulatory mood of the country at the time, it did something its officials now admit was naive. The proposed rule was advanced before the agency had done an economic analysis of whether the benefits of implementing the rule were worth the costs, or had examined if there were any cheaper alternatives that would achieve the same end. "We failed to protect where we were most vulnerable—on the economic side," said Morris. "We put out the regulation and then did the cost-benefit analysis. It did not have the documentation it should have had. We found out what concerned people most was the economics. How naive of us.''

Naive indeed. With its soft underbelly thus exposed, the FDA ventured bravely into battle. Daggers were drawn at almost every turn. With the battle lines thus formed the arguments for and against the inserts came into sharp focus.

Arguments For: Proponents advanced the concept as a partial solution to a number of problems surrounding the prescribing and use of prescription drugs, which had increased fourfold since 1950. They argued that, given simple and accurate written information about the drugs they were taking, patients would make safer and more effective use of those products. One main argument held that patients either did not pay attention to or forgot what their doctors told them. Numerous scientific studies have shown that ''noncompliance'' by patients is extremely high and causes many medical problems. Patients frequently fail to space their doses properly, skip doses, take extra doses, or fail to complete the ordered regimen. . . .

In addition, many argued that the prescribing practices of doctors left something to be desired. Some maintained that doctors, out of ignorance or laziness, have come to rely too heavily on issuing prescriptions, particularly for antibiotics and tranquilizers. Also, critics say, they tend to get much of their information from drug company representatives with a financial interest in pushing one drug or another. . . .

The large number of untoward side effects of drugs was another argument made for PPIs. . . .

Finally, there was the philosophical argument that the patient has the ''right to know'' about his or her treatment. The FDA advanced several opinion surveys showing that people, particularly the better educated, wanted more information about their medications and wanted to play a larger role in their own health care. . . .

Arguments Against: While most people generally agreed that the more information the patient had the better, numerous doubts cropped up. Many doctors complained that the inserts would damage their relationships with the patients, that patients would be alarmed by the information and ask a lot of unnecessary questions, wasting the doctor's valuable time. The doctors feared that patients might rely solely on the inserts, possibly altering the doctor's instructions and even discontinuing the medication.

Both pharmacists and doctors also raised the possibility that the inserts might affect patients psychologically, causing them to develop side effects and adverse reactions merely through suggestion. Or, conversely, they said accurate information might inhibit the desired placebo effect that doctors sometimes strive for. And what about the cancer patient, whose illness has been kept secret for therapeutic reasons, who reads that he or she is taking an anticancer drug?

Druggists and drug makers complained that the inserts, insofar as they constituted warnings, would subject them to more damage and liability suits. And the druggists said they would be forced to respond to many questions from worried customers. . . .

Further, the critics argued that the FDA did not have conclusive evidence that the PPIs would do what they were supposed to do, that any substantial number of people would read and heed them. Nor, they argued, did the FDA know for sure that lack of information was the underlying reason for noncompliance and other problems the inserts were meant to correct. . . .

But the most strident objections were neither philosophical nor medical, but economic. The FDA estimated that the proposal would cost about $90 million a year to implement, adding only about 6.3¢ to the cost of the average prescription. All wrong, declared the opponents. Druggists, drugstore owners, and drug makers said the FDA had grossly underestimated the costs—all of which would be passed on to the consumer, of course. The druggists said they would have to redesign their stores to build huge pigeonhole racks to hold the little flyers, hire extra help to fumble with them, and otherwise alter their operations to cope with the new rules. The American Pharmaceutical Association (APhA), representing 55,000 pharmacists, calculated that the cost would amount to $235 million for the first year and possibly as much as $1.8 billion over five years. The National Association of Retail Druggists, representing 33,000 independent pharmacy owners who fill 70 percent of all prescriptions, came up with a figure of $250 million for the first year and $100 million to $150 million for each subsequent year. The National Association of Chain Drug Stores, to which 194 chains belong, put the price at $312 million to $532 million a year. And Eli Lilly, a leading drug maker, estimated that the cost to manufacturers alone would run about $140 million annually.

The Lobbying Assault

Armed with this and other ammunition, the industry began a concerted lobbying effort soon after the proposed rules were issued in July of 1979. One of the leaders was the American Pharmaceutical Association. . . .

. . . [T]he PPI proposal was perceived as a formidable threat by the druggists. As any cub lobbyist knows, there are many ways to skin a cat—or in this case a rule—and the APhA and other critics mounted a broad attack. Their leaders and lobbyists met with top FDA officials, including the new commissioner, Dr. Goyan, who took over shortly after the proposal was published. They asked their members to write letters to key legislators, and had their affiliated state associations lobby local members of Congress. They consulted with other interest groups that were sympathetic, like the American Medical Association. And they knocked on the executive door, meeting with White House officials and lobbing missives into the Council on Wage and Price Stability (COWPS) and the Office of Management and Budget (OMB), where they found sympathetic ears. Patricia Roberts Harris, the secretary of Health, Education and Welfare at the time, got an earful about PPIs when she addressed the annual meeting of the APhA in Washington.

At the same time, the chain drugstore group was pressing its opposition. As frequent contributors to local members of Congress, local druggists and their organizations expected to be heard by their representatives, and they were. In addition, lobbyists for their national groups went to the FDA, to Alfred Kahn (then head of COWPS) and to OMB. "PPIs may scare patients," said Ty Kelley, chief lobbyist for the National Association of Chain Drug Stores. "They may come back for refunds. It would make more sense to have doctors give the information. Why burden the pharmacist with this responsibility when it should be done in the physician's office?"

The doctors, doing their own lobbying, agreed. Their representatives told Congress and the White House that PPIs might interfere with the doctor-patient relationship. "It might be alarming to the patient," said Al Faca, an AMA representative in Washington. "He may not take the drug because of it. It is our feeling that it is really the responsibility of the doctor to make the patient aware." Like the other opponents, he said he preferred a limited test before a full-scale test was begun. However, the doctors did not take the lead on this issue. . . .

Robert J. Bolger, president of the chain drugstore group, wrote to President Carter to complain of the "immense inflationary impact" of the proposal. He contended it might swell drug prices by 8 to 16 percent—at the very time, he underscored pointedly, when the Carter administration was trying to contain the growth in health care costs. The letter made some impression on the President's health advisers. Meanwhile other members of the administration were getting similar missives. Bolger declared to Kahn, the chairman of COWPS, that the proposal would plunge druggists into a "colossal paperwork jungle."

Other letters landed on the desk of James M. McIntyre Jr., powerful head of OMB. Right or wrong, these arguments were beginning to have some effect in official Washington, partly because the other side did not have the resources to mount much of a counterattack. As Kelley of the chain druggists said with a wry smile, "With the exception of a few consumer organizations, there is not much of a national outcry for this program."

Consumer Groups Weigh In, Lightly

The consumer or "public interest" proponents of PPIs were not inactive in all this, but they were outgunned. While such groups are frequently effective at stirring up issues and provoking general alarm, they do not always have the sticking power of industry. While an industry can marshall all of its resources in support or defense of a few major issues, public interest groups by their very nature must concentrate on several fronts at once. Marsha Greenberger is a lawyer for the Center for Law and Social Policy in Washington who worked on the original petition to the FDA in 1975. "The opponents have enormous resources available to them," she said in an interview. "They have gone to congressmen, the White House, they have filed lawsuits. They do have access. We have access too. But we've got limited staff. No one in the consumer movement can devote sustained and regular attention to this issue."

Drug industry lobbyists were "all over the Hill like locusts," said Fred Wegner, a lobbyist with the American Association of Retired Persons (AARP). With 12.5 million members, the association is not without its own clout. But it is only one voice, Wegner said, while the PMA, all of its member companies as well as the various druggist groups, each employ their own lobbyists, who reinforce each other. Given the amount of money drugs cost elderly people, Wegner said that he hoped PPIs would serve to advise patients of other less costly therapies. . . .

The White House Role

But voices like Wegner's were largely drowned out in the chorus of complaints, which were beginning to be taken seriously at the Carter White House. In the words of a former FDA lawyer who now represents the drug makers, the druggists "lobbed a shell into the White House compound" with an analysis of the economic consequences of the proposed regulation. The complaints struck a responsive chord with the President's Domestic Policy Staff, his science advisers, and the Small Business Administration. The only high-level ally to come to the aid of the drug agency was the President's consumer adviser, Esther Peterson.

Then, on top of all this, the proposal got "rarged" early in 1980—a Carterism meaning that the regulation was subjected to close scrutiny by a special interagency panel called the Regulatory Analysis Review Group (RARG), an arm of the Council on Wage and Price Stability. President Carter had set up the panel to review regulations with substantial economic consequences to make agencies more sensitive to the economic effects of what they did. The panel had no direct authority to alter regulations, but agencies had to respond to its inquiries and pronouncements. The panel, made up mostly of economists, tended to be sympathetic to business needs. . . .

The final RARG report took the drug agency to task, saying it had failed to consider many potential costs of the rule. Moreover, it observed, "We are troubled that FDA has not stated how the knowledge gained in its initial implementation steps will be reflected in subsequent ones." It suggested that the agency consider a limited phased-in test of the inserts rather than starting out with a full-blown program. "We call on FDA to publicly commit itself to testing and evaluation before proceeding to mandate patient labeling for all drugs." . . .

The FDA Yields

At first the agency was distressed over the "rarging." But Louis Morris, the psychologist who headed the insert project, said that the ultimate RARG report was a "reasonable" one. "The decision on how many drugs how fast is basically a political decision," he said. "The FDA welcomes advice on that."

By the fall of 1980, the leadership of the drug agency had changed hands. Dr. Kennedy had left to become provost (and later president) of Stanford University and in his place came Dr. Jere Goyan. A man of 49 years with a gentle manner, Dr. Goyan had been dean of the pharmacy school at the University of California at San Francisco. He came to the FDA job with a reputation as a champion of consumer rights.

He once described himself as a "therapeutic nihilist," and had often said that Americans were "overmedicated." He seemed to many, after some months on the job, to be somewhat out of his element in the highly charged political atmosphere surrounding the FDA.

With his reputation as a foe of overmedication, it was widely assumed that Dr. Goyan would push full-speed ahead on the PPI rule. But shortly after taking office, he surprised everybody by letting it be known that he planned to scale back the regulation to include just 10 drugs on an experimental basis. . . .

In an interview at his office in suburban Rockville, Maryland, where the FDA has its headquarters, Dr. Goyan was frank in making it clear that the political opposition to the proposal was too great to resist. . . .

Goyan also conceded that the agency "did not have good data" on the effectiveness of the inserts and that, as a professor and scientist, he thought it was logical to get a better scientific footing before moving much further. "If all we do is cut down a lot of trees and have little effect, what's the point?"

The Role of Congress

There was also a more practical reason to cut back on the number of drugs to be covered, according to Dr. Goyan. The industry lobbyists had been at work on Capitol Hill and had elicited a positive response from the House Appropriations Subcommittee on Agriculture, which handles the FDA budget. Dr. Goyan found himself under hostile questioning at a hearing of the subcommittee in March of 1980, particularly from Representative Bill Alexander, an Arkansas Democrat who had received a $250 contribution from the National Association of Chain Drug Stores Political Action Committee the year before. Minutes after Dr. Goyan testified that "I would not want to swallow a pill about which I knew nothing," Alexander extracted a promise from him that the PPI program would begin with no more than 10 drugs. . . .

Lest there be any doubts or later misunderstandings, the Appropriations Committee wrote into its report accompanying the FDA appropriations bill for the 1981 fiscal year that the agency should proceed with the insert effort "only in an orderly step-by-step manner," and should keep the committee advised of its actions. It also directed the agency to conduct pilot tests, to investigate the cost implications of the rule, and to avoid "unnecessary inflationary costs to the consumer." It added that it expected the FDA to comply with assurances that it would test no more than 10 package inserts over the next two years.

This brought a sharp protest from Henry A. Waxman, a powerful California Democrat who chaired the Health and Environment Subcommittee of the House Interstate and Foreign Commerce Committee, which handles FDA authorizations. He charged that the Appropriations Committee was using its report to undermine the legitimate authority of the FDA, and he denounced what he called "this intrusion" into the legislative jurisdiction of his committee.

Dr. Goyan indicated in the interview on the PPI issue that he feared that the Appropriations Committee would pass a bill forbidding the insert program altogether and the scaled-back scheme seemed like a politic way of getting half a loaf, or at least a few slices. "Politics is not necessarily a bad word," he said.

Behind Dr. Goyan's thinking, undoubtedly, was an awareness of the rocky recent history of FDA's dealings with Congress. And this underscores another motivation governing regulatory decisions: although it has considerable authority and is widely feared by industry, an agency like the FDA has only so much clout, so much staff time and energy. It can fight only so many battles at once. In recent years the drug agency had suffered several stinging political defeats. It had been put on the defensive repeatedly over such issues as its ban on additives like saccharin, the artificial sweetener, and sodium nitrites, used as preservatives in meats. . . .

At the time the PPI issue was before Dr. Goyan, Congress had already intervened to nullify temporarily the saccharin ban and was threatening to extend the moratorium. In short, the FDA already had enough trouble on its hands with two politically unpopular moves without opening up still another front. . . .

The "Final" Rule

And so the FDA proceeded to hammer out its final, much less ambitious, rule. Given the political stress the rule had caused, it was given the unusual—although not unheard of—treatment of a personal review by the HEW secretary, Patricia Harris. And then on September 10, at a press conference led by Secretary Harris at departmental headquarters in downtown Washington—not at the remote FDA headquarters in Rockville, which reporters always seem to have a hard time finding—the rule was announced with appropriate fanfare. It was to be a three-year pilot program involving new prescriptions for 10 drugs or drug classes. Refills were exempted from the insert requirement. Secretary Harris said the program could result in savings of $80 million in worker productivity lost to drug misuse annually. . . .

If this was the great consumer victory the secretary proclaimed it to be, it was hard to tell from the reactions. Consumer groups denounced it as inadequate, the drug makers said they thought it was terrific, and the druggists muted their grumbles. Lewis A. Engman, president of the Pharmaceutical Manufacturers Association, said the inserts would help deliver "meaningful information to the consumer," and he pledged his organization would "do all we can to help make the project a success."

Two days later, on September 12, the full rules were spelled out in 63 pages of small type in the *Federal Register.* . . .

An Unexpected Ending

All things being equal, this would now be the end of this account. . . .

But all things were not equal at that time. In November 1980, two months after the drug agency issued its "final" rule, Ronald Reagan was elected president on a platform that included the promise to roll back what he called costly, overly burdensome, and ineffective government regulations. The opponents of PPIs, having reached a reasonably satisfactory accommodation with the Carter administration, saw the opportunity to reopen the issue and force the FDA to back off even further. A survey taken by the Commerce Department found the PPI rule among the 20 most odious new or pending regulations left over by the outgoing administration—at least in the eyes of the industry.

Soon after the new administration took office in January 1981, it began to notify the drug makers that they would not have to comply with the deadlines for the inserts imposed by the Carter administration. On April 23, the new secretary of Health and Human Services, Richard S. Schweiker, announced that the FDA would conduct a "complete review of ways to provide health and safety information to consumers about drugs." And to permit this review, he said, the FDA would postpone the effective dates of the PPI pilot program. . . .

By this time, Dr. Goyan had swept out of his job as FDA commissioner along with the rest of the top Carter appointees. The new FDA commissioner was Arthur Hull Hayes, Jr., a cardiologist who had been head of the Hypertension Clinic at the Hershey Medical Center, affiliated with Pennsylvania State University. Soon after taking office, he told an interviewer: "I firmly believe that patient information about the drugs they take is terribly important. It's also important to look at any way this can be done in an effective way, [keeping] the costs commensurate with what you're doing."

The new administration called for an "in-depth" study of the PPI matter, to be headed by Dr. Hayes. He promised a decision by year's end. Thus, nearly a decade after the issue first crystallized, the FDA was back to square one, commanded to restudy an issue it had already studied, restudied, and restudied again. . . .

Meanwhile, while the Reagan administration was reconsidering, a long-awaited study of the efficacy of PPIs by the RAND Corporation was released. The study, done under a $525,000 contract from the FDA, seemed to suggest that PPIs were neither as good as their proponents suggested nor as bad as their detractors feared. It found that 70 percent of patients would indeed read the inserts. But the study also found that they did not substantially influence the way the medicine was used, nor encourage patients to return prescriptions for refunds.

Finally, under court order to announce a decision by December 24, 1981, Dr. Hayes and Secretary Schweiker issued a joint statement in late December saying they would scrap the entire proposal. But in so doing they took pains to stress that they remained solidly devoted to the notion of providing more information to patients. The question, they said, was whether it could be done better at less cost by other means. . . .

To underscore the point, Secretary Schweiker directed Dr. Hayes to set up a special Committee on Patient Education at the FDA to coordinate government efforts in this area and to stimulate private sector initiatives. . . .

And so, after years of painful labor, the regulatory system gave birth to nothing. Nevertheless, although it produced nothing tangible in the way of enforceable rules, it could be said that the entire process probably enhanced the flow of information to patients.

Staffing Reagan's Titanic

Terrel Bell

As you read this case study, consider the following questions:

1. Why does Secretary Terrel Bell draw an analogy between the *Titanic* and the Department of Education?
2. What did conservatives on the White House staff mean when they urged that the "right kind of people" be appointed to the Department of Education?
3. As a former professional educator and U.S. Commissioner on Education, how did Bell's idea of the right kind of people differ from the view held by the conservatives on the White House staff?
4. In what ways did the differing emphasis on political and professional qualifications affect the appointment of subcabinet positions in the Department of Education?
5. During the delay in finding permanent appointments for subcabinet positions, to whom did Secretary Bell turn to temporarily fill these vacancies?
6. To gain some limited currency with the "movement conservatives" on the White House staff and to break the logjam over appointments to the Department of Education, what symbolic action, unrelated to the conflict over appointments, did Bell take?
7. What finally broke the logjam over the appointments?

8. Once the movement conservatives were on board, how did they attempt to undermine and challenge Secretary Bell's management of the department?

9. Why did Bell so strongly oppose the initial appointment of the movement conservatives?

10. To what constituency other than the president was Secretary Bell trying to be responsive?

11. In your opinion, was Bell the "correct" choice to be Secretary of Education?

HAD IT BEEN WIDELY KNOWN PRIOR TO ITS FIRST CRUISE THAT THE *TITANIC* WAS DESTINED TO SINK, WOULD THIS HAVE COMPLICATED THE recruiting chores? My task in attracting quality assistant secretaries at the Department of Education was plagued by the *Titanic* syndrome. All cabinet secretaries struggled with the task of staffing in the first weeks of the new administration, but since my department was to be abolished, the problems of senior staff appointments were obviously more complex.

The president's new cabinet had to get their departments ready to govern. Each of us had to select an undersecretary and a large number of assistant secretaries, each of whom oversaw a specific unit. These units were known as subcabinets. Many of them were large and complex. . . . These were very responsible and often sensitive positions; and, given the critical nature of the programs, I wanted to select leaders on the basis of their qualifications without concern for political ideology.

The president had wisely assured his cabinet that he would not force us to employ senior staff that we did not want. The presidential edict established the setting for a protracted fight over who would serve in the subcabinets of my department. Without this insistent and unwavering position, taken early in the president's term, I would have been immediately surrounded by true believers and I would have been forced out of office in six months. However, I had veto power, and I used it.

White House ideologues urged Personnel Director Pennington James to see that I had the "right kind of people" in the key positions in my department. . . . Ed Meese, during his four years as counselor to the president, prior to his becoming U.S. attorney general, stood out as the keeper of the radical right dogma. The leaders of the extreme right quickly made their way to his West Wing office.

Meese was a confidant of Pennington James. . . . This close association made it difficult to gain clearance of any candidate who did not meet with Meese's approval, a circumstance that also gave added power to movement conservatives close to Meese.

In my effort to solve this problem of appointment of senior staff, I became acquainted for the first time with these *movement* conservatives. Being a lifelong Republican, I had worked for years with both conservatives and moderates. Those I had known were practical politicians; they would work hard for the outcomes to which they had strong commitments, but they would compromise after they had determined that the results of debate and negotiation represented the best they could expect at that particular time. The movement conservatives were scornful of compromise; and those who did so were labeled "pragmatists." To become a pragmatist by compromising rather than waging a fight to the end was a failure to keep the faith and a sign of weakness and wishy-washy convictions. . . .

The undersecretary (the number two position in a cabinet department) and all assistant secretaries are presidentially appointed, and their approval requires the advice and consent of the Senate. This situation set the stage for a bitter and protracted fight over the political versus the professional qualifications of the people proposed for these high-level positions.

When candidates for such presidentially appointed posts were under consideration, the movement conservatives would search the record to see who among them were pragmatists and who were solid conservatives with no history of deviating from the movement ideology. In ED, since they had lost the battle to put one of their own in the secretary's chair, the next best thing was to staff all the other senior staff positions with "the right people." This was a difficult goal to achieve because of that effective veto power the president had given his cabinet over appointments in their departments. Nevertheless, the movement's opposition could be formidable, and my problems were enhanced by the general belief that the department was not involved in anything worthwhile anyway. The more we suffered, the sooner we would be willing to concede defeat and fold up the entire unit. . . .

While we waited and waited for approval of the nominees whose names I had sent the White House Personnel Office, I appointed acting assistant secretaries to fill each vacancy. These came from the career civil service ranks. From my experience as commissioner of education in the old Office of Education (the E in HEW) I knew the capacities and weaknesses of many of the executive-level career people. I simply placed the appropriate person in temporary charge. I had decided that I would take my time with the administration-endorsed political appointees. I was not going to commit political suicide. The approval of the extremists being pushed on me would not only cause many difficulties, it would ultimately embarrass the President.

My first effort was to get the number two person in place. The White House proposed Loralee Kinder to be the undersecretary of education. I rejected this. She had served as a chair of the transition task force for education, many of whose proposals I vigorously disagreed with. Even more important, she lacked the education credentials to command the necessary respect of the academic community. I proposed the name of Christopher Cross. I was certain that his work as a scholar and leader in education would add to the prestige of the department. He was a Republican as well as a respected educator. I had known Chris from my HEW days during the Ford administration, and knew he would fill the post admirably. White House Personnel, still angered by my veto of Loralee Kinder, quickly rejected Chris Cross. . . .

Even under normal circumstances, the selection and ultimate confirmation of a presidential appointee are very difficult, time-consuming, and frustrating for the cabinet officer and the candidate he or she has recruited. But when a fight simmers between the White House staff and a cabinet secretary, the ensuing delay, confusion, and behind-the-scenes tactics can be discouraging to even the most dedicated. Given the determination of Ed Meese and his White House aides to stack my department and my equally fervent resolve to prevent this, it is not difficult to fathom the reasons for the inordinate delays in consummating subcabinet appointments in ED.

I lived through this experience for most of 1981. Indeed, it was late November before we started to see success in getting our presidentially appointed people confirmed by the Senate and functioning in their leadership responsibilities.

How could I fight back? We reviewed our options many times. We knew the ultimate power rested with the President, and Ed Meese and his staff had many opportunities to tell Ronald Reagan how recalcitrant I was in responding to their proposals of names to fill their key positions. Meese could walk into his office at will, while my opportunities were very limited. . . .

However, there was one appointment that seemed to me to have enough high-level White House support to merit approval. David Stockman, director of the Office of Management and Budget, suggested that the very competent Chester Finn be appointed deputy undersecretary for planning and budget in ED. Finn had served in the Nixon White House. I had known him from my Nixon–Ford years, and I knew that I could work with him. Given Stockman's support, I was hopeful that he would be the first one to break the logjam. But despite this endorsement, Finn was promptly rejected by White House Personnel because he was currently serving on the staff of Democratic Senator Pat Moynihan. . . . That was enough to do him in. I failed to win clearance for Finn.

Numerous other attempts at appointment consensus also failed. We simply could not agree on high-level people who required presidential appointment. . . .

In April 1981 I began to get inquiries from the press about my appointments to subcabinet positions. "How many have been cleared by White House personnel and sent on to the president?" The questioners knew the answer. I simply responded that I did not discuss personnel matters. But there was no doubt in their minds that I was being stonewalled at the White House personnel level.

The inquiries continued. Specific instances, including names of rejected candidates, were mentioned. This told me that White House staff members with access to the information were leaking these particulars to the press. Part of the strategy of Washington power politics is to hit your opponents with press leaks. . . .

It was clear there was a deliberate movement under way to destroy my credibility, and I had to counter it quickly and aggressively. Such political power base as I had was being drained. I had to get some appointments consummated or take some other action that would display strength, leadership, and decisiveness.

I needed an attention-getting issue unrelated to the senior staff stonewall. What could it be? I knew it had to be something of significance and also a move that would appeal to the conservative camp. I needed to win some grudging approval from at least the responsible conservatives who were close to the president and important to his power base. . . .

One evening, churning this issue over and over in my mind, I came upon just the right move. My predecessor, Shirley Hufstedler, had sent up to the Hill some regulations concerning the bilingual educa-tion act. These rules were dead wrong. I was supportive of bilingual education, but these regulations prescribed a single method of teaching. In the way they were written, neither of the other two popular and effective approaches to teaching limited-English-proficient children could be used. The federal government was way off base in dictating teaching methodology to the teachers of America. I had known that I would eventually amend those rules, but I had planned to wait until we had settled in a bit more.

I decided, in that moment of illumination, to withdraw the regula-tions immediately and have Ted Sky, acting general counsel of the department, and his staff rewrite the entire package. There had been much nationwide discussion and strong criticism of the Hufstedler ac-tion. It would help my situation to move the timetable up. . . .

. . . I called a press conference in the Horace Mann Center at the Department of Education. I issued a press statement and a fact sheet on bilingual education. I attacked the concept of government prescrip-tion of teaching methods. . . .

This action hit the evening network television news. The next morning the newspapers nationwide carried the story of my attack on bilingual education rules.

My telephone began to ring. School administration, teachers, and school board leaders congratulated me. It turned out to be the right move, and the timing could not have been better.

The following Tuesday, as I walked into the cabinet room at the White House, I received accolades from many of my colleagues. Even Ed Meese and Interior Secretary James Watt nodded their approval.

This simple action, which was ultimately going to be necessary anyway, helped my political position during those initial months when I was in a crisis period in my tenure in the cabinet. I had gained a much-needed respite from my adversaries. They did not stop, of course; the pressure simply eased for a short time. . . .

. . . [T]he bilingual issue . . . helped me only temporarily. Though I was now in the position of having gained a small amount of added prestige, the deadlock on appointments had to be resolved and the subcabinet offices filled as quickly as possible.

So in July, I enlisted the help of Craig Fuller, White House direc-tor of cabinet affairs, to get some momentum. . . .

Craig Fuller talked to Penn James several times about the need to get ED's senior staff on board. He heard White House concerns about what it felt was my rigidity about staffing. He suggested to me that it might be time for a compromise. I agreed. . . .

Ready now to compromise as Craig Fuller had suggested, I agreed
to accept a movement conservative to see whether my proposals might
find a reciprocal acceptance, and I approved Daniel Oliver to be the
general counsel for the Department of Education. Dan was a lawyer,
though most recently he had served as senior editor of the conservative journal, *National Review.*

After he joined ED's senior staff, I had agreement on my candidate,
Dr. Vincent Reed, former superintendent of schools for the District
of Columbia, to serve as assistant secretary for elementary and secondary education. Vincent was a moderate Republican and a well-known
educator in the nation's capital. . . .

The Oliver appointment broke the logjam, and we moved ahead
on appointments. There was never a verbal or a written agreement
on trading, but I knew I had to have experienced administrators who
were thoroughly familiar with the education programs under their
direction in the line positions. Whenever I agreed to an interview with
one of the opposition's key candidates I would emphasize my need
for specific educators, highly respected in academe, in these positions.
Nonetheless, I was apprehensive about the ideologues I had agreed
to, for I realized I was bringing potential trouble into ED. . . .

Not long after the impasse over senior appointments in ED was
broken, the people from the movement realized that they had allowed
control of the federal financial assistance programs to schools and colleges to slip through their fingers. The secretary, undersecretary, and
most of the assistant secretaries who controlled education program
dollars were not movement conservatives. I had deliberately put experienced educators in charge of grants and daily contacts with the
nationwide educational community. But the movement people could
be found in ample number in high-level support-staff positions such
as that of general counsel, in the budget and management offices, in
educational research posts, and in regional office liaison, all posts in
which they could monitor much that went on in the department and
raise questions based on the facts they garnered.

Dan Oliver, general counsel; Edward Curran, director of NIE;
Charles Heatherly, departmental executive secretary; Robert Billings,
chief of our regional office liaison unit; Donald Seneese, assistant
secretary for the Office of Educational Research and Evaluation; and
several other movement people in lesser positions made up the roster
of conservatives in ED when staffing was finally concluded. Some
members of this group started holding weekly Wednesday luncheon
meetings. I had my own infiltrator in their ranks, a high-ranking conservative in whom they had misplaced their trust. He was one of them,

but he was also my friend. From this source I learned that I would soon begin to feel the pressure of a carefully planned campaign to force me out of office. Failing that, the Wednesday luncheon participants planned to strangle the infant Department of Education through actions that attacked those presidentially appointed subcabinet members who worried them. They also planned to discredit the programs of financial assistance to students, schools, and colleges. Those who were on my senior staff fed information and copies of issue papers to their fellow true believers and supplied leaks to the press as part of their campaign.

The Wednesday group was well situated to execute its plans because its members were so well placed in influential positions in OMB, the Justice Department, and the West Wing that it was easy to keep the heat on me. . . .

The ultraconservatives who had been placed in my department had ample opportunity to find horror stories if one looked at our operations from their perspective. . . .

Edward Curran, director of the National Institute of Education, found numerous programs in NIE to criticize. Since he was a member of the movement, he discussed many ills in the research program inherited from the Carter days with his fellow conservatives. . . .

. . . [Curran] decided that he was the head of an organization that was wasting money, doing no good, and should be abolished. Curran knew that under the federal act that created the Department of Education, only the secretary had the authority to change or abolish certain units within it, and NIE was one of these; but I was determined to give the institute the chance to prove its worth. Curran knew that too. . . .

When he decided that NIE should be abolished, he did not choose to discuss it with me. He wrote directly to the president, and he "forgot" to send me a copy. His letter said his institute was wasting money and doing no good and that the federal government had no role in education research. It ended with a plea that NIE be abolished.

The letter was a very clever piece of strategy. The word *abolish* was the most popular verb associated with ED. Since it appeared that I was not moving decisively to abolish the entire department, my director of NIE would nudge me along the way by asking the President to do what he knew I would not do.

I was furious, of course, when Dick Darman, deputy to Chief of Staff Jim Baker, referred the letter to me for review and comment. True to Washington's tradition, the letter was also leaked to the press. The cynics who specialize in cabinet watching started speculating what I would do. . . .

. . . It did not take me long to decide on my course of action, though I could not be certain of the outcome. The challenge to my authority had to be met firmly, without equivocation. Since the Curran letter was transmitted to me without a request for my recommendation to the president, I gave Darman a quick, direct response: . . . I wanted Curran fired.

Curran was presidentially appointed, so such an action had to be taken at the White House. This would be a test for the president and his senior staff. It would be especially hard for Ed Meese to accede to the dismissal of a loyal conservative. . . .

Personnel Chief Penn James called to ask if I was convinced this was the best course of action. Some advisors in the department and one good friend over at the White House suggested it might be more prudent to reprimand Curran and then keep him. I was not about to do that. In the Washington game of chicken you don't blink. This was likely to be only the first of such confrontations.

My executive assistant and chief of staff, Elam Hertzler, sized the matter up when he said: "You can't let Ed get away with this trick. From my phone calls I can tell you that the education community is watching this one to see what you'll do."

"I don't have any choice but to demand Curran's resignation, . . . They want me to reconsider, however."

"Don't do it. Stick to your guns," Hertzler advised.

"What if they refuse?" Sharon Schonhaut asked. Sharon was the other professional staff member who served in the immediate office of the secretary. . . .

"I will go directly to the president. I'll explain the situation in detail. Then I'll resign if he doesn't support me. But that should never go out of this room. I've learned that you never threaten to resign. You either go or you stay."

Sharon was startled. "You mean you'd quit your cabinet job just over this?"

"There is no way that Curran can stay on as director of NIE after it's widely known that he wrote directly to the president and told him the mission of NIE was unnecessary," I told her.

That afternoon I received a phone call from Craig Fuller of the Office of Cabinet Affairs. "Ted, if you need to see the president, just let me know," Craig offered. . . .

"I don't think that this matter needs to get into the Oval Office. At least, not just yet," I said. . . .

To my relief and great pleasure, the decision to fire Ed Curran, or at least to transfer him out of ED to another position, came shortly after my conversation with Craig Fuller. Jim Baker let me know that I would receive full support from the White House. This meant that the Baker side had won, and Meese was not going to see the matter go to the president. . . .

Following the Curran episode I began to feel the full heat of the movement's anger. They continued to receive inside information on virtually everything that went on in ED, and my often unhappy tenure became even more so. After the removal of Curran, I had to propose a new name for NIE director, but in the interim I named Bob Sweet to serve as acting director. (I had no choice, since the deputy director was the only other presidentially appointed official at NIE.) But Sweet used this opportunity to launch his own campaign to be appointed permanently. I received phone calls, letters from senators, and even assurances that the appointment of Sweet would heal all my wounds with the far right.

I knew that Bob was not the right person to head up NIE because he lacked strong credentials in educational research. But my choice also had to have a long history of support for Reagan, if he or she was to win White House approval.

Fortunately I found just the right person. He was Hispanic. He had a record of Reagan support going back to the Ford-Reagan fight for the nomination in 1976. Dr. Manuel Justiz, professor of education at the University of New Mexico, was my choice for this hot spot.

The administration was being criticized for its failure to place minority candidates in top positions. . . . We were particularly deficient in senior-level Hispanic appointees. The president had been popular with Hispanics in the 1980 election, but we needed to do some fence-mending. . . .

I sent Dr. Justiz's name over to the White House, and there were immediate phone calls from the Baker faction praising the choice as a master stroke. The Meese contingent would have trouble opposing such a well-qualified Republican candidate.

The nomination was quickly approved at the White House, and his name was sent up to the Senate for confirmation. But to my surprise, this ideal choice generated opposition in the Senate. The chief source was from Bob Sweet's home state of New Hampshire. His senator, Humphrey, put an immediate hold on the Justiz nomination, and his name languished in the Senate instead of whizzing through under the sponsorship of Pete Domenici and with the support of the chairman of the Senate Labor and Human Resources Committee, my good friend and fellow Utahan, Orrin Hatch.

Movement conservatives opposed Justiz, and that made it difficult for Hatch. Since Sweet was one of their own and since Justiz
was a moderate Republican, it was in their interest to defeat the
nomination. . . .

Happily, there was no upsurge of opposition despite the rumors,
and opposition to the nomination subsided in a few days. The Justiz
nomination was moved out of committee and approved on the Senate
floor. I breathed a sigh of relief. The NIE-Curran episode was over.
It was time to turn my efforts to more productive endeavors.

But my belief that I had seen the last of my NIE troubles was
wrong. After Justiz was sworn in he came to me to say that he could
not work with Robert Sweet as deputy director. I briefed him on the
sensitive matters related to Curran's departure; this was not the time
to discharge another problem conservative. We had them all over the
place, and he would have to endure his fair share of the problems they
created.

Justiz promised to do his best to coexist but a few days later he
was back in my office with horror tales of Sweet and his disruptive
disciples. They refused to take direction from him, and he could not
run the place under such conditions.

He was right, but the fact remained that we had had enough
uproar for a while, and I was very reluctant to act. Since Sweet, too,
was presidentially appointed, I would have to go through the White
House again. I looked around for an alternative job for Sweet, but
nothing seemed to fit. I was weary of the mess, but it stayed with me
like the plague.

And the plague was destined to spread. . . .

The Supreme Court

Contrary to popular myth and public perception, the Supreme Court of the United States is a political institution, and justices who serve on it are political decision makers. Like members of Congress, the president, and public administrators, the justices make decisions that authoritatively allocate values for individuals and groups within our political system and for the system itself. As the pinnacle of judicial power and authority for our constitutional democracy, the Supreme Court regularly hears and decides cases reflecting the controversial political issues and hard choices confronting the nation.

The Supreme Court's role as a political institution is particularly evident when it initiates fundamental policy change, as it did in *Brown* v. *The Board of Education of Topeka Kansas* (347 U.S. 483), or when it enhances, more fully develops, or legitimizes policy decisions made by other political actors either in or out of government (Johnson and Cannon 1984, 269). That the Supreme Court is a political institution is further evidenced by its ability to affect the policy agendas of other policy makers, define the arenas in which some political debates occur, and even, on occasion, influence the political futures of some elected officials.

The Court's decisions regarding abortion provide contemporary illustration of its political impact on other political players. The Court's decision in *Webster* v. *Reproductive Health Services* (109 S. Ct. 3040) greatly altered the political landscape of abortion politics and policy. By allowing the states greater latitude to regulate and restrict women's access to abortion services, the Supreme Court's majority ruling made the fifty state legislatures and governorships the new battleground for the abortion controversy. It reenergized a pro-choice movement that had become complacent after sixteen years of generally favorable Supreme Court decisions. It also helped to determine the success or failure of many political candidates as their positions on abortion increasingly affected their support among the electorate.

Though the Supreme Court is a political institution, this fact is not always clearly evident. It is often masked by another important characteristic of the Court. The Supreme Court is, first and foremost, a legal institution in terms of its structure, manner of operation, and the style and substance of its decisions. Legal jargon such as *jurisdiction, standing to sue, justiciability, precedent,* and *neutral principles* helps to create a false impression that judicial decisions are made solely through an objective process of legal reasoning that is free from the political considerations operating in the legislative or executive branches of government (Goldman 1987, 4). But if we look closely at how the Supreme Court justices are chosen and how they actually reach their decisions, we can refine our understanding and see our nation's highest court as both a legal and a political institution.

When nominating candidates to the Supreme Court, presidents routinely call for a confirmation process free from politics and ideological litmus tests. They ask for a confirmation process that focuses on their nominees' professional qualifications and fitness to serve on the nation's highest court.

Presidential pleas notwithstanding, the reality is that all Supreme Court nominations and confirmations are political (O'Brien 1990, 63). They are political because the addition of a new justice has the potential to change the balance of power on the Court. This change, in turn, can alter the outcome of the Court's decisions by creating a " 'critical mass' among the justices that tips the Court firmly to one side . . . " (Tribe 1985, 35).

The ability of a new, carefully selected justice to create a new critical mass within the Court is evident throughout the Supreme Court's history. President John Adams's appointment of John Marshall to be Chief Justice of the United States moved the Supreme Court toward an early and important role of championing national supremacy over state rights. Similarly, President Franklin D. Roosevelt's appointment to the Supreme Court in 1937 of Alabama Senator Hugo Black, a strong supporter of both the New Deal and the president's ill-fated court-packing plan, greatly altered the balance of power on the Court. Prior to Black's nomination, an economically conservative majority within the Supreme Court routinely declared the economic recovery programs of the New Deal to be unconstitutional. But with the retirement of Justice Willis Van Devanter, the strongest member of the conservative majority, Roosevelt had an opportunity to alter the direction of the Court's constitutional reasoning. By appointing Black, Roosevelt secured a five-to-four majority of justices who favored and supported New Deal economic legislation (Abraham 1974, 197–200). More recently, President Ronald Reagan's elevation of Associate Justice William Rehnquist to Chief Justice and his appointments of Justices O'Connor, Scalia, and Kennedy all illustrate the politics inherent in the selection of Supreme Court nominees. With these appointments, Reagan sought to replace the liberal critical mass evident during much of the Warren and Burger eras with a new conservative critical mass less inclined to extend individual rights and more supportive of governmental power.

President Reagan's clearest and boldest attempt to change the critical mass within the Court was his ill-fated nomination of conservative judge Robert H. Bork to succeed retiring Justice Lewis Powell, a political and constitutional moderate. During his sixteen-year tenure, Powell was often the pivotal member of a Supreme Court sharply divided between conservative and liberal justices. So significant was Powell's role on the Court that Ethan Bronner in his book *Battle for Justice* called the justice "the most powerful man in America," because as "[a] flexible conservative, Powell was the swing vote on a polarized bench. He provided the decisive fifth vote for the liberals on such things as abortion, separation of church and state, and affirmative action. He was with the conservatives on death penalty, protecting business interests, and aiding the prosecution of criminals" (Bronner 1989, 17). Had he been confirmed by the Senate, liberal fears and conservative expectations were that Robert Bork would upset the delicate balance then existing on the high court and dramatically alter the Court's critical mass. These expectations and concerns about Bork's impact on the Supreme Court contributed significantly to his failure to win confirmation as an associate justice.

Like appointment and confirmation, decision making within the Supreme Court and the interactions among the justices are also characterized by politics and political maneuvering. Contrary to popular misperception—perpetuated in part by the justices themselves—Supreme Court decisions are not made in a legal vacuum, isolated from political and other nonlegal concerns and constraints. Rather, those decisions are the products of the small-group dynamics that operate among the justices on the Court.

Supreme Court decisions evolve out of the efforts of nine individuals of equal formal status who attempt collectively to resolve constitutional questions that both clarify and create public policy for our nation. Like other political decision makers, the justices of the Supreme Court possess their own policy objectives and goals that they hope to see implemented. These goals and objectives, in turn, influence their outlook concerning what constitutionally valid public policy should be. Also, like other political decision makers with policy objectives, the justices seek to influence one another in an effort to see that their preferences are incorporated into the constitutional interpretations of public policy issues that come before the Court.

In deciding the cases before them, the justices attempt to influence how the other members of the Court are likely to vote at the Wednesday and Friday conferences. In these conferences, the justices discuss and reach tentative decisions on the cases heard during oral arguments. In addition, the justices seek to influence the content of the Court's written opinions on the cases it reviews. Being able to influence the wording of opinions is important because it publicly states the constitutional reasoning behind the Court's decisions, which will affect the future actions of other federal court judges and other political decision makers.

In seeking to influence conference decisions and written opinions, the justices have both personal and formal resources at their disposal. In his path-breaking book *The Elements of Judicial Strategy,* political scientist Walter F. Murphy discusses how the justices use both types of resources to realize their personal values, policy preferences, and goals in the decisions and opinions issued by the Court. In brief, all nine justices have at least two personal and one formal resource at their disposal: personal esteem, professional esteem, and their vote, that is, their decision whether to join the majority outcome (Murphy 1964, 38).

Drawing upon these resources, the justices employ several different tactics to influence the outcome of conference decisions and the wording of the Court's opinions. The justices may attempt to persuade one another of the legal merit of their own conclusions about the cases in question. Or they may try to exploit the personal regard of other justices whom they feel may already be disposed toward their thinking. They may try to influence the Court's decisions through the use of sanctions by refusing to vote in the majority or by threatening to write a dissenting opinion publicly stating their disagreement with the Court's majority (Murphy 1964, 43-67). These tactics contribute to a decision-making process that is ultimately characterized by a good deal of bargaining and compromising among the justices (Murphy and Prichett 1986, 556-560).

As the justices seek to influence one another's positions in the cases before the Court, some members are inevitably more successful than others in affecting the behavior of their "brethren." Their greater success will be due, in part, to their leadership ability. Political scientist David J. Danelski (1975) notes that there are two types of leadership within the Court—social and task leadership—that influence the justices' decision-making process. Social leadership arises from a concern for promoting and maintaining the social cohesiveness among the justices necessary for collegial decision-making. The justice who becomes the Court's social leader is usually the person who is the most well-liked by the other members of the Court (Danelski 1975, 490).

In contrast, task leadership arises from a concern with the intellectual and policy direction of the Court. According to Danelski, the justice who emerges as task leader is likely to be the one who most aggressively challenges the opinions and legal reasoning of his or her colleagues, directs and orients conference discussions, and most successfully defends his or her own positions, ideas, and legal reasoning before those colleagues (Danelski 1975, 489). Because task leadership involves the policy direction of the Court, it is also likely to generate conflict and competition among justices who hold widely divergent views regarding policy objectives, constitutional reasoning, and the proper role and function of the Supreme Court in our political system. In fact, Danelski points out that competition between two strong-willed and strong-minded justices is likely to cause task leadership to be split (Danelski 1975, 492-493). Divided task leadership may be particularly evident among the justices when there are two competing critical masses on the Court.

The two stories presented in this chapter dramatize many aspects of Supreme Court appointments and decision making. The relationship between the politics of critical mass and Supreme Court appointments and confirmations is the central theme in the first case study. "*The War Begins*" by Patrick B. McGuigan and Dawn B. Weyrich recounts the early and intense opposition to President Reagan's nomination of Robert H. Bork to succeed retiring Justice Lewis Powell. It was this opposition that eventually led the Senate to reject Bork's nomination by a vote of 52 to 48. "*The War Begins*" focuses on the months just prior to the Senate confirmation hearings and, in doing so, tells the story of how supporters of Bork, including those in the Reagan administration, failed to respond quickly and effectively to this opposition, thereby failing to stop its momentum.

The second case study is a story of Supreme Court decision making and interpersonal dynamics. "Saving Souls" by James F. Simon recounts the Court's decision-making process in the 1940 case *Minersville School District* v. *Gobitis* and the small-group dynamics among the justices that led to this case's being overturned by the Court just three years later in *West Virginia Board of Education* v. *Barnette*. "Saving

Souls'' also tells the story of the intense competition between Justices Hugo Black and Felix Frankfurter for the task, or intellectual, leadership of the Court. In describing this rivalry, "Saving Souls" illustrates Walter Murphy's observations of how the justices seek to influence one another and the impact these efforts are likely to have.

Suggested Reading

Friendly, Fred W. 1981. *Minnesota Rag.* New York: Random House. A dramatic telling of the story behind *Near* v. *Minnesota,* an important First Amendment case concerning prior restraint of the press.

McCloskey, Robert G. 1960. *The American Supreme Court.* Chicago: University of Chicago Press. A classic historical account of the Supreme Court through 1959 and the important role that it plays in interpreting the Constitution.

Rabkin, Jeremy. 1989. *Judicial Compulsions: How Public Law Distorts Public Policy.* New York: Basic Books. A discussion and critique of federal court–managed policy making and how extended judicial scrutiny of government programs distorts public policies and weakens majority control of the government.

Rubin, Eva R. 1987. *Abortion, Politics, and the Courts: Roe v. Wade and Its Aftermath.* New York: Greenwood Press. An examination of the impact on American politics of the Supreme Court's decision in *Roe* v. *Wade.*

Schwartz, Bernard. 1990. *The Ascent of Pragmatism: The Burger Court in Action.* Reading, MA: Addison-Wesley. A detailed examination of the Supreme Court and its decisions in important areas of constitutional law during the seventeen-year tenure of Chief Justice Warren E. Burger.

Westin, Alan F. 1990. *The Anatomy of a Constitutional Law Case.* New York: Columbia University Press. A documentary portrait of *Youngstown Sheet and Tube Co.* v. *Sawyer,* an important case defining the boundaries of presidential powers.

The War Begins

Patrick B. McGuigan
Dawn M. Weyrich

As you read this case study, consider the following questions:

1. How important was political ideology in the nomination and failed confirmation of Robert H. Bork?

2. Why would the nomination of Bork have been less controversial if he had been replacing a conservative justice such as William Rehnquist or Sandra Day O'Connor?

3. What groups were actively involved in the anti-Bork crusade, and how did their involvement highlight the important political role that the Supreme Court plays in public policy formulation?

4. What strategies did both the anti- and pro-Bork groups employ to gain support for their positions?

5. Why were the decisions of Senators Howell Heflin and Arlen Specter on whether to support Bork's confirmation so important to both anti- and pro-Bork groups?

From *Ninth Justice: The Battle for Bork,* by Patrick B. McGuigan and Dawn M. Weyrich. Copyright 1990 by Free Congress Research and Education Foundation. Reprinted by permission.

T HE WEEKEND FOLLOWING JUSTICE POWELL'S FRIDAY ANNOUNCEMENT, PRESIDENT REAGAN AND ATTORNEY GENERAL EDWIN MEESE III MET TO discuss possible replacements. The President held another meeting to discuss potential nominees that Monday, June 29, with Meese and White House Chief of Staff Howard Baker. Anonymous White House sources said Baker, a moderate, was ambivalent at that point about the reported first choice, U.S. Court of Appeals Judge Robert H. Bork, fearing that the Democratic-controlled Senate would reject him. Joe Biden praised Baker for his hesitation, saying he "understands the reality of this place." . . .

The following day, Meese and Baker handed Senate leaders a list of about ten possible replacements for Justice Powell. Reviewing the list were Senators Strom Thurmond (R-SC), the ranking Republican on the Judiciary Committee, Minority Leader Robert Dole (R-KS), Majority Leader Robert Byrd (D-WV), and Judiciary Committee Chairman Joseph Biden (D-DE). Biden again hinted at the battle a Reagan nominee might face by noting that the list had "some very good people . . . and some, I bluntly told them, would cause a contentious fight if they came up." Bork remained the Administration's top candidate.

The morning of July 1, 1987, White House Counsel Arthur B. Culvahouse and Judge Bork met at a hotel in Washington, D.C. to chat over coffee. Culvahouse grilled the Judge about his past, but could find no evidence of skeletons or personal problems in his background that might ruin his chances of confirmation later on.

President Reagan then called Bork into the Oval Office for a "chat." Some of his colleagues maintained Bork had been prepping himself for a Supreme Court nomination since Reagan entered office in 1981, but Bork himself had his doubts his day would ever come. . . .

So when the President asked that day if he would be the nominee, Bork answered with a typical quip: "I've thought about it for at least ten or twelve seconds, and I would be highly honored." Reagan rejoined, "Does that mean yes?"

Soon after their meeting, the two entered the White House briefing room for the announcement. . . . As Judge Bork stood quietly beside the President, Reagan introduced him on national television as "a premier constitutional authority," and reminded the audience that "when confirmed by the Senate as an appellate judge in 1982, the American Bar Association gave him its highest rating—exceptionally well-qualified." The President continued, "On the bench he has been well-prepared, even-handed and open-minded. I urge the Senate to expedite its consideration of Judge Bork so the court will have nine justices."

After President Reagan and Judge Bork left the briefing room, White House spokesman Marlin Fitzwater told members of the press, "We recognize that any conservative would receive some opposition, but we believe that Mr. Bork will be confirmed." He said despite the expected opposition, "there doesn't appear to be any deep-seated animosity." Another senior White House official predicted a "tough and lengthy" fight while yet another said the President would actively campaign to secure Bork's confirmation.

Senator Howell Heflin of Alabama, the Judiciary Committee's most conservative Democrat, foreshadowed Bork's confirmation process by predicting, "I think he will have the most complete and exhaustive investigation of any nominee to the Supreme Court in history." . . .

His opponents had focused against Bork days even before the announcement, and skipped nary a beat. Perhaps the most frequently quoted statement was made on the Senate floor by Edward Kennedy (D-MA), one of the Judiciary Committee's most liberal members:

> Robert Bork's America is a land in which women would be forced into back-alley abortions, blacks would sit at segregated lunch counters, rogue police could break down citizens' doors in midnight raids, school-children could not be taught about evolution, writers and artists would be censored at the whim of government, and the doors of the Federal courts would be shut on the fingers of millions of citizens for whom the judiciary is often the only protector of the individual rights that are the heart of our democracy. . . .

Benjamin Hooks, executive director of the National Association for the Advancement of Colored People, and Ralph Neas from the Leadership Conference on Civil Rights, issued a joint statement warning that:

> A very substantial majority of the civil-rights community will strongly oppose the nomination of Robert Bork [whose confirmation would] jeopardize the civil rights achievements of the past 30 years. Well-established law on affirmative action, on privacy, on women's rights and on school desegregation could overnight be substantially eroded or overturned.

Arthur Kropp, President of People for the American Way, a 270,000–member liberal group founded by television producer Norman Lear, announced, "Whatever we have to do to defeat his nomination, we'll do it." . . .

Even the seven Democratic presidential hopefuls got in on the initial Bork bashing by holding hurried press conferences to assert their positions. Senator Albert Gore (D-TN) was the only Democratic candidate who said he would not take a stand until after the hearings. . . .

The quick and furious liberal offensive put Senate Judiciary Committee Chairman Joseph Biden in a precarious situation. Judge Bork, who during the 1982 confirmation hearings to the U.S. District Court of Appeals had received high praise from his colleagues and Senators on both sides of the aisle, had been at the top of the list of those being considered to replace Justice Rehnquist when Rehnquist replaced Chief Justice Warren Burger in 1986. It was shortly after Rehnquist's elevation that Senator Biden had conceded, "If Judge Bork were to replace Judge Rehnquist or to replace Judge Scalia, I would have no problem. I'd have to vote for him, and if the [liberal special-interest] groups tear me apart, that's the medicine I'll have to take."

But Biden, who feared that the powerful liberal interests could wreck his fledgling presidential bid, backed away from his statement when Judge Bork's nomination overnight became the focus of massive liberal outcry. Indeed, on the evening of July 1, Biden said: "I continue to have grave doubts about the nomination and expect it to cause a difficult and potentially contentious struggle in the Senate." Biden also promised at that time, "I will not take a formal position on the Bork nomination before [the] hearings begin."

Eager to explain his 1986 statement, Biden claimed the next day that his meaning had been misconstrued. What he had really meant to say, said the Senator, was that he could support a Bork nomination to the High Court only if the Judge were to replace another conservative. "I would attempt to have diversity on the bench," Biden said. "I would see to it that there was a Scalia on the bench and a [liberal Justice William J.] Brennan on the bench. . . . It is wrong to send someone to tip the balance." . . .

. . . One week after the nomination, on Wednesday, July 8, Biden held virtually back-to-back meetings, with decidedly different purposes. At 10 a.m., he regaled the nominee himself for an hour with stories about his campaign for the presidency. He concluded the meeting by asking the jurist if he had any questions, to which Bork replied, "I thought you might have some for me, Senator." Biden replied, "No, I haven't read your opinions yet."

The Senator then met with lobbyists from the left-wing Leadership Conference on Civil Rights, NAACP Legal Defense Fund and the Women's Legal Defense Fund. He vowed to them that the anti-Bork effort would be his number one priority. Emerging from the private pow-wow, Biden admitted to reporters, "I haven't been able to do anything but have a cursory look at Judge Bork's record," but added, "It's highly unlikely I'll be able to vote for Judge Bork." He said he would not announce his actual decision "probably for 10 more days." But one of the representatives who attended the session later said that Biden had "made it very clear to us that he knows what he's going to do, and that he considers the confirmation fight so important that he's willing to work on this, and not on the presidential campaign." By mid-July, some 75 liberal groups would be in constant contact with Biden's staff.

Even columnists employed at some liberal newspapers expressed disgust as the battle unfolded. Michael Barone's scorching depiction of Biden appeared in the Washington *Post* the day following the meeting: "It was the pro-choice groups which first loudly attacked Bork and whipped the Democrats into line: the National Abortion Rights Action League snapped its fingers and Joe Biden, doing what he said he'd never do, jumped."

Biden's "jump" had actually occurred at least as early as a July 7 meeting at his Wilmington, Delaware home with crucial members of his campaign and judiciary committee staffs, during which he decided to head up the anti-Bork campaign. To aid him in that effort, these staff members began gathering volunteers from Washington, D.C. law firms to provide an analysis of Bork's scholarly writings and legal opinions. . . .

In the days following the Bork nomination, the storm of protest escalated as the opponents vowed to plow all available resources into stopping confirmation of the man they believed might ruin the advancement of their agenda. Ralph Neas of the Leadership Conference on Civil Rights, the Left's capable point man on the nomination, estimated that "probably 300 organizations" would join in Bork bashing activities, and predicted a "grass-roots effort in all 50 states."

"As a political organization we are contacting senators to urge them to consider Bork's ideology," said Irene Natividad of the National Women's Political Caucus. "As a grass-roots organization of 77,000 members we are galvanizing our membership nationwide to work against this nomination." People for the American Way's executive director, Arthur Kropp, was the first to mention money—big money. "People are really upset," he said. "Everyone wants to go to the mat on this one. We expect to spend as much as $1 million on this."

Kropp later explained: "We're talking about a heavy newspaper print-ad strategy and radio strategy, hoping to reach saturation in some of the markets," especially in the "opinion-making markets" of Chicago, Los Angeles, Washington, New York, and Atlanta. "We want the American public to be speaking with anyone who might be wavering. We view it as being probably the most important thing we do this year."

Conservatives had reasons for concern—PAW boasted a $10 million budget. Within a week, PAW's 250,000 members received an "alert mailing" to "get them prepared" for the anti-Bork blitz by advising them to call key senators during the week of the Senate Judiciary Committee hearings. PAW also teamed with the liberal Alliance for Justice and distributed a joint mailing to 1,700 editorial writers across the country, hoping to influence their opinions on the Senate's use of ideology as a reason to reject Bork.

Richard Mintz, spokesman for the National Abortion Rights Action League, said its 42 nationwide affiliates planned to "operate phone banks [and] distribute literature." Meanwhile, the 150,000 members of the National Organization for Women were busy organizing anti-Bork protests and preparing mailings to send to key senators, according to President Eleanor Smeal. NOW also hoped to erect a computerized bulletin board that would provide its members with up-to-date information on the progress of the nomination. . . .

Meanwhile, delegates for the National Association for the Advancement of Colored People (NAACP) gathered in New York for their 78th annual conference. Opening the six-day meeting on the first weekend in July, NAACP Executive Director Benjamin L. Hooks promised, "We will go all out in seeing that Bork is not appointed to the Supreme Court." NAACP officials said their more prominent members, who were busy researching Bork's legal past, planned to schedule meetings with all senators individually before the hearings.

The second day of the NAACP convention, several hundred delegates approved a resolution attacking Bork for his advocacy of the death penalty, and what they believed was his political opposition to public accommodations laws and affirmative action. "We must let our senators know that a vote against Mr. Bork is a prerequisite for our vote in the next election," said Coretta Scott King, widow of the Reverend Martin Luther King Jr. The convention hall erupted in cheers and thunderous clapping. . . .

Several politicians speaking at the convention, including Democratic presidential candidates, promised to fight against the Bork nomination. . . .

Democratic Presidential hopeful Congressman Richard Gephardt of Missouri told convention attendees: "I say that if Robert Bork refuses to find room at the inn for the black citizens of this nation, then the citizens of this nation should refuse to find room for him at the Supreme Court." His rival, former Arizona Governor Bruce Babbitt also pledged to NAACP members that he would fight the nomination adding, Bork "has the right to those opinions. The president has a right to admire them. And the Senate has a right to reject them. In the fullness of time, every Democrat will see that there can be no two ways about this vote." Senator Albert Gore, however, remained publicly uncommitted. "I will render my verdict in the Senate," he told the delegates. "But only after hearing all the evidence." . . .

. . . The National Education Association, the nation's largest teachers union with 1.86 million members, held its 125th annual convention on the same weekend. "Judge Bork is a compulsory pregnancy man . . . too conservative on race, women's rights and reproductive freedom," teacher Jane Stern of Rockville, Maryland complained, prompting the 8,000 NEA delegates to vote overwhelmingly in favor of blocking the nomination. "We intend to work to defeat this nomination through our normal congressional and legislative procedures," said Michael Edwards, manager of congressional relations for the NEA. "We have already in place methods to communicate with our members and members of Congress, so it's just a matter of activating members, not a question of adding new dollars."

Editorials on Judge Bork and the potential "effect" his influence would have on the court ran day after day throughout the battle. The arguments frequently sounded echoed this piece, which appeared in the St. Petersburg *Times*:

> Bork is more extreme in his views than the other ideologue on the court, Chief Justice William Rehnquist. Bork claims falsely to practice judicial restraint; he is a judicial activist for a backward-looking ideology. If he replaces the moderate Lewis Powell, shock waves ultimately will be sent throughout American society. . . .

Meanwhile, pro-Bork conservatives, already days behind in strategy, did not react to Bork's nomination with the same panache the liberals had. An early setback occurred when Senate Minority Leader Robert Dole (R-KS) openly worried about Judge Bork's chances of confirmation. "If you look at the numbers, you look at confirmability, then you've got a tough fight on your hands, I think he's a little better than 50–50." Dole said it was "speculative" whether he would have chosen Bork had he been president.

But conservative leaders who had long supported Bork, such as Patrick McGuigan and Dan Casey of the "721 Group," worked round-the-clock to make up for lost time. Through their coalition, they hoped to employ the same muscle the liberals had threatened to use against them—the grass-roots, including some 110 "various right-to-life groups, law enforcement agencies and various . . . religious groups," such as the National Association of Evangelicals, Casey said.

"We're doing what we did in the [Daniel] Manion and the [William] Rehnquist battles by umpty-umpty-umpt millions more," McGuigan said. The "bottom line is the vote count. There are prob-ably 46 solid votes for, probably 30, maybe a little more, against. The balance is the swing votes, and that's what everyone is going to be targeting." McGuigan added that efforts for Bork had begun "im-mediately. The first meeting of conservative leaders to brainstorm and begin to start action were the very next morning" following the nomination.

Out of that meeting came the following strategy: "First, we will try to alert and influence opinion makers, editorial boards, church leaders, and others with the ear of a senator in order to urge them to weigh nominations on the merits, resist pressures from liberal special-interest groups and exercise good judgment in confirming Judge Bork," Casey explained. "The second track is helping funnel information to grass-roots organizations, so that they in turn can feed it to their ac-tive members to energize . . . efforts." . . .

McGuigan and Casey drew some media attention by calling a mid-July press conference to denounce Senator Biden for taking a lead in the anti-Bork effort before the jurist had a chance to testify in front of the Senate Judiciary Committee.

Some 1,000 American Conservative Union contributors received a "here-we-go-again" mailing, which solicited financial support for the Bork battle. ACU Executive Director Casey said 40,000 to 60,000 more letters would be sent to contributors by July 31. "We're going to go all out," he said. "This is an issue that will fund itself because it's what they would say in the direct-mail world is a 'hot-button' issue. Frankly, the liberals have made this a hot-button issue for conser-vatives . . . with the absolute incredible reaction," he added. "Every dollar that Norman Lear spends is probably more support for Judge Bork." But McGuigan was forced to concede that Coalitions for America, with a total annual budget of only $150,000, would have a tough time outgunning People for the American Way, which had pledged to spend at least $1 million to defeat Bork's nomination. "We haven't yet budgeted any money," said McGuigan. "Our budget may be low-tech, but it's high-brain." . . .

The confirmation fight took on an interesting twist that added some punch to the conservative argument when several self-described liberals went public in defense of Bork. Perhaps the greatest coup in this regard was a pro-Bork commentary that eventually appeared in the July 16 issue of the New York *Times*. The author was Lloyd Cutler, former counsel to President Jimmy Carter and founder of the notoriously liberal Lawyers Committee for Civil Rights Under Law. Cutler wrote:

> In my view, Judge Bork is neither an ideologue nor an extreme right-winger, either in his judicial philosophy or in his personal position on current social issues. . . . I make [this assessment] as a liberal Democrat and as an advocate of civil rights before the Supreme Court. . . . Every new appointment creates some change in the "balance" of the Court, but of those on the list the President reportedly considered, Judge Bork is one of the least to create a decisive one.

Cutler's public defense of Bork created friction within his liberal Washington, D.C. law firm, Wilmer, Cutler & Pickering, where about a dozen lawyers were busy preparing an analysis for the Lawyers Committee attacking Bork. Also angered were officials at the American Civil Liberties Union and Common Cause, organizations he had worked closely with in the past, and other liberals, such as Ralph Nader. . . .

As the battle raged on, Raoul Berger, a former professor at Harvard and a self-described liberal, confessed:

> What it boils down to is if you're a liberal—and I am a liberal—it's my ideology against yours and I don't like yours . . . There are areas where I haven't agreed with Bork, but on whole he will make a fine judge. . . .

Prominent conservatives wrote in eloquent defense of Bork as well, attacking the accusations that Bork was an extremist who would force women to perform wretched coathanger abortions on themselves and send minorities back into slavery. . . .

Remaining true to the flashy fashion that had made it famous, the New York *Post* printed a furious attack on the motives for bashing Bork:

Anti-administration liberals seem intent on provoking a gunfight at the O.K. Corral over President Reagan's nomination of Robert Bork for the Supreme Court. Or maybe it's Custer's Last Stand they want to emulate. Seldom has a nomination to high office produced a reaction so strident in tone and so vicious in content. In near-desperation over the popular rejection of their entire political philosophy, liberals seem to have abandoned rational argument in favor of hysteria and character assassination. . . .

Liberals and conservatives embroiled in the confirmation battle worked furiously to activate the grass-roots members of their organizations. But in the arena of the actual fight—the nation's capital—the four Senate Judiciary Committee members who had remained uncommitted became the focus of the intense lobbying efforts: Senators Howell Heflin (D-AL), Dennis DeConcini (D-AZ), Arlen Specter (R-PA), and Patrick Leahy (D-VT). Conservatives predicted they would win the votes of Heflin and DeConcini, as both had indicated they would generally support a president's judicial nominee. DeConcini explained, "I look at Judge Bork as I do any nomination by any president, and the presumption is with the nominee."

Heflin said that political considerations would not determine his vote. "I do not believe the confirmation will be based solely on ideology, certainly not with me," he said. . . .

Clearly, Heflin was a toss-up. But both sides were acutely aware of the importance his support would carry. "A lot of the Southern Democratic senators look to Heflin on nominations," said a former Heflin Judiciary Committee aide. "They don't necessarily follow him, but they look to him, like people look to [Senator] Sam Nunn [D-GA] on defense." . . .

The five Senators who had united early behind the Bork nomination were Republicans Orrin Hatch (UT), Alan Simpson (WY), Gordon Humphrey (NH), Charles Grassley (IA), and Strom Thurmond (SC). The five committee Democrats whose initial statements were interpreted as immediate opposition were chairman Joseph Biden (DE), Edward Kennedy (MA), Howard Metzenbaum (OH), Paul Simon (IL), and Robert Byrd (WV).

Meanwhile, Chairman Biden had yet to set a date for the hearings. The Democrats, hoping to buy the special-interest groups enough time to penetrate the average household with anti-Bork ads, said the Judge would not receive his hearings fast enough to put him on the high court before the opening of its new term on October 5. Pressed for action, Biden finally announced on July 8 that the Senate Judiciary

Committee hearings had been scheduled for September 15, and would run at least two weeks. . . .

This delay of nearly 10 weeks infuriated most Republican Senators and the Reagan Administration. "The most important consideration is that we need to fill that vacancy by the start of the new term," Senator Humphrey said. "If that seat is empty, many cases will end in deadlock. What we're talking about is justice, not politics, and justice delayed is justice denied." . . . White House spokesman Marlin Fitzwater agreed: "It is regrettable that [Biden] has chosen to politicize the hearings in this kind of partisan fashion and further regrettable that we won't be able to have a full court when the term starts. We are hopeful that they will reconsider." . . .

By mid-July, Biden was focusing on the Bork battle on the campaign trail. During an appearance at Scott Community College in Davenport, Iowa, . . . Biden said that he was worried about Bork's outspoken views on "fundamental questions such as is there a right of privacy," adding, "When the president makes what appears to be a pure political judgment to forward his political agenda . . . it's totally appropriate for the U.S. Senate to challenge that."

The following day, Senate Minority Leader Robert Dole (R-KS) and Senator Gordon Humphrey (R-NH) asked Chairman Biden to set a "date certain" for the Judiciary Committee to cast its vote on Bork. Biden, asserting that "we have no intention to hold up this nomination," turned down the request, but promised to send the nomination to the full Senate by October 1.

An infuriated Humphrey said the 70-day delay between Bork's nomination and the scheduled September 15 hearings was "unprecedented and outrageous," and part of a political game Biden was playing with the American people. Humphrey charged there was "a strong circumstantial case" that Biden delayed the nomination hearings to further his presidential bid and give Bork bashers "more time to conduct a witch hunt." . . .

Bork foes in the Senate tried to sway their undecided colleagues by emphasizing their interpretation of "advise and consent." On July 23, Senator Joe Biden delivered the first in a planned series of speeches on the Senate floor. . . . Biden, who spoke for an hour, asserted that . . . "Political or philosophical issues have played a role, sometimes a dominant one, in the outcome of all but one of the 26 Supreme Court nominations rejected or withdrawn since 1789."

Senate Republicans were furious. Even Minority Leader Robert Dole (R-KS), disappointing to Bork supporters at times, responded aggressively to Biden's assertions, saying, "We could all conjure up an imaginary nominee whose ideology was so bizarre, whose thought processes were so alien, that we would feel obliged to vote against him or her." But such an "imaginary candidate" could not have served in the many prestigious positions Bork had, including U.S. Solicitor General, federal judge, and Yale Law School professor." . . .

The issue of ideology continued to be a topic of debate outside the Senate floor as well. Senator Paul Simon (D-IL), another candidate for his party's presidential nomination, told the Washington Council of Lawyers: "The Senate is broadly representative of the country's political diversity. It does not defer to the president when it thinks his proposed budget or legislation will harm the country, and the same should be true with respect to his judicial nominees." . . .

The third week in July, conservative leaders engaged in the Bork battle held a clandestine strategy meeting in Washington, D.C. to discuss their outrage over White House lack of action on behalf of their nominee. They believed that Chief of Staff Howard Baker and White House lobbyist William Ball were too weak to battle hostile Senate Democrats. Conservatives also expressed concern that their closest ally in this fight, Attorney General Edwin Meese III, was being denied his part in helping the confirmation. And pro-Bork leaders were outraged that conservatives who did take a strong pro-Bork stand, namely Education Secretary William Bennett and Gary Bauer, White House domestic policy advisor, received no support from their own administration. Bennett had only angered the Bakers and the Balls when he demanded that Biden remove himself from his post on the Judiciary Committee. Bauer too, had encountered cold shoulders within the Administration for chastising Democratic Senators who refused to challenge outrageous anti-Bork statements made by Edward Kennedy (D-MA) on the Senate floor. . . .

As the battle dragged into its second month, Senate Minority Leader Robert Dole (R-KS) noted that President Reagan had the authority to give Bork a short-term position on the Supreme Court during the congressional recess, scheduled for August 10 through September 9, on the grounds the Senate had gone too far in delaying the nomination. Dole noted that if the full Senate did not overturn such action by the President, Bork could serve as a Justice until three weeks before the end of the Reagan presidency. Dole told the National Conference of State Legislatures in Indianapolis that the "Constitution allows the President to fill any vacancy on the Supreme Court while Congress is in recess, and provides that the person filling that vacancy shall serve until the end of the congressional session." Dole, who said he was not pressing Reagan into taking such action, said Biden was responsible for "the kind of stall being tried now." Dole offered the replacement scheme as "food for thought" for Biden. . . .

By July 29 it appeared that President Reagan had finally recognized the urgency of the Bork battle and decided to do something about it. In remarks to members of the National Law Enforcement Council, President Reagan asked them to lobby the Senate on behalf of Bork. . . . Conservatives were cheered by several other developments as well. Judiciary Committee swing vote Dennis DeConcini (D-AZ) told his colleagues they should follow his example and allow Bork to testify before making a decision. And Senator Byrd (D-WV) followed suit, seeming to back off what had appeared to be firm initial opposition, admonishing fellow Democrats who viewed Supreme Court nominations as a "litmus test of party affiliation and loyalty."

A big boost for Bork's supporters came when Supreme Court Justice John Paul Stevens, a centrist who often voted with the liberal justices on social issues, told attendees at the Eighth Circuit Judicial Conference in Colorado: "I personally regard him as a very well-qualified candidate and one who will be a very welcome addition to the court. There are many, many reasons that lead me to that conclusion."

A poll commissioned by the *National Law Journal* became good ammunition for Bork supporters: a full 50 percent of the 348 state and 57 federal judges interviewed said they would vote for Bork if given the chance. Only 24 percent said they would not, while the remainder reserved opinion. The judges were split on interpretation of the Senate's "advice and consent" role, as 48 percent said a nominee's philosophy should not be considered during confirmation, while 46 percent said it should. Of the group interviewed, 47 percent described themselves as moderate-to-conservative, 31 percent as liberal-to-moderate, 6 percent as liberal, and 9 percent as conservative. . . .

Saving Souls

James F. Simon

As you read this case study, consider the following questions:

1. What aspects of Justice Hugo Black's early behavior on the Supreme Court did Justice Harlan Stone find alarming and why?

2. What constitutional questions were at issue in the *Gobitis* case?

3. What events ensued between the time the case was originally heard in federal district court and when the case finally reached the Supreme Court?

4. Why were these events significant?

5. With what three personal values did Justice Felix Frankfurter have to contend as he attempted to write a majority opinion in the *Gobitis* case, and which value eventually overcame the others?

6. How did Justice Frankfurter attempt to persuade Justice Stone— the lone dissenter in *Gobitis*—to join the Court's eight-justice majority, and what was Stone's reaction?

7. How did Justice Frankfurter react when he learned that Justices Black, Douglas, and Murphy—who had all joined Frankfurter's majority opinion in *Gobitis*—now believed that the Court had erred and should reverse its opinion?

8. What did Justice Frankfurter do to try to retain a majority for his position?

9. Why does Simon argue that with the reversal of *Gobitis* by *Barnette*, Justice Frankfurter began to lose his position as the task leader for the Court's liberal bloc of justices?

10. How does the *Bridges* case illustrate Justice Black's ascension to task leader for the Court's liberal block of justices?

11. What factors that were beyond his own or Frankfurter's control assisted Black in this ascension to leadership?

12. According to Simon's analysis, why was Justice Black successful in challenging Justice Frankfurter as task leader for the Court's liberal bloc of justices?

13. Why did Justice Frankfurter fail to maintain his role as task leader?

E VERY WEEKDAY MORNING, JUST AFTER DAWN, THE LONE, HULKING FIGURE OF ASSOCIATE JUSTICE HARLAN FISKE STONE COULD BE SEEN WALKING from his palatial northwest Washington residence up Massachusetts Avenue and then returning home for breakfast and a day of work. Sometimes he was joined by Marquis Childs, the ambitious, respected journalist for the *St. Louis Post-Dispatch.*

As the two took their early-morning exercise, Justice Stone talked to his companion about his concerns for the Court. Stone, a strong-minded, plainspoken man, told Childs that he feared the Court was in danger of repeating one of the most tragic mistakes in its history. Only two years earlier, in 1935, the Court majority had very nearly provoked a constitutional crisis by tossing out one piece of New Deal legislation after another in the name of constitutional orthodoxy. Stone, usually joined by Justices Cardozo and Brandeis, had condemned the Court majority for substituting their political views for the legislature's and claiming they were merely interpreting the Constitution.

The Court majority had shifted by 1937 so that New Deal legislation was safe from further interference by politically conservative Justices. But the basic problem of judicial legislation, as Stone saw it, had arisen again. This time the threat did not come from the right, but from the political left on the Court, represented by President Franklin Roosevelt's first appointee, Justice Hugo Black.

Stone conceded that Black was bright enough and certainly hardworking. But he lacked judicial experience or even the broad-based legal practice that would have prepared him for the Court's work. His raw intellect and aggressive methods had served him well in the U.S. Senate. And that was part of the problem—Justice Black seemingly had not changed roles. He was still the populist legislator bent on making economic and social policy with slashing attacks on his colleagues and the vested corporate interests he accused them of protecting. Black's early Court opinions, full of bold ideas and devastating criticism of the status quo and his brethren who maintained it, were an embarrassment to Stone and other, more experienced judicial colleagues.

Black had not yet completed a full year on the Court before he had written more dissents during the term than any other member. That fact alone suggested to Stone that the former Senator did not fully appreciate the history and tradition of the Court or the required subtlety of movement by the Justices. Audaciously, Black had even dissented from an unsigned opinion supported by all eight of his colleagues. By tradition, that simply was not done.

Black's transgression occurred in a case in which the Indianapolis Water Company complained that its rates to consumers had been set too low by a state regulatory commission. The water company had asked the federal courts to set aside the commission's decision, arguing that the rates established were so low as to be confiscatory. The Supreme Court majority accepted the utility company's argument, in effect, and sent the case back to the federal district court for a new rate-making analysis with the clear directive to take into consideration the water company's rising costs. Presumably, with the increased costs considered in the valuation, the public utility would be able to demand a greater return through consumer billing.

Justice Black's written disagreement with his brethren covered nineteen pages. In that space the Court's newest Justice questioned the competence of federal courts to review state utility rates, then committed further judicial heresy by asserting that a corporation should not be protected by the due process clause of the Fourteenth Amendment. . . .

Stone found the Black dissent in the Indianapolis Water Company case disconcerting, but the worst was yet to come. For in a second dissent that term Black submitted a small treatise to follow his earlier notion that the Fourteenth Amendment did not protect corporations.

His position was disarmingly straightforward: The Fourteenth Amendment was drafted after the Civil War to protect the recently freed slaves. It was only later, in a period when the U.S. Supreme Court looked with extravagant favor on corporations, that the Justices discovered a new meaning for "persons" in the Fourteenth Amendment that included Standard Oil and other corporate giants. That was wrong, Black concluded, and that judicial error of sixty-four years' standing should be corrected. Immediately. The amendment, wrote Black, "followed the freedom of a race from slavery," and when it was submitted to the people they "were told that its purpose was to protect weak and helpless human beings and were not told that it was intended to remove corporations in any fashion from the control of state governments."

Marquis Childs listened intently to Justice Stone's criticisms of Black's opinions during their early-morning walks together, and on January 22, 1938, Childs's *St. Louis Post-Dispatch* readers also learned about the Justice's views. "The *Post-Dispatch* has been privileged to gain an inside view of the Court," Childs wrote, "and of the concern for its future of the members who feel keenly the importance of its integrity and continuity." Childs adopted Justice Stone's position of judicial restraint, then discussed the difficulty posed by a neophyte jurist like Black. "A new man on the bench," Childs wrote, "who has had no judicial experience and only a comparatively limited legal experience is not a help to his colleagues in the first two or three years."

"Just what is needed to educate the public," Stone told Childs after reading the article. But why not deliver the message to a national audience? Stone asked. And that is exactly what Marquis Childs did four months later.

In an article in the May 1938 issue of *Harper's Magazine* entitled "The Supreme Court Today," Childs laid out Stone's complaints in considerable detail and revealed, for the first time, that the complaints were directed explicitly at Justice Black. . . .

With the publication of the article, the tight little world at the U.S. Supreme Court was shattered. A Justice had been attacked openly and in very personal terms. And the attacker, a journalist without formal legal training, was so well informed that the conclusion was inescapable that the journalist's informant was a member of the Court. When reporters discovered that Childs had been taking early-morning walks with Justice Stone, the Justice's phone began to ring. . . .

The only person who seemed totally unperturbed by the furor was Justice Hugo Black. A friend of Stone's, Irving Brant, assured Black that Stone "did not remotely support the statements made by Mr. Childs."

. . . "I can assure you," Black replied coolly, "that I am not disturbed in the slightest by the matter to which you referred."

Harlan Fiske Stone's discomfort over the incident passed and his hopes for the future of the Court were significantly lifted by the news that Professor Felix Frankfurter of Harvard was actively being considered as the President's next Supreme Court nominee. Stone had earlier asked Frankfurter to engage Hugo Black in a friendly tutorial on the proper role of the judiciary. And now it seemed that Stone would have Frankfurter nearby to help civilize the renegade Black. In fact, Stone had operated effectively behind the scenes to accomplish that result. At Roosevelt's invitation Stone had visited the White House to discuss a replacement for Justice Benjamin Cardozo, who had died during the summer of 1938. Stone spoke of Frankfurter's eminent qualifications to serve on the Court and the need to select Justices with the intellectual gifts and training to make the Court truly distinguished. The President could do no better than Felix Frankfurter, whose potent mind and liberal bent would serve as an effective foil to the formidable and more conservative Chief Justice, Charles Evans Hughes.

Frankfurter dressed casually in an alpaca coat and slacks for his first judicial conference, but upon entering the well-appointed conference room, he was chagrined to find that all his new colleagues wore suits. At the lunchtime break Frankfurter rushed home, changed into a suit and returned for the afternoon session. He was greeted by Chief Justice Hughes, who had also made a lunchtime change of dress, and now wore *his* alpaca coat.

That small gesture suggests one of the minor reasons that Charles Evans Hughes became a great Chief Justice of the United States. Tall, full-bearded and austere in appearance, Hughes was always the gentleman, and he showed an acute sensitivity toward his judicial colleagues, as Felix Frankfurter discovered that very first day at the Court. But Hughes's leadership qualities ran much deeper. His reverence for the Court as an institution was inspirational, and his conduct of the day-to-day affairs of the Court was no less impressive. He absorbed facts and identified legal issues with phenomenal efficiency and thoroughness. His presentation of the cases to the other Justices in conference, therefore, became a verbal instrument of considerable power.

As Chief Justice, Hughes assigned the writing of the opinion for the Court when he was in the majority, and that authority gave him subtle but not insignificant influence. Selecting the colleague who was most likely to bring to an opinion Hughes's own views as well as the skill to preserve a majority vote required a political savvy that the Chief Justice possessed in full measure. That talent was readily apparent in the spring of 1940 when the Chief Justice assigned the majority opinion in *Minersville School District* v. *Gobitis* to Felix Frankfurter. The opinion, written barely more than a year after his appointment, would indelibly mark Frankfurter's judicial career.

The school board in the small Pennsylvania community of Minersville had required that all public school children salute the American flag before classes began each weekday morning. Although the overwhelming majority of Minersville students routinely accepted the rule, Lillian and William Gobitis, ages twelve and ten, did not. The Gobitis children had been raised by their father, Walter, as Jehovah's Witnesses and had been taught to refuse to worship false idols. In Chapter 20 of Exodus, it was written: "Thou shall not make unto thee any graven image, or any likeness of any thing that is in the heaven above, or that is in the earth beneath, or that is in the water under the earth: /Thou shalt not bow down thyself to them, nor serve them." According to the Gobitis reading of Exodus, Chapter 20, saluting the American flag was therefore forbidden by God, and the punishment for ignoring the biblical command was annihilation.

Lillian and William Gobitis did not join their classmates in the early-morning patriotic exercise and were subsequently expelled from the public school. Their father, as a result, brought a lawsuit against the Minersville School Board, charging that the board had prevented his children from freely exercising their religious beliefs in violation of the First Amendment of the Constitution.

"Our beloved flag, the emblem of religious liberty," wrote U.S. District Judge Albert Maris in his opinion supporting the Gobitis position, "apparently has been used as an instrument to impose a religious test as a condition of receiving the benefits of public education. And this has been done without any compelling necessity of public safety or welfare." The Maris opinion was upheld unanimously by the U.S. Court of Appeals for the Third Circuit. . . .

The case had first been heard in Judge Maris's courtroom in 1937. When the Supreme Court listened to arguments in April 1940, the western world had been radically transformed by the violent ambitions of Adolf Hitler. The Nazi blitzkrieg had devastated large chunks of Europe, and observers on both sides of the Atlantic were dreading the imminent Battle of Britain. In those portentous times the plea by the attorney for the Minersville School Board defending the flag salute as a legitimate form of patriotism assumed a special poignancy.

The *Gobitis* case presented two conflicting elemental Frankfurter values for calm judicial resolution. The first had been argued by the attorney for Lillian and William Gobitis: In the United States it was an article of faith as well as law that every citizen was entitled to freedom of belief and expression without fear of government intrusion. No American living in 1940 could make a greater claim to upholding that seminal proposition than Felix Frankfurther, for he had dedicated much of his professional life to the defense of civil liberties. . . .

But against his strong libertarian beliefs Frankfurter struggled with his equally firm conviction that the judicial branch of government should exercise restraint in reviewing the acts of the popularly elected branches. . . . The Gobitis children's argument could only succeed if the Supreme Court rejected a public school requirement, enforced by a publicly responsible school board, that all public school children, including Lillian and William Gobitis, salute the American flag. Affirmation of the requirement of the school board need not be seen as an abandonment of Frankfurter's libertarian ideals. It could be argued, rather, that those ideals were best preserved by the electorate, not the Court. A flag-salute requirement was a silly rule, but Frankfurter, the civil libertarian who might have opposed it as a member of a small-town school board, might not as a member of the U.S. Supreme Court declare it unconstitutional.

There was a third Frankfurter value at work, which proved to be decisive. Frankfurter was a patriot first and last, and no amount of sophisticated judicial philosophizing could cover up the deep debt that he felt to his adopted country. As he freely admitted, the convert was more zealous in preaching the faith than the native-born, and this Jewish immigrant who did not speak English when he arrived at Ellis Island in 1894 was an unabashed zealot. . . .

Frankfurter was the only Justice who regularly whistled, "Stars and Stripes Forever" as he walked through the corridors of the Supreme Court building. . . .

At the judicial conference following oral argument in the *Gobitis* case Chief Justice Hughes spoke first. "I come up to this case like a skittish horse to a brass band," he said. "I am disturbed that we have this case before us. There is nothing that I have more profound belief in than religious freedom, so I must bring myself to view this case on the question of state power." Having posed the issue skillfully, the Chief Justice concluded that "the state can insist on inculcation of loyalty. It would be extraordinary if in this country the state could not provide for respect for the flag of our land."

Both Justices Black and Murphy had doubts about the wisdom of the school board regulation. But Black and Murphy, as well as other Roosevelt appointees William O. Douglas and Stanley Reed, eagerly awaited the view of Felix Frankfurter, who, by training and experience, had earned their respect on civil liberties issues above all others, including the Chief Justice. Frankfurter did not need to belabor his devotion to civil liberties; it was a matter of public record. Here, he said, the Court was confronted with two clashing constitutional rights: the individual's right to free exercise of religion and the state's right to teach patriotism. For Frankfurter, the only foreign-born member of the Court, a public school's prerogative to nurture national loyalty was constitutionally unassailable. Did any member of the Court seriously think the framers of the First Amendment would have forbidden a flag salute? Frankfurter had no doubt they would not, nor should the Court in 1940. His statement dominated the conference, and seven members of the Court, including every Roosevelt appointee—Black, Douglas, Murphy and Reed—voted with him.

On the eve of World War II, the Court's *Gobitis* opinion undoubtedly would be read with particular care by scholars and lay citizens alike. The Chief Justice's assignment, therefore, became critically important. A safe choice would have been Stanley Reed—intelligent, cautious, centrist. Or the Chief himself. Hughes, in fact, was Frankfurter's choice. The Chief Justice kept his own counsel, however, and without hesitation gave the assignment to Frankfurter. He made the choice, he said, "because of Frankfurter's moving statement at conference on the role of the public school in instilling love of country in our pluralistic society." Although he never said so, the Chief Justice may also have been mindful of the effect that Frankfurter, one of the most celebrated civil libertarians of his generation, would have on his countrymen when he argued in his opinion that the claim of the free exercise of religion protected by the First Amendment should not prevail.

With the support of seven of his colleagues Frankfurter began to draft his *Gobitis* opinion. But the one Court holdout, Justice Stone, so troubled Frankfurter that he attempted anew to persuade the dissenter in a five-page memorandum. "I am not happy that you should entertain doubts that I cannot share or meet," he wrote Stone, "in a domain where constitutional power is on one side and my private notions of liberty and toleration and good sense are on the other." He assured Stone that he was committed to giving "the fullest elbow room to every variety of religious, political and economic view." But here the Court was presented with "the clash of rights, not the clash of wrongs. For resolving such a clash we have no calculus." On balance, Frankfurter was convinced that the responsibility for teaching toleration must come from the people themselves, not the Court. . . .

But Justice Stone was unmoved by Frankfurter's entreaty. "I am truly sorry not to go along with you," Stone wrote, responding to Frankfurter's memorandum. "The case is peculiarly one of the relative weight of imponderables and I cannot overcome the feeling that the Constitution tips the scales in favor of religion."

With the exception of Stone, Frankfurter's draft opinion won high accolades from his brethren. "You have accomplished most admirably a very difficult and highly important task," Chief Justice Hughes wrote Frankfurter. "The Court is indebted to you." Justice Douglas joined in: "This is a powerful moving document of incalculable contemporary and (I believe) historic value. I congratulate you on a truly statesmanlike job." . . .

On the morning of June 3, 1940, the Supreme Court was abuzz with word that Justice Frankfurter would break with traditional practice and read his opinion in Court. The *Gobitis* case raised such momentous issues for all Americans that, the rumor had it, Frankfurter wanted to deliver his opinion orally. Having heard of Frankfurter's intentions, Justice Stone, the only dissenter, determined to read his own opinion out loud as well.

To the disappointment of the large crowd that had gathered in the ornate courtroom, Frankfurter chose not to read his majority opinion aloud. But Justice Stone did not follow his example. Hunched forward in his seat, Stone, normally private and undemonstrative, read his opinion with heavy emotion: "History teaches us that there have been but few infringements of personal liberty by the state which have not been justified, as they are here, in the name of righteousness and the public good, and few which have not been directed, as they are now, at politically helpless minorities." He concluded, "This seems to me no less than the surrender of the constitutional protection of the liberty of small minorities to the public will."

The following day the majority opinion of Justice Frankfurter was available for the nation to study. And those who had long admired Frankfurter's extraordinary analytical skills and verbal locutions could find much to appreciate in his *Gobitis* opinion. . . . Civil liberties, judicial restraint, patriotism—all laudable values in our American democracy and all given careful attention in the Frankfurter opinion. But many of his most devoted friends were stunned by his conclusion that the claim of the First Amendment's protection of religious liberty must fail.

They did not telephone Frankfurter or drop him a congratulatory note. Those gracious gestures were saved for the Court's lone dissenter, Justice Stone. "When a liberal judge holds out alone against his liberal brethren," Benjamin Cohen, one of Frankfurter's New Deal protégés, told Stone, "I think he ought to know when he has spoken not for himself alone, but has superbly articulated the thoughts of his contemporaries who believe with him in an effective but tolerant democracy." Frankfurter's close friend, Professor Harold Laski, seconded Cohen. "I want to tell you," he wrote Stone, "how right I think you are in that educational case from Pennsylvania and to my deep regret, how wrong I think Felix is."

Frankfurter had his supporters, not the least being the President of the United States. While he mixed cocktails for Felix and Marion Frankfurter at Hyde Park a few weeks after the decision, FDR approvingly explained Frankfurter's position to a skeptical Eleanor Roosevelt. The Minersville School Board had acted stupidly, FDR said, but not outside its legal authority.

Eleanor Roosevelt listened patiently and did not question the constitutional argument of her husband and Justice Frankfurter. But there was something profoundly unsettling, she said, was there not, with a Supreme Court opinion that made children in public schools salute the flag in violation of their religious beliefs. The First Lady added that such official intolerance could well encourage a cruder variety in the public at large.

Eleanor Roosevelt's fearful speculation came to pass. Vigilante committees formed to enforce respect for the flag. Rampaging mobs attacked Witnesses in Litchfield, Illinois, and Rockville, Maryland, and other beatings and burnings of Jehovah's Witnesses' property were reported in Maine, Texas and California. No one blamed Frankfurter personally for the violent outbursts but a Justice Department study later traced the lawlessness directly to the Court's *Gobitis* decision.

If he was disturbed by the violence, Frankfurter never acknowledged it. He was, however, hurt by the disapproval of friends and angered by the reaction of the overwhelming majority of the nation's newspapers that condemned his *Gobitis* opinion. The editorial in the *St. Louis Post-Dispatch*, one of the earliest and most enthusiastic supporters of Frankfurter's Court appointment, was typical. "We think the decision of the United States Supreme Court is dead wrong," the *Post-Dispatch* declared. "If patriotism depends upon such things as this—upon violation of a fundamental right of religious freedom—then it becomes not a noble emotion of love for country but something to be rammed down our throats by the law." . . .

Frankfurter would write long and learned opinions in every field of constitutional law over the next twenty-two years, but no compendium of his opinions would be complete without reference to *Minersville School District* v. *Gobitis*. . . . His opinion would also prove to be his undoing as leader of the Roosevelt appointees. In a short time he would lose his majority, including Justices William O. Douglas and Frank Murphy, who would with predictable consistency follow the new liberal leader of the Court, Justice Hugo Black.

At the end of the summer of 1940, less than three months after the *Gobitis* decision had been announced, Frankfurter learned from Justice Douglas that Black had changed his mind and would now favor Stone's dissenting position. . . .

When a second case involving the First Amendment rights of Jehovah's Witnesses, *Jones* v. *Opelika,* came before the Court two years after *Gobitis,* Black took the opportunity to emphasize how strongly he felt about his initial error. The extraordinary public confession was joined by Justices Douglas and Murphy:

> The opinion of the Court sanctions a device which in our opinion suppresses or tends to suppress the free exercise of religion practiced by a minority group. This is but another step in the direction which *Minersville School District* v. *Gobitis* took against the same religious minority and is a logical extension of the principles upon which that case rested. Since we joined in the opinion in the *Gobitis* case, we think this is an appropriate occasion to state that we now believe it was also wrongly decided. . . .

It public, Frankfurter said nothing. But in private, he raged like a wounded animal, attacking his new adversaries with venomous verbal thrusts. He began referring to the trio of Black, Douglas and Murphy as "the Axis," surely the most treacherous sobriquet imaginable during World War II. And this sensitive human being, who touched so many with his kindnesses and generosity, was now regularly reduced to petty clucking about the perceived weaknesses of his adversaries. Frankfurter told little stories to colleagues, including Stanley Reed and Owen Roberts, that depicted Murphy as slow-witted, Douglas as crassly political, and Black, worst of all, as manipulating each of them for his own transparent strategic advantage.

In Frankfurter's mind Black always stood above the rest, the master puppeteer skillfully controlling the actions of the others. . . . Every Black initiative was viewed in the most unsavory light. When Black spoke in conference, it became "a harangue worthy of the cheapest soapbox orator." And when his antagonist changed his position, as he did in *Opelika* . . . it was attributed to naked political motives.

An incorrigible proselytizer, Frankfurter stepped up his efforts in the face of the challenge. He had lost three votes he expected to control, so he intensified his attentions with his other colleagues. Ironically, his most conspicuous weapon of persuasion, flattery, was precisely the tactic he accused his adversaries Black and Douglas of using in an unseemly way. Douglas, he said, was "the most systematic exploiter of flattery I have ever encountered in my life" and Black was not far behind.

In fact, no one could rival Frankfurter in flattering colleagues. He was astounded by their insights, dazzled by their learning, generally in direct proportion to their agreement with his own positions.

Frankfurter magisterially welcomed new appointees, Wiley Rutledge, for instance, as if he governed the institution:

> My dear Rutledge: Judges *are* men—and therefore poor and fallible creatures. But there have been three men since the Civil War whose character—their disinterestedness in its subtlest forms and their humility—even more than pre-eminent intellectual powers, enabled them to transcend men's ordinary limitations. To the fellowship of Justice Holmes, Brandeis and Cardozo I welcome you. And no one can possibly do so more warmly than I do. Yours very sincerely . . .

Rutledge, however, was not impressed. Within a few months of taking his seat on the Court he concluded that Black, not Frankfurter, was the intellectual leader of the Court. . . .

Frankfurter had commanded eight votes with his *Gobitis* opinion but suspected, when the constitutionality of a compulsory flag-salute exercise in the public schools was again argued in 1943 before the Court in *West Virginia Board of Education* v. *Barnette,* that his position would not even win a majority. Black, Douglas and Murphy would certainly join the original dissenter, Justice Stone, as they had promised in *Opelika.* Moreover, two new Court appointees had replaced members of the *Gobitis* majority and were by no means dependable votes for Frankfurter's position. Wiley Rutledge had taken the seat Frankfurter had hoped would be filled by his intimate friend and longtime philosophical ally, Judge Learned Hand, and had already expressed a strong commitment to individual liberties. And Justice Robert Jackson, FDR's eloquent Attorney General, was the man who in 1938 had urged the President to appoint Frankfurter to provide *liberal* leadership on the Court.

Frankfurter prepared for the reversal as a proud but doomed gun-fighter would approach his final shootout. Months before the *Barnette* case was argued in the Supreme Court, Frankfurter was already writing his dissent. He jotted down sentences while shaving, then stuffed them into a dresser drawer. Later, at the office he dictated isolated paragraphs to his secretary and placed them in a manila folder. The paragraphs often seemed disjointed to his law clerk, Philip Elman. But Frankfurter did not ask for or accept drafting or research help from his clerk. "I have to do this myself," he told Elman. Later, he invited Elman to his house for dinner and then to his study, where the Justice dictated his opinion to Elman, who dutifully typed out the words.

The vote was 6–3 for reversal in *Barnette* with only Justices Stanley Reed and Owen Roberts supporting Frankfurter in dissent. Robert Jackson wrote the majority opinion and Hugo Black added a concurrence that underscored his growing conviction that when First Amendment liberties were in jeopardy the Court must intervene. . . .

With the *Barnette* decision, Frankfurter's leadership of the liberal wing of the Court, so confidently assured only three years earlier, was obliterated. Despite Frankfurter's perception that it was the others who had strayed, in fact it was Frankfurter himself who had drifted from the credible libertarian position. Based on a mixture of philosophical and personal convictions, he had insisted that the Court owed no greater duty to the protection of First Amendment freedoms than a reasonable majority was willing to give. But the constitutional standard was so easily met under Frankfurter's rationale that the First Amendment's protection of belief and expression in wartime was rendered meaningless.

Frankfurter's refusal to change his position provided Black with the opening to assume the reins of liberal leadership on the Court. Black's growing conviction that the First Amendment deserved a preferred position in the constitutional hierarchy guaranteed an impassioned debate with Frankfurter that would extend to the end of their days on the Court together. More importantly, Black's commitment to First Amendment freedoms, which evolved into his insistence on absolute protection, became the centerpiece for his advocacy that would assure his place in judicial history. . . .

The Black-Frankfurter debates on the essential meaning of the First Amendment's protection of speech were spread over more than two decades and produced thousands of words, at times vituperative, from the two Justices. . . .

Frankfurter firmly believed that he, as the protégé of Holmes and Brandeis, possessed a clearer understanding of the First Amendment protections than any of his colleagues, and that Hugo Black always got it wrong. When two free speech cases, one involving the radical longshoreman Harry Bridges, and the other the shrill editorials of the *Los Angeles Times,* were coupled for Court argument, Frankfurter and Black squared off, each confidently quoting Justice Holmes to bolster their irreconcilable positions.

Bridge had been fined for contempt of court after sending a telegram to the Secretary of Labor (and to several newspapers for publication) criticizing a California judge's decision that did not favor his union; Bridges threatened a strike if the decision remained in effect. The *Los Angeles Times* had also been fined for contempt for publishing three editorials instructing a state court judge in tough language to punish two members of the Teamsters Union. "Probation for Gorillas?" asked the editorial writer and then rejected the possibility in favor of the "assignment to the jute mill."

The two cases presented the Court with one of its most difficult constitutional dilemmas: choosing between guarantees of free press under the First Amendment and fair trial under the Sixth Amendment, each guarantee considered applicable to the states through the due process clause of the Fourteenth Amendment. California judges had attempted to insure that judicial deliberations took place in an atmosphere untainted by a labor leader's threat or a newspaper's verbal harassment. But by issuing the contempt citations the judiciary itself became an intimidating voice, threatening the free flow of information and opinion in the press.

Frankfurter viewed the two cases, as he did so many that came before the Court, as an exercise in careful constitutional balancing in which neither constitutional guarantee necessarily took precedence over the other. Both free press and fair trial protections were important, and it was the task of the Court to weigh the merits of each case, considering carefully the particular facts and circumstances involved. Beyond that analysis, however, Frankfurter considered the whole history of English-speaking peoples, dating back more than half a millennium, and concluded that judicial tradition compelled respect for a court's contempt power. Centuries of British judges had used it to protect the fair administration of justice, and its right and efficacy had properly been transferred to American courts as well. The Court's exercise of the contempt power, Frankfurter argued, represented an unbroken, incontrovertible commitment to the integrity of the judicial process.

An agitated Hugo Black attacked the Frankfurter position with a bolt of intellectual energy reminiscent of his fieriest Senate days.

Frankfurter was wrong on first principles, Black charged. The Court was not bound by the centuries of British judicial history. The starting point for the *U.S.* Supreme Court was the *U.S.* Constitution, and any other reference to the history of English-speaking peoples was irrelevant. American patriots fought the War of Independence to free themselves from British law; to bind American rights of free expression to the British rules was to deny our history. The framers knew British history well, too well, and consciously chose to protect the colonists' right of free expression with the explicit, uncompromising language of the First Amendment. The contempt citations, Black concluded, should be overturned.

Black persuaded only Douglas and Reed, while the remaining five Justices supported Frankfurter's position. Undaunted, Black prepared a scorching dissent. Working from scribbled notes on a scratch pad, he challenged every basic assumption that Frankfurter had promised to defend . . .

Later in the term, after the Justices had voted in the *Bridges* case, two unrelated events suddenly shook Felix Frankfurter's once-firm majority. Justice James McReynolds, one of the six majority votes, retired, reducing the vote to 5–3. Shortly after the McReynolds announcement, a second member of the Frankfurter majority, Justice Frank Murphy, began to listen with disquieting concern to his law clerk who had argued from the start that the contempt citations should be reversed. The judge in the *Bridges* case had not been intimidated by Harry Bridges's telegram, the clerk contended, and may not have even been aware of it. Murphy reviewed the trial record and ruminated on the larger constitutional issues. Reluctantly he concluded that his earlier vote in judicial conference could no longer be justified. . . .

Significantly, Justice Murphy chose to inform Justice Black of his decision before he told Frankfurter. By this time Frankfurter's early gilded treatment of Murphy had begun to tarnish. His cutting assessments of Murphy's intellectual limitations would soon be no secret, especially to the sensitive Murphy. Justice Black, a consummate politician, could adroitly size up a man's strengths and weaknesses, and his conclusions about Justice Murphy may not have been very different from Frankfurter's. But he kept his opinions to himself and outwardly cultivated Murphy, offering professional respect and personal affection. With his switch in the *Bridges* case, Murphy rejected Frankfurter's leadership for good and accepted that of Hugo Black. . . .

On the first Monday in October 1941, Frankfurter and Black welcomed two new colleagues who would cast the decisive votes in *Bridges.* They also prepared to hear reargument of the *Bridges* case

later in the fall. After oral argument Black discussed the case with his
law clerk, Max Isenbergh, in such a way that Isenbergh thought Black
had not fully made up his mind.

"How do you think I should vote on this?" Black asked.

"Well, you've always had a strong civil liberties record," Isenbergh
said.

"Maybe you're right," Black responded.

Black gave Isenbergh the impression that he was unsure of his philosophical position and was groping for grounds to support his political
sympathies. This impression fit in neatly with Justice Frankfurter's image of Black, an image that Frankfurter freely shared with many others,
including Isenbergh.

More likely, Justice Black was engaging his young clerk in an intellectual dialogue for the clerk's, not his own, benefit. For Black
had already put on paper his exceedingly forceful opinion that First
Amendment rights must prevail. When newly appointed Justice Robert
Jackson supported that view in conference, Hugo Black had won his
majority.

Writing for five members of the Court, Justice Black set aside
all of the contempt citations in *Bridges*. In doing so, Black reiterated
his theory that the Court must give paramount consideration to the
First Amendment, regardless of the instruction of British law. "No
purpose in ratifying the Bill of Rights," wrote Black, "was clearer
than that of securing for the people of the United States much greater
freedom of religion, expression, assembly, and petition than the
people of Great Britain had ever enjoyed." Black continued, "The
assumption that respect for the judiciary can be won by shielding
judges from public criticism wrongly appraises the character of
American public opinion. For it is a prized American privilege to speak
one's mind, although not always with perfect good taste, on all public
institutions." . . .

With his *Bridges* majority opinion, Black had challenged the
former Harvard professor on constitutional theory, and he had prevailed. He had done so by trusting his own reading of constitutional
history and concluding that the First Amendment was an original and
essential American creation. Notice was given, as if it were necessary,
that the Justice with the paltry legal education and narrow plaintiff's
lawyer's experience could operate on the most ambitious intellectual
level. Members of the Alabama bar had known of Black's brilliance
for years, and so had his former colleagues in the Senate. He had now
brought all of the Justices into the circle—not just Murphy and Douglas,

but those like Stone and Frankfurter, who had so woefully under-estimated him a few short years ago.

The *Bridges* decision came down two years after the Court ap-pointment of Felix Frankfurter, and *Barnette,* the second flag-salute decision, less than two years later. Within that relatively short span of time, Frankfurter had not only lost his liberal majority and leader-ship but had been unceremoniously replaced in that position by Hugo Black. How, it must be asked, did this happen so quickly?

First, consider Black's and Frankfurter's effectiveness with their colleagues. Both Black and Frankfurter possessed the powerful intellects to assume leadership roles on the Court, though Frankfurter was slow to recognize that Black's intellect was as formidable as his own. Others on the Court did so less grudgingly. When Black began to carve out his own strong position on the First Amendment, liberal colleagues like Douglas and Murphy were naturally drawn to his arguments. They listened to Frankfurter's lectures on the balancing of constitutional demands, but they voted with Hugo Black. They voted with him not only on principle but also because Black, with his expert political skills, was better equipped to influence the brethren. True, Frankfurter had been an adviser to Presidents. But Hugo Black had worked in the trenches, speaking plainly to lay juries and Alabama voters as well as U.S. Senators. He knew how to talk persuasively without lecturing like a Harvard professor. The more Frankfurter lectured, the less influen-tial he became with his liberal colleagues.

There was also the nasty Frankfurter habit of talking deprecatingly about Justices who did not agree with him. In informal conversations at the Court and with friends, he belittled Frank Murphy's legal ap-titude and castigated Black and Douglas for what he perceived to be their bald political maneuvering. For his part, Hugo Black never tired of promoting his view of the First Amendment, but he did so directly and relied on the force of his argument, not on personal insults.

Black's success transcended his ability to persuade his colleagues to adopt his views in individual cases. More significantly, Black re-sponded aggressively to the most important constitutional challenge to the modern Supreme Court—the protection of individual rights. Before their Court appointments, both Black and Frankfurter had condemned Court interference with New Deal legislation; neither, however, sug-gested that the Court should defer to the legislature on civil liberties issues. Indeed, Frankfurter had made the point in 1938, only a year before his Court appointment, that civil liberties issues came to the

Court with a special claim for constitutional protection. But with *Gobitis* and *Barnette*, Frankfurter appeared to forget his own lecture. Black did not.

Frankfurter continued to express concern for civil liberties, but in the final analysis he relied on the legislative branch for guidance. Black rejected that view. For him, the Court's primary role was to protect the individual liberties guaranteed in the Bill of Rights. In this way, Black believed, the people were best defended against overreaching government control. Once Black had identified this basic constitutional need of the American people, he pressed his colleagues to fulfill what he perceived to be their judicial obligation. And he did so through forcefully lucid opinions that projected an unwavering sense of institutional mission.

Still, the battle was only joined, not decisively won. The flag-salute and *Bridges* cases were decided in wartime, but the civil liberties issues raised then would continue to be placed high on the Court's agenda throughout the Cold War. Every step of the way Black and Frankfurter, evangelical in their pursuit of judicial converts, battled each other for souls—and a Court majority.

Their confrontations were not confined to First Amendment issues but were spread throughout the Bill of Rights. Regardless of the civil liberties issues in the forties, however, Justice Black usually could depend on the votes of Douglas, Murphy and Rutledge. These were labeled the Court liberals, with Black commonly acknowledged as their leader.

But four did not make a majority, and Black found it increasingly difficult to capture the crucial fifth vote. For Justice Jackson, the man who had delivered the Court majority opinion rejecting the mandatory flag salute as well as the fifth vote for Black's majority in *Bridges,* would soon desert him. In fact, he would become Felix Frankfurter's best friend and ally on the Court and would, with Frankfurter's encouragement, take up the cudgels against Hugo Black.

References

Aberbach, Joel D. 1990. *Keeping a Watchful Eye.* Washington, DC: Brookings Institution.

Archer, Jules. 1977. *Police State: Could It Happen Here?* New York: Harper and Row.

Armstrong, Scott. 1990. *Iran-Contra: Was the press any match for all the president's men?* Columbia Journalism Review (May/June), 27–35.

Beard, Charles A. 1913. *An Economic Interpretation of the Constitution of the United States.* New York: Free Press.

Berry, Jeffrey M. 1984. *The Interest Group Society.* Boston: Little, Brown.

———. 1977. *Lobbying for the People.* Princeton, NJ: Princeton University Press.

Botterweck, C. M., and Mary Kate Hiatt. 1990. *People and Politics: An Introduction to American Government.* Wheaton, IL: Gregory Publishing.

Bowers, James R. 1990. *Regulating the Regulators.* New York: Praeger.

Bronner, Ethan. 1989. *Battle for Justice.* New York: W. W. Norton.

Burke, John P. 1990. The institutional presidency. In *The Presidency and the Political System,* ed. Michael Nelson, 383–408. Washington, DC: Congressional Quarterly Press.

Congressional Quarterly Inc. 1982. *Congressional Quarterly Guide to Congress.* Washington, DC: Congressional Quarterly Press.

Conway, M. M. 1983. PACs, the new politics, and congressional campaigns. In *Interest Group Politics,* eds. Allen J. Cigler and Burdett A. Loomis, 110–125. Washington, DC: Congressional Quarterly Press.

Cronin, Thomas E. 1980. *The State of the Presidency.* Boston: Little, Brown.

Curry, James A., Richard B. Riley, and Richard M. Battistoni. 1989. *Constitutional Government: The American Experience.* St. Paul, MN: West Publishing.

Danelski, David J. 1975. The influence of the chief justice in the decisional process of the Supreme Court. In *American Court Systems,* 2nd ed., eds. Sheldon Goldman and Austin Sarat, 486–499. New York: Longman.

Davidson, Roger H., and Walter J. Oleszek. 1985. *Congress and Its Members.* Washington, DC: Congressional Quarterly Press.

Duskin Publishing Group. 1991. *The Encyclopedic Dictionary of American Government.* Guilford, CT: Duskin Publishing Group.

Eagleton, Thomas F. 1991. *Issues in Business and Government.* Englewood Cliffs, NJ: Prentice-Hall.

Edwards, George C., III, and Stephen J. Wayne. 1990. *Presidential Leadership: Politics and Policy Making.* New York: St. Martin's.

Everson, David H. 1982. *Public Opinion and Interest Groups in American Politics.* New York: Franklin Watts.

Fallows, James. 1990. The presidency and the press. In *The Presidency and the Political System*, ed. Michael Nelson, 315–334. Washington, DC: Congressional Quarterly Press.

Fenno, Richard. 1978. *Home Style: House Members in Their Districts.* Boston: Little, Brown.

Fesler, James W., and Donald F. Kettl. 1991. *The Politics of the Administrative Process.* Chatham, NJ: Chatham House.

Gitelson, Alan R., Robert L. Dudley, and Melvin J. Dubnick. 1991. *American Government.* Boston: Houghton Mifflin.

Goldberg, Edie N., and Michael Traugott. 1984. *Campaigning for Congress.* Washington, DC: Congressional Quarterly Press.

Goldman, Sheldon. 1987. *Constitutional Law: Cases and Essays.* New York: Harper and Row.

Goodwin, R. Kenneth. 1988. *One Billion Dollars of Influence.* Chatham, NJ: Chatham House.

Graber, Doris A. 1980. *Mass Media and American Politics.* Washington, DC: Congressional Quarterly Press.

Greenwald, Carol S. 1977. *Group Power: Lobbying and Public Policy.* New York: Praeger.

Hershey, Marjorie R. 1989. The campaign and the media. In *The Election of 1988: Reports and Interpretations*, eds. Gerald M. Pomper et al., 73–102. New York: Chatham House.

Hess, Stephen. 1988. *Organizing the Presidency.* Washington, DC: The Brookings Institution.

Jackson, Brooks. 1990. *Harvest Graft.* Washington, DC: Farragut.

Jewell, Malcolm A., and David M. Olson. 1988. *Political Parties and Elections in American States*, 3rd ed. Chicago: Dorsey Press.

Johnson, Charles A., and Bradley Cannon. 1984. *Judicial Policies: Implementation and Impact.* Washington, DC: Congressional Quarterly Press.

Kamen, Michael. 1986. *A Machine That Would Go of Itself.* New York: Vintage Books.

Keefe, William J. 1988. *Parties, Politics, and Public Policy in America,* 5th ed. Washington, DC: Congressional Quarterly Press.

Loomis, Burdett A., and Allan J. Cigler. 1983. The changing nature of interest group politics. In *Interest Group Politics*, eds. Allan J. Cigler and Burdett A. Loomis, 1–30. Washington, DC: Congressional Quarterly Press.

Lowi, Theodore J. 1969. *The End of Liberalism.* New York: W. W. Norton.

Luttberg, Norman R. 1974. Political linkage in a large society. In *Public Opinion and Public Policy*, ed. Norman R. Luttberg, 1–10. Homewood, IL: Dorsey Press.

Maisel, L. S. 1987. *Parties and Elections in America.* New York: Random House.

Milkis, Sidney M., and Michael Nelson. 1990. *The American Presidency: Origin and Development, 1776–1990.* Washington, DC: Congressional Quarterly Press.

Miroff, Bruce. 1990. The presidency and the public: Leadership as spectacle. In *The Presidency and the Political System*, ed. Michael Nelson, 289–314. Washington, DC: Congressional Quarterly Press.

Morin, Richard. 1991. The no. 2 man is still seen as a poor second. *The Washington Post National Weekly Edition* 8 (May 13–19): 37.

Murphy, Walter F. 1964. *The Elements of Judicial Strategy.* Chicago: University of Chicago Press.

Murphy, Walter F., and C. Herman Prichett. 1986. *Courts, Judges, and Politics.* New York: Random House.

Nachmias, David, and David H. Rosenbloom. 1980. *Bureaucratic Government USA.* New York: St. Martin's.

Nathan, Richard P. 1983. *The Administrative Presidency.* New York: John Wiley & Sons.

Neustadt, Richard E. 1990. *Presidential Power and the Modern Presidents.* New York: Free Press.

O'Brien, David M. 1990. *Storm Center: The Supreme Court in American Politics*, 2nd ed. New York: W. W. Norton.

Oleszek, Walter J. 1989. *Congressional Procedures and The Policy Process.* Washington, DC: Congressional Quarterly Press.

Ornstein, Norman J., and Shirley Elder. 1978. *Interest Groups, Lobbying, and Policymaking.* Washington, DC: Congressional Quarterly Press.

Patterson, Bradley. 1988. *The Ring of Power.* New York: Basic Books.

Patterson, Thomas E. 1990. *The American Democracy.* New York: McGraw-Hill.

Patterson, Thomas E., and Robert D. McClure. 1976. *The Unseeing Eye.* New York: Putnam.

Powell, Norman J. 1967. *Responsible Bureaucracy in the United States.* Boston: Allyn and Bacon.

Press, Charles, and Kenneth Verburg. 1988. *American Politicians and Journalists.* Glenview, IL: Scott, Foresman/Little, Brown.

Price, David E. 1984. *Bringing Back the Parties.* Washington, DC: Congressional Quarterly Press.

Ranney, Austin. 1983. *Channels of Power.* New York: Basic Books.

Ripley, Randall B. 1988. *Congress: Process and Policy.* New York: W. W. Norton.

Ripley, Randall B., and Grace A. Franklin. 1986. *Policy Implementation and Bureaucracy.* Chicago: Dorsey Press.

Roche, John P. 1961. The founding fathers: A reform caucus in action. *American Political Science Review* 55 (December): 799–816.

Rossiter, Clinton, ed. 1961. *The Federalist Papers,* by Alexander Hamilton, James Madison, and John Jay. New York: Mentor Books.

Sabato, Larry J. 1985. *PAC Power: Inside the World of Political Action Committees.* New York: W. W. Norton.

————. 1981. *The Rise of Political Consultants.* New York: Basic Books.

Salmore, Barbara G., and Stephen A. Salmore. 1989. *Candidates, Parties, and Campaigns.* Washington, DC: Congressional Quarterly Press.

Seib, Philip. 1987. *Who's in Charge?* Dallas, TX: Taylor Publishing Group.

Shafritz, Jay M. 1988. *The Dorsey Dictionary of Government and Politics.* Chicago: Dorsey Press.

Sorauf, Frank J. 1984. *Party Politics in America,* 5th ed. Boston: Little, Brown.

Tribe, Laurence H. 1985. *God Save This Honorable Court.* New York: Random House.

Vogler, David J. 1988. *The Politics of Congress.* Boston: Allyn and Bacon.

Waterman, Richard W. 1989. *Presidential Influence and the Administrative State.* Knoxville, TN: University of Tennessee Press.

Wayne, Stephen J. 1988. *The Road to the White House.* New York: St. Martin's.

TO THE OWNER OF THIS BOOK:

We hope that you have found *American Stories: Case Studies in Politics and Government* useful. So that this book can be improved in a future edition, would you take the time to complete this sheet and return it? Thank you.

Instructor's name: _____

Department: _____

School and address: _____

_____

1. The name of the course in which I used this book is: _____

_____

2. My general reaction to this book is: _____

_____

_____

3. What I like most about this book is: _____

_____

_____

4. What I like least about this book is: _____

_____

_____

5. Were all of the chapters of the book assigned for you to read?   Yes   No

   If not, which ones weren't? _____

6. Do you plan to keep this book after you finish the course?   Yes   No

   Why or why not? _____

_____

7. On a separate sheet of paper, please write specific suggestions for improving this book and anything else you'd care to share about your experience in using the book.

Optional:

Your name: _____ Date: _____

May Wadsworth quote you, either in promotion for *American Stories: Case Studies in Politics and Government* or in future publishing ventures?

Yes: _____   No: _____

Sincerely,
James R. Bowers

FOLD HERE

BUSINESS REPLY MAIL
FIRST CLASS   PERMIT NO. 34   BELMONT, CA

POSTAGE WILL BE PAID BY ADDRESSEE

James R. Bowers
Wadsworth Publishing Company
10 Davis Drive
Belmont, CA 94002

NO POSTAGE
NECESSARY
IF MAILED
IN THE
UNITED STATES